# Apparition Fever

MCGILL-QUEEN'S STUDIES IN THE HISTORY OF RELIGION
*Volumes in this series have been supported by the Jackman Foundation of Toronto.*

SERIES ONE: G.A. RAWLYK, EDITOR

1 Small Differences
Irish Catholics and Irish Protestants, 1815–1922
An International Perspective
*Donald Harman Akenson*

2 Two Worlds
The Protestant Culture of Nineteenth-Century Ontario
*William Westfall*

3 An Evangelical Mind
Nathanael Burwash and the Methodist Tradition in Canada, 1839–1918
*Marguerite Van Die*

4 The Dévotes
Women and Church in Seventeenth-Century France
*Elizabeth Rapley*

5 The Evangelical Century
College and Creed in English Canada from the Great Revival to the Great Depression
*Michael Gauvreau*

6 The German Peasants' War and Anabaptist Community of Goods
*James M. Stayer*

7 A World Mission
Canadian Protestantism and the Quest for a New International Order, 1918–1939
*Robert Wright*

8 Serving the Present Age
Revivalism, Progressivism, and the Methodist Tradition in Canada
*Phyllis D. Airhart*

9 A Sensitive Independence
Canadian Methodist Women Missionaries in Canada and the Orient, 1881–1925
*Rosemary R. Gagan*

10 God's Peoples
Covenant and Land in South Africa, Israel, and Ulster
*Donald Harman Akenson*

11 Creed and Culture
The Place of English-Speaking Catholics in Canadian Society, 1750–1930
*Edited by Terrence Murphy and Gerald Stortz*

12 Piety and Nationalism
Lay Voluntary Associations and the Creation of an Irish-Catholic Community in Toronto, 1850–1895
*Brian P. Clarke*

13 Amazing Grace
Studies in Evangelicalism in Australia, Britain, Canada, and the United States
*Edited by George Rawlyk and Mark A. Noll*

14 Children of Peace
*W. John McIntyre*

15 A Solitary Pillar
Montreal's Anglican Church and the Quiet Revolution
*Joan Marshall*

16 Padres in No Man's Land
Canadian Chaplains and the Great War
*Duff Crerar*

17 Christian Ethics and Political Economy in North America
A Critical Analysis
*P. Travis Kroeker*

18 Pilgrims in Lotus Land
Conservative Protestantism in British Columbia, 1917–1981
*Robert K. Burkinshaw*

19 Through Sunshine and Shadow
The Woman's Christian Temperance Union, Evangelicalism, and Reform in Ontario, 1874–1930
*Sharon Cook*

20 Church, College, and Clergy
A History of Theological Education at Knox College, Toronto, 1844–1994
*Brian J. Fraser*

21 The Lord's Dominion
The History of Canadian Methodism
*Neil Semple*

22 A Full-Orbed Christianity
The Protestant Churches and Social Welfare in Canada, 1900–1940
*Nancy Christie and Michael Gauvreau*

23 Evangelism and Apostasy
The Evolution and Impact of Evangelicals in Modern Mexico
*Kurt Bowen*

24 The Chignecto Covenanters
A Regional History of Reformed Presbyterianism in New Brunswick and Nova Scotia, 1827–1905
*Eldon Hay*

25 Methodists and Women's Education in Ontario, 1836–1925
*Johanne Selles*

26 Puritanism and Historical Controversy
*William Lamont*

SERIES TWO IN MEMORY OF GEORGE RAWLYK
DONALD HARMAN AKENSON, EDITOR

1 Marguerite Bourgeoys and Montreal, 1640–1665
*Patricia Simpson*

2 Aspects of the Canadian Evangelical Experience
*Edited by G.A. Rawlyk*

3 Infinity, Faith, and Time
Christian Humanism and Renaissance Literature
*John Spencer Hill*

4 The Contribution of Presbyterianism to the Maritime Provinces of Canada
*Edited by Charles H.H. Scobie and G.A. Rawlyk*

5 Labour, Love, and Prayer
Female Piety in Ulster Religious Literature, 1850–1914
*Andrea Ebel Brozyna*

6 The Waning of the Green
Catholics, the Irish, and Identity in Toronto, 1887–1922
*Mark G. McGowan*

7 Religion and Nationality in Western Ukraine
The Greek Catholic Church and the Ruthenian National Movement in Galicia, 1867–1900
*John-Paul Himka*

8 Good Citizens
British Missionaries and Imperial States, 1870–1918
*James G. Greenlee and Charles M. Johnston*

9 The Theology of the Oral Torah
Revealing the Justice of God
*Jacob Neusner*

10 Gentle Eminence
A Life of Cardinal Flahiff
*P. Wallace Platt*

11 Culture, Religion, and Demographic Behaviour
Catholics and Lutherans in Alsace, 1750–1870
*Kevin McQuillan*

12 Between Damnation and Starvation
Priests and Merchants in Newfoundland Politics, 1745–1855
*John P. Greene*

13 Martin Luther, German Saviour
German Evangelical Theological Factions and the Interpretation of Luther, 1917–1933
*James M. Stayer*

14 Modernity and the Dilemma of North American Anglican Identities, 1880–1950
*William H. Katerberg*

15 The Methodist Church on the Prairies, 1896–1914
*George Emery*

16 Christian Attitudes towards the State of Israel
*Paul Charles Merkley*

17 A Social History of the Cloister
Daily Life in the Teaching Monasteries of the Old Regime
*Elizabeth Rapley*

18 Households of Faith
Family, Gender, and Community in Canada, 1760–1969
*Edited by Nancy Christie*

19 Blood Ground
Colonialism, Missions, and the Contest for Christianity in the Cape Colony and Britain, 1799–1853
*Elizabeth Elbourne*

20 A History of Canadian Catholics
Gallicanism, Romanism, and Canadianism
*Terence J. Fay*

21 The View from Rome
Archbishop Stagni's 1915 Reports on the Ontario Bilingual Schools Question
*Edited and translated by John Zucchi*

22 The Founding Moment
Church, Society, and the Construction of Trinity College
*William Westfall*

23 The Holocaust, Israel, and Canadian Protestant Churches
*Haim Genizi*

24 Governing Charities
Church and State in Toronto's Catholic Archdiocese, 1850–1950
*Paula Maurutto*

25 Anglicans and the Atlantic World
High Churchmen, Evangelicals, and the Quebec Connection
*Richard W. Vaudry*

26 Evangelicals and the Continental Divide
The Conservative Protestant Subculture in Canada and the United States
*Sam Reimer*

27 Christians in a Secular World
The Canadian Experience
*Kurt Bowen*

28 Anatomy of a Seance
A History of Spirit Communication in Central Canada
*Stan McMullin*

29 With Skilful Hand
The Story of King David
*David T. Barnard*

30 Faithful Intellect
Samuel S. Nelles and Victoria University
*Neil Semple*

31 W. Stanford Reid
An Evangelical Calvinist in the Academy
*A. Donald MacLeod*

32 A Long Eclipse
The Liberal Protestant Establishment and the Canadian University, 1920–1970
*Catherine Gidney*

33 Forkhill Protestants and Forkhill Catholics, 1787–1858
*Kyla Madden*

34 For Canada's Sake
Public Religion, Centennial Celebrations, and the Re-making of Canada in the 1960s
*Gary R. Miedema*

35 Revival in the City
The Impact of American Evangelists in Canada, 1884–1914
*Eric R. Crouse*

36 The Lord for the Body
Religion, Medicine, and Protestant Faith Healing in Canada, 1880–1930
*James Opp*

37 Six Hundred Years of Reform
Bishops and the French Church, 1190–1789
*J. Michael Hayden and Malcolm R. Greenshields*

38 The Missionary Oblate Sisters
Vision and Mission
*Rosa Bruno-Jofré*

39 Religion, Family, and Community in Victorian Canada
The Colbys of Carrollcroft
*Marguerite Van Die*

40 Michael Power
The Struggle to Build the Catholic Church on the Canadian Frontier
*Mark G. McGowan*

41 The Catholic Origins of Quebec's Quiet Revolution, 1931–1970
*Michael Gauvreau*

42 Marguerite Bourgeoys and the Congregation of Notre-Dame, 1665–1700
*Patricia Simpson*

43 To Heal a Fractured World
The Ethics of Responsibility
*Jonathan Sacks*

44 Revivalists
Marketing the Gospel in English Canada, 1884–1957
*Kevin Kee*

45 The Churches and Social Order in Nineteenth- and Twentieth-Century Canada
*Edited by Michael Gauvreau and Ollivier Hubert*

46 Political Ecumenism
Catholics, Jews, and Protestants in De Gaulle's Free France, 1940–1945
*Geoffrey Adams*

47 From Quaker to Upper Canadian
Faith and Community among Yonge Street Friends, 1801–1850
*Robynne Rogers Healey*

48 The Congrégation de Notre-Dame, Superiors, and the Paradox of Power, 1693–1796
*Colleen Gray*

49 Canadian Pentecostalism
Transition and Transformation
*Edited by Michael Wilkinson*

50 A War with a Silver Lining
Canadian Protestant Churches and the South African War, 1899–1902
*Gordon L. Heath*

51 In the Aftermath of Catastrophe
Founding Judaism, 70 to 640
*Jacob Neusner*
52 Imagining Holiness
Classic Hasidic Tales in Modern Times
*Justin Jaron Lewis*
53 Shouting, Embracing, and Dancing with Ecstasy
The Growth of Methodism in Newfoundland, 1774–1874
*Calvin Hollett*
54 Into Deep Waters
Evangelical Spirituality and Maritime Calvinist Baptist Ministers, 1790–1855
*Daniel C. Goodwin*
55 Vanguard of the New Age
The Toronto Theosophical Society, 1891–1945
*Gillian McCann*
56 A Commerce of Taste
Church Architecture in Canada, 1867–1914
*Barry Magrill*
57 The Big Picture
The Antigonish Movement of Eastern Nova Scotia
*Santo Dodaro and Leonard Pluta*
58 My Heart's Best Wishes for You
A Biography of Archbishop John Walsh
*John P. Comiskey*
59 The Covenanters in Canada
Reformed Presbyterianism from 1820 to 2012
*Eldon Hay*
60 The Guardianship of Best Interests
Institutional Care for the Children of the Poor in Halifax, 1850–1960
*Renée N. Lafferty*
61 In Defence of the Faith
Joaquim Marques de Araújo, a Comissário in the Age of Inquisitional Decline
*James E. Wadsworth*
62 Contesting the Moral High Ground
Popular Moralists in Mid-Twentieth-Century Britain
*Paul T. Phillips*
63 The Catholicisms of Coutances
Varieties of Religion in Early Modern France, 1350–1789
*J. Michael Hayden*
64 After Evangelicalism
The Sixties and the United Church of Canada
*Kevin N. Flatt*
65 The Return of Ancestral Gods
Modern Ukrainian Paganism as an Alternative Vision for a Nation
*Mariya Lesiv*
66 Transatlantic Methodists
British Wesleyanism and the Formation of an Evangelical Culture in Nineteenth-Century Ontario and Quebec
*Todd Webb*
67 A Church with the Soul of a Nation
Making and Remaking the United Church of Canada
*Phyllis D. Airhart*
68 Fighting over God
A Legal and Political History of Religious Freedom in Canada
*Janet Epp Buckingham*
69 From India to Israel
Identity, Immigration, and the Struggle for Religious Equality
*Joseph Hodes*
70 Becoming Holy in Early Canada
*Timothy Pearson*
71 The Cistercian Arts
From the 12th to the 21st Century
*Edited by Terryl N. Kinder and Roberto Cassanelli*
72 The Canny Scot
Archbishop James Morrison of Antigonish
*Peter Ludlow*
73 Religion and Greater Ireland
Christianity and Irish Global Networks, 1750–1950
*Edited by Colin Barr and Hilary M. Carey*
74 The Invisible Irish
Finding Protestants in the Nineteenth-Century Migrations to America
*Rankin Sherling*
75 Beating against the Wind
Popular Opposition to Bishop Feild and Tractarianism in Newfoundland and Labrador, 1844–1876
*Calvin Hollett*
76 The Body or the Soul?
Religion and Culture in a Quebec Parish, 1736–1901
*Frank A. Abbott*
77 Saving Germany
North American Protestants and Christian Mission to West Germany, 1945–1974
*James C. Enns*

78 The Imperial Irish
Canada's Irish Catholics Fight the Great War, 1914–1918
*Mark G. McGowan*

79 Into Silence and Servitude
How American Girls Became Nuns, 1945–1965
*Brian Titley*

80 Boundless Dominion
Providence, Politics, and the Early Canadian Presbyterian Worldview
*Denis McKim*

81 Faithful Encounters
Authorities and American Missionaries in the Ottoman Empire
*Emrah Şahin*

82 Beyond the Noise of Solemn Assemblies
The Protestant Ethic and the Quest for Social Justice in Canada
*Richard Allen*

83 Not Quite Us
Anti-Catholic Thought in English Canada since 1900
*Kevin P. Anderson*

84 Scandal in the Parish
Priests and Parishioners Behaving Badly in Eighteenth-Century France
*Karen E. Carter*

85 Ordinary Saints
Women, Work, and Faith in Newfoundland
*Bonnie Morgan*

86 Patriot and Priest
Jean-Baptiste Volfius and the Constitutional Church in the Côte-d'Or
*Annette Chapman-Adisho*

87 A.B. Simpson and the Making of Modern Evangelicalism
*Daryn Henry*

88 The Uncomfortable Pew
Christianity and the New Left in Toronto
*Bruce Douville*

89 Berruyer's Bible
Public Opinion and the Politics of Enlightenment Catholicism in France
*Daniel J. Watkins*

90 Communities of the Soul
A Short History of Religion in Puerto Rico
*José E. Igartua*

91 Callings and Consequences
The Making of Catholic Vocational Culture in Early Modern France
*Christopher J. Lane*

92 Religion, Ethnonationalism, and Antisemitism in the Era of the Two World Wars
*Edited by Kevin P. Spicer and Rebecca Carter-Chand*

93 Water from Dragon's Well
The History of a Korean-Canadian Church Relationship
*David Kim-Cragg*

94 Protestant Liberty
Religion and the Making of Canadian Liberalism, 1828–1878
*James M. Forbes*

95 To Make a Village Soviet
Jehovah's Witnesses and the Transformation of a Postwar Ukrainian Borderland
*Emily B. Baran*

96 Disciples of Antigonish
Catholics in Nova Scotia, 1880–1960
*Peter Ludlow*

97 A Black American Missionary in Canada
The Life and Letters of Lewis Champion Chambers
*Edited by Hilary Bates Neary*

98 A People's Reformation
Building the English Church in the Elizabethan Parish
*Lucy Moffat Kaufman*

99 Towards a Godless Dominion
Unbelief in Interwar Canada
*Elliot Hanowski*

100 Finding Molly Johnson
Irish Famine Orphans in Canada
*Mark G. McGowan*

101 Apparition Fever
Observing the Virgin Mary in Belgium
*Tine Van Osselaer*

# Apparition Fever

## *Observing the Virgin Mary in Belgium*

TINE VAN OSSELAER

McGill-Queen's University Press
Montreal & Kingston • London • Chicago

ISBN 978-0-2280-2472-9 (paper)
ISBN 978-0-2280-2496-5 (ePDF)
ISBN 978-0-2280-2497-2 (ePUB)

Legal deposit second quarter 2025
Bibliothèque et Archives nationales du Québec

Printed in Canada on acid-free paper that is 100% ancient-forest-free, containing 100% sustainable, recycled fibre, and processed chlorine-free.

Funded by the Government of Canada | Financé par le gouvernement du Canada | Canada

Canada Council for the Arts | Conseil des arts du Canada

We acknowledge the support of the Canada Council for the Arts.

Nous remercions le Conseil des arts du Canada de son soutien.

McGill-Queen's University Press in Montreal is on land which long served as a site of meeting and exchange amongst Indigenous Peoples, including the Haudenosaunee and Anishinabeg nations. In Kingston it is situated on the territory of the Haudenosaunee and Anishinaabek. We acknowledge and thank the diverse Indigenous Peoples whose footsteps have marked these territories on which peoples of the world now gather.

---

Library and Archives Canada Cataloguing in Publication

Title: Apparition fever : observing the Virgin Mary in Belgium / Tine Van Osselaer.

Names: Van Osselaer, Tine, author

Series: McGill-Queen's studies in the history of religion. Series two ; 101.

Description: Series statement: McGill-Queen's studies in the history of religion. Series two ; 101 | Includes bibliographical references and index.

Identifiers: Canadiana (print) 20250146185 | Canadiana (ebook) 20250146223 | ISBN 9780228024729 (cloth) | ISBN 9780228024972 (ePUB) | ISBN 9780228024965 (ePDF)

Subjects: LCSH: Mary, Blessed Virgin, Saint – Apparitions and miracles – Belgium – History – 20th century. | LCSH: Banneux, Onze-Lieve-Vrouw van. | LCSH: Beauraing, Notre-Dame de.

Classification: LCC BT660.B28 V36 2025 | DDC 232.91/70949309044 – dc23

---

This book was designed and typeset by Peggy Issenman in 11.5/14 Adobe Garamond Pro. Copyediting by Margaret MacQuarrie.

McGill-Queen's University Press
Suite 1720, 1010 Sherbrooke St West, Montreal, QC, H3A 2R7

Authorized safety representative in the EU: Mare Nostrum Group BV, Mauritskade 21D, 1091 GC Amsterdam, the Netherlands, gpsr@mare-nostrum.co.uk

# Contents

# Table and Figures

## Table



## Figures

Images are from the author's private collection unless specified otherwise.

# Acknowledgments

In the summer of 2011, I was working in the archives of the shrine of Beauraing, sitting beside a box containing letters related to the first year of the apparitions. While I was permitted to consult all the other documents in the archive, this box was off limits. Mind you, the box was not sealed or locked in any way, and it was right next to me. I like to see it as a character test, and an incredibly hard one for any historian. It had been a particularly tough week, but I managed not to let my curiosity get the better of me, and I did not open the box. (So yes, there is still material out there that needs to be studied, once the ban is lifted.) That I managed to control myself had everything to do with the other sources that were available and with the trust I was given when permitted into the archives.

These two elements, wonderful sources and welcoming archivists, have been constant features of my research on the Marian apparitions in 1930s Belgium. I have built up a huge debt in the last decade and wish to thank Odette Calay, Marcel Cock, Ludo Collin, Anny Dedyn, Christian Dury, Daniel Meynen, Daniel Ponziani, Patricia Quaghebeur, Christophe Rouard, Nico Van Campenhout, Gerrit Vanden Bosch, and Erna Van Looveren for granting me access to the sources and helping me navigate through them.

As for the writing, Bill Christian has provided unwavering support from the inception of the book up until this final stage. He has been an enthusiastic yet critical reader, not afraid to point out flaws and lacunas, while generous with suggestions, sources, and encouraging words. I am grateful to the two reviewers of McGill-Queen's University Press for their helpful comments. (I have to admit, I like the book better now.)

The manuscript of this book has been a companion of mine for more than a decade. I have worked on it at Leuven University, during a research stay at the Max Planck Institute for Human Development, and here at the Ruusbroec Institute of the University of Antwerp. I found supportive colleagues in all these vibrant academic environments and would like to thank, in particular, Monique Scheer for welcoming me into the Berlin research group; Leonardo Rossi for checking my Italian translations; and Robrecht Neyrinck and Joke De Wilde for helping me with the scans. I have benefitted from conversations with John Arblaster, Henk De Smaele, Paula Kane, Mary Heimann, Natalia Núñez Bargueño, Patrick Pasture, Kristof Smeyers, Lieke Smits, Joris Vandendriessche, and Kaat Wils, amongst others.

I am grateful to "De Bourgondiërs," Annelies, Ben, Elwin, Liesbet and Sam, as our culinary and cultural outings helped charge my batteries, and my thanks also to Karolien, Dagmar, and Moufida for the difference supportive friends can make. My sisters, incomparable forces of energy, resilience, and creative thinking, have been a constant source of inspiration. My parents have been my most fervent supporters in writing this book and throughout the academic ups and downs. This book is for them.

Writing this book was made possible thanks to the generous support of the FWO (Research Foundation – Flanders), the special research fund of Leuven University and the special research fund of the University of Antwerp.

# Apparition Fever

# Introduction

> The triumph will therefore be greater for our successors than for us: we have known the pettiness, the viciousness, the "disarray" of the ideas and the dispute, which has led us to change our minds about many things, notably about the value of people's sincerity, about the lightness of judgment of many experts of the mind, of many "savants," idea leaders … and that has been unpleasant and caused great disillusions. Our successors, in case [the apparition] is recognized, will see nothing else than the pretty side, just as it is for Lourdes. As soldiers, still impressed by the horror of the battle, retain other memories than those who see nothing but the victory.[1]
>
> Louis Wilmet

## Human Faith

In a rather pessimistic tone, the Belgian writer Louis Wilmet looked back in September 1936 on his first years of involvement in pleading and lobbying for the recognition of some of the Marian apparitions reported in Belgium in the 1930s.[2] His words to his fellow investigator and promoter, Abbé Didion, show not only his frustration but also his understanding of how apparition stories are rewritten in the course of the years. Uncomfortable episodes, contradictions, supporters whose involvement is no longer considered beneficial … all are filtered out of the "official" story. For the Belgian series of apparitions, of which only two (Beauraing and Banneux) were eventually officially approved, this meant reducing the number of apparitional sites from more than forty down to the original two; paying no attention to hundreds of other visionaries in order to promote the child-visionaries of the first two sites, and ignoring years of reports on apparitions and focusing only on three months at the end of 1932 and start of 1933. This book is about how this filtering took place, how some of the events came to be deemed credible (by some) and others did not.

Focusing on such filtering processes means studying the ways in which "true" apparitions were set apart, how "credibility" and "authenticity" were claimed and created. This might seem odd, for Marian apparitions are, above all, a question of faith. When the Catholic Church approves of an apparition, this solely indicates "that its message contains nothing contrary to faith and morals; it is licit to make it public and the faithful are authorized to give to it their prudent adhesion."[3] The church does thereby not guarantee the "truth of the fact narrated"[4] and it makes a distinction between "human faith" and "divine faith." The former relates to cases of private revelations approved by the church, the latter is requested for the truth contained in the Revelation or defined as dogmatic truth.[5] Approval of the apparitions only means that the faithful are allowed to worship Mary in a specific way, but it is not an obligation.[6]

The Dicastery for the Doctrine of Faith addressed this somewhat confusing situation in the new *Norms for Proceeding in the Discernment of Alleged Supernatural Phenomena* that were launched in May 2024: "the actual procedures followed by the Dicastery, even in recent times, were still inclined toward the Bishop making a declaration that the event was 'supernatural' or 'not supernatural' … these expressions oriented the faithful to think they had to believe in these phenomena." In the current norms, "as a rule, such declarations of 'supernaturalness' are replaced either by a *Nihil obstat*, which authorizes positive pastoral work, or by another determination that is suited to the specific situation … the possibility of declaring an event as 'not supernatural' remains, but only when there are objective signs that clearly indicate manipulation at the basis of the phenomenon."[7]

The new 2024 norms are meant to speed up the evaluation process and help to control the religious enthusiasm. By focusing on the adequate pastoral response rather than on the question of the authenticity of the phenomenon – the investigation of which could take decades – the dicastery wants to avoid "the use of such phenomenon to gain 'profit, power, fame, social recognition, or other personal interest' (II Art.15, 4°) … or the use of these phenomena 'as a means of or pretext for exerting control over people or carrying out abuses' (II Art.16)" or "believers being misled by an event that is attributed to a divine initiative but is merely the product of someone's imagination, desire for novelty, tendency to fabricate falsehoods (mythomania), or inclination towards lying." Interestingly, while my focus is on apparitions of the 1930s,[8] many of the issues that instigated the recent reformulation of the norms were already at play: religious enthusiasm for non-approved phenomena intensified due to press coverage and was very hard to control, the phenomena themselves were attested in multiple dioceses and attracted enthusiasts from abroad, and the various religious authorities involved held different opinions.

The two apparition series of the Belgian wave that were approved (Beauraing, 1932–33 and Banneux, 1933), were only recognized in 1949. The sixteen years between the initial events and their approval were years of waxing and waning religious enthusiasm. This book is on the long road toward this official statement by the ordinary, the bishop responsible for the site, and the gradual filtering out (and at times explicit rejection) of the other apparition series reported in 1930s Belgium. This final verdict was, however, only the last step in a long process of examining and weighing the apparitions, their messages, and visionaries. It all started the moment a visionary claimed to have seen the Virgin and the word started to spread at different (interacting) levels. I am interested in the longer story, the response at the different levels and the impact that the public character had on the evaluation of the apparitions.

Once deemed "committing professional suicide,"[9] writing on nineteenth- and twentieth-century Marian apparitions has in the last two decades become part and parcel in the study of cultural history and religious anthropology. There were various reasons for the neglect: secular historians looked down on these "manifestations of irrationality" and did not consider them worthy of a historian's attention, and Catholic historians felt uncomfortable about these phenomena and preferred not to discuss them.[10] Gradually however, the attention for apparitions grew as historical interest in religion and, more specifically, in the devotions of "common laypeople" augmented. The increasing interest in popular devotions came with the understanding that Christian norms and values remained influential and important for identity-formation also in modern (allegedly "secular") societies. This renewed attention for popular devotion secured the growth of historical interest in Marian apparitions which are now no longer studied exclusively in devotional and apologetic Mariography.[11] Apart from the rise in the number of case studies on nineteenth- and twentieth-century apparitions and their socio-cultural, religious, and political context and impact,[12] Marian apparitions are also commented upon in studies on Marian devotion, pilgrimage culture,[13] and compared to similar phenomena and analyzed within the context of (secular and religious) "miracles"[14] and the "invisible."[15]

Scholars can focus on numerous cases. It is not an exaggeration to state that thousands of Marian apparitions have been reported in the previous centuries. The standard inventory, René Laurentin and Patrick Sbalchiero's *Dictionnaire des 'apparitions' de la Vierge Marie* (2007) documents 2,400 apparitions.[16] The Marian Library[17] (of the International Marian Research Institute, Dayton/Ohio) provides us with information about apparitions (worldwide) from 1900 up until 2011, and lists a total of 452 cases. The majority of these apparitions did not trigger an examination, but of those that did, eighty-five have been rejected and eight were approved: Fátima (1917, Portugal), Beauraing (1932, Belgium), Banneux (1933, Belgium), Syracuse (1953, Italy), Akita (1973, Japan), Betania (1976, Venezuela), Kibèho (1981, Rwanda), and San Nicolas (1983, Argentina).[18] While some of these apparitions have attracted more scholarly interest than others, we cannot say that the approved apparitions have monopolized the attention. On the contrary, some of the most interesting anthropological and historical studies have focused on the (non-approved or rejected) events in Ezquioga, Marpingen, and Heede.[19]

The series I focus on includes both approved (Beauraing and Banneux) and rejected apparitions. It was a nationwide modern series of apparitions and followed the pattern set by Lourdes in 1858: They were public and serial. Since the visions of Bernadette Soubirous, apparitions have evolved from private visions to public events, where the visionary/ies were surrounded by bystanders who could "see" the apparitions by reading the body language of the visionaries.[20] The enthusiast spectators knew when to be present, for – often – the visionaries claimed that Mary had told them when she would reappear. Many of these events were covered by the press, and the journalistic interest often increased the appeal the apparitions (and sites) had on the public.[21] Apparitions were rarely single incidents and were attested in series.[22] There were often several seers who entered an altered state during the apparitions.[23] Moreover, at modern apparition sites, the Virgin often communicated "universal" messages that were of importance beyond the local level.[24]

These modern characteristics held inherent challenges for the acceptance of apparitions. As William Christian noted, "for proponents of a given seer or vision site, the existence of multiple replications is a drawback, as it risks trivializing the entire phenomenon." Some of these iterations were only covered by hostile press because they knew "it would reflect badly on the entire phenomenon."[25] Moreover, the presence of other people at the site made the visionaries vulnerable to criticism. Seeing the Virgin with bystanders present exposed the seers to public scrutiny. Their openness could also work to their benefit however. In the case of the Lourdes visionary Bernadette Soubirous, "the public nature" of her experience, so Ruth Harris wrote, "was considered key to her veracity."[26] She had allowed people to examine her. This social aspect of modern Marian apparitions, the fact that they are witnessed by others and spoken of by non-seers, is what makes them so interesting for historians. The event needed to be shared (verbally, visually, …) in order to be authenticated.[27]

Studying Catholic evaluations of religious phenomena, I can draw upon the expanding research on the history of knowledge.[28] This still fairly new approach does not solely focus on academic science but can include whatever contemporaries thought of as knowledge.[29] While some scholars hesitate to include belief systems (for lack of focus on the rational),[30] others like Simone Lässig have argued that it is difficult, even impossible, to draw sharp contrasts between knowledge and belief and one should focus rather on "the dialectical relationship and interconnections between them" as "[r]eligion is, to varying degrees, a matter of both faith and knowledge."[31] Before expanding on how I plan to address this interaction in the following chapters, I want to highlight two aspects that can further clarify how we should look at "religion" here. First of all, as this book explores Catholic evaluations of a wave of Marian apparitions, it is good to keep in mind that also within Christianity (the production and circulation of) knowledge differed along confessions.[32] Secondly, knowledge can be delegitimized and, as Lässig has suggested, it might be interesting to look at the interconnection between "the deligitimation of 'superseded' religious knowledge" on the one hand, and "the call for 'pure'" religious knowledge on the other.[33] Here I am particularly interested in how different types of Catholic knowing were activated in the evaluation of the apparition wave. So, while focusing on the evaluation of the series of alleged supernatural phenomena, I will not be studying solely the medical experts and their evaluation of the apparitions and miraculous cures. Instead, I aim to address questions of credibility, trust, and epistemology within diverse types of evaluation. These included, for instance, the lay response by eye witnesses (analyzing their own sensory experiences) and the theological evaluation in the diocesan commissions. What types of knowledge were drawn upon in what setting? Did the types operate independently or did they interact, and, if so, how?[34] By taking this broader approach, I adopt Martin Mulsow's suggestion to see the history of knowledge as an opportunity "not simply to contextualize scholarly and scientific knowledge, as has been done up till now, but to bring this knowledge into contact with other forms of knowledge"[35] and to explore how highly a particular form of knowledge is valued.[36]

In other words, I follow the lead of Boute, Badea, Cavarzere, and Vanden Broecke who asserted "that the credibility of religious truth can be captured by reconstructing the unglamorous work floor where it was manufactured and administrated by a multitude of historical actors." Unlike their study about making truth in early modern Catholicism, however, I will not be focusing solely on the "learned Catholicism of elites,"[37] but will include the ideas of lay (non-expert) Catholics as well. In addition, I will pay particular attention to the public setting of the series and their reception. Rather than solely looking at the public announcement of the result of the evaluation processes as a means to control religious enthusiasm, I want to reflect more thoroughly on the public setting of the apparitions and examine if and how it had an impact on the evaluation of the phenomena.

## Public Apparitions – Public Evaluations?

"Marian apparitions are not simple events with self-evident meanings," Sandra Zimdars-Swartz wrote in her study of six modern apparitions. "These are very complex phenomena that have been pared down and subjected to a considerable amount of interpretation by those who have sought to make them publicly accessible."[38] This editing process in the creation of the official story, the reframing of the apparitions to enhance their credibility, has been addressed in case studies on the nineteenth and twentieth century.[39] Scholars thereby emphasized that this (re)writing was not devoid of power struggles: By erasing some voices (such as those of competing visionaries) and privileging others, one could assert the right to act as custodian of a shrine.[40] Likewise, the official approval of an apparition was a determining moment for the official story line. Authentication often meant imposing an official version of the story (for instance the visionary as an obedient vis-a-vis the church authorities).

Such stories had an impact on the credibility of other apparitions. The more apparitions were known, the clearer the expectations concerning the visionaries, divine messages, and sites became. Apparitions or visionaries that did not fit model types (of, for instance, La Salette, Lourdes, or Fátima[41]) had more difficulties being accepted (at different levels). The improving means of communication played an important role in this standardization of Marian apparitions.[42] The mimesis effect (similar visionaries for instance) was part of the transnational character of modern apparitional culture. Catholic devotees saw apparitions as related to one another and there was cross-referencing and -fertilization.[43]

Credibility not only depended on the apparition's recognizability but also its acceptance by the ecclesiastical authorities. Scholars like Joachim Bouflet, Patrick Sbalchiero, and Daniel Klimek have looked at the decision makers and the different ecclesiastical procedures, and have provided us with an overall view of accepted and rejected apparitions.[44] In their studies, they reflected on how and why the church categorized some of the apparitions as fraudulent while authenticating others. We will discuss the decision-making process of the ecclesiastical examinations more in detail in our section on authority, but let us point out a few elements here.

First of all, in the nineteenth century and a large part of the twentieth century, there were no fixed regulations on how to proceed and examine Marian apparitions. There was no standard format for the ecclesiastical examination and, as we shall see in the Belgian case, the commissions could take on various shapes. Nonetheless, some general rules were already in place. Since the Fifth Council of the Lateran (1517) and the Council of Trent (1563), the official investigation required the creation of a diocesan commission.[45] However, while the examination was the responsibility of the local bishop, in cases of national importance "the national Conference of Bishops or the Apostolic See may intervene."[46] The bishop's duty to oversee the examination was not explicitly addressed in canon law, but, as Michael Smith Foster explained, his responsibility in these matters "is evidenced in the laws pertaining to his liturgical office, his regulation of the liturgy, and his oversight of the authenticity of prayers and devotion."[47] For instance, in the 1917 code, the one that is of interest for the 1930s Belgian series of apparitions, "Canon 121.2 exhorted bishops to ensure (1) the avoidance of superstitious practice in the daily life of the faithful, (2) the exclusion of anything alien to the faith, (3) the termination of anything which may be out of harmony with ecclesiastical tradition, and (4) the avoidance of anything which promotes commercialization."[48] The examination was part of the pastoral care a bishop needed to provide. The fact that the decision was in his hands and not in those of the Magisterium ecclesiae already implied that a potential recognition of an apparition had not the same impact as the statements by the Magisterium and did not elevate the decision to a dogmatic truth or obligate the faithful to believe in it.[49]

Secondly, even before the (then named) Congregation for the Doctrine of the Faith issued *Norms Regarding the Manner of Proceeding in the Discernment of Presumed Apparitions or Revelations* in 1978,[50] a "criteriology" had been developing. The examination focused on the phenomena themselves, the personality of the visionaries, the context (among other miracles), the message (is it theologically sound?) and the effects for the seer and the people.[51] Given the line of questioning and the interest in the personality of the visionary and the miraculous cures, commissions also engaged physicians, psychiatrists, and psychologists in the decision process.

Was the official verdict really that important for the further evolution of the devotion (and site)? If the decision of the ecclesiastical authorities was affirmative, the cult was institutionalized, but was rejection always lethal for the religious enthusiasm the apparitions generated?[52] The many "wild" pilgrimages (related to apparitions that have not yet been approved or even have been rejected) seem to suggest otherwise.[53]

Moreover, the church did not always intervene. So what did it mean when it chose to do so? Some scholars thought of an official proclamation and authentication a form of church control,[54] others see it as a strategic use of Marian devotion and pilgrimages to protect Catholics against the temptations of the modern world.[55] Joseph Laycock thinks of the rejection of apparitions by the Catholic Church authorities primarily as boundary-setting, a moment when the "fault-line between the vernacular practices of lay Catholics and the doctrinal positions of the Church hierarchy" became apparent. He added that "[w]hile these two faces of Catholicism share much in common, they often see the world in different ways. Where vernacular Catholicism blurs the lines between sacred and profane, finding the miraculous in the local and the everyday, the hierarchy generally works to consolidate access to the sacred within prescribed times, spaces, and rituals. They employ different mechanisms and traditions for evaluating truth claims, especially claims of the supernatural and the miraculous."[56]

This book addresses the interpretative work and the decision-making by diocesan authorities *and* lay Catholics. Heeding Ann Taves' advice, I want to avoid reiterating the dichotomy between "educated elites" who are "depicted as explaining (away) religious experience in abstract terms, while ordinary people, embedded in traditions of faith and practice, are depicted as having them."[57] The interpretational efforts by devotees have been a topic of interest primarily in studies of religious anthropology. Scholars have explored the ways in which the visionaries and witnesses made sense of what happened "by referring to shared Christian doctrine, well-known historical precedents, and familiar iconographies." The outcomes were unique for each of the religious events, as all these evaluations took place in different historical settings.[58] The motives and methods for authentication differed from those of the ecclesiastical authorities. Still those witnessing an apparition knew about previous cases and "the conventions which are used to argue for the validity of an apparition for Roman Catholic believers."[59] "Those who did not see" looked for signs (for instance a miraculous healing, sun miracle, ecstasy of the visionaries) to legitimate the truth of the event.[60] Their means to "prove" authenticity claims evolved and new technologies of authentication (for instance Polaroids) made it easier for them to share knowledge and more, challenging the clergy's monopoly of interpreting the revelations.[61]

Drawing upon these studies, this book adopts a broad view of the evaluation process of Marian apparitions and does not focus solely on the diocesan official examinations. This more inclusive approach stems from the observation that the format of Marian apparitions has changed throughout the ages – they became more public – and that this shift also had an influence on how and by whom the apparitions were evaluated. For modern – that is public and serial – apparitions, the other levels (those of the first witnesses/laymen and of the medical experts) seem to be just as important as that of the diocese.

If we want to understand how modern (public and serial) apparitions were evaluated at these different levels, we need to reflect also on the impact that this public character had. This means paying attention to the public setting of the apparition that allowed for the creation of an apparition site where people could come and see the phenomena for themselves, a site where people publicly showed their trust in what happened (for instance by leaving ex-votos or bringing their sick), and paying attention to the public discussions that developed in the press and journals, amplifying the voices of those who wanted to share their opinion. So it is not just about adding a new layer to the analysis and seeing how the different levels interact, it means examining the effect public discussions, statements, and actions had on the evaluation of the apparition. As we shall see, those involved in the final stages of the decision-making did not abstain from expressing their opinion also in those first years of the reception – and they did so publicly. The kneeling of a bishop at a non-approved apparition site, for instance, had no small impact on the later decision process.

## Studying the Belgian Apparition Series: Focus and Outline

The apparitions in Beauraing and Banneux are two of the very small number of apparitions that have been approved by the church (by bishops and/or Rome). Their recognition was exceptional in various respects. Banneux and Beauraing were the only apparition sites approved during the pontificate of Pius XII, and the two cults that developed at the site were approved already in 1942 and in 1943 (hence in the midst of World War II), while the approval of the apparitions followed in 1949. Still, rather than focusing exclusively on Beauraing and Banneux, the following chapters include also the evaluations of the rest of the series.

The series-aspect calls for some caveats. First of all, while this book focuses on the Belgian "wave," the following chapters do not want to suggest that this was necessarily the level of analysis that the contemporaries adopted. The apparitions were first and foremost local events that were – only later – integrated into a bigger, national, series. Secondly, the wave-aspect might generate a misleading impression of uniformity. As we shall see, the various phenomena reported in different locations all over Belgium showed no small variety. So why then address the apparitions as a series and not focus solely on the approved events? The main reason is that, for contemporaries, the series became a point of reference, and the reports on Beauraing and Banneux were embedded in the story of a bigger, nationwide, series. Secondly, by focusing on the series in general, this book wants to give importance also to the non-approved apparitions. These were likewise regarded as religious experiences by many devotees, albeit not by those who had the final say.

The public and serial character of the Belgian series of apparitions calls for an integrated analysis addressing the different levels of response and also the interaction between the various types of respondents. An exclusive focus on the response of the episcopal authorities (even though they had the final word) would give us a distorted view and might confirm the idea of "two" Catholicisms, an official one and a lived reality, whereas we want to look at the interaction between the various actors – the laity, clergy, episcopal authorities, and medical experts. The final verdict was not created *ex nihilo*, but also built upon grassroots evaluations. The faithful participated in the meaning making, and at different moments in the decision-making process (before and after the various official evaluations and verdicts).

This book is not about the individual religious experience of the seers and the expression thereof; the voices of the visionaries are seldom quoted. It is, rather, a book about the people who chose to believe them (or not) and their reasons for doing so. The public Belgian apparitions drew the attention of lay people, of medical professionals in particular, and of church authorities (diocesan, national, and international). The evaluation and filtering thus took place within different epistemological systems. Experiences could be deemed "religious," or cast aside as fraud, hallucination, or illusion.[62] A study of the Belgian apparition series thus allows us to look at how different types of evaluation processes interacted when judging phenomena like Marian apparitions. We will examine to what extent the adopted criteria and ways of observing and evaluating at different levels converged, whose authority in these matters was accepted or challenged, and how the public character of the events impacted the evaluation.

Two elements need to be pointed out here: First of all, an evaluation can take on different forms and does not need to be limited to formal investigations or written text. Mockery and pilgrimages, for instance, also inform us about prevalent ideas. Secondly, my focus is primarily on the Catholic response (positive and negative) to the apparition series. While a focus on the outsider-perspective would indeed be an interesting approach, for the evaluation of the apparitions and the filtering out of Beauraing and Banneux, a focus on the Catholic trajectory is already an exceptionally broad endeavour. As the selection and examination of the apparitions was a long-term process, this book covers a period ranging from the start of the apparitions in late 1932 until the late 1940s when Beauraing and Banneux, the first two sites, were officially recognized.

The various sections track the gradual formalization of the inquiries. We start with the laity that attended the apparitions or visited the sites after the visions were over, and we will look at the arguments they developed to convince each other and the ecclesiastical authorities. In the next section we move on to a more formal examination of the events as we address the medical professionals who discussed the events not only through publications, but also at public meetings. We then consider the commissions that were convened by ecclesiastical authorities in Belgium and Rome to study the events and inform the decision that was eventually left in the hands of the bishops. The final section focuses on the aftermath of the apparition series and examines the impact of the official statements of rejection or approval.

The sections focus on the main characters of each phase but it is important to point out in advance that the epistemologies referred to were not exclusive for each of the phases or type of people involved. Furthermore, while we address the different levels consecutively, we should be careful not to present the evaluations as too linear a process. Some visionaries were rejected by ecclesiastical authorities long before other apparition sites reached this level of discernment. Finally, the book builds on four central concepts: trust, competence, authority, and time – the foundations on which the actors of the different sections built their statements and actions. But they should not be tied to them exclusively, as most of them play a role in the different book sections.[63]

## *Trust*

The first section focuses on the laity's view of these events and looks at how trust was a key issue for their actions and evaluations. At a moment of political and economic crisis, trust in the Virgin's presence symbolized a hope for a better future. Willingness to believe was not unconditional, and in these chapters we will see how the contemporaries decided to trust in the veracity of the visionaries' statements, the apparitions, and miraculous cures. We will see how they publicly showed this trust and how that inspired imitation. "Lay" (non-clerical and non-expert) Catholics, who by this period were largely literate, did not hesitate to write to their spiritual shepherds (and to each other) about Marian apparitions. Their letters let us look through what Lisa Bitel calls "the eyes of the believers"[64] and allows us to examine the way in which the devotees experienced and evaluated the apparitions and their aftermath, to situate them in their religious world, and to see how they regarded the claims of ecclesiastical and medical agents.

To understand this lay perspective (both of visionaries and supporters) we have a broad range of documents at our disposal. Letters and reports were collected by the various diocesan commissions that show how supporters and visionaries tried to convince the clerical authorities of their opinion. There are also several collections of documents not related to these commissions. These illustrate the interchange of information between the various supporters and the visionaries and offer a less censured means to access their religious world and their opinion about the apparitions. The collection gathered by Honoré Vermeire,[65] for instance, documents the network of Flemish visionaries and their supporters. Similarly, that of Louis Wilmet[66] provides information about the lay visions on the apparitions in Beauraing and in Onkerzele, and shows the tension that existed between the various groups of supporters. The parish archives of Onkerzele and those of the Beauraing and Banneux shrines provide information about the impact of the clergy on the laity, but also about the divine favours people claimed to have received.[67]

## *Competence*

The second section studies the medical professionals. In the commotion about the apparitions and miraculous cures, they took different positions. Doctors who did not hesitate to guarantee the authenticity of the events with medical tests faced materialist colleagues who pathologized religious experiences. Both sides were present at the sites, and both expressed their opinions afterwards in medical meetings and in newspapers and periodicals. Some doctors were more welcome than others at the apparitions. Those who had been invited by the supporters of the sites had better access and thus a better view of the visionaries; they could subject the visionaries to various tests and received the permission to attend, or even participate in, the post-vision questioning of the seers. Whereas the involvement of doctors was initially sporadic and spontaneous, it developed a firmer structure after a few years when a group of Catholic Belgian doctors suggested the formation of a commission. Church authorities soon agreed and gave them permission to question and examine more closely the visionaries and those healed. The church's willingness to involve the doctors fit a trend toward an increasing emphasis on medical tests in the evaluation of exceptional religious events.

We can trace the activities of the medical professionals through their publications (their books and articles in medical and religious journals), but doctors also left their traces in archives. Part of their correspondence has been preserved in diocesan, shrine, and Vatican archives. The focus is primarily on the doctors who explicitly called themselves "Catholic," but did not necessarily "believe" in the apparitions. The discussions they had with the lay supporters and members of the clergy shows the difficulties some of them had in combining their Catholicism and their medical science, two epistemologies capable of "explaining" and "defining" the apparition series.

## *Authority*

A third section focuses on the Catholic clergy and how they responded to and evaluated the series. After an initial silence, the bishops did not hesitate to intervene as the apparitions received more and more public attention and caused commotion. Reports of the series reached Rome as well and, at the command of the Vatican, the Belgian bishops eventually created diocesan commissions to investigate the matter more closely. The ways in which these commissions examined the events were not uniform: While some based their findings on formalized hearings of witnesses, others collected reports of "specialists" on certain episodes (for instance the bleeding objects) or read through the letters and reports that the visionaries and their supporters had created. Even though these commissions had been initiated by the bishops, the bishops were not bound to follow the commissions' conclusions. It was eventually up to the bishop – on his authority as ordinary of the site – to decide whether or not to approve them. Interestingly, the activities and the decisions of these commissions were hardly known to the public, so the discrepancy between their opinion and the bishops' actions would not always have been easy to see. In fact, the bishops' public comportment – both in this final phase and in the previous stages of the evaluation – caused a few stirs in ecclesiastical circles and had an impact on how the events were evaluated.

The various commissions left a substantial paper trail, and we can examine their actions and discussions through the various reports that have been preserved. Apart from these sources we also have correspondence among the bishops, between the bishops and the clergy, and between the bishops and Rome. This more formal investigation of the apparition series was, however, only one side of the clerical reaction. Various members of the clergy also expressed their opinions in letters to the bishops and to the laity, and we will examine these non-official stances as well.

## *Time*

To grasp the effect of the official decisions of the ecclesiastical authorities, the fourth section relates to time. We examine the consequences of the official recognition or rejection of the religious experiences and the associated cults and study both the non-approved sites as well as Beauraing and Banneux and the development of their sanctuaries over time. Even before the recognition, the "official" stories started to circulate and authentication was made visible in rituals and material signposts, guarantees for the interest of future generations. Moreover, as we shall see, official approval was not a *conditio sine qua non* for the survival of the site and some devotees believed that if they waited long enough, the truth about the apparitions would come out. Time erased memories and filtered out the debris of apparitions leaving only edited stories so that, in the end, even an abandoned site could be rejuvenated.

In the concluding chapter I reflect on what it means to study the evaluation of the Belgian wave of apparitions as that of an intrinsically modern, and, thus, public, series. I summarize how this public format of the alleged supernatural events impacted the Catholic evaluation processes and show how paying attention to the public setting allows us to go beyond the depiction of modern Catholicism as a homogenous and firmly structured hierarchical knowledge system.

First however, we need to enter the "horror of the battle," as Louis Wilmet described it in September 1936, and start with the chaos of the initial years. In order to understand the meaning of the series of apparitions and the individual events, we need to place them in their historical context.[68] The following pages will, therefore, provide the reader with some information on the religious, political, and economic scene in Belgium that Mary entered in late 1932. We will thereby study the series as the complex phenomenon it was: a product of the age of Mary, mediatized on a national level, and loaded with political and economic meaning.

# 1

# Apparitions

## Mary in Belgium

### *Popularity of Marian Devotion*

The 1930s were a period of flourishing Marian devotion of an intense Catholic organizational life in Belgium. The Catholic laity participated in Catholic mass meetings and joined Catholic movements that covered different aspects of their lives, not solely their religious needs.[1] Still, the nationwide incidence of visions in the 1930s is somewhat surprising given variations in the observance of religious practices in the different regions of Belgium. In the most agricultural regions of Belgium the observance was still about a 100 per cent, but in larger cities and industrial centres (as for instance, Brussels, Antwerp, and Liège) only a small number (between 20 to 25 per cent) attended church. The number of Catholic baptisms, marriages and funerals were diminishing there as well.[2] Furthermore, there were also differences in the type of Catholic political involvement between Dutch-speaking Flanders and francophone Wallonia. Social differences were more pronounced in Wallonia than in Flanders and Christian democracy never really flourished there. Church strategy in Wallonia had a more missionary stance. In Flanders, social segregation was more attenuated and, in contrast to Wallonia, the (antidemocratic) conservatives did not dominate Catholic politics.[3] Nonetheless, in both parts of the country initiatives for the re-Christianization of society had emerged under the umbrella of Catholic Action. "The overall impression," so Martin Conway concludes in his depiction of Catholicism in interwar Belgium, "remains one of a powerful and well-organized church which through its vast network of affiliated organizations – such as schools, youth movements, farmers' leagues and trade unions – exerted a preponderant influence of many areas of Belgian life."[4]

Marian devotion had always been strong in Belgium and often centred on different incarnations and local versions of the Virgin.[5] "Love Gave You a Thousand Names" ("*Liefde gaf U duizend namen*"), as a popular song for the Virgin put it.[6] The Virgin could be appealed to for different reasons and illnesses, the various local Virgins all had their names and specialties. Our Lady of Mesen in Edingen, for instance, was called upon for cases of rheumatism, while Our Lady of Donk was said to help conception, and Our Lady of Rozebeke helped against dandruff.[7] Although these local variations remained popular, the Belgian devotional landscape started to shift in the nineteenth century due to the strong centralization and uniformization of the Catholic Church. This "Romanization" also had an impact on Marian devotion. Supported by new mass media, a more uniform image of the Virgin Mother circulated.[8]

Our Lady of Lourdes was one of these international devotions that, supported by Rome and modern media and means, evoked a rapid and broad response. The Catholic Church's swift approval (18 January 1862) and the particularly quick (commercial and religious) development of the site in the last quarter of the nineteenth century were exceptional.[9] The shrine's popularity was partly due to the many miraculous cures that were reported at the site, which were carefully evaluated, listed, and disseminated by the local medical office.

The response to the Belgian apparition series of the 1930s cannot be fully understood without reference to the popularity of the Lourdes cult in Belgium. Initially Lourdes only attracted French pilgrims, but with the support of Rome it soon developed into an international pilgrimage site.[10] Belgium had its own Marian shrines, but the Pyrenean apparition shrine proved to have a particular attraction for Belgian Catholics. Up until the Great War, Belgium was the country that, after France, sent most pilgrims to Lourdes (where they made up a quarter of all the foreign visitors).[11] By the 1870s Belgium had its own periodicals focusing on the events near the grotto, *Les Gloires de Notre-Dame de Lourdes*, the *Almanach de Notre-Dame de Lourdes* and *Belgisch Tijdschrift van Onze-Lieve-Vrouw van Lourdes*. The huge success of the Lourdes devotion was, according to the *Belgisch Tijdschrift van Onze*

*Lieve Vrouw van Lourdes,* primarily the result of the popularity of the book of the Catholic jurist and zealous ultramontane, Henri Lasserre.[12] His *Notre-Dame de Lourdes,* published in 1869 with the approval of Pius IX, was an immediate success and subsequently translated into no less than eighty-three languages. By 1900 about a million copies had been sold. Part of the book's popularity was due to its many accounts of miraculous cures.[13] Such stories were also included in the Belgian Lourdes periodicals about Lourdes but also in others like *Bode van het Heilig Hart.*[14]

The Lourdes devotion left its material marks in Belgium: statues of the "Immaculate Virgin" were put up in Ghent and Liège[15] and imitations of the Massabielle grotto became local places of prayer. Some of them were exact copies on one-quarter scale (the measurements acquired from the Bureau of the Oeuvre du Roc), others were free interpretations. There were two "peaks" in their creation. The first was the era in which the apparitions became famous and the first pilgrimages were organized (last quarter of the nineteenth century). The second was in the 1920s and '30s, when the Lourdes visionary, Bernadette Soubirous, was canonized.[16]

When Bernadette was officially included in the ranks of the saints, on 8 December 1933, Belgium was in the midst of its own series of Marian apparitions. It was exactly near such an imitation Lourdes grotto that the Belgian wave started with a first series of apparitions to five children in Beauraing in November 1932.[17] In the series of apparitions that followed and lasted up until 1935, Lourdes was regularly a reference point, and several visionaries were compared to Bernadette Soubirous. During one of the apparitions, in Sclayn, Mary was said to have asked for a Lourdes-grotto (instead of the more common "small chapel"). Lourdes had become a standard that the Belgian apparitions were measured against.[18]

The Lourdes apparitions were, however, not the only ones that the Belgian Catholics could have heard about. In the decades before Beauraing and Banneux, other Marian apparitions had been reported in Belgium.[19] Compendia of Marian apparitions include Belgian events in Rochehaut (1927, a young girl), Faroeulx (1925, a priest), and Malmédy (1919, where Mary was said to have scared two burglars away). But these reports of apparitions received little attention and were certainly not approved by the church. Apart from these episodes

Figure 1.1 Postcard depicting the Lourdes-grotto of Beauraing and a drawing of the Virgin appearing to the five children.

in Belgium, there had been apparitions reported elsewhere, as in La Salette (1846), Pontmain (1871), and, more recently, in Fátima (1917). It is difficult to define how much Belgian Catholics knew about these foreign apparitions.[20] Some of the witnesses called to testify about the Beauraing apparitions stated that these foreign apparitions were not well known in Belgium.[21] This is in line with recent scholarship on the Portuguese apparitions suggesting that Fátima only started to attract international attention in the 1940s (although the cult of Our Lady of Fátima was approved in 1930).[22] A recent apparition series that Belgian Catholics *did* refer to when evaluating the credibility of Belgian apparitions was that of Ezquioga, which began in 1931. As in Belgium, in the Spanish series hundreds of visionaries had reported seeing the Virgin during public and serial events at various locations.[23] Similarities with the Spanish apparition site were used as arguments for and against the Belgian visions.

Overall however, it seems important to make a distinction between what an "average" Catholic knew about Marian apparitions and the expert knowledge of a small number of faithful who were interested in mystical events and were particularly keen on hearing about them. The Belgian apparition series that started in late 1932 did not cater solely to these "experts"; they caused an enthusiast response among Belgian Catholics in general. These were people who had heard about earlier apparitions, but those apparitions were always in bygone eras or somewhere distant, not in their "own" environment.

## *Apparition Fever*

While the large number of Marian apparitions during the "age of Mary" (between the dogma of the Immaculate Conception in 1854 and that of the Assumption of Mary in 1950) has caught the attention of scholars, the Belgian series of apparitions has aroused relatively little interest. Even though it was exceptional in extent and diversity,[24] it is mentioned only briefly in surveys of Marian apparitions and research on the cult of Mary in Belgium, or in passing in studies about other European apparitions in the 1930s.[25] Only the two initial events, Beauraing and Banneux, have been the object of more extensive studies.[26]

The series started late November 1932 when five children of Beauraing claimed to see the Virgin Mary near a hawthorn tree in the garden of a school run by the nuns of the Christian Doctrine. These visions were quickly followed by reports of Marian apparitions in Banneux (since January 1933) involving a young girl. Both of these initial series of apparitions took place in Wallonia, the French-speaking part of Belgium.[27] Other sites were soon reported in both the French- and Dutch-speaking areas of Belgium. By the mid-1930s, the sites of apparitions that appeared in the news covered most of the country. Some contemporaries described the complex series of events that followed as a "wave," a "fever," and even an "epidemic."[28] It was not always the Virgin Mary who appeared to the visionaries, other saints and heavenly and infernal beings were involved as well. What is more, even though the various sites generally started with an apparition episode, other phenomena were also reported, including diamonds falling from the sky and then disappearing.[29] These and similar phenomena indicate that the series of apparitions that followed the rather sober, Lourdes-like episodes in Beauraing and Banneux had a somewhat different tone and physiognomy. Whereas some, as in Uitkerke and Chaineux, were as restrained as the initial series, others, as in Lokeren, Onkerzele, and the followup visions of Beauraing, were more exuberant. Various visionaries insisted that they had experienced more than a hundred apparitions

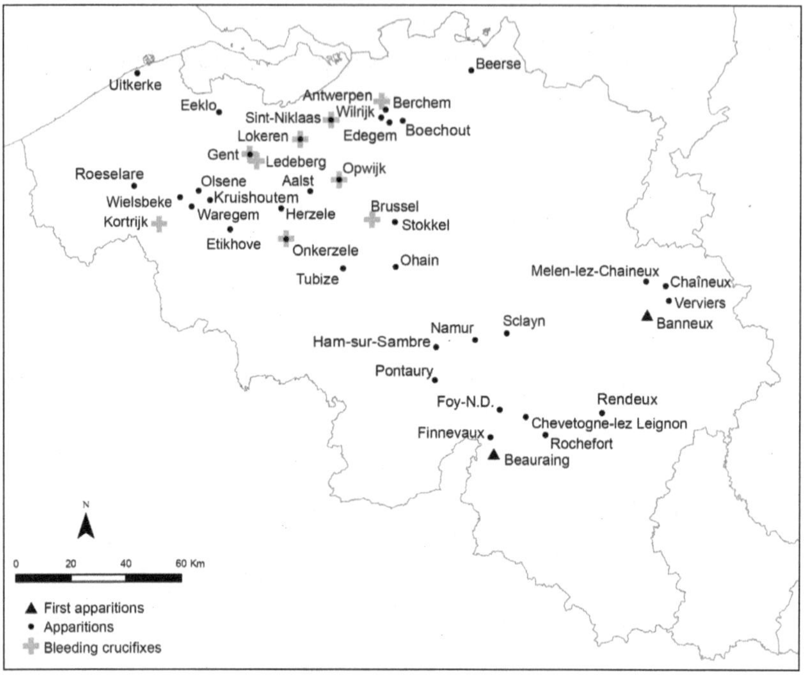


Figure 1.2 Map of sites of apparitions and bleeding crucifixes.

and saw not only Mary, but also Jesus, the Devil,[30] Saint Anthony, Saint Joseph, the Archangel Gabriel,[31] the heads of angels,[32] flying globes,[33] green and red birds fighting,[34] blood on their own hands,[35] and so on. Some of the episodes resemble those at foreign apparition sites. For instance, the boy-visionary of Lokeren, Gustaaf Van Driessche, stated that he had played with a younger version of the Virgin. The claim was similar to that of the visionaries at Spanish and German apparition sites at the start of the twentieth century.[36] Bleeding and moving crucifixes and other devotional objects were reported as well. These resembled, as the contemporaries remarked, earlier reports on bleeding crosses in Spain (Gandia, Limpias, and Piedramillera, 1918–22), Templemore in Ireland (1920), and Asti in Italy (September 1933).[37]

Various visionaries (mostly adults) assumed leading roles at the apparition sites. As they claimed to have been singled out by Mary, they promulgated the Virgin's messages but told what they had heard during these apparitions about contemporary politics (both national and international) or even the whereabouts of a recently stolen work of art.[38] One unlucky visionary insisted that Mary had told him to dig a hole for the spring she would eventually create there. After three days of digging however, all he had to show was the mockery of his neighbours.[39] Still, most of the time, the visionaries conveyed religious messages, often referring to the need to repent and sacrifice.[40] Not only the survival of the Belgian nation depended on people's repentance, the Catholic Church also faced a gloomy future.[41] In apocalyptical terms, they hinted at secrets that the Virgin had told them that had to be locked away for the next decades.[42]

Several of the visionaries, male and female, indicated that the Virgin had asked them to sacrifice themselves.[43] Whereas these calls for prayer, suffering, and sacrifice were still in line with the stress on sacrificial penance in Catholic teachings of the time, some of the visionaries did not shrink from introducing new practices and devotions whose orthodoxy was more adventurous. The visionary of Onkerzele, Leonie Van den Dijck, for instance, emphasized that the faithful had to worship the drops of blood that Jesus had lost during the Passion and in doing so they would be saved from purgatory.[44] On other occasions, she (and other visionaries) referred to a hitherto unknown wound of Christ that had to be venerated.[45] Similarly, the Lokeren girls insisted that whoever embraced a certain pair of stones would obtain eternal life,[46] and a visionary from Namur claimed to be an intermediary in miraculous cures.[47]

In this respect, the various visionaries can – in the words of Chris Maunder – be depicted as "popular theologians." Their "visionary mode of theologizing is distinctive: following mystics of the Catholic past, visionaries have employed an epistemology in which the instigator of all propositions was a supernatural person dictating them – in this case, a supernatural female figure, the Virgin Mary."[48] Mary was often said to confide messages and these emphasized existing Christian doctrines, but also pointed at new elements. It was particularly these "new contributions" to the Catholic teachings that left their mark in the archives because of the reaction they provoked among the religious authorities. Inspired by the instructions the visionaries claimed to have received from above, supporters did not hesitate to change the words of the "Ave Maria" prayer or to promote unapproved devotions. A particularly notorious case was the support of the devotion of the Sacred Head as the seat of divine wisdom.[49] Seers and their supporters founded a confraternity (which is beyond the authority of laymen), and distributed devotional medals and pictures. They announced a new feast day on 1 July in honour of that devotion, organized the associated festivities and pilgrimages,[50] and promised that everyone that wore the medal with its image would be protected from harm.[51]

Subsequent to the initial events in Beauraing, thirty-three sites developed where visionaries had a first apparitional experience. Visionaries had additional visionary experiences in seven other locations.[52] There were two other sites where bleeding objects were signalled that were not also sites where apparitions had been reported (apparitions and bleeding objects often converged).[53] The total thus comes to forty-two, but might have been higher as it's probable not all such events left traces in the archives. Most of these followup apparition sites did not develop immediately after news of the events in Beauraing and Banneux. Even though there were reports of visions in Verviers in Rendeux already in January 1933, the peak in the emergence of new sites was almost a year later, in October 1933. In that month nine new locations were reported: Chaineux, Etikhove, Foy-Notre-Dame, Herzele, Lokeren, Melen, Olsene, Uitkerke, and Wielsbeke. These sites in October were centred around two main nuclei: Banneux and Onkerzele, a site in Flanders where the first apparitions had been signalled in August 1933. In the vicinity of Beauraing, other sites developed as well, but their creation was less concentrated in time. Keeping this temporal clustering in mind, it seems as though the Onkerzele apparitions (linked to the apparitions of Tilman Côme in Beauraing) functioned as a kind of catalyst for reports on other apparitions in Flanders. The importance of these followup sites should not be underestimated. Even though Beauraing and Banneux are the best-known sites today, the other locations generated as many or more visionaries. While Beauraing stands unrivalled with sixty-nine persons claiming to have experienced a mystical event, Banneux could only boast three while Onkerzele had thirty-six, Olsene twenty, Lokeren twelve, and Etikhove and Chaineux both five.[54]

As our map (figure 1.2) shows, apparitions were reported in Wallonia, the French-speaking part of Belgium, and in Dutch-speaking Flanders. There was, however, a difference in the incubation of the epidemic between Flanders and Wallonia. The reports in Flanders peaked about ten months after the initial events in Beauraing and two months after the Flemish apparition site of Onkerzele had started to attract attention. It may be that even though Beauraing and Banneux had been well-covered in the press, the proximity of a Flemish example stimulated reports of new sites in Flanders.

As noted at the start of this chapter, there were some differences in religious observance between Wallonia and Flanders and more industrial and rural regions. Did the differences between Wallonia and Flanders also show in the Marian apparitions? At first glance, the various accounts seem to be more similar than one might expect. The majority of the apparitions (with exception of Brussels, Ghent, and smaller cities such as Lokeren, and Eeklo) took place in villages (of 1,000 to 3,000 inhabitants)[55] in rural areas. For a more detailed description of the sites, Abbé Didion's list is a good starting point. Referring to the garden setting of the apparitions in Beauraing and Banneux, Didion noted that, "the others took place at identical kinds of locations":[56] a garden in Melen and Beerse; a hedge in Chaineux, Onkerzele, Etikhove, and Lokeren. Looking at Didion's list and that of Louis Wilmet, we can add that there were similar sites in Ohain and Herzele. As for the Lourdes grotto in Beauraing, the apparitions in Onkerzele, Wielsbeke, and Eeklo were near imitation grottos as well. Apart from these garden settings, there was also a rural aspect to the sites in Uitkerke and Olsene. The arcadian atmosphere this overview evokes might however leave the wrong impression: The modern era was not completely absent and announced itself in the railroad bridge in Beauraing, or in the visionaries arriving by train in Lokeren.

There were also important differences between the sites, and not all of them reported apparitions that continued for a long period of time. In Beauraing new visionaries and apparitions continued to be reported from November 1932 until March 1934; in Onkerzele the reports span from August 1933 to October 1934; and in Lokeren apparitions and other phenomena were reported from October 1933 until October 1934. The peak of the mass phenomenon of religious enthusiasm was 29 October 1933. On that evening the Virgin appeared in Onkerzele, Lokeren, Etikhove, Herzele, and Melen. In Melen 5,000 people were present, in Etikhove, 40,000. After that, the "epidemic" seems to have declined. The events were now primarily located in Onkerzele (second series) and Lokeren. And no longer was it the general public who went to watch, but rather a specialized audience, almost always the same.

Figure 1.3 The visionary Emelda Scohy in front of the "tunnel" in Ham-sur-Sambre.

This decline, so Dr August Ladon remarked in his study of the series, might have had something to do with the fact that the Virgin did not keep her promises: In Etikhove she did not show herself to the public, and in Melen no spring miraculously appeared.[57]

While the sites had some similarities, the profile of the visionaries involved showed considerable variation. The best way to describe the diversity of the visionaries involved is to start in November 1933 when Nestor Brasseur felt his whiskers become singed in Verviers. However bizarre in hindsight, in 1930s Belgium the event made the news since Nestor's burned moustache seemed to be physical evidence of the apparition he claimed to see in the Verviers cemetery. The thirty-six-year-old unemployed factory driver reported that, when counting his money to see if he had enough for cigarettes, he came across a religious medal in his wallet. He got angry and threw it away, complaining that it had not brought him any luck. Instantly something burned his moustache and he felt compelled to kneel and pray. Then he saw Jesus who told him to pick up the medal and use it to bless "all the unhappy people" he would subsequently encounter. When other men made fun of him, Nestor stood by his story and emphasized that he had the burned moustache as proof.[58]

Nestor is an unlikely introduction to the visionaries that were involved in the Belgian series given the seers of the initial two episodes, Beauraing and Banneux, that dominate the official accounts on the Belgian series. In Beauraing, there were five children involved: Fernande (fifteen), Gilberte (thirteen), and Albert Voisin (eleven); and Andrée (fourteen) and Gilberte Degeimbre (thirteen). In Banneux, Mary was said to have visited a young girl named Mariette Béco (eleven). As all of them came from a rural background and were still rather young, they fit with the model nineteenth-century visionary identified by David Blackbourn. In this model, the visionaries were female rather than male, children rather than adults, and laity rather than the clergy, whereas the prototypical visionary of the Middle Ages had, up to 1400, most often been adult, male, and often a priest.[59]

The Belgian series, however, continued after Beauraing and Banneux and the number of visionaries involved is rather impressive. At least 185 persons claimed to have seen Mary and/or other saints during the wave of apparitions and their profiles often did not fit that of the prototypical female child visionary. While the list of visionaries retrieved from the archival documents can never be complete, it does give us an indication of the type, age, and sex of the visionaries: sixty-five male and sixty-seven female adults, as opposed to twenty-five girls and fourteen boys.[60]

The gender distribution of the adult visionaries is arresting. And it becomes even more remarkable when we look at the thirty-two sites where an initial Marian apparition took place (excluding the sites where visionaries only had a followup apparition). For twelve of these, men have been named as the initial visionaries, in nine cases the first visionaries were women (twice in combination with younger visionary/ies); on seven occasions girls were involved (twice in combination with other visionaries); while another four sites were linked to boys (twice in combination). So men like Nestor Brasseur not only started new sites, but they tended to do so on their own. In this they differed from the male visionaries in the Spanish Basque Country, who functioned primarily as a confirmation of apparitional sites, but did not start them.[61]

We know the professions of some of the male visionaries that started new sites in Belgium. They included an unemployed factory chauffeur, a waffle maker, an unemployed mason, an innkeeper, a housepainter, an agricultural worker, a factory worker, and a weaver. Their professional backgrounds resemble that of the majority of the male followup visionaries we know about. By far most of them made their living by manual labour as factory workers (six), weavers (five), agricultural workers (three),[62] and others. Most of them thus belonged to the classes that felt the effect of the economic crisis, as the description of two visionaries as "unemployed" indicates. Likewise, some visionaries alluded in letters to their difficult financial situation when they thanked their correspondents for the money they sent, or tried to explain their reasons for accepting the money from pilgrims.[63]

The professions of the female visionaries is seldom mentioned, so it is harder to place them in society. In those cases where a job is referred to, the sources indicate a working-class background (servant, female worker).[64] When class is explicitly mentioned, the tone of the mention varies. Whereas on some occasions the emphasis is positive, describing the difficult and hard life they had up to the first apparition, on others the emphasis is derogatory. Leonie Van den Dijck, the first visionary from Onkerzele, is a good example. Her supporters emphasized the hardships she had suffered after her husband left her and their children. The local priest, on the contrary, repeatedly used her

Figure 1.4 Group portrait of the visionaries from Onkerzele, 15 June 1934, from left to right front row: Jules De Vuyst (?), Berthonia Holtkamp, Leonie Van den Dijck; second row: man with hands folded in prayer, Gabriel Quatannens; in the back: Henri Kempenaers.

background in order to explain her eagerness to be in the limelight.[65] In his opinion she acted out of "a desire for attention in line with what could be expected from such low-class working-class women."[66]

A closer look at the Belgian series shows how interconnected visionaries and sites were. The same visionaries were involved at different sites, and there were other links as well. For instance, the Onkerzele sequence of apparitions that seems to have been a sort of catalyst for the creation of Flemish sites was linked to the apparitions in Beauraing. More precisely, the Onkerzele series started on the eve of the day on which a new series of apparitions had been promised to Tilman Côme, a followup visionary from Beauraing. The first Onkerzele visionary, Leonie Van den Dijck, had given her parish priest money for a mass to be said on 5 August in honour of Our Lady of Beauraing and started reporting apparitions the evening before.[67] Contemporary observers noted these and other connections as well, especially those among the Flemish sites.[68]

One of the Onkerzele visionaries, Berthonia Holtkamp, for instance frequently claimed to have visions at other sites where visionaries had already reported apparitions. Her first experience was in Beauraing, and later she reported visions in Onkerzele, Lokeren, Etikhove, and Olsene.[69] Beauraing was important for other itinerant visionaries as well:[70] The so-called Sœur Marie-Régine claimed apparitions in Beauraing, Brussels, and Onkerzele;[71] similarly Laure Dulière had her first series of visions in Beauraing and continued having them in Brussels and Kortrijk.[72] Jules De Vuyst, the Herzele seer, reported apparitions in Destelbergen, Lokeren, Staakte, Onkerzele, Opwijk, Gentbrugge, Bergenkruis, and Sint-Amandsberg.[73] The visionaries often travelled to the other sites when they were looking for support they did not find in their place of origin.[74] Some even moved to these (more popular) locations: Onkerzele, for instance, attracted Berthonia Holtkamp and Gabriel Quatannens, but also "Sœur" Marie-Régine.[75] Apart from peripatetic visionaries, the various sites were also linked through the reported messages of the Virgin and the similarities in their content. Some of the visionaries asserted that the Virgin had given them information about other visionaries or other paramystical phenomena, for instance telling them which of the bleeding objects was "authentic."[76]

Considering that each of these sites involved one or more visionaries, and sometimes up to thousands of enthusiastic Belgian and foreign bystanders driven by curiosity and piety, it is safe to say that the number of persons involved in the vision series was considerable. Its magnitude is best illustrated by the comments of Abbé Didion, in correspondence with Louis Wilmet. On 27 November 1934, two years after the initial events, Didion reflected on the Belgian series. By that time he had already written two major reports on the apparitions, which he sent to the archbishop in Malines. He counted nineteen sites. Noting that in the last century there had only been six or seven apparitions with a public repercussion (Rue du Bac, Pontmain, Loo, La Salette, Lourdes, and Fátima), he worried about this large number of locations reported in such a small country. According to his count, the total number of visions reported was by then more than a thousand. Moreover, in these visions the Virgin was said to have asked for at least nineteen chapels and sanctuaries. As the country was in the midst of an economic crisis and already building the national Basilica of the Sacred Heart in Koekelberg (Brussels), this was no small number. Six or seven pilgrimages had been requested, three springs announced for healing the sick, and numerous secrets confided. Mary had changed her appearance more than once and called herself, among others, the Virgin of the Poor; the Mother of Christ, The Virgin that stands above all women, Our Lady of the Sacred Face, Mother of the Rosary, Our Lady Mediatrix, and Our Lady of Flanders.[77] Some of these names referred to older traditions, while names such Our Lady of Bôring or Virgin of the Poor were new. Unrivalled in extent and diversity, it was the scale of the events that worried Didion.

## *Apparition Scenes*

The Belgian series of apparitions was a series of a series of apparitions. Each of the different sites had its own visionary/ies who saw the Virgin several times. A few sites, some of which I introduce below, had several sets of visionaries and, as such, resembled the Ezquioga apparitions as there were multiple visionaries (this was, as William Christian has shown, an innovation in comparison with the Lourdes apparitions).[78] What was exceptional about the Belgian series however was that the events were not limited to a specific region (as the Spanish series was confined to the Basque country), but eventually covered large parts of Belgium. In that regard, they were similar to the Italian "wind of miracles" as Robert Ventresca describes the 1948 series of apparitions and other events (moving statues, miraculous cures).[79] While Ventresca points to different locations, he treats the series on a national scale. The following chapters follow his approach as this makes a study of the complete series more feasible. The grouping of the diverse series is not only a post-factum approach, something we see in historiography on the series. Contemporaries also saw the diverse apparition series as part of a bigger Belgian wave of apparitions. One of the challenges in studying this Belgian apparition series is, therefore, that while all attestations were eventually linked to the nationwide series, each of these cases started as a local event. All apparitions had specific features (visionaries, messages, locations) that made them unique, yet because of their chronology, they were grouped together and weighed against each other.

Before adopting an umbrella view, the next pages elaborate on this difference between the local and national level, the unicity of each apparition series and their similarities. Through a short description of eleven of the Belgian reports I want to elucidate the diversity *and* interconnectedness of these apparitions. The selected cases are the most well-known and longer ones. Three of the case studies concern followup apparition series, that is a second series of apparitions centred on a new group of visionaries at a site that had already been the scene of a previous series. This allows me to point at the importance of the sites of the apparitions and the fact that the dots on the map (figure 1.2) only show the different locations and the total number of apparition-series within this wave is even higher.

### BEAURAING

This wave of apparitions started at the end of 1932. That same year the first references to the upcoming canonization of Bernadette Soubirous, the visionary of Lourdes, appeared in the Belgian newspapers.[80] Given the popularity of the Lourdes devotion in Belgium, the Belgian series of apparitions began at an appropriate location, near an imitation of the Massabielle grotto. It was, however, not the Lourdes Madonna that was spotted on the evening of 29 November 1932. Even though she later confirmed that she was the Immaculate Conception, the Virgin in Beauraing looked quite different from the one in Lourdes. In fact, it would take a while (until 2 December 1932) before the young visionaries received the confirmation that they were indeed meeting the Virgin.[81]

Beauraing was the juridical centre of the canton and had, at the time of the apparitions, about 2,000 inhabitants. The city was a petit bourgeois town with civil servants, retired people, and merchants making up a good part of the population. Some inhabitants were employed in the local quarries and lime kilns, but the majority worked in the factories in nearby France. Animal husbandry in the agricultural area was the main activity.[82]

That first night in late November the five children saw a young lady, shining brightly just above the Lourdes grotto in the garden of the Sisters of the Christian Doctrine. Albert Voisin (eleven years old) spotted her first. Together with his sisters Fernande (fifteen) and Gilberte (thirteen) and their friends Andrée (fourteen) and Gilberte Degeimbre (nine), he continued to see the Virgin until 3 January 1933.[83] Communication started as well. On 23 December, the Virgin, whom the children described as having rays of light around her head[84] and a golden heart on her chest indicated that she appeared in Beauraing "so

Figure 1.5 Postcard of the apparition according to the information provided by the children.

that they might come here on pilgrimage."[85] She later also promised to "convert the sinners," encouraged people to pray, asked for a chapel, and conveyed personal messages to the visionaries.[86]

The apparitions in Beauraing seem only to have been a private, intimate affair on the first evening(s). The rumour spread quickly. Gradually more and more people were involved. As the apparitions continued and the newspapers reported about the events, the news spread on a national scale and attracted also some pilgrims from France, the Netherlands, Luxembourg, and Germany. The curious and the devout flocked to the apparition site by car, train, and buses … Toussaint and Joset estimate that about 150,000 people went to Beauraing between December 1932 and the first days of January 1933.[87] When, on 3 January 1933, the Virgin said goodbye to the children, between 25,000 and 30,000 people were present.[88]

In the months following the apparitions, the stream of publications continued, with booklets and periodical articles on Beauraing. As we will see in the following chapters these publications contained intense polemics.[89] Even after the series of apparitions ended, the site continued to attract attention. Reports of miraculous cures at the site consolidated its importance.[90] One of these alleged cures became the start of a new series of apparitions in Beauraing (see Beauraing II). The personality of the visionary, Tilman Côme, and the character of his visions and messages rekindled the controversy.

### BANNEUX

Only a few days after the apparitions in Beauraing ended, the Virgin was sighted in Banneux, a village in between Tancrémont and Louveigné. She appeared on Sunday, 15 January 1933, near the small worker's house of the Béco family, next to the forest near "La Fange."[91] The Béco family was poor. Father Béco (a bricklayer, shale decker, and mechanic) had been unemployed for five months. The oldest of seven children, Mariette Béco (age eleven) was not very religious, had given up on her catechism classes, and had not stepped inside a church for two months. Yet, when she stared out the window that evening and saw a very beautiful young lady standing outside, she believed she saw the Virgin.[92]

According to Mariette Béco, the Virgin was dressed in white, and had a blue veil and a cloud around her feet. One brief glimpse at her feet suggested that there were golden roses on them. Around her head was

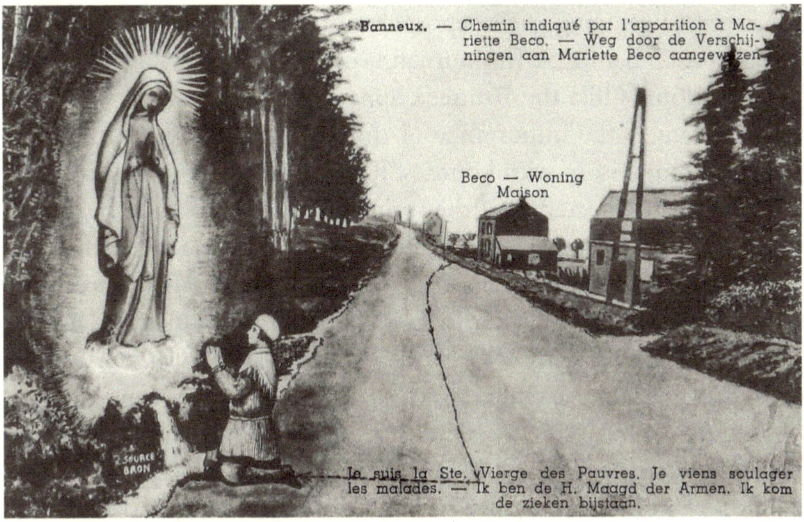


Figure 1.6 Postcard of the road the Virgin indicated to Mariette Béco.

a semi-circle of rays of light.[93] The Banneux Virgin thus showed greater similarities with the Lourdes Madonna than with that of Beauraing. Mariette Béco saw the Virgin eight times (the last time on 2 March 1933), at first in the small front garden of the family. The Virgin also led her to a small spring near her house saying "This spring is reserved for me,"[94] and "This spring is reserved for all nations … to alleviate the sick." She identified herself as "the Virgin of the Poor" and asked for "a little chapel."[95] The following weeks the Virgin did not appear. She remained absent until Saturday, 11 February 1933, the seventy-fifth anniversary of the apparitions in Lourdes, when she told the young girl that she had "come to ease the suffering." The final apparition took place on Thursday, 2 March 1933. Once more, she encouraged Béco to pray a lot, she blessed her and then disappeared.[96]

The small number of people present during the apparitions stands in sharp contrast with what happened in Beauraing. There, the visionaries found themselves near a busy road, surrounded by thousands of people, physicians and journalists present, and special trains bringing those interested in the apparition to the town. However, like Beauraing, Banneux also developed into a pilgrimage site and cures were reported early on.[97]

The newspapers seem to have responded rather slowly or not at all. *De Standaard,* the Catholic newspaper that had most diligently covered the Beauraing series, reported only weeks after the events on the apparitions in Banneux. The journalists first wanted to conduct a proper investigation. While the Banneux apparitions were seen to be linked to Beauraing,[98] the importance of the spring in the Banneux series inspired comparisons with Lourdes. It was probably not a coincidence, so a journalist reflected, that the spring was on the "Bois de Banneux" that belonged to the poor and could therefore not be bought or sold.[99] This connection with the poor, gave, so one of the articles said, the bishop of Liège, Mgr Kerkhofs, good hope for the future: It could be a devotion "to Our Lady of the Poor, converting the workers who have drifted away from the church."[100]

### BEAURAING II

After the Virgin said goodbye to Mariette Béco, new apparitions were reported at other locations (Rendeux, Verviers, Finnevaux, Tubize). One of the first followup series of apparitions to gain its own momentum in the press was the apparitions to Tilman Côme in the summer of 1933. Côme's apparition series in fact started out as a miraculous cure at the original apparition site in Beauraing, the garden of the Sisters of the Christian Doctrine. Côme saw the Virgin twelve times between 11 June and 15 August 1933. That final day more than 100,000 people came to witness.[101]

Tilman Côme was a fifty-eight-year-old metal worker from Pontaury-Mettet, but had not worked since December 1932 because of a light case of spondylitis of the vertebrae. On 11 June 1933, at 9.00 a.m., Côme was praying near the Lourdes grotto. When he was about to leave, a warm feeling went through his body from head to toes and he saw the Virgin on the exact same spot where the children had seen her. She told him "until tomorrow" and left. This brief vision restored the corporeal functions that Côme had lost in the previous months. He returned the next day and this time, the Virgin informed him "I have come for the glory of Belgium, to preserve this land from the invader … Make haste!"[102]

Tilman Côme saw a lady in white, with a white veil, not a crown of golden rays as the children had seen. Her feet were in a cloud and she had a ribbon as a belt. When he asked her, on 15 June, what they should call her, she did not answer but Côme saw gold letters on the ribbon and read "Notre-Dame de Bôring" or "Böring." She did, however, tell him that she wanted "a chapel."[103] The initial enthusiasm inspired by Côme's cure was soon followed by suspicion. Tilman Côme communicated with the Virgin, but what he heard her say mainly put *him* in the spotlight, for instance, "Show yourself among the people. Your wishes will be fulfilled. Pray."[104]

The Virgin asked Côme to organize a pilgrimage on 5 August, her feast day, and announced a secret. This kindled the imagination of the faithful and curious and thousands of people travelled to Beauraing that day. They returned disappointed as they did not witness a miracle and the Virgin only asked for a chapel and annual pilgrimage on 8 May. It was a rather incoherent request, and some people recalled that before Tilman Côme had his first apparition in Beauraing, he already received a message of Saint Therese of Lisieux.[105] Moreover, no one spelled Beauraing as Böring. Why would the Virgin do that? Was that not a very German spelling?[106]

Côme's cure and apparitions rekindled the controversy the original Beauraing apparitions had generated. The apparitions featured in the press after the first reports and were covered on an almost daily basis.[107] His supporters and opponents published in the periodicals that were linked to the apparition site (*Les Annales de Beauraing et Banneux, L'Officiel de Beauraing*) and produced a series of small booklets.[108]

### ONKERZELE

In the final days of the apparitions to Tilman Côme, the centre of the apparition series started to move north toward the Flemish part of Belgium, to Onkerzele in the diocese of Ghent. Explicitly linked to the events in Beauraing, the apparitions to Leonie Van den Dijck shared characteristics with the original apparition series and with the series in Banneux.

Onkerzele was a town of 2,300 inhabitants, most of them small farmers and cigar makers. Louis Wilmet, who covered the series, noted: "there are many socialists, stubborn ones, who are concerned about social demands and moderate ones that are merely worried about material concerns. A third of the members of the Workers party goes to church." Most of them had voted Catholic, however, when the "Reds" started to attack religion and the confessional school. "They all die in the arms of the church, by the way."[109]

Near the church of Onkerzele was a small imitation of the Massabielle grotto with a small chapel next to it consecrated to Our Lady of Lourdes.

This is where Leonie Van den Dijck (1875–1949) first claimed to see the Virgin on 4 August 1933. Van den Dijck was fifty-eight years old, mother of thirteen children, nine of which survived infancy, and had been left by her husband. She had visited Beauraing in June and a month later she had saved enough money to pay for two masses to be sung for Our Lady of Beauraing, "the Virgin with the golden heart." The priest however decided to hold the masses in honour of Our Lady of Snow as the Beauraing events had not been approved yet. The masses were sung on Saturday, 5 August, and Sunday, 6 August 1933.[110]

Around eight in the evening of 4 August 1933 – the evening before the first mass she paid for – Van den Dijck was praying in the small chapel together with some of her friends when she first saw Mary. The next day, the date of the great pilgrimage organized by Tilman Côme in Beauraing, she observed the Virgin again. New apparitions in the chapel followed. After a few visits Mary made herself known as "Our Lady of the Poor" adding "I have come to convert the sinners and to stop the blasphemies."[111] In later apparition messages we hear echoes from other apparition sites like La Salette (the Virgin not being able to keep back the arm of her son if the blasphemies did not stop) or Beauraing II ("I will protect your country"),[112] and like the children in Beauraing and Banneux, Van den Dijck received a secret. Van den Dijck saw different types of Virgins: Our Lady of the Sacred Heart, Our Lady of the Seven Sorrows, Our Lady of the Roses.[113] However, the Onkerzele apparition Virgin is most depicted as Mary standing on a globe (figure 1.9)

Initially, only a few women were present during Van den Dijck's visions. Gradually, the number of bystanders grew (on 8 September 1933, for instance, there were about 10,000 people present).[114] Not all meant well, and there was a fair amount of mockery and cursing. A journalist concluded, "to maintain in Onkerzele that one sees Our Lady, in itself requires an exceptional amount of courage and stamina."[115]

Press coverage started with a little delay, as the first articles in the national press appeared almost a month after the initial events.[116] From the onset, there were comparisons with Beauraing. Furthermore, the articles and the booklets that were published on the site stressed the fact that this time the Virgin appeared in Flanders (Magain 1933; Sindic 1933). This "Flemish character" also seems to have been somewhat cultivated at the site since there were small flags on sale that showed the Virgin of the Poor of Onkerzele and were printed in the Flemish colours.[117]

Van den Dijck was not the only one who saw the Virgin during this period. Other visionaries also came forward. None of these however gained much attention. For this first series Leonie Van den Dijck was and remained the main visionary. That would, however, change after an "Antwerp" invasion (Onkerzele II).[118]

## HOULTEAU-CHAINEUX

The series of apparitions in Houlteau-Chaineux (a hamlet near Dison, not far from Verviers)[119] was smaller than the previous apparition series. Even though the series had features similar to other apparitions – child visionaries, a poor family and a spring – there were serious doubts about the authenticity of the events from the start.[120] Still, the Chaineux-events attracted hundreds of people and this was one of the apparition sites where public authorities intervened.[121]

The series started on 5 October 1933, near the house of the Emonds family, in a corner of Corbeau-Dison Road. That first evening, sometime between 8:00 and 9:15 p.m., five-year old Jeanne Emonds went into the garden to get some nuts from her father's ice cream and candy cart that was parked in the shed. Returning to the house, she saw a bright light in the hedge, pointed it out to her sister Marie (age nine) and said: "Look, the Virgin."

Their parents, followers of Antoinism, a Spiritist movement with Catholic elements,[122] were skeptical, but had never seen their oldest daughter so distraught. Moreover, the girls were not the only ones who saw the Virgin dressed in white, with a blue veil, brown girdle, great brown rosary, and her feet in a cloud. One of their neighbours, Bertine Weusten, also claimed she saw something that night. In the following days, two more people saw the Virgin: Charles Gillet, a 15-year-old mechanic apprentice in Verviers, whose family lived nearby, and the mother of the two original visionaries.

An increasing number of people attended the apparitions. According to one of the promotors, on Tuesday, 17 October more than 5,000 people were present.[123] (It was easily accessible by train.)[124] The mayor thought that things were getting out of hand and on 21 October 1933 announced a prohibition on gatherings of more than five people and the parking of cars. The visionaries and their supporters (a provisory committee called Pro Virgo Maria) then moved their activities away from the public road to a nearby field and created a parking lot whose

Figure 1.7 Postcard of Marie Emonds, one of the visionaries of Chaineux.

fee would be used for the construction of a chapel.[125] The messages the Virgin communicated during the apparitions resembled those at the other sites and referred to a spring as well as the threat of war.

ETIKHOVE

"The Virgin is making the tour of Flanders," the socialist newspaper *De Vooruit* remarked on learning of the new apparition site in Flemish Etikhove, a farming village between Audenaarde and Ronse.[126] From 9 October 1933 until the end of that month, two adult men, Maurice Van Roeckegem (a worker, age thirty)[127] and Omer Eneman, saw the Virgin. Omer Eneman, also known as "Merke Gosseye" was thirty-five, married, a painter/worker, a singer in the church choir, but also an entertainer with his accordion at wedding feasts and neighbourhood fairs.[128]

Hearing about the events in the other towns, Eneman had allegedly quipped that Our Lady first had to appear in a tree near his house before he would take the apparitions seriously. As in many apparition sequences, his skepticism was about to be tested. On 8 October 1933 he was on his way to an inn when he suddenly saw the Virgin in a meteor shower in a set of trees. His wife joked that he was probably seeing his "beers" rather than the Virgin.[129] Eneman however insisted he saw the Virgin – dressed in white, with a blue mantle, and a crown of golden roses – also the following evenings. Eneman had to tell the people to go to confession and receive communion, and to encourage the priest to convert the sinners.[130]

Initially, there were only twenty-five people witnessing his apparitions, but the number soon increased up to thousands of bystanders. Press coverage started after a delay. Newspapers like *De Standaard* were somewhat slower in responding, as they first wanted to make sure that it was not a case of fraud or included shallow messages.[131] Not all bystanders believed in the apparitions, as one reporter remarked there were some who "mocked, cursed, ripped the clothes of those who were praying etc., but apart from these there were also thousands who were beautifully reserved, and undisturbed continued with singing, prayers and litany."[132] From the 18 October onwards, Maurice Van Roeckegem, a Walloon living in Ronse, also claimed to see the Virgin.[133]

As with Tilman Côme and the child visionaries of Beauraing, Eneman had been given a specific date on which to return, the Feast of Christ the King, on 29 October. The local authorities saw the enthusiasm the apparitions generated on "normal" days and prepared accordingly.[134] They installed loudspeakers, provided Eneman with a microphone to say his prayers and brought in the Red Cross. The Belgian railway organized eight pilgrimage trains to Etikhove. About 20,000 people were present that day, among them people from Wallonia. Many sick who hoped to be cured came, but no miracle happened. Eneman did not even have a vision that day. In the following days, some hundred pilgrims continued to travel to Etikhove. After 2 November, the press no longer covered the events and interest declined.[135]

### LOKEREN

The first series of apparitions in Lokeren started when nine-year-old Gustaaf ("Stafke") Van Driessche, son of a coal merchant, saw Our Lady in a chestnut tree in the Naastveld district at 9:00 p.m. on 25 October 1933. After that night, he returned every evening to pray and saw the Virgin several times. Interest in the apparition grew gradually and people of the surrounding municipalities came to Lokeren to witness the boy praying. Some came, as one journalist remarked, "out of curiosity" while others came "out of conviction."[136] There was even a special bus service.

The apparition in Lokeren drew press attention, albeit minimal. When covered in the national press, the Lokeren events featured as part of the series of apparitions that was reported in Belgium.[137] Of the three local Lokeren newspapers, only one reported about the apparitions; the others (Catholic) did not even mention them. As the weather worsened and the roads turned into pools of mud, the interest diminished. The number of bystanders dropped from 2,000 to between 150 and 100 people.[138] Lokeren disappeared from the apparition radar. That is, until the summer of 1934 when three young girls claimed to see the Virgin as well (Lokeren II) and the events took a far more dramatic turn.

### OLSENE

On 29 October 1933, the day Omer Eneman's visions attracted so many visitors to Etikhove, another Flemish apparition site developed as well. In comparison with the other sites discussed here, it was one of the shortest series for it continued just over a week until 7 November 1933, when the Virgin said goodbye, blessing the crowd.

Maurice Van den Broecke (1907–2000) was from "a good Christian family" with nine children. When he first saw the Virgin he had already been working as a weaver for ten years at a factory in Olsene.[139] Well-liked by his fellow workers, he was almost illiterate, but – as his boss emphasized – intelligent. He went to church on Sundays (although he preferred to stay in the portal during mass), but allegedly did not believe in the apparitions in Beauraing and elsewhere and had not visited any of these sites.[140]

That Sunday evening 29 October 1933, around 9:45 p.m., Van den Broecke was cycling home after visiting several pubs, expressing his own disbelief when people talked about the apparitions. He was taking a short cut on a dirt road when he saw the Virgin floating eighty centimetres above the ground, her hands folded, next to a small poplar, her feet on some sort of brown pillar, with a golden crown, blue robe covered with stars, and in front of her "golden tongues of fire." She would later call herself, on 4 November, "Our Lady Above All."[141]

When Van den Broecke told his family members what he had seen, they asked him not to make himself the laughing stock of the neighbourhood. He, however, continued to go to the site in the hope of seeing the Virgin, and others went with him. On Tuesday evening (31 October), his colleagues from the factory gathered at the apparition site. The next days the crowd grew and according to the police there were at least 4,000 on some evenings.[142]

In the case of Maurice Van den Broecke, his good reputation helped him to gain credibility among his co-workers. His boss later declared that even though they initially mocked him, they did believe him in the end, because they trusted him and he was known not to lie.[143]

### ONKERZELE II

On 19 October 1933 a new series of apparitions started in Onkerzele, where Leonie Van den Dijck claimed to see the Virgin in August 1933. This time the visionaries were Bertha ("Berthonia") Holtkamp (between twenty-five and thirty-years old), Henri Kempenaers (forty), and Martha M. (fifty-four).[144] All three lived near Antwerp (Berchem, Wilrijk, and Edegem) and were, therefore, called "the Antwerp people" ("les Anversois").

The three visionaries seem to have been part of a pilgrimage from Antwerp to Onkerzele that had as its main goal to pray for Kempenaers, who had a damaged lung. The initial statement of Holtkamp reads like the account of a day-trip: She went on a pilgrimage to Onkerzele, visited the grotto, had a sandwich, saw the visionary Leonie Van den Dijck, returned to the grotto, and then had her first vision.[145] The other visionaries, Martha M. and Kempenaers, had visited apparition sites before. Martha M. had been to Beauraing seven times and Banneux four times.[146] Kempenaers seems to have visited Banneux once, but had never been to Beauraing. The files on Onkerzele show that on this first day and in the following weeks, the initial visionary Leonie ("Nieke") Van den Dijck continued to report apparitions but that this new set of visionaries, especially Holtkamp and Kempenaers, gradually took the centre stage. On 21 November 1933, for instance, Van den Dijck who was praying in a loud voice was asked to remain quiet the moment the ecstasy of Holtkamp started.[147]

The series of apparitions continued for months and gradually the phenomena became more diverse: Holtkamp saw "The Virgin of the Holy Face"[148] and Jesus in different versions (with a two-pointed beard, as the Sacred Heart, as the child Jesus) and Kempenaers relived Christ's Passion.[149] What is more, the public "saw" as well when, on 18 December 1933 around noon, about 5,000 people thought they witnessed a supernatural solar phenomenon similar to what happened in Fátima. They saw a spinning "disc" in front of the sun and the sun changing colour from green to purple to blue.[150]

Onkerzele II was one of the longest series of apparitions of the whole Belgian wave. While the other visionaries only reported a fixed number of apparitions, Kempenaers and Holtkamp seem to have continued to see the Virgin in the following years. The number of bystanders diminished however, and in the late 1930s there seems to have been a loyal group of followers that gathered in Onkerzele primarily on special occasions (newly invented rituals, anniversaries).

### LOKEREN II

In the summer of 1934, Lokeren was once again the central stage of apparitions when three young girls, Elisabeth Cornelis (from Sint-Niklaas); Tiny Kool (Kemzeke), and Maria Van den Plas (Antwerp), also claimed to see Mary. The tumult that developed around this second series – forcing the public authorities to intervene – resembled what happened in Houlteau-Chaineux.

The girls not only reported apparitions of the Virgin (and other saints); they also claimed to play and talk with the child Jesus, predicted miraculous cures, and relived Christ's Passion. Moreover, the crucifixes they carried when reliving Christ's Passion were not only said to bleed but also to move and speak.[151] In this regard, the apparitions were quite similar to what had been reported about the apparitions in Ezquioga in 1931. At the Spanish apparition site, the visionaries likewise saw Mary and relived Christ's Passion.[152] Contemporaries noted these similarities and used them as a negative example, since Ezquioga had been rejected by the diocesan authorities.[153] Lokeren was similar to Ezquioga from another perspective as well: In Ezquioga, a platform for the visionaries had been constructed so that the masses of bystanders could follow the apparitions more easily. In Lokeren, tribunes were built that allowed the visitors to have a better view, and entrance tickets were sold.[154] Apparently, this was not the most stable construction, and on 21 August one of the tribunes collapsed – causing extra hilarity among the critics of the site.[155]

The behaviour of the visionaries did not improve the situation. Their threatening gestures and words like "wretched people, punishment awaits you" disturbed bystanders.[156] When the police had difficulties controlling the mob on 24 and 31 July,[157] the events alarmed the public and ecclesiastical authorities. After an emergency meeting of the city council on 2 August 1934, all gatherings of more than five people were forbidden.[158] Even though the visionaries and their followers continued to meet, the religious enthusiasm the apparitions had once generated started to cool down. The miraculous cures that had been promised for 21 August 1934 did not materialize, and the only thing reported that day was a fight between the visionaries.[159] Moreover, the ecclesiastical authorities decided to intervene as well and circulated a letter (2 September 1934) rejecting the events in Lokeren-Naastveld.[160] The visionaries obeyed and stayed away from Lokeren.

### HAM-SUR-SAMBRE

In many ways, the apparitions in Ham-sur-Sambre are somewhat different from the rest of the series. First of all, the apparitions began four years after the initial events in Beauraing, on 22 March 1936, hence rather late in comparison with the other sites. Secondly, there was an intense involvement of French Catholics that resulted in a separate cult

Figure 1.8 The apparition site in Lokeren.

site in France.[161] In comparison with most other series of apparitions, the Ham-sur-Sambre series was exceptionally long, as the series continued throughout the following years in Belgium and in France.

The apparition series started when a twelve-year-old girl, Emelda Scohy, the daughter of a miner, came back from a walk in the woods with one of her friends. At around 5:30 p.m. they passed the entrance of a small irrigation tunnel[162] in a place called "La Praule," where her friend detected only a strange light, but Scohy could see "someone illuminated by a ray of light"[163] (figure 1.3).

Up to a thousand bystanders joined Scohy's prayers the following days as she kneeled down in the water. On 30 March the "Virgin of the Virgins" told Scohy to come pray at the tunnel dressed like her, in a brown robe, a white veil, and a crown of roses. Photographs of the apparition site show Scohy surrounded by one child dressed as Ste Thérèse of Lisieux, one as Ste Elisabeth, and another one as St Jean – all carrying paper flowers.[164] From that day onwards the girl saw not only Mary but also the saints around her and Jesus the Good Shepherd, who had allegedly come to Ham-sur-Sambre to recruit good and saintly priests. Linking the apparitions to Beauraing II, Scohy noted that while the Virgin had announced in Beauraing that Belgium would be spared from the intruder, it would become clear during her own apparitions what type of trials Belgium was to expect. The young girl claimed she had to suffer for Belgium, build a church above the tunnel, and organize a yearly pilgrimage to Ham-sur-Sambre.[165] Some newspapers (primarily the regional ones) covered the series, albeit in rather negative terms. They mocked the similarities with Beauraing,[166] Scohy's visions, and the fact that she and her friends were dressing up like divine beings.[167]

Scohy was, however, not the only visionary in Ham-sur-Sambre. On 11 April 1936, a young woman, Adeline Pietquin, declared she saw "Our Lady of the Poor Tunnel" ("la Vierge du Pauvre Tunnel") as well. Her visions focused on France where, according to the Virgin, Spanish communists would start a revolution in the late 1930s. In this turmoil, evidence would turn up that would allow the Bourbon-Naundorffs, who pretended to be the heirs of Louis XVII, to claim the French throne and restore the Bourbon dynasty. Belgium would be absorbed by France and the old Carolingian realm would be restored. Pietquin was to help the Bourbon-Naundorffs and replace the pope with one of her followers. Apart from a focus on the Sacred Heart devotion, poverty, humility, and charity were of central importance in her visions. In this respect, she shied away from the public attention and commercialization that Emelda Scohy seemed to be seeking.[168]

In 1937, Pietquin went to France, in Bouxières, at the invitation of the parish priest Césard, and her apparitions continued there.[169] In Ham-sur-Sambre, Emelda Scohy's apparitions became the central focus point. The numbers of pilgrims diminished in the following years however, but there seems to have been a loyal core of followers. This persistence of the enthusiasm for the (continuing) apparitions needs to be read against the background of the repeatedly announced negative verdict of the episcopal authorities.

## *Cross-section*

These summary overviews of a portion of the apparition series reported in Belgium in the 1930s demonstrate the diversity and the interconnections of the different sites. The two approved apparition series (Beauraing I and Banneux) show similarities with other approved sites as they included child visionaries (similar to Lourdes and Fátima for instance), "sober" Marian visions, a request for a chapel and pilgrimage, and the reference to a spring. Even though the two initial series resembled each other (in comparison with the other Belgian reports), the reception of the two sites was quite different. While thousands of curious and faithful flocked to Beauraing during the apparitions, the series in Banneux was low key with only about fifteen people bearing witness to the event. Banneux followed after Beauraing and was, therefore, immediately tainted by the accusation of imitation, but it was also less accessible, as it was unconnected to the railroad network.

In the case of Beauraing, Lourdes seems to have been the most important reference point. Given the upcoming canonization of the Lourdes-visionary Bernadette Soubirous, the newspapers had already been reporting on the mid-nineteenth-century Lourdes apparitions again. Beauraing was heralded as a "new edition of the Lourdes miracle"[170] and the visionaries were "new Bernadettes."[171] Given the prominence of Beauraing in the press, the Walloon site became the reference point for the following Belgian apparition reports. None of these locations was discussed as an independent site, they derived their relevance and meaning from comparison with and connection to the other Belgian apparition sites and they were always *post*-Beauraing. The Flemish Onkerzele site, for instance, first made the news as a "Flemish Beauraing."[172] The link with the rest of the series made smaller apparitions visible (that might have stayed under the "radar" – in the words of William Christian[173]), but also stimulated accusations of imitations.

When we look at the different locations of the apparitions, it is quite telling that, in many instances, the events took place near a site that was already linked to Marian devotion. This connection had been established either by the presence of a small chapel (Etikhove) or Lourdes grotto (Beauraing, Onkerzele) and/or by previous apparitions that had been reported at the site (Lokeren). This vouches for the importance of the site, later sometimes also captured in the emphasis on one (natural) element, touched by the Virgin: the hawthorn in Beauraing, the elms in Etikhove, and the water in Ham-sur-Sambre.

Every new apparition site was automatically linked to previous events. Still, each case had its own unique characteristics that its promoters would emphasize as it differentiated "their" site from others and mitigated accusations of imitations. One of the ways in which apparition series differed from one another is the way in which the visionaries described the Virgin Mary. In cases like Beauraing, Banneux,

Onkerzele, and Olsene this led to fixed visual representations – the iconization of the Virgin.[174] These multiple images of the Virgin fit the polymorphous character of Marian devotion, and pointed to different aspects of Mary that appealed to different audiences. In Banneux, Mary introduced herself as "The Virgin of the Poor," who had come for "all the sick" and "all nations."[175] In Beauraing she confirmed she was the "Immaculate Conception," but also the "Mother of God, the Queen of Heavens," while she was "Our Lady Above All" in Olsene. Each identity came with specific material markers. There were some echoes between the sites, however, and "the Virgin of the Poor" appeared in Banneux and in Onkerzele. Likewise, the messages the Virgin communicated at the different apparition sites displayed similarities, and yet also had their own specificity. She asked for a chapel at different sites (Beauraing, Beauraing II, Chaineux); a pilgrimage (Beauraing, Beauraing II); she promised to convert the sinners (Beauraing, Onkerzele) or encouraged the visionaries to pray for the conversion of sinners (Onkerzele, Chaineux); to help the sick (Banneux; Beauraing II, Chaineux); to ease those who suffer (Banneux); and she pointed to a local spring (Banneux, Chaineux). Apart from these more general cult-related messages, there were also some messages that related to the political context of the time: The Virgin warned of an invader (Beauraing II, Chaineux), and promised to protect the country (Beauraing II, Onkerzele, Chaineux). In combination with the messages promulgated at the different sites, each version of the Virgin had its own "story," its own appeal. There was a dependence and coherence, but also competition among the sites.

The specificity of each apparition series also becomes apparent when we look at the unfolding of the local drama. Reports of apparitions found more willing ears at some locations than at others. Responses of local authorities involving the prohibition of public gatherings (as we saw in Lokeren and in Chaineux) had not only to do with the number of people the series of apparitions attracted, but also with the local political dynamics. As we learn from the reports on Lokeren and Onkerzele, the series worsened existing tensions. Other towns were more welcoming. The Beauraing pilgrimage of 5 August 1933 and the Etikhove pilgrimage of 29 October 1933 show how public authorities (and transport companies) had learned to respond to the mass enthusiasm the apparitions generated. In this respect, it is important to emphasize that while all of these series were public events, some were more publicly known than others. Still, most sites seem to have benefitted from the momentum created by the other apparition series and people were curious to see their own "local" variations on the theme. The majority of the series described above indeed started as completely "local" events with visionaries who lived in the vicinity of the apparition site. Three series were exceptions: At Beauraing II, Lokeren II, and Onkerzele II visionaries from other towns travelled to the already well-known apparition site and claimed to have their "first" apparitions there.

## *A Public Series: Media and Politics*

The 1930s Belgian incidents quickly made the news and their sites were visited frequently. Thanks to an elaborate railway network (which laid on extra trains) and the eager response of the bus companies, Belgian pilgrims were quite mobile.[176] They crossed the country to visit a certain apparition site or even went on "apparitional tours" to several sites in one day. The frequency and public character of the events turned the apparitional sites into stages for what one could almost call religious spectacles. Arriving hours in advance, crowds grouped together to catch a glimpse of the visionaries. Seeing them was chancy, and it was not unusual to go home disappointed.[177]

The apparitions were promoted in announcements of pilgrimages in various newspapers and magazines. There were, however, other means of promotion, not all of them appreciated. When, for instance, the Onkerzele visionaries and supporters went to Beauraing in May 1935, the visionaries were dismissed as "fanatics" and the aggressive promoting by those who accompanied them criticized. One witness, for instance, saw "[t]he leaflets distributed to the crowd in favor of the 'Living Rosary' with the large poster placed on … (I apologize for having to say this to you!) the belly of the promoter lacks all good sense and taste."[178] Some supporters of apparition cycles were enterprising in this respect. As noted, during Lokeren II people had to buy tickets to enter the apparition tribune (figure 1.8). Other sites attracted ancillary commercial activities. Booths with food or devotional objects were set up at the sites of long-running series of apparitions or at those where apparitions had been announced in advance. Creative entrepreneurs even produced new religious objects such as postcards of the visionaries. Some of the new "mystics" (for instance Leonie Van den Dijck and Tilman Côme) got involved in these commercial activities themselves.

Figure 1.9 Postcards of some of the forms in which the Virgin was said to have appeared: Banneux, Beauraing, Onkerzele, and Olsene.

Figure 1.10 Visitors of the Beauraing apparition site before the gate of the garden where the apparitions took place.

Figure 1.11 Pilgrims at the Banneux apparition site.

Figure 1.12 Postcard of the first visionary of Onkerzele, Leonie Van den Dijck.

Figure 1.13 Postcard with the stalls at the apparition site in Onkerzele.

Their mercantile spirit made their opponents question the credibility of their claims of the supernatural.[179]

The events were well covered by the Belgian and international press.[180] In Spain, for instance, the supporters of the apparitions in Ezquioga (1931) compared the Belgian visions with their Spanish counterparts.[181] In Belgium, the first articles about the apparition series were published only a few days after the initial events in Beauraing (10 December 1932). Newspapers of different ideological tendencies (liberal, socialist, and Catholic)[182] enthusiastically covered the series, forcing the ecclesiastical authorities to intervene. In a directive of 20 October 1933, the Belgian bishops tried to contain the stream of information and asked those who had witnessed something extraordinary to report it to the clergy and not the press. They emphasized that all texts that deliberately discussed the apparition series had to obtain the imprimatur since the matter pertained to religion and morals. However, as the Jesuit J. Creusen remarked, newspaper articles were difficult to control. The imprimatur – a guarantee of orthodoxy and morality, not scientific truth – was never appended to newspaper items, even if it had been requested and granted.[183]

In spite of this episcopal directive, newspapers continued reporting on the visions well beyond the autumn of 1933. Catholics like Jan Filip Boon, the editor-in-chief of the Catholic newspaper *De Standaard*, however, promised to limit their reports to the "journalistic" side of the events, that is, to "all that can be seen and heard by the common bystanders … as has been prescribed"[184] without adding an interpretation of the phenomena. Still, not all articles published after the bishop' intervention were written in this documentary manner. On 8 February 1934, Georgina De Myttenaere of the Catholic *Nieuws van de Dag* made a telling apology. Even though the paper had initially reported on the apparitions in a sober manner, it had changed its approach for fear of losing readers to other newspapers like the liberal paper *Het Laatste Nieuws* or the socialist paper *De Vooruit*. She added that they had already lost readers to *De Standaard* (Boon's paper) because of its extensive reports on the apparitions in Onkerzele. De Myttenaere nonetheless promised to remind the journalists to keep the episcopal directives in mind and not to dramatize the gestures and actions of the visionaries involved.[185]

While journalists commented on the "apparition fever," supporters of the events composed, sponsored, and distributed their own substantial promotional literature of tracts, brochures, and books that helped spread the fever. They also composed songs, poems, and prayers that they circulated among the pilgrims.[186] Here the effect of the episcopal requirement for an imprimatur could be felt. The letters of would-be promoters of various apparitions show how potential authors were hindered in publishing about the events. The archives of the archdiocese of Malines, for instance, contain the text, already typeset, of a book by Jan Filip Boon on Tilman Côme that was never published because the author could not obtain the imprimatur. Similarly, Alfred Magain was not allowed to publish a French version of his book on the apparitions in Onkerzele, even though a wealthy donor was ready to pay for its distribution.[187] Nevertheless, the number of publications that did get published was large enough that Rome formulated its own instructions two years after the bishops did. On 25 March 1935, the nuncio Clemente Micara addressed a letter to Archbishop Van Roey, referring to the prescriptions the Holy Office had formulated on 9 January 1935. Micara was adamant that publications (books, booklets, and articles) on the vision series should be forbidden and the Belgian bishops should make sure their 1933 instructions were observed.[188]

Figure 1.14 Poster announcing a presentation by Abbé Didion about the apparitions in Beauraing and Banneux and three Flemish apparition sites.

Print was only one of the means through which information on the Belgian series circulated. Supporters like Louis Wilmet also contributed to spreading the story of the apparitions and travelled the country to talk about the events. Their opponents, of course, did so as well[189]. The visual media also showed interest, and already in September 1933 a newspaper article referred to a sensational film called *Beauraing, ses apparitions, ses guérisons, ses miracles (Beauraing, Its Apparitions, Cures and Miracles)* and indicated that the Catholic Film Centre (*Katholieke Filmcentrale*) was also preparing a documentary on the topic.[190]

### *Rex: Selling the Supernatural*

> The "Rex" editions have published the most complete and efficient pieces of evidence about the "Apparitions" in Beauraing and Banneux.[191]
>
> Excerpt from an advertisement

Given the coverage the wave of apparitions received, the Catholic publishing house of Rex was making no small statement in their advertisement of 1933. Rex substantiated the claim with a list of books it had already published in French and Dutch on the Belgian series of apparitions.[192] The following years, Rex continued to publish booklets on the series[193] and dedicated articles to the topic in its periodicals (*Rex*, *Soirées*, *Pour que les Catholiques lisent*). The publications covered the most famous trio of apparition sites – Beauraing, Banneux, and Onkerzele – but also commented on smaller series like Chaineux.[194]

Books on the apparition series could be a very lucrative business. Rex was nearly bankrupt when news about the apparitions in Beauraing reached its director, Léon Degrelle (1906–1994). He decided to invest in publications about the visions and asked the local Beauraing doctor, Fernand Maistriaux, to write an account. The doctor's booklet was published even before the apparitions were over and it was an immense success. According to Degrelle, the doctor's two booklets (published in Dutch, French, and German) sold no less than 700,000 copies. Degrelle was a notorious exaggerator and it is hard to confirm that number, but the booklets must have sold well, since Rex was soon out of danger of going bankrupt.[195]

Rex was the publishing house of the Catholic Action youth movement. Catholic Action represented a new type of lay apostolate that was introduced by Pius X's encyclical *Il fermo proposito* (11 June 1905). Under the wings of the ecclesiastical hierarchy, and with an eye on Rome, the laity was to act as *milites Christi* and rechristen modern society that was allegedly secularizing.[196] The movement was very successful in Belgium, especially among the young.[197] The Belgian Catholic Action youth movement was not strictly unitarian, as it functioned as a coordinating movement for other – existing – organizations such as those focusing on students, scouting, young farmers, and parish youth.[198]

The publishing house of the Catholic Action youth movement existed since 1926. It communicated the church doctrine to the young (publishing papal encyclicals), provided some of the campaign material of the Action Catholique de la Jeunesse Belge (ACJB), and even published various novels, but had only limited impact. That changed when Léon Degrelle was appointed at its head in October 1930. Expanding its reach, Degrelle launched new periodicals, among them for instance *Soirées* in December 1931, a weekly magazine for the young.[199]

The financial situation remained precarious but things started to change for the better when Rex's booklets concerning the Belgian apparitions became a success. It is unclear why Degrelle decided to start publishing booklets on the Marian apparitions in Beauraing. His memoires and those who collaborated with him at the time recount different explanations. Discussing the topic in an interview fifty years later, he noted: "People often laugh about those stories, not me: we hardly know anything about spiritual forces." He added that the night he heard about them, he went to see with his own eyes (Beauraing was about forty kilometres from his native town of Bouillon).[200] Degrelle later claimed that he went every night, but apparently he only attended a few of the apparitions, and on one occasion (1 January 1933) he also witnessed the questioning of the child visionaries.[201] While some of his contemporaries confirmed that he was overwhelmed and believed in the apparitions without the slightest hesitation,[202] Degrelle also gave another version of his involvement at the time. In a series of interviews with Wim Dannau (published in 1973), we read: "I told myself, this is the solution! We are going to make very popular editions and sell those in all the Catholic schools, to the bigots, from Arlon to Ostend."[203] Ridiculing the public's enthusiasm, he posed as more critical: "It is by the way very typical how people hurried to the garden of the sisters by thousands, only on the basis of statements, that were rather ridiculous. Our Lady appeared every day. I often wondered whether this whole business was not a scam done with slides. Anyway, we made a lot of money. At Beauraing at least the miracle of Rex took place."[204]

Robert de Vroylande, one of his collaborators, remembers it somewhat differently in the booklet he published in 1936, the year he cut ties with "Léon Bluff" (as he called him).[205] He wrote that he and a colleague had a hard time persuading Degrelle to publish something about the event. Degrelle became convinced the moment he saw the ecstasies of the visionaries with his own eyes and recognized the potential in publishing about it.[206] The former Rex employees, however, all agree that the Maistriaux booklets were an immense success.[207] Given the success of the Beauraing booklets, it is no surprise that once the apparitions of Banneux, Beauraing II, and Onkerzele became public knowledge, Rex published on those as well.

When Degrelle and his colleagues heard about the apparitions taking place in Ezquioga,[208] a team of writers travelled to Spain in September 1933. In the *Soirées* issue of 22 September 1933, Degrelle gave a short summary of the Spanish events. His text was accompanied by a series of compelling photographs, zooming in on the visionaries and the response of the public. Degrelle announced a series of articles that would be "the most fantastic research that ever appeared in the world, since it combines at the time the horror of the most dreadful predictions and the heart-breaking tableau of the hundreds of visions that are undeniably supernatural."[209] However, when the date for the launch of the series arrived, the bishop of Vitoria, Mgr Mateo Múgica, had already warned in an episcopal letter against the Ezquioga apparitions. Louis Picard, founder and general almoner of the ACJB, therefore wrote a short note on how they were not going to publish their reportage, since the respect for a bishop was not "a matter of discussion or dosage." However, Picard's note was extensively illustrated over several pages that *Soirées* – so the text read – only added as "documentation."[210] So while Rex did indeed obey the bishop, it did so in a "creative" way. It is interesting to add here an observation made by the Carmelite Bruno de Jésus-Marie in a letter to the Holy Office, dated 15 October 1933. Reflecting on the negative comments he and other writers had received for their critical position on Ezquioga, he mentioned that when Degrelle announced the fantastic reportage, Ezquioga had in fact already been condemned by the bishop (the letter was read out loud in the parish churches on 17 and 24 September and once again in October).[211]

The decision of the Belgian episcopal authorities of October 1933 to require an imprimatur for all the texts that covered the apparition series had an impact on the publications of Rex.[212] Rex asked Archbishop Van Roey for an imprimatur for the French translation of Alfred Magain's booklet on Onkerzele, but he refused. *Soirées*, which had regularly addressed the series of apparitions from the start until early November 1933, stopped publishing on the topic. The only exception was an article in June 1934 in which Léon Degrelle described the situation at the Beauraing apparition site where, in his opinion, faith in the apparitions survived and "The wise prescriptions of the Bishops and Archbishop have swept away the imprudence, mercantilism, hysterical outbursts. This great tranquility is necessary to be on the one hand, able to study, and on the other, to pray and hope."[213]

In sum, in the first years of the Belgian apparition series, the Rex publishing house contributed to the spreading of information on the apparition series and provided their readers with articles that leaned toward a positive evaluation. For the Rex collaborators, the Marian apparition series were an opportunity to remedy their precarious financial situation. However, the publications and the later biographical accounts also suggest a religious motivation for covering the apparitions. As we shall see, the involvement of the Rex publishing house in the communication and promotion of the apparitions became problematic after Rex developed into a full-fledged political party.

## *Marian Politics*

The intense media coverage of the series seems to confirm William Christian's assumption that there are certain periods in which apparitions are more frequent, or, to be more precise, periods in which people are more interested in hearing about them, "it is as if the level of skepticism drops." In his opinion, "once a major episode makes visions topical, other minor cases become newsworthy or at least mentionable."[214] Some apparitions only draw attention because they are reported together with or shortly after a major episode is reported and discussed. Referring to these "sleeper apparitions," Christian notes that "what happens in the upward curve, both in the short and long attention cycles, is that visions that would otherwise remain private, be shrugged off, or maybe even laughed at, are taken seriously … At all times there is a continuum of credibility as to what constitutes an authentic apparition, but the criterion shifts, becomes more rigorous or more relaxed, according to the times."[215] He links this shift in criterion, the lowering of the "level of scepticism" to economically and/or politically unstable times when people were more likely to be craving for heavenly support. This convergence of apparitions and political or economic uncertainty has been noted for twentieth- as well as nineteenth-century reports on apparitions.[216]

The 1930 Belgian series clearly seemed to fit a pattern and the 1930 commentators noted that as well. Louis Wilmet, for instance, observed in a presentation held in Brussels that the Virgin had first appeared in Belgium while the nation was in the midst of an electoral struggle (the elections of the parliament were held on 27 November 1932).[217] He noted that Mary frequently appeared in situations of political uncertainty. That had been the case for the Marian apparitions in Paris, La Salette, Lourdes, Pontmain, Fátima, and Ezquioga. On these occasions the Virgin had warned the people about political upheaval and urged them to pray and repent.[218]

The connection between the series of apparitions and the political and economic uncertainty that Belgium was facing has been emphasized by several scholars. Their summary descriptions involve references to Rex's role in the promotion of the apparitions, the imminent threat of Hitler's invasion, and the economic depression and socialist advance.[219] While I largely agree with these descriptions, I believe that we need to delve a little deeper to fully understand the challenges the Catholic Church and political party were facing at the time of the apparitions and how these affected the faithful and their perception of the apparitions.

The Beauraing apparitions began, in an atmosphere of Catholic unity, two days after an intense electoral battle framed as a Catholic struggle against an anticlerical cartel. The elections had not been prompted by this ideological battle, but by the economic and financial distress that the government had not found a solution for. The crash of the American stock market in October 1929 had not immediately set the Belgian economy into a downward spiral. In the first months of 1930 the economy was still thriving. But this changed in the second half of the year, when factories had to close their doors and unemployment increased. By the winter of 1931–32 the economy hit a low point. The production of the metal and textile industry dropped 25 per cent and 19 per cent, respectively, in one year; there was an overproduction of coal; the potato crop could no longer be exported to Germany; and as an export economy Belgium felt the consequences of diminished international trade. The number of unemployed rose from 76,000 in 1930 to 400,000 in 1934 (and since these were only the numbers of the insured unemployed, the numbers probably need to be doubled). Salaries dropped, government pensions diminished, and married women lost their unemployment support. After the government fell because of the commotions and unease caused by these decisions, new elections were held on 27 November 1932.[220]

As Emmanuel Gerard has shown in his analysis of the electoral battle, the campaign and outcome held some unexpected elements. While the Catholic party did not have a good starting position (it had lost some seats to the Liberals and the Workers' Party during the previous municipal elections), things took a turn for the better when Prime Minister de Broqueville managed to distract the attention of the Catholic voters from the financial and economic situation of the country and focus it on the "school battle" instead. This school battle had been a rallying point for Catholics in the previous decades as it involved public funding for (Catholic) schools and concerned "the beautiful soul of the child." In other words, de Broqueville was mobilizing the voters to be good Catholic voters. The tactic paid off: The Catholics won some seats and de Broqueville formed a new government.[221]

The new government wanted to introduce drastic government cuts and received special powers from the parliament in December 1932. This resulted in a "black fortnight" ("*quinzaine noire*") of cuts in salaries and social services, the raising of a number of indirect taxes, and a new national crisis tax. During this fortnight, the apparitions of Banneux started. As Jean-Pierre Delville has put it, "Mary appeared thus at the most tragic moment in the crisis in Belgium."[222] Her apparition, so the faithful believed, showed that the Virgin cared for the people in the midst of an economic crisis. Tellingly, in Banneux, Mary called herself "Virgin of the Poor." The economic condition remained dire in the following years, as none of the frequently changing governments could provide an adequate solution for the malaise. The situation took a turn for the better when, in March 1935, a new government under Van Zeeland (an independent) came in power and introduced a new economic policy based on devaluation. Trade and industry benefitted from the new oxygen this provided and the unemployment diminished.[223]

In the meantime, new political challenges had risen. At the start of 1936, the economic situation had improved, but the parliamentary democracy was under attack.[224] Among the critics were Léon Degrelle and his Rexists. Since its engagement with the apparitions, Rex had become more and more political (in its publications and public meetings). As the ACJB was meant to be apolitical, the movement dissociated itself from Rex.[225] Rex's political engagement threatened Catholic unity in the 1930s and divided the francophone Catholic voters.

Degrelle and his party members represented a generation of Catholic youth, trained by the Catholic Action and no longer at ease with the status quo represented by an older, democratic generation. They strove for a more militant Catholicism characterized by anti-liberal and traditionalist features. Rex regarded the Belgian Catholic Party as outdated and unable to create change. Their militantism showed, for example, in the "coup of Courtrai." On 2 November 1935, Degrelle and some of his followers travelled to Courtrai to a meeting of the national party leaders and criticized them for their self-righteousness and alleged corruption.[226] As a response, the Belgian bishops published a statement concerning Rex on 20 November 1935. They stressed that priests and members of the religious orders were not allowed to participate in its meetings or contribute to its periodicals, and that directors of youth institutions were to shield the youth from Rex. It was, as the historian Lieve Gevers has shown, not yet a full condemnation, but the statement was meant to create a clear difference between Rex and the Catholic Action movement.[227]

The formal break with the Catholic political party followed a few months later. When Hubert Pierlot, the new president of the Catholic Party, made clear that he did not want to negotiate with the rebels, Degrelle responded by announcing that Rex would participate in the May 1936 elections as an independent party. As a "catch-all protest movement" it attracted voters that hoped for a change in an economically and politically instable time. Rex was remarkably successful (11.49 per cent of the votes, and twenty-one out of 202 seats in the chamber), primarily at the cost of the Catholic Party.[228]

In October 1936, Rex entered an agreement with the anti-Belgian Flemish nationalists. This move shocked its primarily francophone voters who feared for its impact on the already fragile unity of the Belgian state. The Belgian bishops responded in the winter of 1936 by publishing a letter in which they condemned not only communism, but also right-wing dictatorship. They stressed that only strong Catholic social organizations could protect against the red peril and that a strong government was needed to defend religious freedom and fight anti-democratic powers. The letter also had an impact on the Catholic youth who started to express fewer criticism on the existing political structures.[229]

The position of Rex became even more precarious in the winter of 1936–37 when the Premier Paul Van Zeeland challenged the Rexist troublemakers with his coalition government of socialists, Catholics, and liberals. Militia in uniform were forbidden and Rex members were banned from the radio.[230] During intermediary elections in Brussels in spring 1937, Degrelle made a capital mistake when he suggested that Cardinal Van Roey's silence about Rex was, in fact, a sign of his sympathy. The archbishop, who had remained hopeful that a conciliation between Rex and the Catholic Party would be possible, now publicly warned the faithful that Rex was a "threat to Church and country" and encouraged them to vote for Van Zeeland. The party lost most of its voters in the election of April 1937.[231]

After all hope for an alliance between Rex and the Catholic Party disappeared,[232] Rex almost completely lost its original Catholic foundation and developed quickly into an extreme right movement. In the elections of April 1939, Rex only received 4.43 per cent of the votes – which brought its total number of seats down to four. As Conway concludes, by the end of the 1930s, due to its own mistakes and international events, Rex had become a marginal movement that posed no threat to the political status quo. Rex would, however, become one of the most important francophone collaborationist movements of Belgium during the German occupation (1940–44).[233]

The political evolution of Rex is important to mention here as it had an impact on the perception of the Belgian apparitions. Rex and Beauraing were in the minds of the people closely linked to one another because of the many publications and because of Dr Maistriaux, the author of the first booklets on Beauraing featured on the electoral list of Rex in his region.[234] Rex's link to the Beauraing-episode featured prominently in the newspaper articles covering the political upheaval. Some journalists even suggested that Léon Degrelle had staged the Beauraing apparitions[235] and accused Degrelle of choosing Dr Maistriaux as a Rex electoral candidate in order to benefit politically from religious enthusiasm.[236] An article entitled "After the Condemnation of Rex" ("*Après la condemnation de Rex*") in *Les Annales de Beauraing et Banneux*, published on 15 May 1937, gave a list of newspaper articles making these allegations. The recurring theme was that in publishing on the apparitions, Degrelle had commercially exploited the credulity of the faithful. The author concluded two things: First, that the sheer number of articles on the Beauraing-link that were published after the condemnation showed that even if it was already years after the first sighting, these newspapers were still obsessed with Beauraing and wanted to discredit the apparitions. Secondly, that the Catholic journalists and politicians who were counting on the political advantage these insults would cause observed a guilty silence. In the author's opinion, they should be as quick to protest against the slandering of the Virgin Mary as they were to defend a political personality of their own clan.[237]

Apart from sharpening intra-Catholic tensions in Belgium, the Belgian 1930s apparitions and their numerous enthusiasts exacerbated from the onset the existing political tensions among Catholics, (liberal) anti-clericals, and socialists. The liberals and socialists regarded apparitions, miraculous cures, and other phenomena as archaic remnants of the past. Journalists of socialist and liberal newspapers adopted a "linear narrative" of a secularized modernity and regarded the piety that was on display at the sites as out of date and "medieval."[238] A journalist of the liberal newspaper *Het Laatste Nieuws* expressed his surprise at how the pilgrims at a time of "radio and electricity, of plane building and other scientific achievements"[239] could "live in an atmosphere as if there are miracles brewing every day and the apparitions might occur every moment?"[240]

The commercial activities that developed at the apparition sites likewise provoked comments from the socialist and liberal newspapers and became a topic of derision. As such, the mockery and aspersions of the Belgian non-Catholic press did not differ much from what their nineteenth-century anticlerical colleagues had reported on older apparitional sites. Wondering about the swift acceptance of the events by the locals, they saw material self-interest as the main motivation.[241] Others thought the apparitions were to distract the workers from the fact that they were starving.[242] The apparitions also inevitably reflected the tensions between the Dutch- and French-speaking parts of Belgium. Even though Flemish Catholics travelled to the Walloon sites almost from the start of the events, some commentators saw the tension between Flanders and Wallonia at work in the vision series. They pointed at the Flemish pilgrims singing "Our Lady of Flanders" at the Walloon sites and called the first Flemish apparitional site, Onkerzele, a case of "Flamingantism."[243] In their opinion, a site that developed solely in reaction to the Walloon site at Beauraing could not and should not be taken seriously.[244]

The tensions were reported and nourished in the press, but also caused brawls, material damage, and threats to the devotees. At more than one site, the police and gendarmes were stationed to monitor the crowds.[245] In two places, Lokeren and Onkerzele, the situation got out of hand. In Onkerzele it was a harmless episode on 24 August 1933 when students from Geraardsbergen threw stink bombs and sneezing powder during an apparition.[246] The Lokeren case, however, ended in physical violence. The visionaries and their supporters were verbally and physically abused by anticlericals but also by other Catholics. The negative atmosphere that surrounded the second series of apparitions in Lokeren is illustrated by the anonymous note threatening the visionaries sent to the city council in the summer of 1934:

> Dear Sirs,
> In the name of all outraged co-citizens I ask you earnestly and kindly to send all the people's agitators, who are the instigators of all the sad events in the neighbourhood Naastveld, home during the next demonstration or to arrest them, if not, I order myself to shoot them all on the spot. With high regards.[247]

The author of the note did not carry out the threat. But their warning captures the disapproval of the local population – also voiced in local papers referring to the actions of a "fanatical sanctimonious hypocrite" and the "swindle." They called upon the religious and worldly authorities to put a stop to the vision series.[248] On Sunday, 29 July 1934, things flared up. The adjunct police commissar posted at the site reported the following:

> From around nine p.m. onwards, we noted an agitation in the crowd, that did not seem to be controllable: the people pushed more and more forward, hostile cries rose from the crowd, at any time there could be an assault of the law enforcement, with an attack on the prayers, and when at a certain moment, the three so-called visionaries came from the pathway close to the public road and spoke to the people (and I have been assured that they addressed the people with insults) only an extremely firm action of law enforcement was able to maintain the order and avoid violent events.[249]

With these events in mind, the police force prepared for the next visions on 31 July. They put up a rope on both sides of the alley in order to keep the crowd away. This time 4,000 people came to the site of the apparitions. There was a continuous howling and whistling and the rope was broken several times. Time and again the police were able to restrain the crowd, but at 9:15 p.m. the police could no longer maintain control[250] and warned the devotees to flee. The journalist and fervent Lokeren supporter Jan Filip Boon was among those who tried to escape to the train station together with the girl visionaries. He reported how they walked in silence amidst the "murderous crowd" yelling at them, threatening them, throwing stones and dirt, and spitting on them.[251] Four people were hurt before they reached the station. Two gendarmes and a railroad employee intervened, and the crowds dispersed. The riots led the Lokeren city council to take action and on 2 August they forbade meetings of more than five people on the public thoroughfare. Those who did not obey these orders would be charged or put in prison. The decision was publicly announced by a note at the apparition site, but it did not keep the devotees from gathering in a nearby garden as the number of arrest warrants in the town archives indicates.[252] Church authorities took action as well, and at the beginning of September both Bishop Coppieters of Ghent and Archbishop Van Roey condemned the Lokeren apparitions in a public letter.[253] Their intervention is exceptional, for it was the first time in the Belgian vision series that the bishops publicly expressed their opinion on one of the apparition sites.[254]

Not only Belgian political tensions influenced the reception of the apparition series, the political developments on an international scale were disquieting as well. Hitler and Nazism were looming, and Stalin's five-year plan to eradicate religion (destruction of churches, arrest of the clergy) increased distrust of communism. As Chris Maunder has noted, the Beauraing apparitions started the same month as a series of elections through which the National Socialists became the largest party in Germany (6 November 1932). Not much later, Hitler was appointed chancellor on 30 January 1933. Maunder links the fact that Beauraing was the first site of the apparitions to its history during the Great War. German troops had invaded and occupied Belgium during these years of warfare, and harrying of the German troops by the Belgian resistance had led to the population – primarily in Louvain and Dinant (close to Beauraing) – suffering atrocities in reprisal. "In these circumstances" so he adds, "it is reasonable to suggest that the Roman Catholic community in Wallonia in areas affected by the First World War would have been sensitive to the possibility of divine intervention and consolation."[255]

In the context of increasing international tension, Mary's message in Banneux that she wanted to set a local spring apart "for all nations, for the sick" was striking.[256] The Union Internationale de Prière, the international prayer society that was created in 1934 and linked to the apparitions in Banneux, strengthened this unusual message. Its members promised to pray the rosary each night for the poor, sick, and suffering, and for the peace among nations as well.[257]

The political and economic instability also left its mark on the apparitions reported in the wake of Beauraing and Banneux. As in other European apparition series, the Virgin presented herself as motherly and/or a more militant figure.[258] On some occasions she appeared to avert the threat or help fight an enemy (who changed throughout the centuries from freemasons and liberals to communists and rival armies), at other sites she functioned as intermediary for the downtrodden and neglected.[259] Some of the Belgian apparitions fit the type of public apocalyptic visions described by Sandra Zimdars-Swartz as warnings that divine chastisement was imminent "unless people repent and do penance for their sins."[260] In Belgium, the form of chastisement, the imminent threat, was often not specified. The fear of an invader was however a recurring theme, not surprisingly after Belgium's traumatic experience in World War I. A telling example of this continuing fear (and changing enemy) were the reports of the visions of the Virgin's words to Tilman Côme, the fifty-eight-year-old Beauraing visionary. According to Côme, Mary had told him that she had "come here for the glory of Belgium and to preserve this land from the invader."[261] In the first months and years after this apparition the "invader" was interpreted as the German army, since Hitler had just become the German chancellor and his political and military moves were regarded with mistrust. However, after Belgium was invaded, the meaning attached to this word gradually evolved into the communist threat, and in the years after World War II, Côme's supporters could still claim that the Virgin had indeed saved Belgium from the "invader," this time defined as the communists.[262] The changing interpretations of the "open" messages of Mary document the changing fears and Mary's role in controlling them. In any case, warnings against an "invader" were also heard at other Belgian apparition sites in the 1930s. In July 1935, the Flemish visionary Jules De Vuyst warned of "an invader," "a man of anger, of the division of the people, a usurper."[263] He also reported visions of Archangel Michael destroying flags with a swastika-design and soothing messages from St Joseph assuring him that he would free and rule "your land of Belgians."[264] The apparitions in Chaineux similarly warned of a menace coming from Germany and, Leonie Van den Dijck believed her country to be in great danger, though she said that Mary would protect it.[265]

Some of the visionaries believed that since they had direct interaction with heavenly beings, they should guide politicians in their actions. The woman who called herself Sœur Marie-Régine de Jésus-Marie, for instance, wrote a letter to the bishop of Ghent and enclosed two letters, one addressed to Neville Chamberlain and other to Adolf Hitler. In these letters, she gave them political advice. While she praised Hitler for his army and wondered whether Saint Michael had helped him, she reprimanded Chamberlain and told him to seize power again and sign the compromise.[266] For these visionaries and their supporters it was obvious that the Virgin intervened in earthly politics and used the voices of the faithful to convey her requests. Conjoined trajectories of the political and the devotional were not new. Marian devotions and Catholic devotional culture in general had, for centuries, a political aspect that did not go uncontested.

## *In a Nutshell*

So there we have it. A rough sketch of the apparitions and their historical context. Flawed and limited as every overview is, but hopefully rich enough to provide the necessary background for the following chapters in which we will be focusing on the evaluations of the series by different types of people (laymen, medical experts, and the clergy). What is important to keep in mind when reading the next chapters is that the Belgian apparition series of the 1930s built on a rich tradition of Marian devotion and renewed interest in the Lourdes apparitions. The faithful, mobilized in the Catholic Action, tried to restore society in Christ, and while the Catholic voters had presented a more united front in the previous elections, political tensions were building.

It was hard to ignore the series of apparitions. The press covered the events extensively (even though some sites did receive more press than others). Thousands of faithful and curious attended eager to catch a glimpse of what was happening. The messages the Virgin communicated at the sites tallied with the concerns of people. The Virgin of the Poor spoke to those suffering because of the economic malaise, and the warnings of the "invader" and looming war found willing ears. The ecclesiastical authorities tried to temper the enthusiasm by controlling the publications and demanding authors obtain the imprimatur before publishing. Local authorities (as in Lokeren) attempted to monitor the stream of visitors the apparitions attracted and diminish the tensions they caused with the local population and the socialists.

In sum, almost everyone had an opinion about the wave of apparitions. In the next chapters we will explore how the lay men and women who found their way to the apparition sites made up their minds, evaluated what they were witnessing, and publicly showed their convictions.

Table 1.1 List of apparitions and visionaries

| Location | Date | Name of visionary* | Gender |
|---|---|---|---|
| Roeselare | Already in May 1930 but continues throughout the next years. | Gerard C.† | 1 man |
| Namur | Already in October 1932 but continues throughout Beauraing period. | Marie Pousset-Dodémont† | 1 woman |
| Beauraing | November 1932 | Fernande, Gilberte, and Albert Voisin; Andree and Gilberte Degeimbre | 4 girls 1 boy |
| Banneux | January 1933 | Mariette Béco | 1 girl |
| Rendeux | January 1933 | Hermit of Marcourt | 1 man |
| Verviers | January 1933 | Nestor Brasseur | 1 man |
| Finnevaux | Spring 1933 | – | 2 girls |
| Tubize | May 1933 | Mrs Beeckman | 1 woman |
| Ohain | June 1933 | Julia Dessy | 1 woman |
| Kruishoutem | July 1933 | Joseph Bekaert-Weytens | 1 man |
| Onkerzele | August 1933 | Leonie Van den Dijck | 1 woman |
| Rochefort | August 1933 | Mrs Bucher and her son | 1 woman; 1 boy |
| Etikhove | October 1933 | Omer Eneman | 1 man |
| Olsene | October 1933 | Maurice Van den Broecke | 1 man |
| Chaineux | October 1933 | Jeanne Emonds, Marie Emonds | 2 girls |
| Herzele | October 1933 | Jules De Vuyst | 1 man |
| Wielsbeke | October 1933 | Jeanne Martin | 1 girl |
| Uitkerke | October 1933 | Mrs Goossens, her daughter and her friend | 1 woman; 2 girls |
| Melen | October 1933 | Matthieu Lovens | 1 man |
| Foy-Notre Dame | October 1933 | ? Malet | 1 girl |
| Lokeren | October 1933 | Gustaaf Van Driessche | 1 boy |
| Aalst | November 1933 | Hendrik de Greeve | 1 man |
| Beerse | January 1934 | Bertha Embrechts | 1 woman |
| Stokkel | March 1934 | Joseph Cloetens | 1 man |
| Brussels | March 1935 | Marie Fontenoy | 1 woman |
| Sclayn | May 1935 | Joseph Monjoie | 1 man |
| Ham-sur-Sambre | March 1936 | Emelda Scohy | 1 girl |
| Chevetogne | 1934 | – | – |
| Waregem | 1933? | s.n. | – |
| Opwijk | 1933? | A member of the religious congregation of the Black Sisters | 1 woman |
| Eeklo | 1934? | – | 3 children |
| Ghent | ? | Sons of the Pesse family | 2 boys |
| Boechout | ? | Bernard Van Eeckhout | 1 man |

* Initiating visionaries.

† These visionaries, although already "active" in an earlier period, get involved with the series of apparitions that started with the reports on Beauraing.

# 2

# Trust

## Lay Enthusiasm

> I thought these notes might interest also the future historian who, after our generation, undertakes to retrace the origins of the cult of our Lady of Beauraing. He might find here some unpublished details and, above all, see how the start of Beauraing appeared to a contemporary observer, so much more at liberty to say what he knows, since he does not think about publishing his account. … before writing this chapter, one has to be able to visit the archives of the dioceses of Namur, Liège, Malines, and those of the Holy Office. But they are well guarded and the secret they hold will not be lifted so soon.[1]

The lay men and women involved in the 1930s Belgian series were writing history and, as the above quotation indicates, they were well aware of it. Even though it still feels a little awkward to come across such sources that are explicitly addressed to the future historian, studying the series has made clear that this was no single incident. Various supporters and opponents of the series took care that their voices were still heard decades after the official story had been created and explicitly mentioned this intention when leaving their documents in the various archives. In their opinion, their voice was as important as that of the ecclesiastical authorities.

This section will address the ways in which these lay commentators (promoters, lay supporters, and opponents) wrote about the series. The documents leave a somewhat chaotic impression of this lay field. As new sites developed, new visionaries raised their voices and often travelled from one site to another seeking contact with other seers. They were supported by promoters, grouped in various organizations, capable of switching loyalties as easily as they switched movements. During the entire series and the first years afterwards, an initial filtering was taking place at various levels (concerning, for instance, visionaries and their messages) and the clerical authorities already rejected some of the apparitions. Such a public decision left its mark also on the lay reception.

Even though the laity is discussed here as one entity, it is important to stress from the onset that the way they interpreted the visions was not independent from their place of origin and status, and could differ according to region, nation, gender, class,[2] and so on. This section tries to capture some general trends. What is of interest here are the criteria and methods they adopted in their evaluation process, their type of reasoning, and the categories they thought fit in their examination. Studying their choices and argumentations will tell us something about how they made sense of the world and the transcendent.[3]

The following pages introduce the lay men and women involved, the stages on which they acted, and the ways in which they communicated their opinions. This introduction will allow a better contextualization of their argumentations and evaluations in the next two chapters.

## *Trust in the Virgin*

In the discussion of the lay involvement and evaluation, trust is a central notion. Admittingly, on first sight trust seems a vague and rather elusive concept. It is never defined in the sources and yet, at the apparition sites, trust was the main currency. As we shall see, the "trust" or "distrust" of Catholic devotees informed their actions, comportments, and evaluations.[4] People put their trust in the Virgin (for instance, hoping for a miraculous cure or a conversion); they trusted and mistrusted visionaries, the ecclesiastical and civil authorities, and their own eyes; and they trusted each other with information. Trust could be an individual as well as an interpersonal feature stabilizing the relationship between people and a collective phenomenon (for example, trust in the church or state). It was stronger than hope[5] and a motivation for action (for example, trust in the supernatural, a feeling of certainty). Trust was not a given but needed to be earned and communicated. The documents therefore show trust "at work" *in situ* and *in actu.*[6]

Scholars like Ute Frevert and Geoffrey Hosking have shown how trust and distrust have different meanings and take different forms in different historical contexts.[7] So before we look into how trust functioned in the evaluation processes, we first need to address the context in which they manoeuvered and worked for the recognition or rejection of an apparition site. The devotees trusted in the Virgin, and this trust sets the emotional scene for their actions. As we have seen, the Belgian devotional landscape of the 1930s was a place where the gloomy thoughts about the political and economic future met the hope the Virgin embodied. Two levels are of importance here: the collective level of shared fears and sufferings, and the individual level on which trust in the Virgin's interventions eased worries about family members or one's own well-being and provided hope.

A good way to get a feeling of the atmosphere at the apparition sites is to look at the devotional cards that circulated and communicated the Virgin's central message to the faithful. A Banneux devotional card read: "I am the Virgin of the Poor. I have come to ease the suffering." A souvenir card produced at the same site contained a quotation from Scheuer: "The future is dark, but this torch will brighten it" ("*Bien sombre est l'avenir, mais ce flambeau l'éclaire.*"). Finally, a devotional card linked to Tilman Côme's apparitions spread the more politically inflected message of his apparitions: "I have come for the glory of Belgium and to preserve this land from the invader."[8] The present was looking bleak with a looming military threat, political tensions, and economic malaise, but the Virgin brought hope and a promise of a better future, and the faithful wanted to pray to her at a site where she had shown her continuing interest in the well-being of the people and where the intervention of the supernatural seemed to be possible.[9] This line of thinking also motivated the actions for the approval of the sites by the ecclesiastical authorities years later. At least, that is what the following fragment suggests. In November 1939, when the danger of war increased, one commentator remarked that the bishop of Liège informed him that "in these moments of global agitation, threats of war that throw us into distress, the recognition of Beauraing and Banneux would give an impulse of piety and hope that would comfort the hearts and bring the hope that the Holy Virgin will interfere, she who in Banneux declared she came for all the nations."[10]

Trust in the Virgin also inspired individual actions. The reports of the promoters document how Catholic devotees, hoping to improve

Figure 2.1 Devotional card from Banneux.

Figure 2.2 Devotional card from Beauraing (Apparitions to Tilman Côme).

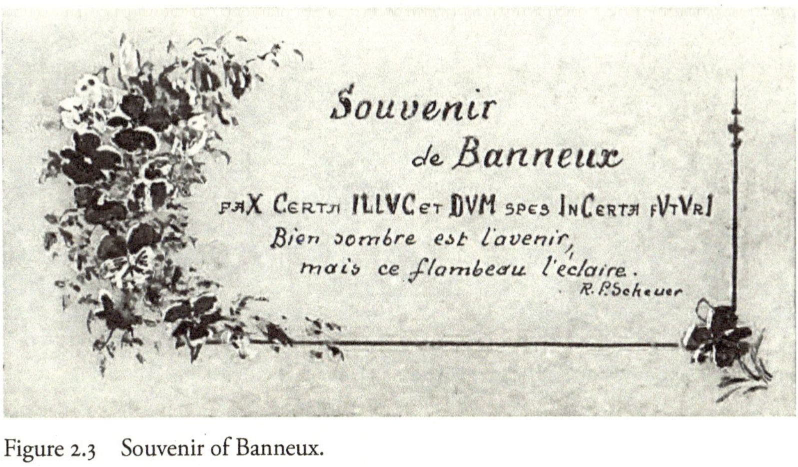


Figure 2.3 Souvenir of Banneux.

Figure 2.4 Postcard with pilgrims next to the Banneux spring.

Figure 2.5 The sick at Banneux (15 August 1933).

their situation, found their way to the apparition sites. Louis Wilmet, for instance, described how a father carried his sick daughter "with great love and trust to Onkerzele to implore her healing."[11] Wilmet added that the father clearly differentiated between the various sites and refused to bring his daughter to Lokeren, as he thought the apparitions there resembled those at Ezquioga (that were not approved). Such fragments thus not only inform us about how trust in the Virgin's potential future interference translated into actions, but also how the actions of this Catholic father in fact mirrored his evaluation of the sites. He knew which sites he trusted and where he wanted to bring his daughter.

Such trust had a multiplying effect, especially when miraculous cures were reported. When the bishop of Liège was invited by the papal nuncio in Belgium, Clemente Micara, to reflect on the enthusiasm for the Banneux site in 1934, he noted that one of the main reasons for its appeal and the "growing trust" were the "[f]avors of a temporal nature, in particular healings have been very numerous. A part of them is registered with great care. The beneficiaries thereby testify of a great gratitude towards the Virgin of the Poor."[12]

## *Creating a Sacred Site: Promotors, Pilgrimages, and Material Development*

By travelling to these sites and praying there, devotees set these locations apart as religiously meaningful – a place where the supernatural had been attested and could be attested again (for instance as apparition or miraculous cure). The focus on the site shows how – from a devotional point of view – it was not the individual visionary that was important, but rather the apparition and its location. People went to "see" an apparition, stare at the visionaries, and maybe catch a glimpse of the divine themselves. A telling example is Louis Wilmet's description of the public at the apparitions in Onkerzele. He described the situation in December 1933, almost a month after the bishops circulated a letter in which they encouraged a more cautionary stance.

> At the bottom of the slope, at the top where I find myself, some utterly comical scenes occur; men, women, most of them elegantly dressed, try to climb the path to the top of the slope in

> order to have a better view of what is going on near the chapel; but the ground, icy and muddy, glides and slides away under their feet; some of them fall full length on the ground; others make superhuman efforts to keep their balance, but end up by flopping themselves and their beautiful clothes out in the mud, to the guffaws of the people who look at them from above, mocking and incapable of helping them in their perilous ascent. Some of them fall belly down, and then glide to the bottom of the slope, their little bags with lunch open up, spilling over the muddy ground the now inedible victuals. It was a pitiful spectacle, about which one laughs in order not to cry; the laughter was therefore the nervous laughter of people who were not occupied and were impatient, rather than inappropriate mockery.[13]

Wilmet described the curious and faithful in a poignant scene, hinting at their idle waiting and the difficulties they had in finding a good spot. He noted that it had only taken a few newspapers writing about the apparitions to trigger the curiosity of the people who are always thirsty for the "wondrous."[14] Wilmet's detailed report hints not only at the continuity of the interest in the apparitions and the limited effect of the bishops' guidelines, but also describes how those who did not belong to the same class as most of the visionaries made their way to (or gravitated toward) the various sites. The public consisted of a mixed set of people, including various classes, genders, and ages.

Among those witnessing the apparitions, we find a number of enthusiastic Catholics who wanted to spread the news about the apparition series or a specific site. The reports on their activities and their network have largely been preserved, informing us about those lobbying for the various apparitions. These men and women, now long forgotten, were energetic in their campaigns and left behind numerous documents about the apparitions. What little we know about the background of these promotors comes from their letters to each other, to the visionaries, and to the clergy.[15] These letters also inform us that each travelled to several sites and supported various visionaries. Wilmet, for instance, described how he recognized "many fervent supporters of other apparitional sites"[16] in Lokeren. These "fervent" supporters knew each other, kept in touch, and comforted each other, but they also battled and criticized each other.[17]

Some of the promoters are more easy to track because of their omnipresence and prominence. Wilmet was a regular visitor, as were Princess Madeleine de Croÿ,[18] the journalist Jan Filip Boon, and the writer Germaine De Smet.[19] These engaged Catholics produced unofficial eyewitness accounts and interviews that they circulated among fellow supporters and sent to church authorities.[20] The Catholic authors, members of the nobility, and other vision-promoters had a social or professional status in common that allowed their voices to have more impact than those of the visionaries, who had limited visibility and public projection.[21] Moreover, their status as active supporters ensured them front-row seats at the public mystical events. They published their articles in the daily press, but also in the new periodicals that developed at the initial apparition sites such as *Les Annales de Beauraing et de Banneux, L'Officiel/La Voix de Beauraing* and *Banneux Notre-Dame.* Some of them wrote books. Boon published one about the first apparitions in Beauraing (*Getuigenis omtrent Beauraing: ervaringen van een journalist,* 1933) and prepared another about those of Tilman Côme, which did not receive ecclesiastical approval. Wilmet published *Beauraing, Banneux, Onkerzele* (1933) with the permission of the ecclesiastical authorities. By writing about the apparitions (or financing them), the supporters helped to create what Ellen Badone has called a "corpus of narrative evidence."[22]

As the eyes and ears of the public, these writers provide us with detailed descriptions of what was going at the apparition site: what the visionaries looked like; what they communicated; who was present; and how the public responded. In addition, the addressees of these reports (sometimes episcopal authorities, but also fellow supporters) provide us with information about how the evaluations on this level took place and whom the writers of the reports thought needed to be informed. The reports tell us about the religious world from which the phenomena derived their meaning, who claimed authority, and discrepancies in regard to religious agency.[23] The involvement of these promoters is what, to a large extent, makes the apparitions "visible" even today. In focusing on their accounts in the following pages, we do not want to suggest that their voices should be the dominant ones, but for this level of evaluation, their voices are often the only ones that have survived.

Whereas all had their own reasons for supporting visionaries, these promoters did not only act individually. On the contrary, almost from the start onwards, they grouped together. In the initial stage, the gatherings at the apparition sites were not formally organized. However, if the apparition series at a certain site continued over a longer period, supporters of the events took initiatives to improve the circulation of the pilgrims, the popularity of the individual sites, and the material organization of what they believed to be an important locus of Marian pilgrimage.

Different types of organizations emerged, most often with a geographical focus. There were several committees centred on the Beauraing apparitions. Some focused primarily on promoting Beauraing as the site where the five children had experienced a Marian apparition (Les Amis de Beauraing, Comité Pro Maria[24]); others also embraced the visions of Tilman Côme (Union Notre-Dame de l'Aubépine et du Chêne[25]). Some of these Beauraing movements also included Banneux when organizing pilgrimages and other means of promotion (Amis de Beauraing et de Banneux). The Banneux apparitions also led to the creation of other associations (Caritas Banneux) in Belgium and abroad.[26] Similarly, in Flanders, the apparitions of Lokeren and Onkerzele stimulated the formation of several lay organizations (for instance Comité voor de verheerlijking van Onze Lieve Vrouw van Onkerzele; Comiteit Naastveld/ Comité van Lokeren)[27] while some of the promoters from Audenarde even moved from apparition site to apparition site (Comité d'Action d'Audenarde).[28] The promoters of the apparitions reported near Banneux, in Melen, in Chaineux, and Ham-sur-Sambre also formed their own committees (the committee Virgo Maria; the committee of Melen; Virgo Virginum).[29] Other sodalities and associations primarily promoted the new devotions or devotional emphases that visionaries had introduced and organized pilgrimages (Confrérie de la Tête Sacrée et de Notre-Dame des 7 Douleurs,[30] Vereniging voor het H. Aanschijn, also called Bond of the Sacred Head[31]). Bleeding images and crucifixes were the cult focus point of at least two lay associations. The Brussel-based Le Cénacle de Notre-Dame Médiatrice, Reine de la Paix shared some of its members with the Confrérie de la Tête Sacrée et de Notre-Dame des 7 Douleurs. A break-away from the former was the organization of Les Pèlerins Serviteurs (Pénitents) de Marie, whose leader, Mr Renard-Champenois, believed the latter to be fanatical and dangerous.[32]

The supporters took care to make the sites accessible to pilgrims. By turning the sites into a "destination" to be reached after walking several kilometres or travelling by train or bus, they set the sites apart

Figure 2.6 Photograph of the chapel and pilgrims in Onkerzele.

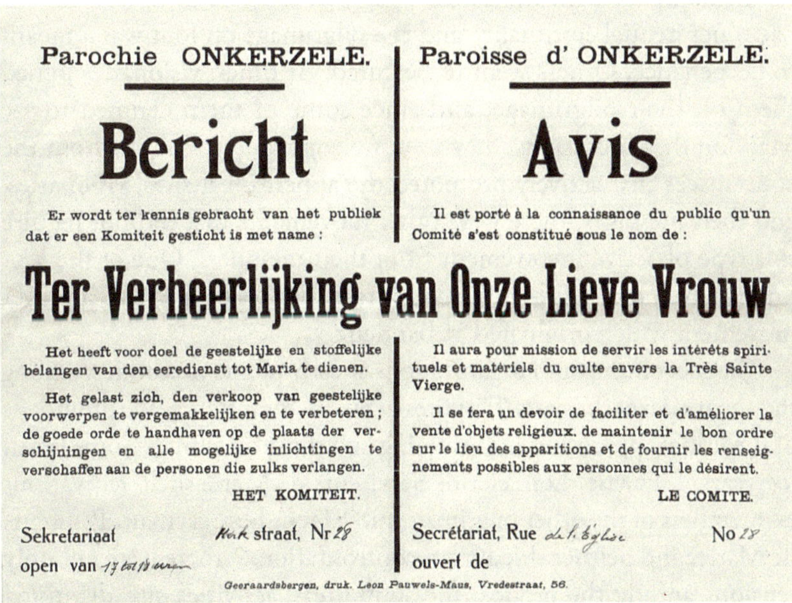

Parochie ONKERZELE.

# Bericht

Er wordt ter kennis gebracht van het publiek dat er een Komiteit gesticht is met name :

Paroisse d' ONKERZELE.

# Avis

Il est porté à la connaissance du public qu'un Comité s'est constitué sous le nom de :

## Ter Verheerlijking van Onze Lieve Vrouw

Het heeft voor doel de geestelijke en stoffelijke belangen van den eeredienst tot Maria te dienen.

Het gelast zich, den verkoop van geestelijke voorwerpen te vergemakkelijken en te verbeteren ; de goede orde te handhaven op de plaats der verschijningen en alle mogelijke inlichtingen te verschaffen aan de personen die zulks verlangen.

HET KOMITEIT.

Sekretariaat Kerk straat, Nr 28
open van 17 tot 18 uren

Il aura pour mission de servir les intérêts spirituels et matériels du culte envers la Très Sainte Vierge.

Il se fera un devoir de faciliter et d'améliorer la vente d'objets religieux. de maintenir le bon ordre sur le lieu des apparitions et de fournir les renseignements possibles aux personnes qui le désirent.

LE COMITE.

Secrétariat, Rue de l'Église No 28
ouvert de

Geeraardsbergen, druk. Leon Pauwels-Maus, Vredestraat, 56.

Figure 2.7 This announcement of the creation of the committee of Onkerzele indicates that the committee's goal was to "facilitate and improve the sale of religious objects; to guarantee the good order at the place of the apparitions; and provide all kinds of information to the people who request them."

as exceptional, sacralizing them.[33] Pilgrims came primarily on the days on which Marian apparitions were announced. But even after the series of apparitions stopped, pilgrimages could continue and the committees took care to organize them either on days requested by Mary or on days that were considered "special" (like the anniversary of an apparition or cure).[34] In other words, they were already identifying what they believed to be the most important, noteworthy, events. The best known of these post-apparition anniversary pilgrimages were those of 18 May and 5 August in Beauraing and that of 19 October in Onkerzele. For the first two, the Beauraing connection may be misleading, since these pilgrimages had little to do with the apparitions to the child-visionaries that were eventually approved. The two pilgrimages were both linked to the apparitions of Tilman Côme. That of 18 May (the anniversary of *Rerum Novarum* and *Quadragesimo Anno*) was organized at least until 1943 by the energetic Princess de Croÿ and her helpers.[35] That of 5 August was organized at least until the 1990s.[36] Both dates, according to the visionary's promoters, were requested by Mary.

The pilgrims often had personal reasons for travelling to these sites. As the names of their movements suggest, some of these associations had a penitential spirituality and the pilgrimage on foot was a means to do penance. Others went to be cured. At times, visionaries joined them on their pilgrimage, and since some of them claimed to see Mary on these occasions, they were welcome guests.[37] Apart from the committees that actively promoted the apparitional sites, visionaries, and their messages, there were other movements that did not require this type of active involvement from their members. One of the best known, even today, is the L'Union Internationale de la Prière, a prayer movement which originated at Banneux.[38]

The sheer number of organizations already points to conflicts among the apparition enthusiasts. Disputes between, for instance, the promoters of the initial apparitions in Beauraing and those to Tilman Côme lasted for years. Likewise, Les Pèlerins Serviteurs de Marie sheltered various ex-members of the other pilgrimage movement Les Serviteurs Pénitents de Marie, and neither shied from confrontation.[39] There were not only tensions among the groups; the supporters' activities also disrupted their relations with the clergy and diocesan authorities. Members of the clergy had been ordered by the ecclesiastical authorities not to organize pilgrimages to the apparition sites without the approval of their local bishop. The laymen involved were thus not intermediaries between the ecclesiastical hierarchy and the pilgrims (as was/is, for instance, the case in Lourdes).[40] On the contrary, the laymen saw themselves as the ones in charge of these sites. They were, however, not entirely beyond clerical control and reprimands.

The lay supporters took on different tasks, but mostly their initiatives started by investing time and energy in the development of the apparition site. The sites were considered places where contact with the divine had proven to be possible, and had the potential of offering again that breakthrough of the transcendent.[41] At those locations where the apparitions did not take place on a site with religious meaning – for example, inside a chapel or near a Lourdes grotto – the first step of the lay promoters most often consisted of creating a landmark, placing a sign to point out where exactly the Virgin appeared. This could be a small statue of the Virgin, but in the case of the apparitions to Tilman Côme, his supporters wanted to place a cross at the site. Photographs preserved in the diocesan and parish archives document these provisional signposts, as do the letters of the supporters and other people involved, including local clergy.

As long as the apparitions were taking place, these lay committees "managed" the sites. For instance, in Etikhove, on 29 October 1933, a day announced by Mary, they made sure that the hundreds of pilgrims followed the route marked out for them by fences and crowd managers wearing a distinctive bracelet.[42]

A second step could consist of trying to create the shrine, chapel, or even the grotto that the Virgin was said to have requested.[43] The formal organization of the supporters in "committees" formed an important stage in this material development of the sites.[44] They were most often the ones who collected the necessary funds.[45] The architectural plans in diocesan and parish archives are eloquent examples of their ambition, illustrating dreams of basilicas and other shrines. Lay persons at times even purchased the property on which they believed these new sanctuaries had to be built, or convinced the owners to donate them. In Onkerzele and Olsene, where archival sources have been preserved, church (and also municipal) authorities intervened to block their execution.[46] Still, the promoters did not necessarily stop their plans for buildings when the bishops announced the rejection of the apparitions in 1942.

Figure 2.8 Indication of the location of an apparition site, the original site in Olsene.

Figure 2.9 Indication of the location of an apparition site, Banneux.

At those locations where various visionaries were "active," the plans could take different forms depending on the promoter group. A telling example is the case of Onkerzele: The archive preserves the plans for two different shrines. The first is based on the visions of Henri Kempenaers and depicts a basilica with Christ's role as saviour of his church as central image. The second is based on the apparitions to Jules De Vuyst and shows a "religious park" with several chapels in honour of Mary's sorrows and even the little shop that the visionary claimed Mary had reserved for him.[47] Neither of these plans were executed, but their very presence in the archives indicates that the lay supporters were quite willing to take these steps toward institutionalization even without clerical guidance or support. Moreover, as the two plans have been preserved, it becomes clear that whatever criteria the laymen adopted, these eventually also must have led to discussions among rival groups of supporters. In the Onkerzele case, the discussion about the visionaries' ranking (there was no space for two such religious sites on the same spot) was clearly not settled.

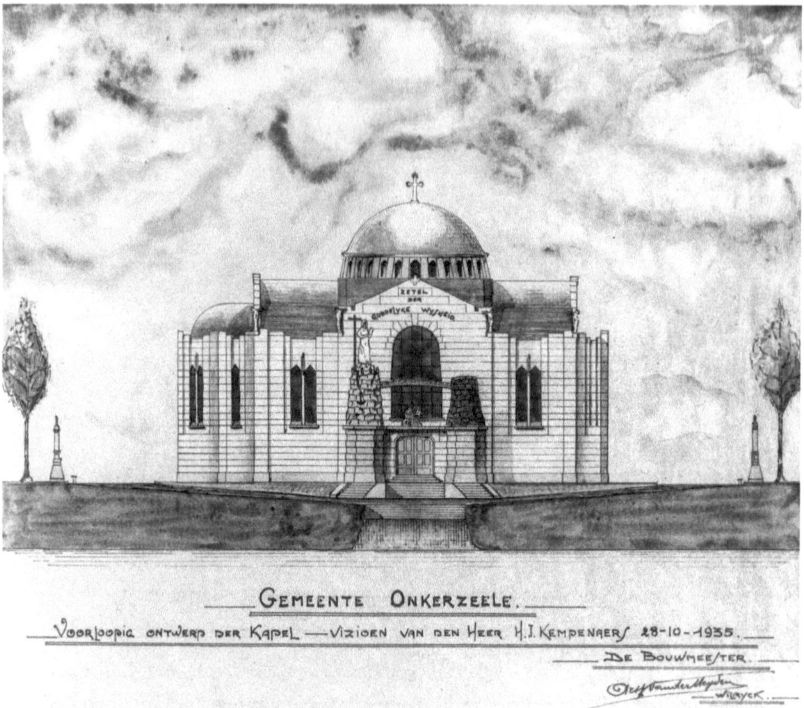


Figure 2.10 Design of the Onkerzele basilica with a central spot for the Lady of Sorrows, with corners for the Sacred Heart and Our Lady (according to visions of Henri Kempenaers).

Figure 2.11 Same site – plan according visions of Jules De Vuyst with the re-erection of the chapels in honour of Mary's sorrows.

## *Communicating Trust and Distrust*

> Know that I often rather made a long journey, than left a letter behind, nowadays I do exactly the opposite. I intend my writings to last. I know why.[48]
>
> Léon Sebruyns-Desmet

On 12 February 1936, a promoter of various Flemish sites, Léon Sebruyns-Desmet, wrote to a fellow-promoter of the sites, Honoré Vermeire. Sebruyns-Desmet had decided that it was better to create a record of his involvement to document his position, rather than leave it to others to speculate and make suggestions. Both had learned by then that rumours and suggestions could be as effective in polarizing opinions as first-hand reports. The importance of communicating findings and arguments to the public is a central theme of the reports of the lay promoters. Accounts of the change of heart of two promoters, Alfred Magain and Louis Wilmet, provide telling examples. Both cases involve lay promoters who had initially fervently promoted the cause of a visionary and subsequently turned against them.

Alfred Magain wrote a book about the apparitions in Onkerzele, and while the book focused on the first series of apparitions in Onkerzele to Leonie Van den Dijck, he also supported the visionaries of the second wave, especially Berthonia Holtkamp nicknamed "the queen of the visionaries."[49] It was Holtkamp's lies and "improper" behaviour that led Magain to change his mind about the Onkerzele series as a whole and lose faith in Van den Dijck as well.[50] Berthonia Holtkamp's real first name was Bertha, but after a religious crisis resolved by the intervention of Saint Anthony, she decided to add his name to her first name as a sign of gratitude.[51] Before she became a visionary, she had unsuccessfully attempted to enter four different religious orders.[52] When her visions in Onkerzele commenced she met Gabriel Quatannens, an ex-seminarian with whom she entered in a "spiritual union" and started a religious group of women (led by Holtkamp) and men (led by Quatannens). They claimed that Jesus had appeared to Holtkamp and given her instructions on how to lead her "honorary sufferers" who were to be part of the Passionist order.[53] Holtkamp had even sent one of them to the Passionists' cloister in Tielt to ask for the rules, and she and her followers were wearing the emblems of the order. The Passionists in turn stressed that they had nothing to do with this new group. After pastor Thyssen complained that Holtkamp had already sixteen female followers in Berchem, Mgr Van Roey intervened on 25 August 1934.[54] He circulated a letter in which he asked "the clergy and the faithful not to attach any importance to the visions, revelations, predictions, that are ascribed to the persons Berthonia Holtkamp of Berchem-Antwerp, and Jozef-Henri Kempenaers of Wilrijk."[55] In doing so, Mgr Van Roey made Onkerzele II together with Lokeren II one of the few apparition series that were rejected even before the official examination. Holtkamp and Quatannens were not discouraged. Their semi-religious lifestyle continued to trigger episcopal responses in the various dioceses where they settled in the following years.[56]

To make matters worse, Holtkamp and Quatannens also promoted the devotion to the Sacred Head of Jesus. This devotion had not been approved by the ecclesiastical authorities. Changing names again, Holtkamp now called herself "Maria Veronica," most probably because of Saint Veronica's prominent role in the devotion to the Holy Face of Jesus.[57] Mgr Coppieters, the bishop of Ghent, therefore also explicitly warned the laity not to pay attention to the devotions and religious practices initiated by these individuals. More specifically, in June 1938, a public letter of his cautioned the faithful of the deanery of Geraardsbergen about the devotion to the Sacred Head of Jesus.[58]

Even before the archbishop intervened, Magain wrote about his disenchantment. He reported that he now believed that the second Onkerzele series was the result of hallucination or diabolic intervention. Moreover, after long deliberation he had come to the conclusion that Van den Dijck's visions could not be authentic either: they were too closely connected to those of the "Antwerp people," of the second series. Furthermore, Van den Dijck had obtained (material) "fruits" from the events, and these were quite different from the improvement in piety one might expect. Magain clearly believed in the power of the written word and he used the media to circulate his opinion and/or at least counteract the promulgation of ideas he no longer believed. He wondered what he should do about his Onkerzele book. It was still in circulation and he feared that it could mislead people. To his relief Rex, the publishing house, had promised not to sell any more of *Our Dear Lady among the Flemish* (*Onze Lieve Vrouw bij de Vlamingen*).[59]

Figure 2.12 Photograph of Berthonia Holtkamp with an image of the Sacred Face.

The theme of the power of the written word also runs through Louis Wilmet's fallout with Tilman Côme in August 1933. Only a few weeks after the major apparitions to Côme on August 5, Wilmet described his impasse to a priest.[60] In his letter he noted that he had found out that the Beauraing visionary had reported visions of a chapel before this date even though he then claimed to see it for the first time. Disappointed in Côme's actions and statements, Wilmet was frustrated that his book on Beauraing was already at press, and he did not know what to do. If he kept silent, a single word of his opponents would suffice to demolish his whole work, but if he said something about the case before they had the chance to criticize him – what should he say? He no longer knew what to do, "now that he had learned the dangers of silence and speech."[61] Côme's case certainly divided the promoters of the Beauraing site and this friction also showed in their publications. The means and ways people used to voice their opinion of him, or rather, the access they had to means of spreading their ideas, were of particular importance. Ten years after Tilman Côme's apparitions, one of his supporters remarked how they could no longer publish, as they used to, in *L'Officiel de Beauraing*, one of the periodicals distributed by the lay supporters of the Beauraing site. According to Côme this was because Côme's supporters were too numerous, and the prime goal of the periodical was the promotion of the child visionaries of Beauraing.[62]

Periodicals like this indeed played an important role in promoting the apparition series and pilgrimage sites. When one wanted one's miraculous healing to be publicly known, one could do so by reporting the events to periodicals connected to apparition sites. Those linked to Beauraing and Banneux often included reports of miraculous cures. They regularly included "proof," that is, photographs of the *miraculé(e)s* before and after their cure, like those that circulated about Lourdes.[63] Numerous accounts of these events have been preserved, thanks to the principle of reciprocity whereby those who experienced a miraculous cure had to thank Mary for her intervention. There were other means to show gratitude. While some donated money for the improvement of the apparition site, others left ex-votos or their crutches at the apparition site,[64] and still other miraculés thanked Mary by paying for a mass. This in turn could have a multiplying effect. In one of the letters preserved about the Onkerzele cures, a small annotation notes that the masses could be accepted, but – given the fact that the apparitions had not been approved – were not to be announced as such.[65]

In conclusion, the faithful's two main means to publicly show their trust in the apparitions were investing in the sites, and publishing about the apparitions and cures. By doing so they meant to influence others and broaden the impact of the apparitions. As we shall see, the bishops of Namur and Liège thought of this religious enthusiasm as indispensable for judging the apparitions in a fair way: the fruits of the apparitions were as important as the initial events. Others believed them to encourage non-approved devotions. Before we explore the evaluations of this lay enthusiasm however, we first need to trace how the faithful decided on the authenticity of an apparition. What did they look at?

## Criteria

### *The Danger of a Criterion*

> Examine and believe, those are two different things. One has to start with examining, with sympathy surely, but with distrust, yes, with distrust, knowing that the devil is master of the world and that he has even tempted Christ and that history shows abundant proofs of his power. Here, one believes from the onset, one wants the supernatural to exist at any price and one gets lost in the most delicate and perilous domain in the world.[66]
>
> Louis Wilmet

On 14 August 1934, Louis Wilmet complained to Princess Madeleine De Croÿ, his fellow supporter of the apparitions of Tilman Côme, that the examinations of the other Beauraing visionaries were insufficiently critical. He doubted that the examiners had the courage to study everything concerning the child visionaries and wondered whether they made public whatever was not in line. In his opinion, the other visionaries were not examined properly, as if the decision had been made before the examination. But what is relevant in evaluating an apparition? Two years later, in September 1936, Wilmet reflected on the use of various criteria in these matters, such as *sensus fidelium* ("sense of the faithful"). In his opinion, it was "dangerous to trust what one thinks is a 'criterion,' since one then explains everything in function of the idea one believes one needs to defend."[67] Wilmet thereby showed his distrust of a priori "relevant" criteria, such as those formulated by Pope Benedict XIV in 1744[68] and applied in the evaluation of the Beauraing apparitions by Wilmet's contemporary, the Jesuit Jean-Baptiste Lenain.[69] These included, among others, that there be nothing "bizarre" in the apparition, and that the visionary have a sense of certainty (God let his presence be felt), and a feeling of happiness about the encounter. Other criteria included the behaviour of the visionary, miracles, and the persistence of popular sentiment.

In interwar Belgium, no official rules for discernment circulated and laypersons applied varying criteria. Each of the lay commentators had their personal luggage and the "eyes of the beholders" were different, since each of them had their own memories and background that coloured their perception.[70] Still, the reports and letters of the supporters show that they did share certain ways to evaluate an apparition.

Lay evaluation and filtering of the apparitions are the focus of this chapter. Largely independent of the evaluation of the apparition series in more formalized assessments of the medical and diocesan commissions, these non-expert and non-clerical men and women reflected on the apparitions. As we shall see, laypersons sometimes referred to what they believed to be medical and religious referents and cited the "authorities" in question, but often they did not build on external expertise. The archives permit a glimpse of the diverse means they used to plead their case. Apart from the textual sources on which the majority of the next pages are based, other sources included drawings and paintings of visions, and photographs of bleeding crucifixes. Convincing others of the trustworthiness of one's argument required words and images.

## *Trustworthy? The Visionaries.*

The network of the apparitional sites and its supporters was close-knit. Whether or not someone who claimed to have experienced a divine intervention could become part of it depended not only on the strength of their case, but also on the willingness of the lay supporters and other visionaries to accept them. The visionaries and their reports had to be deemed trustworthy in order to have an effect.[71] In a mediatized environment, people were well informed about what to expect from a "real" apparition. As a result, those apparitions that resembled authenticated cases had a better chance of being accepted. The knowledge of other sites thus had a uniformizing effect. In other words, a visionary only attracted sufficient attention if they fit the profile of the type of a seer deemed credible.[72] In the Belgian series, the "humble" background of some of the seers allowed them to be compared to other cases. In 1944 (when his case had already been rejected), a supporter of Jules De Vuyst described the visionary as follows: "This is a simple farmer, of an uncultivated intelligence, of rudimentary instruction and education, who speaks only a rough Flemish dialect; and is thus on the level of the majority of the visionaries, almost always chosen among the most humble and insignificant, because they are incapable of deriving by themselves or from previous studies the messages that they bring."[73]

Still, it is important to note that even though De Vuyst's background did indeed make him an easy fit with other, better-known, cases, his gender should have made him stand out as exceptional. Oddly enough, however, the reports on the Belgian series do not reveal an unease about the male visionaries: They were not considered out of place at the apparition sites even though they did not fit the contemporary topos of girl visionaries from a rural area.[74] One can only suggest various reasons for their acceptance. First of all, the 1930s was a period of an increased emphasis on Catholic lay involvement: Both men and women were called upon to participate in the lay apostolate of the church. Moreover, the clergy was particularly keen on publicly staging men's involvement in, for example, the Leagues of the Sacred Heart and organized public meetings and ceremonies. The leagues were male sodalities centred on devotion to the Sacred Heart of Jesus, which emphasized the need for atonement and penance, for example by means of group communions. The moment the first male visionaries of the series were reported, men had thus already been publicly linked to a devotion with a focus on atonement and suffering – a message often conveyed during Marian apparitions. Secondly, the Catholic tradition included male mystics. Even though many of these had been members of the clergy (Henri Suso, Bernard of Clairvaux), their cases demonstrated that it was not a novelty that men reported mystical experiences. Thirdly, the social class of the male visionaries fit the Catholic ideology of the time, and when Tilman Côme was described as a "worker apostle"[75] this manner of speaking fit the emphasis that was put on the apostleship of all of the laity since the start of the twentieth century in the Catholic Action movement.[76] The working classes were focused on, in particular, as they were considered endangered by socialist ideas. Accordingly, one of the visionaries reported that Saint Joseph appeared to him dressed as a worker. He called this very appropriate since it was above all workers who could benefit from the Christian message.[77]

In addition to a humble background, humble behaviour played an important role in the evaluation of the visionaries. Craving too much press attention was an indication of a lack of authenticity, as the Onkerzele case clearly illustrates. In January 1934, hence, after the second series of apparitions had started there, a commentator from Auderghem compared the two Onkerzele vision sequences. He noted that during the apparitions to Leonie Van den Dijck almost no press was present; there were no attempts to create a spectacle and still "Nieke" earned people's respect and men removed their hats whenever she passed by. Berthonia Holtkamp, on the other hand, sought to create a mystical impression and was surrounded by numerous journalists, people from the higher classes, and gendarmes. None of that resulted in the same level of respect, and no one removed his hat when near her. Besides, the commentator was quite sure that Our Lady of the Poor did not want all that commotion.[78] Similarly, drawing too much attention to oneself as mediator with the world above also led to a negative response and doubts about credibility. It did not help the case of Henri Kempenaers, another Onkerzele visionary, when he claimed that Our Lady said that he was her servant and "whoever harms you, will have harmed me."[79]

There was less consensus about other criteria, and what one commentator perceived as positive (for instance, a high level of piety) could be interpreted by another as negative (a high level of piety can make one more vulnerable to being fooled by apparitions). There seems to have been no conditions about the minimum level of piety of the visionaries prior to the apparitions. On the contrary, some even suggested that a total lack of religiosity even argued in favour of the authenticity of the events. No non-believing visionary would have claimed to have seen Mary if they were not convinced of what they had seen, as they faced criticism and mockery from their immediate environment.[80] However flexible they may have been about the pre-apparition piety, believers held stricter expectations for the post-apparition religiosity and behaviour. The encounter with the divine should have a positive effect on the seers.[81]

Morality and character were important categories. For Alfred Magain, the discovery of the mendacious side of Berthonia Holtkamp was sufficient reason to change his opinion about the Onkerzele events in April 1934. He did not think much of the first Onkerzele visionary either: "Nieke" was greedy and lacked charity for the husband who had abandoned her and other members of her family, and she showed little respect for the ecclesiastical hierarchy.[82] Not only did the visionaries' morals during and after the apparition count, but also the pre-apparition history of the visionaries was taken into account. Tilman Côme's case is notorious in this respect, for rumour had it that he had collaborated with the Germans during World War I. His reputation made several commentators critical of his claims of receiving messages from Mary, for they thought it unlikely that the Virgin would choose such a person to protect the nation.[83]

Nonetheless, even though some believed that character flaws were a clear indication of untrustworthiness in a seer, others were more flexible.

The Beauraing children were not perfect, so a local stationmaster noted, but in his opinion their "flaws" did not necessarily make them less fit to see Mary.[84] Wilmet phrased it most eloquently when he tried to lobby for Van den Dijck's visions with the Onkerzele parish priest. He cautioned him not to pay any attention to "Nieke's" current behaviour. Our Lady did not necessarily bestow excellence upon her visionaries, as the La Salette case proved. The families of the Beauraing and Banneux visionaries could be criticized for their attempts to obtain financial benefits as well; they were, after all "only human."[85]

## *Corporeal Proof?*

> The wave of great trust and faith in Banneux was constantly fed by all the graces that were attributed to the prayers towards Mary, the Virgin of the Poor.
>
> *Banneux Notre-Dame – Record of the Graces*, 1934.[86]

As the above quotation shows, trust in the apparitions (here Banneux) increased with every new report of the Virgin bestowing graces upon her devotees. Some of these miraculous cures were well known and well documented. According to the promoters of these cases it was not hard to see the Virgin's intervention, one only had to look closely.

Henri Kempenaers' case was convincing in the eyes of many supporters. Before his first vision, on 19 October 1933 in Onkerzele, the "ambulant visionary"[87] had been suffering from tuberculosis for 18 months (others said since 1929); he had been a "human wreck" with a hole in his right lung. During his first encounter with Mary, however, he was cured miraculously and could breathe normally again.[88] His supporters believed his body to be the material proof of his statements, and they assembled ample documentation in order to convince others. A photo album of the apparitions in Onkerzele (sent to the bishop of Ghent by one of the supporters) included a picture of Kempenaers just after he left the sanatorium where he was treated (unsuccessfully) and a picture of him after his miraculous cure.

Kempenaers' body functioned as "proof" in other ways as well. On Christmas Day 1933 he allegedly embodied the stations of the cross in Onkerzele in the presence of numerous spectators. Accounts on the event – among others by Jan Boon, Alfred Magain, and Honoré Vermeire – document how carefully all of Kempenaers' facial expressions and body movements were scrutinized and recorded. Boon, for instance, narrated how the seer placed the cross of his rosary on his left shoulder with both hands, bowing under its weight and how he stumbled, his knees trembling, under the weight of the cross. He described how Kempenaers met his mother and kissed her just like Jesus kissed Mary, and removed his shawl, coat, and tie (in accordance with the tenth station of the cross when Jesus' clothes are removed). "All slowly and solemn, without any convulsive movement – opening for instance with a very precise movement the button of his collar." All of this took place outside; but for the final episode, Kempenaers went into the local church and in front of the image of the Immaculate Conception fell down, showing his bruises in ecstasy, "his arms a little above his head (as in a cross) not horizontal, but slanting, rather wide-open closed at the top, closed eyes, tongue out of the mouth – bitter expression."[89] Adding to this detailed descriptions even the direction to which Kempenaers looked, his pace, and the style of his movements, Boon seems to have been convinced that these small details were of importance in evaluating the authenticity of what was happening. In *De Standaard*, the newspaper for which Boon reported on the series of apparitions, an article on the Christmas Day events noted that biblical historians were astonished at the "historical accuracy" of the details and sequence by which Kempenears "showed" Jesus' way of the cross.[90]

There were no physical marks on Kempenaers' body after this episode, but he claimed that this was not the case when he relived Christ's passion again on 10 and 17 June 1934. This time, he experienced it all in the privacy of his rooms. Boon also wrote a detailed report on this episode, but could only refer to Kempenaers' statements. Quoting the seer, Kempenaers remarked that after the excruciating pain, he ran his fingers over the surface and he could feel how beneath the skin of his hands a hole had developed. "Then I saw the following on my hands: these seemed to have become hollow inside, as if there was only skin left on the palm and at the back. When I pushed it, there seemed to be no more flesh. There was a big red spot (slightly red, a brighter color than blood) on the inside of both hands, there were signs as if something that had been torn apart and of which the flesh is torn into pieces."[91]

As a self-proclaimed stigmatic, Kempenaers is rather exceptional, for most of the reported stigmatics of the last centuries were women (with the notable exception of Padre Pio) even though the first stigmatic, Saint Francis, was male.[92] The visionaries of the Lokeren apparitions were more in line with the "standard" female profile of the stigmatic. During the second series of apparitions there, three young girls publicly "relived" Christ's passion several times a day.[93] Again, the details of the re-embodiment were considered of outmost importance, and when one of the visionaries ended with the "wrong" foot (in comparison with the two other girls) on top of the other in the final phase of the crucifixion, it was enough to cause a serious commotion among those present.[94]

Not only the visionaries' own bodies, but also those of others could add to the credibility of an apparition. Miraculous healings were reported at various sites and not only at those that later gained the bishops' approval. In addition to the heavily documented cures in Beauraing and Banneux, healings were reported in Onkerzele,[95] Lokeren, Chaineux,[96] and Melen.[97] In Côme's case, even though he became a visionary himself, some supporters considered his cure a confirmation of the authenticity of the apparitions to the child visionaries.[98]

There were two types of cures: One type was the instantaneous cure at the apparition site – as with Tilman Côme and Henri Kempenaers, who were cured on the spot where Mary had appeared; the other type was the miracle at a distance,[99] when the cure was linked to a relic brought (or ordered) from the apparition site such as tree fragments (in the case of Beauraing, Lokeren, and Onkerzele) or water (Banneux and Onkerzele).

The sheer number of apparition sites, and the diversity of means and procedures that could be "used" while praying for a cure, had an unexpected side-effect. This becomes apparent in the case of Sister Rose. She had been healed after using both the water of Banneux and leaves from the hawthorn of Beauraing, and supporters of both sites wanted to claim her cure as proof to strengthen the case of their apparition site.[100] Similarly in the case of Hubert D.W. there was no consensus as to which site was "responsible for his cure": he had been to Lourdes; twice to Beauraing; and had been washed with Banneux water. The only thing for sure was that he had been healed by Mary.[101]

Miraculous cures were considered "testable," unlike other kinds of "favours" like, for instance, temporal ones (getting a job, winning the lottery) and conversions, which did not leave "proofs" that were tangible. The supporters of the site took their cue from Lourdes, where a medical bureau took care to collect medical reports to support their cases. At Beauraing this interest resulted in standardized forms to be filled out for exceptional cures.[102]

Figure 2.13 Leaves of the apparition tree in Beauraing.

The list of cures in 1934 published in *Banneux Notre-Dame* is remarkable for the care with which each ailment is noted. Whereas there are some general descriptions such as "illness" ("*maladie*"), in most cases the affliction is mentioned in detail: Pott's disease; burning tenosynovitis of the right index finger, cephalalgy, pyelitis, and so on. It almost seems as if mentioning these particulars adds extra importance to the cure. They attest that one knows exactly what was amiss and was not ascribing miraculous qualities to the disappearance of a vague phenomenon that could have healed without the intervention of Mary. Mention of the exact medical term suggested that the patient had visited a doctor who had diagnosed the ailment but had not been able to offer an effective cure.[103]

As Suzanne Kaufman has noted for the miraculous cures in Lourdes, this involvement of modern medicine and the medical narratives that developed "also made the cures themselves more spectacular."[104] The stories about the miraculés published in the devotional periodicals seldom failed to name the doctor who examined the sick or invalid before and/or after the cure and thereby document the limits of medical knowledge. "Specialists" had been consulted without any success.

More general descriptions were used in the comments about the visionaries. The lay commentators seemed to be well aware that apparitions and related phenomena as stigmata were linked to hysteria and hallucination, and when they questioned the credibility of certain visionaries descriptions such as "hysterical,"[105] "hallucinated,"[106] and "neuropathic"[107] reoccur. Most often these passages refer to the female visionaries, but similar remarks were made about the men as well.[108] In other words, the bystanders seemed to know that visions were not only limited to the domain of religion and that medical findings could contribute to building stronger cases or rejecting others. This generalized "medical knowledge" influenced the way in which these contemporaries talked about the apparitions and criticized them.

They not only adopted the vocabulary, they knew the appropriate tests as well. The medical tests were primarily imitated in order to "prove" the authenticity of what was happening. It is not clear where the bystanders who did the tests picked up this knowledge, whether they saw the doctors who were present at some apparition sites execute these tests, or whether they knew them from reports on other (foreign) apparition sites. In any case, in the absence of doctors, some of the spectators started to perform the tests themselves. Most of the time they wanted to find out whether or not the visionaries were really in ecstasy. For instance, on 26 August 1933, a bystander near Leonie Van den Dijck pinched her hard during her apparition, but, as the local priest noted, she seemed to feel nothing.[109] Likewise, the spectators shone electric lights in the eyes of the Onkerzele visionaries Berthonia Holtkamp and Martha M. on 21 November 1933 – again with no reaction from the visionaries.[110] Similar reports were made about other sites. The most invasive tests seem to have been performed in Lokeren where one eyewitness testified how strangers cut the boy visionary between the nails and in the cheeks, burned a candle under his hands, and cut his knee.[111]

Still, even though the vocabulary and tests were eagerly adopted, and reference to mental and physical health (ideally with the support of a medical certificate) was a recurrent strategy in pleading for or against the authenticity of an event,[112] the role of the doctors at the site and their authority on the matter were not unquestioned. In July 1933, for instance, a commentator from Hamont noted that he believed far too much attention was given to the opinion of the doctors, just as with the stigmatic Theresa Neumann. "They invoke so easily suggestion, hallucination, hysteria, hypnotism … the doctors are a little … materialistic. One consults too much the medical science that God and the Holy Virgin precisely want to overthrow."[113] What is more, he was convinced that the Virgin might even use someone whom the world believes to be crazy, someone whom the scientists have declared "hysteric" just to "confound that human science."[114] Aurélien Pierroux, the first secretary of the Pro Maria Committee of Beauraing, likewise questioned the exclusive status of the doctors. He held that questioning the visionaries should be a task for convinced laymen and not the sole competence of the doctors.[115]

The visionaries' physical appearance and emotions were considered important markers of authentic apparitions. Ideally, the bystanders could read Mary's presence from the bodies and faces of the visionaries – for example, their faces radiated the sudden joy,[116] or there was a change of voice.[117] On 21 November 1933, Louis Wilmet witnessed an apparition scene in Onkerzele. Describing Berthonia Holtkamp's actions, he remarked: "I note that during the prayers in front of the tree, I had difficulty distinguishing the ecstatic state from that of the non-ecstatic state. Only her fixed look gave me indications, for her physiognomy kept its normal aspect without a particular expression. The smile was soft, her gestures were slow, no paleness, no vivid emotions, no transfiguration."[118]

The way their bodies were supposed to reflect this encounter was object of fervid discussion. A "changed" state was not enough: Their bodies had to remain – or rather become – beautiful during this phase. Beauty seemed to be an indisputable criterion, and various supporters referred to it when formulating their opinion on visionaries (male and female). Germaine De Smet, a fervent supporter of the Flemish apparition sites, remarked about Holtkamp's ecstasy on 6 January 1934: "As always, she is very beautiful,"[119] others called her features "fresh" and "angelic."[120] By the same token, the absence of beauty could lead to doubt and even function as an argument when describing visions as "false" or devilish. When Leonie Van den Dijck was experiencing an apparition in October 1935, Jan Boon remarked that she had "false vision" because she was "ugly" during the event.[121] Still, even though it might be undisputed as criterion, beauty was relative. Louis Wilmet, for instance, thought that Boon was exaggerating when he described the "beauty" of the Onkerzele visionaries in ecstasy.[122] Watteyne, in turn, minimized the importance of this criterion in his letter to the dean of Beauraing. He admitted that Laure Dulière was not the most beautiful creature during her apparitions, but in his opinion, Tilman Côme had not been either.[123]

Beautiful features and dignified manners were ideally combined with a change in tone of voice and emotional expressivity. The emotions reflected on the visionaries' faces and expressed through bodily movements were of central importance for the visibility of the apparitions. Only by "reading" these could the bystanders comprehend what the visionary experienced. This public character of the apparitions allowed a certain "exaggeration"/"intensification" of the emotions experienced during the event. By publicly showing their emotions on their faces and in their bodies, the visionaries made them possible for others to see. This emotional expressivity was also accepted for the male visionaries, despite the prototypical distinction between rational men and emotional women.[124] All had to remain within limits; however, the moment the apparition ended, the male visionaries were expected to be in control of themselves again. It was their rationality and calmness in their "normal" condition that was used as an argument in favour of their credibility. Likewise, in the case of female visionaries, in some descriptions it was emphasized that they were "sensitive" but not "sentimental,"[125] suggesting there was nothing in their character that tended toward an exaggerated emotionality. Nonetheless, this emphasis on the "visible" emotions of the visionaries, and their self-control when not in ecstasy, illustrates the thin line between control and exaggeration. Similar ideals circulated about the body language of the visionaries. Their movements were scrutinized with the same care during the apparitions. Too much theatricality and too many grand gestures seemed to indicate fraud. The movements had to be smooth and dignified.[126]

The emotions and bodily experiences of the eyewitnesses were of importance as well. One of these bystanders remarked comparing the apparitions of the child visionaries in Beauraing to those of Onkerzele, that whereas he had felt compelled to fall on his knees during the Beauraing visions, he did not feel the same thing in Onkerzele.[127] In Lokeren, where the three girls relived Christ's passion, various bystanders started to weep and thus, according to Louis Wilmet, they actually participated in the re-enactment.[128] What is more, some of the male bystanders even expressed their reverence for Mary (and thus their belief in the truth of what was happening) by removing their hats. They adapted movements with which they had learned to express reverence in church or when encountering a procession for this new situation.[129]

Bystanders were not only moved by emotions; some of them also believed they experienced physical sensations that supported the claims of the visionaries. References to exceptionally sweet fragrances smelled during the apparitions are among the most common reports in this respect. Notes on the interviews held by a collaborator of *De Standaard* document how bystanders noticed a very sweet fragrance of roses in Onkerzele in October 1933.[130] Others reported smelling something like "Armenian paper"[131] or "balm odour."[132] While Marian apparitions were said to be accompanied by this sweet fragrance, those of the devil could be detected by the smell of burned flesh. This unpleasant odour most probably hinted at the smell of burning bodies in hell.[133] The reports on odours at the sites and the bystanders asking each other whether they smelled the same thing fits what Philip Davis and Jacqueline Boles have called pilgrim apparition work: The "interpretive interactive efforts" of the pilgrims "to attend to their religious environment, manoeuver their way through that environment, identify reverable objects, and engage others about the signs of divine being's immediate presence."[134]

Odours were impressions that only bystanders could perceive. Fragrances were hard to capture, but visual impressions were another matter.[135] Even though the postcards sold at the site did not show the visionaries in ecstasy (as did those of Ezquioga for instance[136]), this does not mean that there were no photographs taken during the apparitions. Most of the pictures that have been preserved are from Flemish apparition sites: Lokeren (both series), Onkerzele (the second series), and Etikhove. The majority of those that were preserved had been sent to the bishops by laymen to support their cause. It is thus safe to assume that a certain selection had already taken place and only the most "convincing" ones were sent. In the case of the Onkerzele apparitions, it is interesting to note that the pictures show more similarities with the Ezquioga visions than with the formalized (reconstructed) photographs of Lourdes.[137] They show the visionaries in trance with their arms wide open or gesturing, displaying emotions. Their bodies, behaving out of the ordinary, pleaded their case (figure 2.15). As William Christian has noted in his work about the Ezquioga pictures, the selection of photographs tells us something about the template that the supporters want to fit into: a stereotypical and ideal image resembling pictures of the saints in trance. Spanish variations on this theme had been covered by the Belgian press only a few years before. It is not unlikely that the Belgian promoters selected the photographic material that resembled the images they believed to be "typical" and thus convincing.[138]

## *A Catholic Repertoire*

The smell of roses and ecstatic beauty of the visionaries – these were all aspects of apparitions that were known from other sites as well. That they were noted and singled out as relevant in the Belgian series indicates how they were among the "plausibility structures" that, according to Philip Davis and Jacqueline Boles, "link immediate apparition experiences to wider religious meanings and membership." They can be regarded as an "interpretative roadmap." The smell of roses is such a sign of divine presence, but so are the so-called "miracles of the sun": "the idea that during an apparition … the sun 'dances,' 'spins' or 'twirls' is a preformed and widely publicized sign that the Virgin Mary is present."[139]

On at least five occasions so-called miracles of the sun were reported at Belgian sites.[140] Collectivity seemed to contribute to the credibility of the event and enhanced one's trust in what one had seen at the site. At the same time, however, reports on this shared experience also created doubt, and a witness could start to wonder about what he had seen because he remembered it in different colours than others did.[141] The best-documented miracles of the sun are the events on 6 August 1933 in Beauraing and 18 December 1933 in Onkerzele. Newspaper articles about the August events in Beauraing made comparisons with the well-known miracle of the sun reported in Fátima on 13 October 1917.[142] The press covered the Beauraing episode in detail, and when, half a year later, similar phenomena were signalled in Onkerzele, the Beauraing episode figured as a point of comparison. Enthusiastic witnesses[143] reported how they had seen a (purple) circle slide in front of the sun, compared it to what had happened in Fátima, and emphasized that no one could doubt it.[144] Other voices were more critical and called it "typical" that a miracle of the sun was reported at the site of an apparition.[145]

As the Fátima comparison indicates, older apparition events functioned as reference points for the Belgian series. Lourdes was a classic example. When Albert Voisin, one of the first child visionaries, prayed with someone else's rosary and the Virgin did not appear to him, this was compared to what was said to have happened to Bernadette Soubirous.[146] Likewise, as Soubirous confirmed through her apparitions the doctrine of the Immaculate Conception (four years after its promulgation), so did the Lokeren visionary Elisabeth Cornelis confirm the idea of Maria Mediatrix.[147] Whereas the apparitions of Lourdes functioned as a positive model, the non-approved apparitions of Ezquioga served as a negative template. References to Ezquioga were most often made in descriptions of the second series at Lokeren, where the girl visionaries went through Christ's passion (and people bought tickets to see them do so).[148] One commentator remarked that it was high time they put a stop to this "new Ezquioga" that had undoubtedly been triggered by women's exaggerated pious readings.[149]

The devotees thus had different ways of determining the authenticity of an apparition. They could go and see (even conduct "tests"), and compare their findings and the stories on the Belgian series to what was known from previous cases, and ponder about what they themselves experienced. We have seen that the "criteria" were quite diverse and their importance was evaluated quite differently by opponents and supporters. Still, as the next chapter will illustrate, there were some cases where (almost) all agreed and the reported phenomena were rejected. The following pages will show how important such a rejection, or more precisely, an official rejection, could be.

## Lay Examinations and Selections

### *"The Land of the Credulous": Formulating Doubts About Apparitions*

On 15 October 1933, still in the first year of the apparition series, the Catholic newspaper *De Standaard* referred to three sites that had not survived a close examination: Verviers, Herzele, and Rochefort. According to the article, a Catholic journalist had been able to discover that the first one, the Verviers apparitions, involving the burned moustache of Nestor Brasseur, was based on deceit.[150] In Herzele, a socialist barkeeper staged the apparitions and was exposed by the local population.[151] The third one, the apparitions in Rochefort, had been set up by the socialist newspaper *Le Peuple,* and the clergy of Rochefort had discovered the fraud. The *De Standaard* journalist concluded: "We are not in the land of the credulous, nor in that of people who accept apples for lemons, the Flemish people in particular look at all this with a sound mind."[152]

The Rochefort case is particularly interesting. Various groups and persons have been credited with its disclosure as an illusion, fraud, or the "stunt of the socialist press." This multiplicity indicates how important it was to express not only an opinion on what one believed to be true or not, but also to claim the discovery of the "truth" for one's own side. The "apparitions" began on 23 August 1933, when, at about 9:00 p.m., a fuzzy image of about one metre twenty-five centimetres high appeared on one of the houses in the Dewoin neighbourhood. The phenomenon repeated every evening and numerous people came to see it.[153] The news coverage was not as intense as in the other apparition events, and a week after the start of the series, the socialist *Le Peuple* commented that even though the Catholic press gave "exceptional publicity in favor of the Beauraing apparitions, its reporters remained silent as far as Rochefort was concerned."[154] Their Catholic colleagues of *De Standaard* later noted that none of the Belgian Catholic newspapers had been fooled by the reports of *Le Peuple*[155] and only a few foreign journalists had fallen for it. The Rochefort clergy had uncovered the "socialist fraud."[156] A journalist of *Le Peuple*, on the other hand, named the journalist Alfred Bouckaert of *Le Soir* as the person responsible for exposing the delusion. He had discovered that the phenomenon was caused by the reflection of the light of a street lantern.[157] *La Libre*

*Belgique* in turn claimed that a group of Catholic youngsters had helped discover the truth. Climbing upon an automobile, they had held a jacket in front of the moon which had kept the vision from "appearing." Even though he could not decide what had eventually produced this image, the journalist listed several possible explanations: a projection from an apparatus hidden in a nearby house; or the reflection of an electric lamp upon a hidden mirror or the windows.[158] All thus claimed their truth and all referred to people they held responsible for discovering what "actually" happened.

The information we have about the other sites that were filtered out of the apparition series is far more fragmented. For the Chaineux apparitions, which involved two little girls and a young mechanic apprentice, the only indications about the fraud are to be found in the reports of the diocesan commission that two years later was responsible for the examination of the events in Banneux.[159] Two of the witnesses called to the stand referred to the staging of the Chaineux apparitions. One of them indicated that the people responsible had asked a young woman to play Mary. The other witness suggested that those who were behind the Chaineux fraud might also be responsible for what happened in Banneux.[160] Their doubts were not exceptional, for even at the time of the apparitions, the Chaineux series came under criticism. The newspaper articles at the time, the autumn of 1933, indicated that the local parish priest called it a "comedy of which the actors hardly knew their parts" and believed the children to be lying. Moreover, so the journalist noted, someone who frequented the local pub had suggested that in order for Chaineux to be prosperous it had to have its own apparitions – that all was staged for financial profit.[161] Other contemporaries questioned the lack of originality, and some of the supporters of the sites of Beauraing and Banneux noted that the messages Mary communicated in Chaineux, referring to the German menace and the persecution of clergy there, contained nothing more than what any informed person would know.[162] An anonymous note, dated most probably around November 1933, suggested that the Chaineux apparitions, like those in Melen, were "*assez louche.*"[163]

Other visionaries never won much attention and their apparitions seem to have provoked above all scorn and mockery (for instance those of Saint Steven's Woluwe involving "the beard";[164] those of Rendeux involving the "hermit of Marcourt,"[165] those of Uitkerke,[166] and the apparitions at Melen that were attributed to "a sick mind"[167]). Of the remaining episodes, we will discuss two in detail as they provide exceptional insight in the "fieldwork" of the lay men and women evaluating the series. The cases inform us about their use of criteria, relation to the authorities, and the importance they attached to an open communication. Both cases, a "miraculous" cure and a series of bleeding objects, were in fact side-effects of a series of apparitions. In each case, the central character managed to attract supporters for several years. Both individuals involved can be described as confidence men/women or tricksters who misused the trust of their followers.[168] In both cases, lay men and women compiled extensive files to convince the ecclesiastical authorities that fraud had been committed and action was needed in order for the apparition sites not to be tainted by these events. We will examine their reasons for asking more closely.

### BENITO PELIGRI

On 22 August 1933 a pilgrim couple, Benito Peligri and his wife, reached Banneux. They claimed they came from Barcelona and had been walking for days to reach the shrine to ask Mary for a cure. Peligri, so he asserted, was an unemployed labourer who had worked with heating systems until he hurt his arm in a work accident and had not been able to use it since. According to the story, the unlucky worker was an atheist anarchist who had only gone on the pilgrimage to please his wife. When they arrived in Banneux, the couple was not able to approach the spring due to the large number of people. Seeing their distress, a willing bystander brought them a bucket with Banneux water. Benito Peligri then allegedly said to the Virgin: "Look upon my arm, cure it, demonstrate that you are truly Our Lady of the Poor. I came from so far for you to cure me!" And behold: After plunging his arm in the water, he could move his hand again. "Enough prayers," he called out, "I am cured!"[169] A few days after his cure, he was said to have married his wife in a church wedding held in Banneux, with the visionary Mariette Béco at their side.[170]

Peligri's story was seen as a confirmation of Béco's apparitions and initially many people were happy to accept it as genuine. But rumours quickly started to spread, especially since the miraculé did not remain discreetly silent on the topic but instead embarked on a tour of the country. In September 1933 we find him in Oostakker (a Lourdes-connected

Figure 2.14 Benito Peligri.

pilgrimage site famous for the miraculé Pierre de Rudder), Lede, Sint-Amandsberg, Onkerzele, and Etikhove. In Etikhove he claimed to have seen the Virgin. A month later he was in Mons, in January 1934 he was back in Onkerzele, and in June 1934 he was in Beauraing and La Hulpe. His tour illustrates how he, famous from press coverage, was a welcome guest at meetings. Gradually, however, he became more and more problematic and by September 1933 some Catholics seemed to know that Peligri actually had a lawful wife in Spain and sometimes received communion twice a day.[171]

Peligri had developed a little "trick" that helped him make money out of his "cure." There were variations, but the basic idea was that he sold his supporters a coin that had allegedly "fallen" into the water and made him plunge his hand in. The believers bought this coin from him for several times its value. At other locations, he sold bracelets that he said were blessed in Banneux. In addition, he claimed to be well-acquainted with the archbishop and stated to have slept in the bed of (the late) Mgr Mercier.[172] He also declared that he had inspired the conversion of a "Père Abbé of Forges-lez-Chimay" who, so Peligri stated, dropped dead after singing the *Te Deum* holding his hand. As the "Père Abbé" in question was still alive when the parish priest of Onhaye contacted the archbishop, the priest wondered whether Peligri might have been mistaken and actually wanted to refer to a "Père ordinaire trappiste" of Chimay?[173] The reason that Peligri could continue to trick the people into buying his objects and still find believers was that he was not publicly exposed (even though the first indications of his deceit were reported by September 1933).[174] Those who knew him to be capable of lying and deceit did not denounce him, holding that to be the job of the bishops. It is hard to reconstruct when exactly these laymen started to notice the irregularities in Peligri's stories and attempted to obtain an official response. A note among the documents of Louis Wilmet suggests that he had already contacted the bishop of Ghent on 7 December 1933. As Peligri had also managed to mislead the religious of Oostakker with his story, Mgr Coppieters seems to have been convinced that it was necessary to involve civil authorities in order to expel Peligri, "who is a crook."[175] There seem to have been no official sanctions however.

There were new lay actions against Peligri a few months later. By June 1934 Princess Madeleine de Croÿ had started investigating Peligri's activities in La Hulpe. She did not want the affair to have a negative effect on the other miraculés and complained that, even after proving the man was lying, she was shrugged off with the answer, "He's a Spaniard, they all exaggerate and make things up."[176] Pushing for an official response, in early July she contacted the bishop of Liège (the diocese of Banneux). She told him that the bishop of Tournai, Mgr Rasneur, had already forbidden Peligri to give talks in his diocese and that Peligri had retreated to France but returned regularly for the pilgrimages of Onkerzele and Beauraing. On 13 July 1934, she received the answer that Peligri's cure had to be separated from his deceit. In other words, the cure did not necessarily have to be false, even though the beneficiary had proven deceitful. Moreover, the Banneux committee had already asked Peligri to leave the region.[177]

By August 1934, the de Croÿ family had put together an entire dossier against Peligri and were wondering what to do with it. Should they

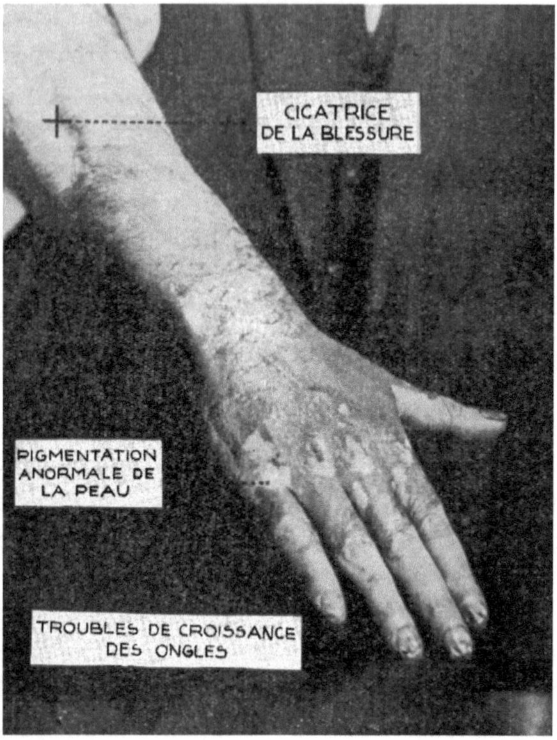


Figure 2.15 Photograph of Benito Peligri's arm in an article on his miraculous cure.

send it to the bishop of Namur? They first gave it to Louis Wilmet, who then forwarded it to Archbishop Van Roey. The documents they collected give an idea of the extent of Peligri's deceit. First of all, the Spaniard Benito Peligri was actually an Italian named Luigi/Louis Oriani, Oriano, or Oriana. Secondly, he had made the wound himself; he had been injured in a work accident, but instead of letting his arm heal he had infected it with urine to hinder it from healing and ensure that it would be a means of financial support. He himself had produced the medical report he was showing around. While Peligri had indeed been treated by Dr Trueta in Barcelona after his accident, the doctor had never seen the medical report the miraculé was showing around. The doctor had written one in Catalan, but this version only contained the clinical characteristics and not the elaborate story in Peligri's version. As for his activities in Belgium, the file compiled by the princess included, among others, letters from a woman of La Hulpe who had been tricked by the cunning miraculé into buying the piece of money he claimed to have dropped in the water of Banneux, as well as belts blessed by the water of Banneux. Moreover, he had persuaded her to give him a piece of jewelry. Similar reports came from the Poor Clares in Tournai. The Trappist fathers of Forges-lez-Chimay, on the other hand, were happy to report that even though Peligri had indeed visited them, everyone was still alive and one should not pay too much attention to what this poor soul was saying. As to Peligri's alleged church wedding to a certain Elise Simons in Banneux, this marriage was refuted by the chaplain of Banneux. The lady in question wrote that she was married to another man, and that as for the concubine of Benito Peligri who allegedly "had entered the Poor Clare convent of Verviers," this convent "does not exist."[178]

The file seems to have been sent to Malines, but much to the annoyance of the princess, the response was silence. The archbishop did not warn the people about "*ce filou*" even though he had not hesitated to warn them about the likes of Berthonia Holtkamp and Henri Kempenaers.[179] The silence of those who managed the Banneux site annoyed Wilmet and the Princess de Croÿ as well. In their opinion, this lack of response was due to the fact that the Banneux supporters did not want to damage the reputation of the Banneux apparitions (for which Peligri's cure had served as a confirmation) and discourage pilgrims. Wilmet and the princess agreed that if his cure was questionable, then others had most probably not been investigated properly as well.[180] Other contemporaries claimed quite the opposite. They believed the story had been staged by those who wanted to cast doubts on the Banneux apparitions. On 10 October 1934, a retired priest contacted the archbishop and noted that in his opinion Peligri's story – his life as a communist, his marriage to a Belgian woman, his journey to Banneux, his cure, and his conversion (all written down by a Poor Clare) – was far too romantic and most probably the invention of the enemies of Banneux who wanted to discredit the apparitions.[181]

Still, in spite of this silence, it was not the last that was heard from Benito/Luigi/Louis. In December 1934 he made the newspapers again. From these articles we learn that Louis Oriani had been arrested at the request of the Spanish government. The articles show us yet another side of "Benito." He had been born in Naples thirty-eight years before and had been expelled from Belgium in 1923. Since then he had lived in Barcelona posing as an Italian captain and lawyer. After his cure and tour in Belgium, he must have returned to Spain, for in March 1934 he was arrested in Barcelona suspected of participating in a bomb attack. He was able to escape on 17 June and had fled to France and Belgium where he gave his lectures. He was arrested by the state police in Marbais during one of these lectures for using a false name. When held by the public prosecutor of Nivelles, Oriani's extradition had been requested by Spain.[182] Another journalist seemed to know that Oriani, as a political opponent, had been obliged to flee Italy in 1928 and fought against the revolutionaries in Morocco.[183] In May 1935, the "Italian fraud" appeared before the court in Nivelles and was convicted for using a false name and taking money under false pretenses.[184]

It is hard to verify these findings; every journalist seemed to know something new. Nonetheless, regarding the Banneux series and Peligri's dwellings in Belgium, his story shows how not all incidents that were discovered to be fraudulent were publicly revealed as such. The silence was interpreted in a negative way by those who had worked hard to uncover the "truth." Their remarks and attempts to bring the ecclesiastical hierarchy to an official response demonstrate the importance they attached to transparency and the distribution of information. In their opinion, this was a task and duty of the ecclesiastical hierarchies, since the managers of the Banneux site had proved not brave enough to do it.

### LAURE DULIÈRE

In the wake of a series of Marian apparitions in Belgium (1932–35), paramystical phenomena such as stigmata and embodiments of Christ's passion etc., were reported as well. Among these was a series of bleeding images in which various "foyers"[185] were detected. Such "living" images of Jesus and Mary were already an age-old phenomenon. Similar incidents had been narrated already in the fifteenth century and especially since the seventeenth century.[186] Only a few years before the Belgian events, living images had been reported, for example, in Spain (Gandia, Limpias, and Piedramillera, 1918–22), France (Mirebeau, 1913), and Italy (Asti, September 1933).[187] In Belgium, the bleeding crucifixes were in the news since the autumn of 1934, more than a year after the initial Marian apparitions in Beauraing and Banneux.

The bleeding crucifixes differed from the other phenomena of the series as they did not manifest themselves in the bodies of the new "mystics," but provided material "proof" – thus permanently "testable" – of divine interventions. Nonetheless, the importance of the presence of these "mystics" should not be underestimated. A contemporary witness, the Franciscan Father Oswald Royen, for instance, described the four foyers of crucifixes (both statues and images) that bled, sweated, and moved in 1936, as follows: "a foyer is constituted by a single person. It is not required that that person is actually, corporally and physically present in order to make the crosses bleed; neither does he have to touch the objects, that strangers bring and deposit before the person in question. Furthermore, it is not necessary that the objects leave the hands of their owners, the cartons, the packing material, the frames that enclose them."[188]

The four foyers he mentioned were Maria Van den Plas (Kiel-Antwerpen), Jules De Vuyst (Sint-Niklaas, Lokeren), Maria B. (Eeklo, Lovendegem), and Laure Dulière (Beauraing, Brussel, Kortrijk). His list can be enlarged to include, for instance, Elisabeth Cornelis (Sint-Niklaas) or Mrs V.L. (Sint-Niklaas), Tiny Kool (Kemzeke), and Berthonia Holtkamp (Berchem, Gent, Onkerzele).[189]

A few weeks after he had made this inventory, Father Oswald had to admit that already one of them had proven to be fake, and he denounced Maria B. as a fraud and hysteric.[190] We will focus here on a more successful fraud, Laure Dulière. "Successful," not only because she was able to attract national and international media attention to her and her crucifixes for over a year, but also because of the loyalty of her followers, and – one must admit – her immense productiveness (hundreds of bleeding crucifixes and devotional images). As the clerical investigation of Dulière's case ran in parallel with that of the laymen, they will be discussed together.

Laure Dulière was about fifty years old[191] when she started to make the news. She worked as a maid,[192] and while she could read and write she had little notion of grammar and orthography.[193] Dulière thus fits the profile of "humble mystic." Her supporters frequently stressed the hardships she had to endure, her husband abandoning her in 1921,[194] and her voluntary suffering.

Before she attracted attention with bleeding crucifixes, Dulière had already made a name as the seventh visionary of Beauraing,[195] albeit a far from prominent one. Her visionary experiences commenced on 2 July 1933 during a picnic in the area. Although the popularity of her

Figure 2.16 Laure Dulière during her apparitional experiences.

visions was minimal in comparison to that of the other adult visionaries, Dulière continued to have them until 20 October 1935. She always saw Mary on the same location, the garden of the Sisters of the Christian Doctrine, and at the exact same time, five o'clock. Before long, both Mother Théophile, the mother superior of the convent, and the local sexton, Willems, forbade her to enter the garden.[196] Afterwards, she no longer claimed to see the Virgin, but insisted that she heard the Virgin's voice – not just in Beauraing but also elsewhere. Her lack of popularity as visionary was referred to both by her supporters and adversaries. Whereas the former believed it to be due to the fact that she was not really beautiful during her visions (in contrast to other visionaries), the latter ascribed it to the banality of her messages and the contortions of her body whenever she purported to go into ecstasy.[197] With her visions, Dulière in fact resembled other "producers" of bleeding images – Jules De Vuyst, Berthonia Holtkamp, and Maria Van den Plas. All were, or had been, "visionaries."

Nonetheless, though hardly popular as visionary, her bleeding crucifixes did win her much of the support she craved. Dulière's supporters belonged to all ranks of society, including – it was rumoured – royalty and aristocracy.[198] The Marquise of Beaufort even turned her house in Rue Joseph II in Brussels into a little "museum" of bleeding crucifixes open to the public. Her grandson later recalled that the visitors were able to purchase on the spot "at a reasonable price" a fragment of cloth marked by the blood of Christ and carrying the imprint of the Sacred Face.[199] However, the museum did not last very long; surprised by the large crowds that came to visit after *La Nation Belge* had printed an article about the phenomenon, the marquise – so Dulière's supporters claimed – decided to shut it down.[200] The grandson of the marquise, however, remembers that it was the police that put an end to the episode.[201]

Although curiosity was mentioned as motive of many of the visitors to the "museum," the images elicited quite different emotions in Dulière's supporters. Some called upon the bleeding images for comfort, while others believed they were an indication of someone's piety and that the dwellings that held these images were blessed.[202] Dulière herself hinted that Mary had indicated that the blood had healing qualities and would help to convert the sinners.[203] Moreover, she even sent one to the Ethiopian king to protect him and his soldiers in the Italo-Abyssinian conflict.[204]

The bleeding crucifixes seemed to function as "proof" of the reality of what Dulière and her supporters were saying. In fact, because of their link with visionaries, they were more problematic than bleeding images that had been reported abroad where – so William Christian remarked in his work on the bleeding crucifixes in Spain – "there was no human being suddenly elevated to the category of divine ambassador (hence no threat to existing hierarchies)."[205] In the Belgian cases, Dulière and her "colleagues" (Jules De Vuyst and Elisabeth Cornelis for instance) also claimed to receive messages from Mary who informed them about the meaning of the bleedings.[206]

Dulière's supporters tried to convince the ecclesiastical hierarchy of the authenticity of what was happening, and in the letters they sent, a number of arguments are recurrent. First of all, they point to the number of bleeding objects. At certain times there were hundreds, even thousands, of devotional objects bleeding at the same time in Belgium. Those connected to Dulière's foyer sometimes counted more than one hundred and it seemed impossible that only one person could be responsible for all of them.[207] Moreover, these objects bled without Dulière or any of her "colleagues" touching them. Second, the scientific analyses (allegedly more than twenty) of the substance that was dripping down the objects indicated that even though it was not paint, it was never blood with "normal proportions" either.[208] Third, the character of the individual to whom all of this was ascribed lived

Figure 2.17 Bleeding Sacred Heart statue in Courtrai.

up to certain expectations. According to one proponent, Dulière was "of naive simplicity and freshness … in spite of her fifty-one years she has preserved her childlike soul and pure spirit in the midst of a coarse milieu." In his opinion, Dulière seemed to be aware that she was a "humble thing" that Mary used to "develop her lovely plan of love."[209] Fourth, some of Dulière's supporters had personal reasons to believe her. Some had received a divine favour through her mediation; others claimed that she knew things about them that she could not have known without heavenly inspiration.[210] Finally, some of them referred to the "miraculous" quality of the bleeding images and described healings by the "precious blood."[211]

By October 1935 Dulière's fame seemed to have reached its apex, with her bleeding crucifixes becoming the subject of newspaper articles,[212]

Figure 2.18 Cover page of *Soirées*, 11 October 1935.

and even a special issue of *Soirées* (11 October 1935) dedicated to her. Nevertheless, the tone of most of these articles was skeptical.[213] By late 1935, criticism of Dulière's character increased, most probably because her actions grew bolder. By the end of October 1935, it was no longer just small-scale, indoor statuettes and images that bled. On 31 October of that year the almost life-sized image of the Sacred Heart of Jesus on the corner of the castle park in Courtrai started to bleed, just after owners hired Dulière as their new maid.

The local clergy responded immediately and on 2 November a small delegation – including two doctors – took some samples of the substance that was trickling down the statue. On the same day, a message from the bishop of Bruges arrived at the castle: Dulière was to leave immediately and the clergy were to warn the faithful and – if necessary – take the statue with them. They did not go that far, but the statue was covered with a layer of oil to prevent any substance being painted on it. Dulière was allowed to stay on a few more days until she had found a place to go to. Two days later, the statue – now "safely" inside a newly erected fence – bled again even though Mrs de la Croix, Dulière's employer, had placed a silk thread over the corridor to hinder anyone leaving the castle without being noticed. She vouched that it had not been broken during the night, but only in the early morning when all had been rising.[214] The stains were removed and still, on 7 November, the day of Dulière's departure, they reappeared. However, laboratory tests indicated that it was not blood. Moreover, the three witnesses who, according to Dulière, could confirm her story about the first bleedings could not be located, even though there was a reward of 1,000 Belgian francs promised to them if they came forward.[215]

The archdiocesan commission created by order of the Holy Office to examine the series of apparitions and related phenomena held its first session on 11 May 1935. Dulière's case, discussed in eight sessions (18 November 1935 – 23 June 1936), was presented by Mgr Tessens, the general vicar of the archbishop of Malines and vice-president of the sessions, assisted by members of the secular and regular clergy.[216] At some of these sessions witnesses for and against were heard.[217] From the testimonies during the various sessions, it is clear that even though Dulière's adversaries were convinced of her fraud, they had no idea how she was doing it. She had not been caught in the act, and so they were left to guess what was happening.

All of this changed in the second half of March 1936. The impetus came through a "divine intervention." Jules De Vuyst, one of the Flemish visionaries and himself a "foyer" for bleeding images, had been invited by Dulière to see her. Uneasy about making contact, De Vuyst had nevertheless visited her on 13 March. In her presence, the cross of his rosary started to bleed. However, on his return home, Mary allegedly appeared to him, wiped the blood off the cross, and told him to stay away from places she did not order him to go. Distressed, De Vuyst had turned to Jan Boon, one of his supporters and – as we have seen – favourably disposed to Dulière. De Vuyst's message gave Boon pause, and he decided to investigate in conjunction with Rev. Bilcke, the parish priest of Kortenberg, the parish to which Dulière had moved on 25 November 1935. Over two months Boon and Bilcke grew convinced that Dulière lied about her messages from Mary and fabricated the bleedings. They decided to lay a trap and suggested to her that all the bleedings would most probably stop on the Feast of the Holy Sacrament. Dulière seized on the idea and after a while claimed that she had received a divine message that all would come to a halt on that day. On 9 June 1936, Mr Doyen, a manufacturer from Kortenberg and Dulière's employer, together with the Deacon of Kortenberg, De Lantsheere, caught Dulière red-handed. She had desperately tried to make the numerous images and crosses – which people had given her in the hope of having them bleed – start "bleeding" before the appointed day. She had been less cautious than usual and even started preparing them in the kitchen and her room.[218] Doyen and De Lantsheere found her in the midst of a workshop for bleeding images: "flacons of paint of iodine, ether, glycerin, soot, brushes, images and objects, some of them already painted, the other ready to be so, pieces of silk carrying imprints that Laure Dulière feigned to be supernatural and that she fabricated by means of medallions and figures in relief that were found in her room, that she used to make the imprints, as the comparison of one with the other showed."[219]

It was eventually Boon, her former supporter, who convinced Dulière to make a full confession. He was particularly eager to do so as he was afraid because of the sheer scale of the alleged events, people would continue to believe that at least some of them had been real, even after the events of Kortenberg had been made public. On 17 June 1936, Dulière confessed that she had fabricated all the bleedings with her own blood, colours, other blood (of which she refused to indicate the provenance) and that her nephew had helped her obtain medical alcohol and ether with which she created them. He never knew what it was for, Dulière added, for she told him it was for the wound from the amputation of her breast. She said that she could not explain how she had learned to prepare all these chemical preparations. Boon was unsure how sincere she was in this respect. Likewise, he did not believe her statement that she had been forced to fabricate the bleedings and that someone had supplied blood to her while she was in Kortenberg. Dulière was asked to leave Kortenberg and went to live with her sister in Charleroi.[220]

Boon sent her confession to Dean Lambert of Beauraing (where it had all started[221]) and to the commission. On 23 June 1936, during the eighteenth session, the members concluded that Dulière was guilty of "manifest fraud by making people believe in the so-called bleeding of crucifixes, pious objects and images." In the name of the archbishop, Mgr Tessens declared that none of the so-called miraculous events that had been provoked by Dulière could be attributed to divine intervention and that objects carrying a trace of blood should not be venerated for carrying these marks, but rather should be destroyed or the traces of blood removed.[222]

Three months before this final verdict on Dulière's case, during session 15 on 11 March 1936, the commission had already drafted a text in which they rejected all bleeding images, medals, and crosses and forbade persons to "expose, circulate or venerate these on pain of sin." So even though catching Dulière in the act did not seem to have been necessary to form their opinion, it did, of course, confirm and substantiate their findings. Six years later, on 25 March 1942, Cardinal Van Roey publicly announced the results of the archdiocesan commission. He declared that in almost all cases that had been reported in Brussels, Antwerp, Courtrai, and elsewhere, there had been fraud and none of them should be ascribed to divine intervention. It was forbidden to hold, distribute, or venerate any of them while they showed signs of bleeding.[223] However, even before that date, supporters of the Marian apparitions of Beauraing and Banneux could get an idea about the opinion of the bishop of Ghent, for in September 1936 *Les Annales de Beauraing et de Banneux* published a letter by one of his staff members that was said to correspond with the bishop's opinion. The last paragraph of the text – which referred primarily to the actions of two other "visionaries" – read as follows: "There is much deception in the affair of the bleeding or weeping Christs, the affaire of Courtrai was a vulgar scam."[224]

Nevertheless, Boon's prediction about the persistency of the belief in the bleedings was borne out. For even as late as 25 April 1944, a letter was sent from Germany referring to a bleeding sacred heart of Courtrai and how the current events (including the bombing of Lokeren on 11 May 1944) fit the warnings communicated by the various visionaries.[225] Dulière herself would never get the opportunity to appreciate the persistent loyalty of her supporters, for she died, according to Boon, "a blood-curdling death" on 11 December 1936.[226]

## *Selection and Rejection*

In the cases of Benito Peligri and Laure Dulière, laypeople took care to inform the ecclesiastical hierarchy of their findings and expected them to react publicly. To these lay men and women the bishops had sole authority in this matter. Or, as one article in the episcopal letter of autumn 1933 explained: "The simple faithful – erudite or ignorant – lack the particular assistance that the Holy Spirit accords to the clergy and, so whatever their conclusions might be, they have only their own personal credit for imposing them."[227]

Fraudulent events could undermine other episodes and were thus better publicly denounced. The promoters' efforts to force a public rejection of fraudulent seers are related to what Ann Taves has called "taboos against mixing and comparing." Referring to Bernadette Soubirous, Taves notes that, "When the claims of competing visionaries threatened to undermine the specialness of Bernadette's experience, her backers responded by discrediting her competitors' visions as inauthentic. In doing so, they reasserted the singularity of her visions and set them apart from others they deemed inauthentic."[228] Rejecting untrustworthy events strengthened the events of others.[229]

On the lay level then, the public character of the apparition series was of central importance in the evaluation process. The faithful could go and see for themselves, gaze at the emotionally expressive visionaries, smell roses or burned flesh, and maybe watch the sick being healed. They could take pictures and create their own "proof," do their own "medical tests," or look at the ex-votos that were left behind and buy pictures of the visionaries or of reconstructions of the apparitions. They could read about these events in newspapers and periodicals and compare them with older and new cases, drawing on a Catholic repertoire and adopting criteria they knew from other apparitions they had heard about. They showed their trust and distrust at the apparition sites, carried their sick there, burned candles and prayed, or protested and scorned.

They were well aware of the impact the public communication about the events had on the faithful. This awareness shows in their pleas for transparency about demonstrated frauds such as Benito Peligri and Laure Dulière, and in their efforts to take laudatory booklets out of circulation when they could no longer vouch for the messages these texts conveyed. But they also worked and lobbied behind the scenes and sent their reports to their bishops. For they knew enough about other cases to realize that the final decision was not up to them, and that apart from their eyewitness knowledge, other expertise was needed.

Rejection and approval required close observation and examination. As the journalist Fernand Remisch noted in 1933, "aside from the Christian revelation, all our truths demand to be acquired." The implementation of "intuition, fate" or "inspiration" did not generate confidence. Remisch added that since the field of human knowledge had expanded and they were living "under the reign of the specialist," collective efforts were needed.[230] His dream team for the examinations of such events therefore ideally consisted of, in a first phase, specialists in observation and criminal sciences (trained in uncovering fraud) and historians (specialists in criticizing facts); in a second phase, medical experts of an undisputed authority who verify the findings and materiality of certain phenomena; and finally, in a third phase, when the natural explanations prove to be insufficient, theologians who differentiate between divine or diabolical intervention.[231] As we shall see, the various categories of specialists were indeed called upon, but their expertise in the matter did not remain undisputed.

# 3

# Competence

## Medical Interest in the Apparition Series

### *The Medicalization of Miracles*

On 24 September 1933, in the first year of the vision series, *De Standaard* published an article on the apparitions in Onkerzele noting that there was no "medical or other scientific observation" and only the parish priest was studying everything close at hand. "The Catholic physicians apparently do not deem it worthy to bother about: *a priori* and from a distance they know that it is 'a mental illness,' without taking the trouble to check the facts or observing the comportment of the woman."[1] This critical comment on the initial lack of involvement by doctors in Onkerzele shows the importance the journalist attached to medical evaluation. No exceptional phenomenon could ever be considered trustworthy if physical or psychological defaults could be pointed out. The first check had to be by medical experts.

The request for medical expertise came not only from the lay Catholics, nor was it new in interwar Belgium. The Catholic Church had been displaying a similar interest and requested – before denoting a phenomenon as "exceptional" – a medical examination. This (in Foucauldian terms) "medicalization of the miracle"[2] has primarily been associated with the nineteenth century and the diagnosis of hysteria.[3] The creation of the Lourdes Bureau of Medical Verifications (Bureau des Constatations Médicales) in 1883[4] and, for Belgium, the medical interest in the stigmatic Louise Lateau are well-known instances.[5]

In fact, the church had shown an interest in medical testimonies long before that era. From 1588 onwards there was increased attention in canonization proceedings for physical healings supported by medical testimony.[6] This interest continued to grow and the tumultuous conflicts of the late nineteenth century provided the church with extra reasons for caution and skepticism regarding mystical phenomena. Medical examinations requested by the church not only filtered out the false or pathological cases but also provided a first line of defense against anti-Catholic attacks.[7]

At the same time that the church called upon medical expertise, there was increasing interest in religious phenomena from the various branches of medicine.[8] New psychological disciplines provided new diagnoses[9] and apparitions, miraculous cures, and stigmata were now described as induced by suggestion, hypnosis, or as something similar to hallucination and eidetic phenomena. Similarly, psychoanalytical readings of apparitions linked them to the Oedipus complex, especially in those cases where there was a matriarchal family structure, or explained them in Jungian terms as the projection of the collective unconscious.[10] The bishops, experts in mysticism who belonged to the regular clergy, specialists at the Vatican, and Catholic doctors kept track of the new developments in the study of religious phenomena. Conflicting diagnoses and hints at the misdiagnosis of hysteria, for instance, were used by the defenders of the miraculous cures of Lourdes in order to minimize the cures' dismissal as pathological.[11] Moreover, as Agnès Desmazières has pointed out, there were changes within religious teaching that had an effect on how mysticism was perceived. In the early twentieth century, mystical studies were increasingly differentiated from theology and focused on the individual experience of mysticism.[12]

In Belgium, this neo-scholastic experimental psychology found a promoter in the Belgian Mgr Mercier, whose Institut supérieur de Philosophie became one of the main centres of the new discipline.[13] It is important to note here the specificity of the Belgian context. Research addressing the hysteria diagnosis and religion has focused primarily on France, but France was a very particular case in its sharp division between church and science. Catholic universities were only allowed in that country after 1875 and, as Sofie Lachapelle has remarked, "never attained much recognition for their faculties of science," whereas in Belgium, the universities of Louvain and Liège had an excellent reputation. "Collaboration between scientific and religious authorities," she adds, "was perhaps more amiable in Belgium than elsewhere."[14] A study of Belgian medical periodicals has pointed out that these publications do not show an explicit polarization between believers and non-believers in matters like "hysteria." Catholic doctors were often on the same page as their free-thinking colleagues.[15] Still, exceptional religious phenomena led to vehement debates in Belgium as well, starting especially in the last quarter of the nineteenth century. The phenomena were discussed in the Royal Academy of Medicine and at international congresses on forensic medicine, psychiatry, physiology, and nervous illnesses.[16]

In the period after the Great War, the contact between church leaders, moral theologians, and doctors led to the creation of a Catholic medical ethics and a medical code of obligations based on Catholic norms.[17] An association of particular importance in this promotion of the medical ethics and the reflection on the moral consequences of new medical developments was the Saint-Luc Society. This society originated in France in 1884 (Société médicale Saint-Luc, Saint-Côme et Saint-Damien) and a Belgian branch was created in 1922 with the support of Cardinal Mercier.[18] Its members played a leading role in the discussions on the apparition series involving theologians and members of the clergy as well as medical experts. They did this among others in the periodical of the movement, *Saint-Luc Médical/Sint-Lucasblad*, which was launched in 1922.[19]

This section will first reflect on medical competence and show how not all doctors were considered fit to judge the apparitions. After that we will dive into the public side of the discussions, questioning the results of some of the examinations, and show how difference in opinion could develop into very personal attacks. These public debates also had their effect on the various commissions where the questions put to the medical professionals not only related to their field of expertise but also to their public comportment at the sites and in the press.

### *On Competence: Local Doctors and "Great Doctors"*

On 6 December 1932, Dr Goethals contacted his colleague in Beauraing, Fernand Maistriaux, to ask about a series of strange incidents that took place in the garden of the Sisters of the Christian Doctrine in Beauraing. As Goethals provided medical support on the pilgrimages to Lourdes, he was well acquainted with apparitions and miraculés and eager to hear more about the so-called apparitions happening nearby.

Maistriaux was curious as well, and the two doctors went for a look. Arriving a little too late to be able to witness anything that evening, the following nights provided ample opportunity for them to observe what was happening.[20] As the Beauraing series continued, more and more colleagues joined them, and when Louis Wilmet gave a presentation on the Beauraing series at the end of January 1933, he noted that the police had been obliged to interfere because too many doctors, over one hundred, had obtained permits to enter the garden of the nuns, where they had the best view.[21] Maistriaux and his colleagues came to observe and, hopefully, perform experiments during the apparitions and participate in the questioning of the visionaries.

The presence of medical experts was not limited to the Beauraing site and doctors attended other, smaller, sites as well.[22] Newspaper articles document for instance a modest number of doctors interested in the two visionaries of Etikhove (Omer Eneman and Maurice Van Roeckegem).[23] The four local doctors from Etikhove and its district (Ronse, Audenarde, and Eine)[24] accompanied Omer Eneman before, during, and after the apparitions. They monitored the physical signs Eneman always displayed when the time of apparitions was near: He felt "pulled" to the site, he started to sweat, stopped talking and – as the doctors perceived – his pulse quickened. The doctors also observed Eneman during the apparition; checking his sensitivity, they pricked him on the cheeks and arm and shone a flashlight in his eyes.[25] All this medical interest was not enough for Eneman, however, and he complained, "I would like to be examined by great doctors. Who knows, maybe I have an illness that makes me act and see this way." The *De Standaard* journalist who reported his comment observed, "Since the visionary himself wishes it, such an examination by psychiatrics and other specialists is certainly not out of place. That man has the right to such an examination, which is also in the interest of our holy religion."[26] And to back up his statement, the journalist added: "We ourselves have noted that he is rather susceptible to suggestion."

Eneman's request for an examination by "great doctors" – even though local doctors had been monitoring his apparitions – hints at his ranking of doctors. The journalist made the hierarchy even more explicit indicating that "great" doctors were to be read as psychiatrists and other specialists. Still, the presence of local doctors already seemed to add significance to the Etikhove apparitions.[27] This line of reasoning

Figure 3.1 Omer Eneman (right) and Maurice Van Roeckegem (left) during an apparition on 28 October 1933.

probably also explains Dr Maistriaux's interest in listing in his second booklet on the Beauraing series how many doctors had been present at the site during each episode.[28] As for the "type" of doctors visiting the sites, by far most of them seemed to be the local doctors. The list of those who came to the Beauraing site shows that the most frequent visitors were those who did not have to travel far. Still, the "big names" who led the discussion on Beauraing, the university professors, also came to watch, if only once or twice.[29]

The presence of the doctors at the apparition site heightened the apparitions' importance; the same effect applied in the evaluation of the allegedly miraculous cures. A medical report gave them more credibility. Pilgrims were cured, or were said to have been cured, and not only at the sites that were later approved (Beauraing and Banneux), but also in Chaineux,[30] Onkerzele (Jan Van Saelen, Henri Kempenaers), and in Lokeren (by means of the leaves of the apparition tree). Lourdes seems to have set the norm for the Belgian miraculés,[31] and, well aware that medical reports of before and after a miraculous cure were needed, supporters made an effort to assemble them (for instance in Lokeren[32]).

Maistriaux in Beauraing seems to have gathered the most extensive collection; he travelled to Lourdes to study the format and content of the Bureau of Medical Verification dossiers.[33]

The doctors' degrees and professional rank certainly played a role in the evaluation of the examinations. The evolving medical field had created specialists, and with this specialization came certain expectations. The lay men and women pleading in favour of (some of the) apparitions, were eager to refer to scientific findings in building their cases.[34] At the site, they displayed a similar eagerness for medical evaluation of what was happening. In promotional campaigns, they tactically publicized the doctors' interest in the apparitions. However, as the series continued, the laypeople's reference to the doctors' opinions shifted into what some scholars have referred to as "a paradox of scientific authority."[35] The more the doctors' knowledge was called upon, the more it was questioned. Enthusiastic reports of the doctors' puzzlement at, for instance, the ecstatic comportment of the visionaries made way for more critical comments. As soon as doctors started to suggest the presence of hallucination, hypnotism, hysteria, and so on, their involvement was no longer considered self-evident to the supporters of the site. Even if their attendance at the sites or their involvement were not questioned, their examinations and objectivity came into issue.[36] These formed the basis on which the laymen built the doctors' competence; criticizing them undermined the doctors' authority. As a result, responsibility and authority for the discernment of the apparition series shifted toward the ecclesiastical hierarchy, which had a different, power-based, kind of authority.

When we take a closer look at how the doctors saw their own involvement and competence, it becomes clear that they took great care in defining the limits of their capacities. Emphasizing that it was eventually up to the diocese to make a final decision, they nonetheless stressed that it was their task to exclude events that could be explained by natural causes. Étienne De Greeff, one of the most important doctors in the whole Belgian series, formulated his role as a Catholic doctor as follows:

> It is not up to the doctor to prove the supernatural, no more than it is his role to oppose it. He has no competence at all concerning that question. But, however secondary, his influence

> can be enormous. One knows that in the case of events like those of Beauraing there is room for a number of hypotheses; the only goal that a Catholic doctor might have when he occupies himself with such a case is to find out whether one can find a natural explanation for those events, and which one, and thus to clarify, from a scientific point of view, the sum total of what was examined. The more exigent he has been in choosing his proofs, rigorous in his investigations, pitiless in the dismissal of parasitic events that have no importance, the more his conclusions may be of use if they end up saying: one cannot account for that from a natural point of view.[37]

Dr Louis Vervaeck, the general director of the service for penitentiary anthropology in Liège started his book on the role of doctors in the evaluation of "miraculous" cures with a similar description. He noted that "the intervention of the doctor has a sole goal to demonstrate that the cure is or is not natural, that it has occurred in the margin of biological causes or is in opposition with them, finally, that it cannot be explained by the action of a treatment or by a psychological cause."[38]

Still, as we will discuss more elaborately in the next section, taking a critical stance did cause trouble for the doctors. The English Jesuit Herbert Thurston commented on this in his *Beauraing and Other Apparitions*. It was unfair, he wrote, to cast suspicion on "the good faith of these honorable Catholic scientists" for they (in this case the Louvain professors) had "nothing but unpopularity to gain by their skepticism." In his opinion, the shrewd and temperate observations of these eyewitnesses could not be neglected, as due to "their knowledge of experimental psychology," they spoke with a "certain authority."[39] Thurston's remarks fit in with the distinctions made in other sources. However unlikely it was that a doctor had first-hand experience with Marian apparitions, doctors still believed that some of their colleagues were better prepared for studying them than others. Among the better equipped were those who were trained in medical subdisciplines that had been able to provide answers and explanations for phenomena similar to those that were occurring in Belgium. Tellingly, when we look at the comments on Dr Maistriaux, who was the local Beauraing doctor, some of his critics seem to have been convinced that he only claimed that there were no interesting cures in Beauraing because he did not want to enter into arguments with his better-qualified colleagues.[40] The same rumour spread about Dr Gouy, who had examined the miraculous cure of Tilman Côme and changed his mind after meeting Prof. Van Gehuchten. Rumour had it that he had been cowed by the "learned professor."[41]

## The Public Side of the Examinations and Debates

In spite of the differences in medical disciplines and the distinction between "great doctors" and "local doctors," when it came to the debates on the apparition series, all doctors involved commented on their colleagues' theories, examinations, proofs, and criteria. The remarks were – as we shall see – at times rather tough and could become personal, resonating even louder because of the public character of the debates. This was also the case for criticism by laymen and clergy, and some doctors came out of the experience with their reputations damaged. The focus of the next pages is on the debate in Belgium, and more in particular on the discussions of the Catholic doctors and the public side of their examinations and debates.[42] First however, we will explore the benefits the public character of the apparition series provided: Doctors could travel to apparition sites and study the phenomena themselves, and some of them even got to do experiments and conduct interviews.

### *Facts, Proof, and Truth*

"The doctor is often like Saint Thomas, he only believes what can be grasped by the senses; his pascalian intuition is in opposition to his geometrical spirit."[43] This is how Henri Gailly, a psychiatrist from Charleroi, bluntly put it in 1933. His colleagues' actions suggest that there was truth in what he was saying, for the doctors wanted to observe and – ideally – see with their own eyes. The type of apparitions reported in Belgium, both public and serial, offered ample opportunity for observation, and doctors went on "field trips" to see the visionaries during their encounters with the Virgin.

The doctors directed their critical gaze on the visionaries, observing and registering what they believed to be significant elements in the visionaries' behaviour. For instance, when Fernand Maistriaux described what he saw in Beauraing to his colleagues, he emphasized how the appearance of the child visionaries changed the moment they saw Mary: They at once fell onto their knees; their voices became higher and rushed when they started to recite the rosary; and their eyes fixed on a single point.[44] Different observers saw different things, however (for instance, there were disagreements about simultaneity of the visionaries' response), and they paid attention to other details. Defining what one had seen was a rich, initial source for their discussions.[45] The absence of such a medical gaze in the first days of the apparitions in Beauraing was one of the major frustrations. In comparison with other sites, however, the doctors' presence in Beauraing was quite sustained; the Banneux apparitions, which began shortly after those in Beauraing, aroused little interest among doctors, and at other sites they were only sporadically present.

Some of these doctors went beyond mere observation and conducted experiments. The physiological tests they performed were similar to those conducted on Bernadette Soubirous in Lourdes and primarily sought to detect whether or not the visionary was in ecstasy. The tests done in Beauraing and Onkerzele are well documented in the reports and testimonies of the doctors. They consisted of pricking the visionaries with knives and pens, burning matches underneath their hands, opening and bending their hands and fingers, pinching their calves, shining a flashlight into their eyes, or holding an object in front of their eyes.[46] Their tests show that insensitivity to sensorial stimuli was assumed and looked for during the visionaries' ecstasy. When detected however, it was not always enough to indicate the supernatural. It could, for instance also be ascribed to severe cold weather.[47]

Whereas collecting "facts" and physical evidence was of central importance in the observance and physiological observation of the visionaries during the apparitions, "truth" and reliability seem to have been key words in the questioning of the various visionaries. While the gathering of physiological information often began only when a series of apparitions was well underway, questioning began almost immediately after the first events had been reported at a site. All types of people could participate in the interrogations. There was no clear rule, and it often depended on who was present at the site, or the phase of the apparitions. In an initial phase the individuals who questioned the visionaries were often the local parish priest and family members, later they tended to be journalists, doctors, and members of the clergy from outside the parish.

The best documented interrogations are those of Beauraing. At the Walloon site, the question sessions, held immediately after each apparition, were attended by numerous doctors.[48] These interrogations were of particular importance since this was the only way the doctors were allowed to gather further information. The Beauraing child visionaries had forbidden further physiological testing after hearing what type of experiments they had been subjected to during the apparitions on 8 and 12 December 1933. As Agnès Desmazières has pointed out, this shift in emphasis – from physiological tests to questioning – increased the interest in a psychological approach.[49] We are well informed about what happened during these interrogations thanks to the local notary Laurent who took notes. Packed together on chairs and tables, those present seemed to have asked very diverse and also repetitive questions – not always waiting their turn to speak. The questions seem to have been structured around two hypothetical causes of the apparitions: fraud or pathology. To exclude the first possibility, the children were kept apart before and after the apparitions and were asked misleading questions (referring, for instance, to answers that their fellow visionaries had not given). As for the second, pathology, to gain a better insight in what happened the children were asked more details about how they "saw" (With their eyes or in their minds? Did they see a special light?). Often the interrogations started with a very general question like: Was there something special today?[50]

The improvised character of the examination and the rather harsh approach of some of interviewers soon led to debates on how to conduct the questioning.[51] Even though one might consider the Beauraing case exceptional because of the youth of the visionaries, which required a specific age-appropriate treatment, the way in which the visionaries were to be questioned was an issue at other sites as well. The comments on the questioning referred to the tone and the level of detachment of the interrogator, the type of questions (open or "guiding"), attention or the lack thereof to the reaction time of the visionaries,[52] and the need for a written record.[53] Each of the participants had his own background, education, and ideas about how to proceed. In the interrogations, Étienne De Greeff, trained from years of working with young delinquents, expected three basic qualities in an interviewer: competence, moral independence, and intelligence: "It is necessary that he have a certain intellectual development, for he must not only be an instrument of registration; at certain moments, the examiner must be active; he penetrates the conscience of the one who is examined, he surveys it, scrutinizes it, influences it, masters it. If he is not at least as intelligent as the subject he examines, it will be the latter who will conduct the examination without him realizing it."[54]

While De Greeff's warnings might have been influenced by his experiences with juvenile delinquents, his cautious stance differed markedly from the empathy and trust that had been key terms for the local doctor Maistriaux in gathering the children's testimonies.

Doctors were also involved in the examination of the so-called miraculés who emerged at the various apparition sites. The medical bureau of Lourdes seems to have set the model for the type of examination. Louis Vervaeck, who in 1934 published a book on the role of doctors in such cases, defined what he believed to be the necessary characteristics of a miraculous cure. Based on the documentation of the *Bulletin de l'Association Médicale Internationale de Notre-Dame de Lourdes*, he placed emphasis on the rapidity of the healing, the importance of the result, and the vestiges left by the disease or affliction. As for the medical criteria, the doctors should weigh the impossibility of the healing, the incurability of the disease, the instantaneity of the healing, the suppression of the recovery, the absence of all means of medicine and all influence of a psychological order, and the irregularity of the way in which the healing took place.[55]

Among the most famous miraculous cures of the Belgian series are those of two men who also claimed to have seen Mary: Tilman Côme at Beauraing and Henri Kempenaers at Onkerzele. These men, especially Côme, attracted numerous people to the apparition sites and their popularity at times overshadowed that of the original seers.[56] Among those who travelled to these locations were the afflicted and sick. Encouraged by the widely publicized "cures" of the two men, these invalids were – in the words of Herbert Thurston – eager to "try for a miracle" themselves. The higher the number of pilgrims, so Thurston added, the greater the probability of a cure happening at the site, and he mentioned several of them reported in the newspapers. These cures "clearly" called "for examination by a committee of experts." As the English Jesuit remarked: "I hope it is no slur upon the medical profession at large to doubt the competence of the ordinary general practitioner in a small country town to pronounce a final verdict."[57]

Eventually it was the need for these cures to be investigated more properly that led the Saint-Luc Society to ask the bishops to set up a medical commission.[58]

Finally, the immense crowds present at the sites and their collective interaction caught the doctors' attention as well. How could one explain the high numbers and collective experiences like miracles of the sun and the smell of roses? Dr August Ladon, who addressed this topic several years after the last phenomena had been reported, called it a "modern mental epidemic."[59] Referring to mass psychology (and the works of Gustave Le Bon and McDougall) he tried to explain how the Belgian population, well-known for its good sense, could have been caught up in such a mass phenomenon and become convinced that the phenomena were of supernatural origin.[60] He personally witnessed the "apparitions" in Etikhove on 29 October 1933, and noted that the "impression of a collective feeling" was so strong that for an individual who stood outside the crowd, it left "a very uncomfortable, physical feeling of incompatibility and maybe latent hostility."[61] Still, "real, true piety was the dominant characteristic of the masses who had gathered, and that religious aspect was so earnest that several of the supporters of the supernatural origin of the events could use it as the best argument in favor of their thesis."[62] This deeply felt religious conviction, combined with a lack of a critical attitude, a "paroxistic emotivity," and a remarkable suggestibility led him to characterize the assembled pilgrims as "lower" masses (as opposed to organized masses).[63] Even many years after the events had been rejected, Ladon found it hard to believe that so many adults, and not only those with a low intellectual capacity, put their trust in "the miserable individuals who acted as visionaries."[64] Among the factors stimulating the expansion of the phenomenon, he mentioned the "general disarray that weighed on the world; the belated liquidation of the anxieties of the war; aspirations for a spiritual equilibrium, in the midst of that reversal of values that had caused the actual instability." All of that, combined with the religious traditions of Belgium (the perpetual presence of the wondrous in daily life and "mystical atavism"), might have contributed to the phenomenon but was not enough to create it. The trigger, the initial condensation, was Beauraing – a series of apparitions he believed to have been set off by a visual illusion of Andrée Degeimbre and transferred through suggestion to the other children.[65]

### *Transparency of the Discussions*

In December 1934, Henri Gailly recalled how he had commented upon the work of Étienne De Greeff at a meeting of a medical society: "It does not have any scientific value. All his elucubrations to defend his thesis, I have termed them a scientific novel in his presence in front of sixty doctors at Saint-Luc. I retract nothing, except maybe the word 'scientific' that seems to me truly superfluous."[66] As this fragment illustrates, the medical debates could take on a sharp tone. The doctors disagreed about how to evaluate the events and did so in public. They also used periodicals and newspapers to spread their opinions and argued them at lively meetings of the Saint-Luc Society.[67] Saint-Luc not only welcomed medical professionals, but also members of the clergy investigating the series.[68] Thanks to this openness, we have information on the sessions that is a little less sterile than the formal reports in the journal. On 31 May 1933, the Jesuit Jean-Baptiste Lenain participated in a session in Brussels and reported back to his friend Louis Wilmet. After noting the somewhat disorganized nature of the discussions, he elaborated on the contributions of the various participants of the debate. De Greeff took a rather critical stance. The Louvain professor stated that even though his position might not yet be appreciated, he believed that in a year or six from now, people would be grateful that the Catholic doctors had been so skeptical. Dr Jan Frans Fransen from the University of Ghent, on the contrary, had ended his statement with an act of faith toward our Lady of Beauraing. Still, in Lenain's opinion, Henri Gailly had clarified his position in a better way, noting that in the Beauraing case there was something that "medical science cannot explain." In Lenain's opinion, this was "French clarity as opposed to the mist of German science."[69]

Saint-Luc was not the only group of doctors that organized meetings on the apparitions. Karel Van Acker (subsequently involved in the Onkerzele series) gave a presentation on the Beauraing apparitions at a meeting of the Provincial Medical Society of East-Flanders (Provinciale Geneeskundige Vereniging van Oost-Vlaanderen) in May 1933,[70] and August Ladon from Ghent spoke about the apparition series at a meeting on religious psychology in France in April 1935.[71] Those unable to attend these meetings had the opportunity to follow the discussions in the texts of the presentations published in a monographic issue of *Saint-Luc*

*Médical*. In its introduction the editors emphasized that it was not their intention to take a position in the debate, but simply to participate in the collection of documents and ideas that might contribute to the study of the events. For "the Saint-Luc Society has always believed that in order to study a question with a true critical mind and with a truly scientific method, it is indispensable to be able to investigate without taking a side and without passion, all opinions and all proposed solutions."[72]

Some of the authors of this special *Saint-Luc* issue also contributed to one of the most notable publications on the Belgian series, the April issue of the *Études Carmélitaines*[73] – later republished as *The Mysterious Events of Beauraing: Studies, Documents and Answers* (*Les faits mystérieux de Beauraing. Études, documents, réponses)*, that came to be nicknamed "the blue book" ("*le livre bleu*"). While it was not an exclusively medical periodical, attention for these debates and issues was not new for the journal, which had already shown an interest in the psychological study of mystical phenomena. Bringing together contributions of medical professionals and theologians, the editors emphasized that the goal of the publication was neither an attack nor a defence of the events, but to establish the facts in their objective reality and explain them in accordance with the rules of the criticism of testimonies, with the principles of theology. More specifically, they referred to the doctrine of the Carmelite Saint John of the Cross, who counselled an attitude of extreme prudence regarding the extraordinary – especially the visions and locutions perceived by the external senses.[74]

The doctors' opinions and arguments were not only disseminated through these specialized journals.[75] The general public could read them in newspapers and magazines.[76] De Greeff, for instance, made a statement in the press in December 1932 in which he rejected the hypothesis of collective hysteria and formulated doubts about the supernatural origin of the Beauraing events, suggesting instead an explanation involving an initial shock. It was already too late, he said, to gather information about the initial cause from testimony of the children. Only a long and intense examination of the external circumstances of the apparitions could provide more details. However, even that information would have to be treated with utmost caution. Maistriaux reacted with a statement in the press on 20 December, emphasizing that the events in Beauraing required careful attention and study and that it was too soon to reach any conclusion.[77]

As might be expected, the "rank" of the doctors also played a part in the evaluation of their examinations. When Karel Van Acker, a psychiatrist from Ghent, attended the questioning of the child visionaries in Beauraing on 31 December 1932, he counted about thirty doctors present, noting that the four psychiatrists were clearly outnumbered. He added that among the physicians present, ten (at most) still remembered the basics of psychology and psychopathology they learned at the university. He complained; "Precisely those colleagues who know nothing about psychology and psychiatry are the ones in charge of the case. The examination is dreadful … Beauraing has been examined by those who were absolutely unqualified and in addition to being depressingly unscientific, the information provided to psychiatrists is also depressingly incomplete."[78]

But it took more than hierarchy and specialization in order to be well-positioned to talk about what was happening – at least according to Fernand Maistriaux. When we take a closer look at the criticism that the doctor formulated regarding his colleagues "who spoke at meetings of Saint-Luc or wrote in journals and periodicals," it becomes clear that he did not criticize their arguments, but rather their behaviour and their presence – not surprisingly the aspects in which he believed he did better. He criticized them (1) for arriving "in general, too late"; (2) and some of them, like De Greeff, for "preconceived ideas"; and (3) for having a negative effect on the children (due to a pretentious air). He also noted that (4) "almost all" did not see enough of the children in their everyday state to be able to conclude anything at all.[79] He thus criticized the ways in which his colleagues conducted their examinations, their professionalism, and their objectivity.

Maistriaux was not the only one to deplore the limited presence of the eminent scholars at the Beauraing site. In his book *Testimony on Beauraing* (*Getuigenis omtrent Beauraing*), Jan Filip Boon made a similar remark. V.A. (most probably Dr Karel Van Acker) picked up on it in his review of Boon's book for a medical journal. He noted that Boon calculated that he had spent more hours in Beauraing than any psychiatrist, and thus knew the case better than they did. V.A. mockingly added that if Boon should ever decide to look into a microscope for a while, he would know infinitely more than the trained histologist who only looked for a couple of minutes.[80] An informed, trained, eye could see more and needed less time to do so.

## *Morality and Ruined Reputations*

"The first law of history is to try not to lie; the second one is not to fear telling the truth" (Leo XIII).[81] With such an opening line, it is clear that the editors of the *Études Carmélitaines* special issue on Beauraing knew that they were in for trouble. The campaigns against the *Études* were so personal that they ended in ruined reputations. The themed issue of April 1933 included articles by theologians (the Carmelite Bruno de Jésus-Marie and Aloïs Janssens, of the Congregation of the Immaculate Heart of Mary), doctors (De Greeff and Van Gehuchten), a philosopher (Roland Dalbiez), and a historian (Pierre Debongnie, signing Gustave Leurquin).[82] The overall tone of the articles was skeptical and a few months after the issue came out, the authors had to turn for help from the Belgian archbishop and Rome.[83] In a letter on 15 October 1933 to Mgr Canali, assessor of the Holy Office, Bruno de Jésus-Marie complained about the actions of the "partisans of Beauraing." He reported how the Beauraing supporters threatened the authors in an attempt to reject all they reported in the themed issue about the comportment of the visionaries. They threatened them with losing certain advantages for their projects, tried to intimidate them with the prospect of a process for defamation, and attacked them publicly. Father Bruno contrasted their behaviour with that of "sensible" people who had congratulated them on publishing the issue. In their opinion, the *Études* authors had done the right thing, for otherwise anticlericals could easily have started a campaign against the ecclesiastical exploitation of "popular credulity."[84]

In January 1935, Bruno de Jésus-Marie again wrote to Rome and explained why *Les Études* published a second edition of their "blue book." While they had initially decided against a new edition (even though they had received the necessary permissions), they changed their minds after the Redemptorist Gaston Maes launched a new severe attack in the book on Beauraing. Published with the imprimatur of the bishop of Liège, *Beauraing. Observations on the Study of Mr De Greeff 29 November 1932–3 January 1933* (*Beauraing. Observations sur l'étude de M. De Greeff 29 novembre 1932 – 3 janvier 1933*) was a detailed critique of the blue book. Bruno de Jésus-Marie and his colleagues had therefore decided to write a response to that attack and called it "Our Answer" ("Notre Réponse"). Their issue was published with the imprimatur of the archbishop of Paris.[85]

What was the trouble about? Most of it can be traced to statements of De Greeff on the morality of one of the visionaries from Beauraing, Albert Voisin. At the time of the publication of his statements (1933), Étienne De Greeff (1898–1961) was working at the School of Criminal Sciences, in the central prison of Louvain and in the university psychiatric centre Salve Mater in Lovenjoul.[86] When he heard about the apparitions in Beauraing, he took an interest as he was convinced that it was the duty of a Catholic doctor to exclude natural explanations and to conduct a rigorous investigation. Together with his colleague from Lovenjoul, Charles Rouvroy, he travelled to Beauraing on 11 December 1932. He returned a few days later for more intensive research 15–17 December. During this period he spoke with the children and family and visited the various locations. On the evening of 17 December, he also participated in the questioning of the child visionaries after the apparitions. Afterwards, he made a statement to the press declaring that hysteria, collective hallucination, and hypnosis could be rejected, but it was possible that the phenomenon was due to natural causes; perhaps the apparitions had been caused by fear in combination with unconscious pressure of one of the older children. In his opinion, the so-called perfect accordance of the children (the simultaneity of their actions) had not been sufficiently verified and their statements were rather vague and vacillating.[87]

Whereas other doctors had also been critical about what was happening, De Greeff seems to have become the personification of the "nonbelievers."[88] While his fear hypothesis was criticized, most of the debates eventually centred on his remarks published in *Les Études* and *Saint-Luc Médical* about Albert Voisin's morality. In his article "Rectifications, Completions, Confirmations Concerning the Documents in the 'Notes,'" he was still rather vague in referring to what had happened, as he limited himself to noting that "since the 'apparitions,' certain events have taken place in Beauraing that, for reasons of delicacy, we thought we needed to keep quiet, in the hope that the responsible authorities would be informed about them." However, by the time of this publication, he believed he could no longer remain silent. He was not the only one who possessed documents concerning the "sad affair," and he feared that the nonbelievers who had similar documents in their possession would not hesitate to use them when the right moment came.[89] De Greeff was less cryptic in his article in

*Saint-Luc Médical.* He indicated that in April 1933 Albert Voisin had been accused by some fellow students of improper behaviour, and that was even *after* he claimed to see the Virgin.[90]

His allegations caused a stir, and in October 1933 De Greeff addressed the Belgian Archbishop Van Roey in distress, asking him what to do about the accusations made against him. In particular, he complained about the "hateful campaign" of Mgr Schyrgens even before questions about Voisin's morality had arisen.[91] De Greeff felt like he was treated worse than Émile Zola after publishing *Lourdes* and complained that he had been accused of falsifying his maps of the apparition site and publishing misleading photographs of the children. Even worse, he had been summoned to retract his statements and donate a generous contribution for the building of the Beauraing chapel. De Greeff wanted to know if – to spare his family from a trial – he should agree to publish a retraction.[92]

A month later, De Greeff contacted the archbishop again as matters had taken a turn for the worse. By then, a public retraction – signed by De Greeff – had already been published on 7 November on the front page of *Vers l'Avenir*: "It has been indicated to me by a trustworthy source that a serious examination has refuted certain accusations directed against the little Albert Voisin and that I, following others, have disclosed in some of my articles: 'The mysterious events of Beauraing' and 'Saint-Luc Medical.' In the presence of this contradictory testimony, I do not want to let that question concerning the honour of Albert subsist in my publications. I also want to declare that I never wanted to insinuate anything concerning the other children."[93]

In his letter to the archbishop, De Greeff emphasized that he had been pressed into publishing his retraction. Dom Isidore Bodart (from the Abbey of Maredsous), with whom he had been corresponding since the end of August,[94] had forced him to do it. After a previous (epistolary) attempt to make him retract had failed, Dom Isidore had shown up on De Greeff's doorstep on 6 November. He pressed him for three hours to retract while suggesting that he was a messenger from Mgr Heylen, the bishop of Namur. Bodart had been asked to communicate that Voisin's parents were furious about De Greeff's statements and a lawsuit was imminent. Indicating that the ecclesiastical authorities wanted to avoid the scandal that a public trial would cause, Bodart asked De Greeff to reflect on the negative impact this trial would have on the church. For "by slandering Albert, I had committed a mortal sin for which absolution could only be given to me after a complete reparation." Bodart apparently even added: "I speak to you in the same position as a confessor." De Greeff wrote that he had eventually given in out of respect for Bodart's sacerdotal character and for the episcopal authority. However, as soon as he had started to comprehend how his good faith had been abused, he had tried to withdraw the retraction with a telegram he had sent the next morning to Bodart, and in the afternoon to the newspaper Bodart had been talking about. Both telegrams had, apparently, arrived too late. Aware of the impact this public retraction might have on the official examination of the apparitions and horrified by the abuse of spiritual powers, De Greeff once again wanted to assure the archbishop that he could indeed substantiate his statements about Albert Voisin with overwhelming evidence.[95]

The correspondence between Prof. De Greeff and Dom Bodart has been preserved in several copies and documents what was at play in this clash between the Benedictine monk and criminologist, one a Beauraing supporter and the other a Beauraing critic. No clear-cut religious division existed between them: De Greeff was a practising Catholic and a self-proclaimed Catholic doctor. Moreover, as noted above, he was willing to obey the ecclesiastical authorities (as all Catholic laymen were supposed to). And this obedience eventually brought him to retract his statement. Bodart, however, wondered whether his being a *doctor* had not pushed him into a search for natural explanations at all costs – was he not deformed by his profession? Ruled by skepticism? Irresistibly pushed toward a systematic contradiction?[96] De Greeff admitted that he might be looking for a natural explanation before everything else. Still, he emphasized, he was a *Catholic* doctor and had always presented himself as such – also at scientific meetings. Moreover, he felt that he could not afford himself the luxury to keep quiet when he knew something and believed he could make a valid statement – even though he saw others remain silent.[97]

Apart from criticizing the doctor's skepticism, Bodart also criticized the way in which De Greeff had pleaded his case, the proof and arguments he used. One of their disagreements centred on De Greeff's use of the photographs of the children that he included in his article in the *Études Carmélitaines*.[98] These were not pictures of the visionaries during their encounter with the Virgin, but portraits the children had posed for subsequently. De Greeff referred to these photos in his article in *Saint-Luc Médical*, noting about the Voisin children that their grandfather had been an alcoholic and the pictures illustrated how this hereditary material had only partially been corrected.[99] Dom Isidore Bodart however believed that the pictures did not give a fair image of the children. He accused De Greeff (or Rouvroy, who had accompanied him on his trip to Beauraing) of asking the children to lower their heads a little when posing for the photographs. This pose had made them look slightly dazed.[100] De Greeff responded that this was a pose recommended for portrait pictures (for instance in movies). With his explanations of the pictures, he did not want to suggest that the effects of syphilis or alcohol were in play, only the signs of alcohol abuse of an ancestor.[101] His answer apparently did not satisfy Bodart,[102] for De Greeff returned to the issue in one of his subsequent letters. He noted that he could not remember whether or not he asked the children to lower their heads when posing, but this was such a logical thing to ask when taking pictures. He could not say that the pictures Bodart had sent were in fact more flattering for the children. Moreover, he added, the children had been very happy about their pictures when he showed them the negatives.[103] Both correspondents thus were well aware of the subjective character of photography. Neither presumed a one-to-one relationship between photographs and "reality," and both were aware of the effect that photographs could generate. De Greeff's post-factum portraits were not exceptional in medical publications. Even though photographs of visionaries during the encounters with Mary were primarily published in periodicals linked to apparition sites, we have indications that some doctors took photographs as well. (No pictures were allowed to be taken at night in Beauraing – the flashbulbs had confused more than one bystander who then wondered whether they had "seen").[104]

As for De Greeff's criticism about the way in which the examinations and interrogations had been conducted in Beauraing, Bodart answered: "It is so difficult to conduct an interrogation of children … besides allow me to tell you that you cannot pretend to have the monopoly on the way to do so nor can you hope to impose your criteria and testimonies as the only authentic ones, the only acceptable ones. There have been, so you say, errors in judgment, omissions, vices in the methods of the examinations; that is possible, but note that I hold exactly the same reproach against you."[105]

When we look into their argument about the Albert Voisin matter, it becomes clear that what they were actually talking about was the level of transparency an examination should have. If it damaged the reputation of a child, should an argument that pleaded against a case be made public? De Greeff stressed that he did not use a reference to the boy's morality to build his argument against Beauraing. But even though Albert Voisin's actions and statements were not that exceptional for a boy his age, De Greeff still felt like he had to mention them because, from a religious point of view, they were of significance.[106] This factor of ruining a child's reputation often came up in the discussions on whether or not De Greeff should publish a retraction. A central question in the discussion was whether or not one should be transparent about what one had discovered. Soon, however, transparency about the discussions themselves became a central issue in the debate between De Greeff and Bodart as well.

While the discussions and manoeuvres leading up to De Greeff's public retraction had been a private matter, De Greeff and Bodart fought their battles in a more public way after the disputed public statement. In February 1934, De Greeff published an account of his meeting with Bodart in *L'Avant Garde* describing him as nothing less than "a gangster of the supernatural."[107] Similarly, in the October edition of *Études Carmélitaines*, he used the term "gangster procedures" when he referred to threats of a lawsuit or press campaign and the forms of blackmail he had been subjected to.[108] In this article, De Greeff also tried to explain how the photographs of the visionaries had been taken and how delighted the children had been with them. He added that the complaints about the child visionaries not understanding his questions in the 11 December 1932 interrogation did not make sense. If his interference had really been that exceptional and incomprehensible, then the children should have remembered him more vividly. But when he met them a few days later, they did not seem to recall who he was.[109] De Greeff's answer was not the final word in the matter, however, and a month later, in November 1934, Bodart responded to De Greeff's public complaints about his withdrawal with a new public statement called "The Regrets and Silences of Dr De Greeff" ("Les regrets et les silences de Dr De Greeff"). Mockingly calling him the "wise professor," he criticized the instability of De Greeff's mind that now caused him to regret his retraction. De Greeff might complain about being persecuted by the "circle of Beauraing," but in his complaints he also made accusations – so who was insulting whom?[110]

In short, De Greeff was caught up in an intense and ugly discussion and Mgr Ladeuze, rector of the University of Louvain, and Professor D'Hollander, director of the Lovenjoul Centre, did not think lightly about the whole affair. In August 1935 the conflict allegedly almost cost De Greeff his job.[111] According to his biographer, Joris Casselman, it eventually took the intervention of the minister of justice, Emile Vandervelde, who was the minister responsible for the psychiatric institution Salve Mater in Lovenjoul and the Louvain prisons, to prevent this. Without his support, De Greeff most probably would have been asked to leave the School of Criminology as well.[112]

In the end, De Greeff's retraction not only affected his own credibility but also that of the other authors of the journal: a text called "Science or Blackmail?" ("*Science ou chantage?*") also cast doubts about the statement of Dr L.G. [L. Goedseels] that had been published in *Saint-Luc Médical*. If the statements of De Greeff were not to be trusted, why the others?[113] Indeed, De Greeff was not the only one of the *Études* group whose motives and ideas were questioned by members of the clergy. The Dominican Pie Bonhomme maintained that the only goal of the *Études* authors was commercial success. While he believed in the sincerity of some of the professors of the Catholic University of Louvain, he had the strong impression that, as psychologists, they had let themselves been carried away by preconceived ideas against the possibility of the apparitions.[114]

In sum, the public character of the apparitions both held benefits and dangers for the doctors involved. While it allowed them to see these exceptional phenomena for themselves, and conduct tests and interviews, the public resonance their debates had seems to have intensified the discussions, not only among one another, but also with members of the clergy as De Greeff's public retraction illustrates. Still, as noted before, the doctors' expertise was called on – even by the ecclesiastical authorities. We will see how this involvement became more organized and authorized as the series of apparitions developed.

## The Formalization of the Medical Interest

Almost a year after the first reports, as new apparitions and miraculous cures continued to be signalled over Belgium, the doctors decided to concentrate their actions and organize a medical commission. This chapter explores this formalization of the medical interest and the presence of medical experts in the examinations of the inter/diocesan commissions of the following years. As we will see, the public debates and commotions concerning the doctors had two repercussions. First of all, because of their involvement in these discussions, some of the doctors were thought of as biased and jeopardizing the credibility of these novel examinations. Secondly, this involvement resulted in their being questioned as witnesses not solely for their medical expertise but also in regard to the disputes between the promoters and opponents of the various apparitions. In stark contrast to the public setting of the previous debates, these novel examinations of the various commissions took place behind closed doors. What is more, the outcomes were sometimes not even shared among the various commissions.

### *In the Interest of the Catholic Church: the Medical Commission*

In September 1933, Dr Wibo, the head of the Saint-Luc Society, addressed a letter to the bishop of Namur, Mgr Heylen, asking for the creation of a medical commission. Referring to the cures that continued to be reported at Beauraing, he noted: "It is … absolutely necessary, in the interest of the Beauraing event in itself, in the greater interest of the Catholic Church, that those cures be properly verified, controlled and not hushed up, as in the Bureau of Verifications in Lourdes, when they carry the evident signs of a supernatural intervention. Only this way of acting will dispose of all tendency toward opposition in the skeptics, and will give the friends of Beauraing a fundamental reason to support their opinion and piety.[115]

The Belgian bishops seem to have agreed with the doctors on this matter and a few months later, in December 1933, a medical commission was created with the support of the Archbishop Van Roey.[116] The commission had two major goals: examine the apparitions, and study the miraculous cures that were reported at various sites. The primary aim was to decide whether or not the reported phenomena could be explained in a natural way. If the commission members could not find an explanation, then the phenomena would be subjected to a theological examination.[117]

The commission had three members: Jan Frans Fransen (professor of psychology at the University of Ghent),[118] Henri Gailly (a psychiatrist from Charleroi),[119] and Paul Van Gehuchten (professor of neurology in the medical faculty of Louvain).[120] The commission thus consisted primarily of scholars with an interest in psychology. All three of them were "great doctors" (in the visionary Omer Eneman's terms), who were, as seen above, considered more "fit" to examine apparitions. Interestingly, the members of the commission were all men who had already publicly expressed their opinion on the apparition series at meetings of Saint-Luc or in articles in themed issues in *Saint-Luc Médical* or *Études Carmélitaines*.[121]

Paul Van Gehuchten was rather skeptical: He had attended an apparition in Beauraing (31 December 1932) and participated in the questioning. Referring to the rather "indifferent" tone of the children's prayer, their appearance during the apparitions (not really reflecting contemplation of the Virgin), but also the emotional turbulence after the last apparition (tears and crying), he concluded that there had been a more or less unconscious simulation enhanced by autosuggestion. As for his role in the examination, he believed it to be his job to raise doubts. The sole goal of his efforts was to let the truth triumph.[122]

Henri Gailly had never attended an apparition in Beauraing but had strong opinions about the scientists who had visited the site.[123] He criticized those who had made up their minds (and rejected the apparitions) after only one visit (among them Prof. Van Gehuchten). He remarked that the colleagues who had spent more time and witnessed several apparitions had been shaken by what they had seen. After hearing the various hypotheses – the "tour of psychiatry" as Gailly called it – he believed that science could not solve the Beauraing question. The "scientific novel" fell apart as soon as one started to focus on the details and "something inexplicable remained."[124]

While Jan Frans Fransen admitted there were arguments in favour of an "unconscious simulation combined with autosuggestion" (as Van Gehuchten suggested), he saw no good explanations why this had suddenly commenced and stopped. In his opinion, no satisfactory medical label had been given to the Beauraing case; there had been hints at hysteria, induction, mythomania and also hypnosis, but the scientists had all lost themselves in the details. Fransen's personal opinion tended toward a supernatural explanation, even though he believed that absolute certainty was impossible.[125]

Because of their previous statements, the choice of doctors for the medical commission did not remain uncontested. Members of the clergy as well as laymen commented on their involvement and questioned the commission's impartiality. All three of them were in dispute: Gailly was a known partisan of Beauraing, Fransen was (sometimes) considered one as well, and Van Gehuchten had already identified himself too explicitly as an opponent of the apparitions.[126] Louis Wilmet, for instance, left no doubt about what he thought about the commission in his letters to Father Lenain. In his opinion, "Van Gehuchten had already provided so much proof of his impressionability and his superficiality that his opinion can no longer have any value in the eyes of those who are not name fetishists."[127]

The three members of the commission had well-defined tasks. Van Gehuchten – the secretary of the commission – was responsible for the examination of the miraculous cures; Fransen studied the Flemish sites (in particular Etikhove, Olsene, Onkerzele, and Lokeren), and Gailly studied Beauraing (the child visionaries and Tilman Côme) and Banneux.[128] When the commission was constituted in December 1933, many of the phenomena that were under discussion had already ended (about twenty sites had already been identified). For these cases the commission depended on retroactive examinations and called upon the help of the doctors present at these sites when the events were taking place.[129] As for the sites where apparitions and cures were still being reported, here the commission members went to investigate and carefully observed the reactions and appearance of the visionaries.[130] As their reports indicate, they received assistance from other doctors in conducting their research.[131] The experiments (with matches, flashlights, and knives) to test the visionaries' senses were similar to those described in the previous chapter. Their and their helpers' activities were carefully scrutinized. Apart from comments on the dangers of the experiments, similar to those referred to in the previous chapters, criticism focused on the limited presence of the doctors at the sites.[132] In addition, the commission members were – just like the other doctors – criticized for having made up their minds before they had conducted an examination,[133] for their "professional deformation,"[134] and for conduct unbefitting at a religious site.[135]

Supporters of the various sites tried to ensure that the commission members did not miss the cures that were interesting.[136] A telling example is that of Mr Van Saelen, allegedly miraculously cured in Onkerzele on 9 February 1934 of a "general osteomyelitis" that had forced him to walk with crutches. His case was examined by Dr Careels, who was well informed about the events and had performed some tests during Onkerzele II, and by Dr Vrints, who had previously treated Van Saelen. A report on the cure was sent to Prof. Fransen (responsible for the Flemish sites) and a month later, on 20 March 1934, Dr Vrints drove Van Saelen to Ghent to see Prof. Fransen. According to his colleague, Fransen was stunned to learn that Van Saelen was cured.[137] Vrints therefore waited impatiently for an official approval and complained: "I regularly read the 'Bulletin de l'Association Médicale Internationale de N.D. de Lourdes' and I confirm that if Van Saelen had been cured in Lourdes he would have been accepted long ago."[138] Van Saelen's cure, however, never did pass the official examination. In the final report of the medical commission (dated 4 November 1934) it was suggested that he had been almost completely cured before he went on his pilgrimage to Onkerzele. He therefore did not fit the basic criteria for a cure that was miraculous. As formulated in *De Servorum Dei Beatificatione et Beatorum Canonizatione* there were seven conditions: (1) the affliction had to be severe and difficult to cure; (2) the affliction must not have reached its final stage; (3) medication must have remained useless and insufficient; (4) the cure had to be immediate or in an abnormally short timespan; (5) the healing had to be complete; (6) no noticeable amelioration should have preceded it; and (7) the healing had to be definitive unless the sick had only asked for a temporal relief from it.[139]

In the end, none of the cures in Beauraing, Banneux, and Onkerzele were deemed miraculous. "For each of them," so the medical commission added as general conclusion, "to the extent that we were able to gather sufficient information, we have developed commentaries and conclusions. For certain cases, we were able to establish a diagnosis and prove that the cure involved nothing extraordinary. For other cases, because of a lack of precise information, we could only make some hypotheses. In none of the cases were we under the impression that we were in the presence of phenomena that were inexplicable to science."[140] As for the visionaries, they examined their medical and psychological well-being. The commission members emphasized that their findings did not permit any conclusions about the nature of the visions themselves. While confirming that the children resembled other children, they added an evaluation for each of them addressing four aspects (nervous system, intelligence, character, and physical health). After an examination on 9 May 1934, the commission concluded regarding the Banneux visionary Mariette Béco that there was a certain degree of "psychic disequilibrium" ("*déséquilibre psychique*"). In addition, they rejected the other apparition series they had examined (Beauraing II and Onkerzele II). Beauraing's visionary Tilman Côme was criticized for his egocentrism and need to show off,[141] while for the Onkerzele apparitions, "a natural explanation, pathological for the three of them" could be detected as well as "imitation simulated in accordance with Beauraing and Ezkioga." The solar phenomena on 18 December 1933 and 6 January 1934 could be explained naturally and the insensibility of the visionary Berthonia Holtkamp had proven not to be real: She had been burned during the tests on 21 January 1934 and the scars were still visible a month later.[142]

While the medical commission was thus unwilling to accept any of the cures as miraculous, their evaluation of the child visionaries left room for the possibility of a supernatural origin of the apparitions. This formulation may have been a compromise between the two members Fransen and Gailly, who – before the commission started – did not want to exclude a supernatural origin, and Van Gehuchten, who had suggested the visions were a more or less unconscious simulation. For the Flemish visionaries and Tilman Côme, the commission rejected a supernatural origin. It did not come as a surprise that the supporters of these adult visionaries disagreed with the report. In their opinion, the outcome was what might have been expected from a group of doctors who started their investigation with their minds made up.[143]

## *Doctors on the Stand: "Medicolatry" in the (Inter-)diocesan Commissions?*

The medical commission's negative findings did not stop the creation of five commissions on the apparition series: two in the diocese of Namur (1935–36; and 1942–48); two in the diocese of Liège (1935–36 and 1942–47); and one in the archdiocese of Malines (1935–38). We will discuss these commissions in more detail in the following chapter, but for our analysis of the medical evaluation of the series, it is important to understand that the doctors' findings and analyses were not accepted without dispute, and additional doctors, who were not members of the medical commission, were asked to testify as well. Furthermore, while doctors were called in as experts in these commissions, some of them were also scrutinized regarding their comportment, tests, questionings, and evaluation. Three commissions call our attention here.

In the first diocesan commission of Namur (evaluating Beauraing), the assessment of the medical examinations resulted in observations on the testimonies of doctors and an evaluation of De Greeff's case. To this end the commission members consulted several doctors, primarily local ones who had witnessed the apparitions several times and participated in questioning the visionaries.[144] In a concluding report on the medical examinations, they first addressed "the doctors specialized in psychiatry." Most of these doctors, so they noted, had taken positions against the supernatural origin of the apparitions. According to the Namur commission there were various reasons for that: First of all, the children, who had not been very keen on being questioned yet again, had welcomed them rather coldly and that might have given the doctors a bad impression of the children. Second, these men had too often started off with scientific prejudices that affected their conclusions. For instance, some of them were under the impression that the supernatural required "ecstasy" and that the ecstasy made the subject completely insensible to what happened around him. The commission opposed both views. Finally, they wondered whether the specialists themselves were not the victims of some unconscious tendency to attribute importance to fragmentary and poorly verified findings.

A second set of observations regarded Dr De Greeff. He had refused to testify because he did not believe in the impartiality of the diocesan commission and – after the actions taken against him – he did not trust the people involved.[145] De Greeff's views were, however, very present during the sessions of the Namur commission, whether implicitly or explicitly. For instance, when Dr Gailly took the stand on 21 February 1936, he noted that photographs did not have any pertinence as evidence of defects and that the children, in his opinion, seemed to be more stable than their parents.[146] The commission also asked Dr Albert Rondelet about De Greeff's questioning of the child visionaries. The doctor noted that De Greeff had put very specific questions to the children, who were already quite tired, and while he did not ask them in a brutal way, the tone was still rather rough. Rondelet had the impression that, in the end, the children no longer knew what to say.[147] In a concluding report on the matter, the commission deplored De Greeff's refusal to testify, since it would have given him the opportunity to comment on documents he frequently referred to but did not consider fit for publication. His sincerity was not questioned, but, according to the commission, one could not deny the partiality of his examination and the deformation of his observations. Anyone not led astray by the "scientific airs" of De Greeff or his literary merits would have to conclude that his contribution to the whole story was at least suspect. He had not even checked his facts properly (for instance, in his allusions to a spiritist circle in Beauraing).

The commission of Malines, which examined all apparition sites apart from Beauraing and Banneux, also called upon doctors. In fact, the importance the commission members attached to psychiatrists led one contemporary to remark that the commission showed signs of "medicolatry."[148] Medicolatry (the veneration of medical expertise) is, of course, an exaggeration, but the commission was certainly interested in medical findings[149] and seems at least to have inspired sufficient confidence for Étienne De Greeff to testify about his experiences and findings in regard to Beauraing.[150] In his statement, De Greeff mentioned the witnesses and testimonies he had concerning the Albert Voisin affair and summarized the threats he had received because of his stand in the Beauraing episode. In a note appended to his testimony, he explained how he and Dr Rouvroy soon realized that as far as the first apparition was concerned, nothing had occurred on 11 December 1932 in the manner the children described.[151] Apart from stereotypical descriptions, he believed they told nothing but lies and excuses. "When one had a certain experience in examining such phenomena, reactions and deformations – then such an investigation was not a 'tour de force,' but rather banal, easily pointing to the conclusion that nothing supernatural had taken place."[152] Comparing notes, the doctors concluded that something else must have happened that first day and they called it phenomenon X. De Greeff returned to Beauraing to find out what might have happened, but he soon realized the children could not tell him anything more. In the end, it was the work of Gaston Maes that helped him to interpret the apparitions as a combination of fear and unconscious pressure.[153] For him it was children's make-believe, "fed, pushed and finally exploited by adults."[154] His colleague Charles Rouvroy generally backed up De Greeff at the next session (1 April 1938). Commenting on the way in which they had questioned the children, he noted that they had applied the medico-legal procedures that they were used to, and that no serious examination had been conducted before they arrived. While he did not agree with De Greeff on every point, he also believed there was nothing in the Beauraing case that could not be explained naturally.[155]

Not only De Greeff's procedures were questioned in the diocesan commissions, other doctors were under scrutiny as well. The reports of the second diocesan commission of Namur indicate that the findings of the medical commission of Saint-Luc were still open for question a decade later.[156] In April 1949, the commission members contacted Dr Van Gehuchten and asked him about the medical commission's procedures. He clarified that they had not examined each of the cases themselves. They had primarily relied on the testimonies of other doctors, who in some cases could not be located. He admitted that due to their professional obligations, the 1934 commission members might not have spent as much time on their research as might have been desirable. When asked whether or not he agreed that part of the research of the medical commission would be done again by the diocesan commission, he consented.[157]

Re-evaluations of previous medical decisions and approaches were also central to the examination of one of the two miraculous cures that eventually won the diocesan commission over. The cure of Mrs Acar was a new case altogether, but that of Maria Van Laer (Sister Pudentia of the Franciscan Sisters of the Holy Family) had not been selected as interesting enough to be studied by the medical commission in 1934. Fifteen years later however, the narrative of her cure seemed to hold every ingredient of a convincing case. Maria Van Laer had been seventeen when she fell ill (from tuberculosis, Pott's disease, or osteomyelitis). With great confidence in the power of Our Lady of Beauraing, she went on a pilgrimage to the apparition site on 23 June 1933, when she was about thirty-three. It was said she had hardly been able to pray because of her feeble condition. However, after meeting the visionaries and being taken to the hawthorn tree of the apparitions her condition improved, and as the evening fell she could join the prayers of the visionaries.[158] The commission consulted two experts for the case: Eugène Picard of the University of Louvain, who was a forensic consultant of the Louvain court, and Albert Robaux, neurologist of the Institute of Beau-Vallon near Saint-Servais, a psychiatric institute in Namur. Given Maria Van Laer's affliction, these might seem odd choices, but since one of the major points of criticism on miraculous cures was the "nervous" or "hysterical" character of the miraculés, they were logical ones. They concluded that it was certain that Van Laer "was afflicted by a severe infectious illness of a tuberculous or staphylococcic nature, most probably osteomyelitis." Because of this diagnosis, the fact that Van Laer did not have a hysteric or nervous character, the rapidity of the cure, and its definite nature, the cure could not be explained by natural causes.[159]

This positive evaluation by the two experts was, however, not enough reason to include Van Laer's case as argument in favour of the apparition. That the cure had not been selected as worthy of attention in the previous years, and had not been discussed in the medical commission of 1934, seemed to form a particular reason for concern for the diocesan commission.

> Supposing that the experts knew about it, the fact that they did not accept it is not a precedent that should worry the commission of Namur. The experts themselves admit that they examined the cases that looked the most interesting to them. But that first appreciation had only a relative value; it depended more particularly on the state in which they found the documentation and the possibilities for examination. The commission of Namur should not bother itself about what might be their impression of the Van Laer case, since the documentation now contains so many objective elements to determine the nature of the illness and the circumstances of the cure.[160]

Another reason for concern was that Dr Vogels, the doctor who had treated Van Laer while she was ill and had examined her after her return from Beauraing, still believed that a natural explanation of her cure was possible. The commission members however decided to follow the experts they had engaged since their assessment explained all the symptoms reported by the various witnesses. The doctor's change of his diagnosis did not argue in favour of his credibility. He had first diagnosed Van Laer as afflicted with Pott's disease in the cervical part of the dorsal spine but had come to a different conclusion after her cure. Why he had changed his mind was hard to say. The X-rays Dr Vogels consulted had disappeared.[161]

A third "strange" element in the whole affair was that Maria Van Laer's case was so late in attracting the attention of the diocesan commission of 1935 (not the medical commission). In the commission's opinion this was because the first Namur commission had primarily been interested in "the events of Beauraing," rather than the cures. When they eventually started to examine the cures, the Second World War had already begun and hindered their activities. Moreover, Dr Maistriaux, the head of the Comité Pro Maria, was then a prisoner in Germany and the archives of the Comité were in a lamentable state. It was eventually a publication by Kinzinger that drew the attention of the present commission. However regrettable the delays, they had at least the advantage that they allowed a personal contact between the commission members and Maria Van Laer at a time when her cure seemed proven and definitive.[162]

Once these three objections had been countered, there seemed to be no reason not to approve the miraculous nature of Van Laer's cure. In July 1949, the bishop of Namur publicly announced that Van Laer and Mrs Acar had indeed "been healed suddenly, perfectly and definitively."[163]

In conclusion, the public character of the apparitions provided medical experts with an opportunity to see and examine exceptional religious phenomena. Their presence at a site gave importance to the apparition. However, the visibility of the apparitions and the concomitant phenomena also made their involvement (or lack thereof) an argument in discussing their professionality. Were they present often enough? What did they examine and how? Moreover, by publishing their findings in specialist journals and also in newspapers there was a certain transparency in their discussions, but with that came public polemics and repercussions.

The involvement of doctors in public debates hindered them from joining commissions and opened them up to accusations of aprioristic verdicts and doubts as to impartiality if they did indeed engage in the formal examinations. The transparency of the initial involvement of doctors stands in contrast with their activities in this more formalized commission setting. The public was not informed about the outcome of the evaluations and the procedures of the Saint-Luc medical commission. Nor, apparently, were the diocesan commissions that were constituted a few years later, since the second commission of Namur asked for more information about their procedures.

While some of the doctors were heralded as experts in these matters, their knowledge was not uncontested, as the cases of De Greeff and Van Laer show. Doctors who had received a certain authority – engaged as experts by the ecclesiastical authorities – were as subject to criticism as their other colleagues had been. Some, but not all, of their conclusions were readily accepted: Their reports on the first generations of miraculés in Beauraing and Banneux seem to have found willing ears at the level of the diocesan commissions (with the exception of the case of Maria Van Laer). But their ideas on the Beauraing and Banneux children were another matter, as we will see.

# 4

# Authority

## Clerical Involvement

Almost from the start of the Belgian apparition wave of the 1930s, the members of the clergy travelled to the sites and actively engaged in the debates concerning the authenticity of the phenomena. Their public involvement (either pro or contra) caused concern among the ecclesiastical hierarchy (on the diocesan and Vatican level), but intrigued also the faithful. Was the clergy allowed to have and convey an opinion on these matters and could that be any opinion?

### *Those Who Should Have Been Absent*

In December 1932, Father Léon Lambert travelled to Namur. As dean of Beauraing he wanted to inform the bishop about the Marian apparitions reported in the town since late November. He also needed advice on how to deal with the clergy who showed an interest in the case. Since the bishop was away in France, it was the auxiliary bishop, Mgr Cawet, who met Lambert and advised him to ask the clergy not to attend the apparitions or visit the site, for the church had always been very cautious in these matters.[1] Lambert obeyed, and asked his fellow townsmen to check the apparition site carefully for "soutanes." At first the clergy of the diocese seem to have obeyed the rules, but the situation changed, so Cawet reported, as soon as they saw that French priests *did* visit Beauraing.[2]

The bishops of other dioceses were just as cautious. Absence and avoidance of public statements were the central guidelines for the Belgian clergy during the series of apparitions. The Belgian Archbishop

Van Roey, for instance, warned the deans of his diocese during a meeting on 3 May 1933. While he believed that priests, like laymen, were entitled to their own opinions, he advised them to be cautious and reserved about the phenomena. He could not approve of anyone who took a public stand, gave presentations, and wrote articles.[3] The same message was contained in the joint letter of the Belgian bishops published in autumn 1933. After reminding the clergy that none of the events could be considered as approved or recommended by the church, the bishops asked the priests to remind the faithful of the rules of caution that the church was trying to uphold. They reminded them that priests were not allowed to organize or lead pilgrimages to these sites without the authorization of the local bishop. For, "whether or not he wants to, the priest gives in all his public interventions the appearance of approbation."[4] Referring to Canon 1385, paragraph 85, the bishops added that whatever text discussed the phenomena – be it books, brochures, or newspaper articles – it could not be published without ecclesiastical censorship since these matters pertained to religion and morality. Those who discussed the matter *ex professo* (with the competence one would expect from an expert, or a professional) were going against the will of the bishops if they had not obtained the imprimatur, and the same rules applied to images and prayer.[5]

The bishops' letter and warnings were well known, and as correspondence in the diocesan archives indicates, the letter kept several priests from accompanying pilgrimages to the apparition sites.[6] Still, as the series of apparitions continued, some members of the clergy found it difficult to obey their bishops. During a meeting on 14 May 1934, the archbishop therefore once again reminded his deans that he did not approve of priests leading pilgrimages on days allegedly "singled out" by heaven. The bishops' restrictions were not successful. In a report on the Beauraing apparitions of December 1934, the nuncio Clemente Micara concluded that the bishops' warnings had remained "*lettera morta*" and the clergy neither stayed away from the site nor refrained from publishing on the matter.[7]

In spite of the bishops' repeated warnings, members of the clergy, both secular and religious, did get caught up in the apparitions – some eager and keen to act as promoters, others less voluntarily. Among the latter were the priests of the parishes where the apparitions were reported.[8] The priests of Onkerzele for instance, seem not to have known

Figure 4.1 Photograph of Abbé Didion in front of the promotional material for his lectures, 1933.

how to stop the visionaries and their supporters from disturbing parish life, and looked to their bishop for guidance. The parish priests were confronted with numerous pilgrims who not only visited the apparition sites but also sought to organize gatherings and practise unauthorized devotions. The apparition supporters asked the local clergy for masses in honour of the Virgin of the apparitions or in thanks for what they considered miraculous cures. As neither the apparitions nor the cures had been approved, the priests could not fulfill their requests, and this created tensions.

Clergy could be found on either side of the debate. In Lokeren, for instance, the local clergy seems to have publicly denounced the apparitions (the second series) and mocked the faithful who visited the site.[9] Some members of the clergy were more than mere witnesses of the apparition series, however. Abbé Didion (from Bonneville, Sclayn) crisscrossed the country to talk about the apparition series.

According to the invitation letter that announced his talk in Brussels on 15 January 1934, he had attended seventy-two apparitions at Beauraing, Banneux, Onkerzele, Etikhove, and Olsene and was one of the best informed persons about the vision series, possessing 163 photographs.[10] Members of the clergy also wrote about the series in periodicals read by their colleagues (like *L'Ami du clergé*), but also more general Catholic publications like the *Revue Catholique des Idées et des Faits*[11] and periodicals linked to a specific apparition site like *L'Officiel de Beauraing*.[12]

Some of these clerical authors published under their own names, but others did not want their identity to be known, and their anonymity could lead to heated arguments about authorship.[13] One of the debates centred on the author of the brochure *And What if It Was the Devil?* (*Et si s'était le Diable?*) published on 14 January 1933, a few days after the last apparitions in Beauraing. In the promotional note sent to bookshops on 18 January 1933, the publisher, Édition Universelle, warned about the emotions and enthusiasm caused by the events in Beauraing and called for a more reserved approach on the basis of an "objective study, done by M. l'Abbé Derselle, after an impartial examination."[14] As these promotional ads were published in Catholic newspapers, the staff of the bishop of Namur felt compelled to respond. They asked those who published the announcement to add a few lines indicating that the brochure did not have the imprimatur that the author was required to obtain. The editorial office of *La Libre Belgique* responded that they had contacted the publisher and had been informed that the booklet was in fact written by Dr (and not *Abbé*) Charles Derselle and that there was thus no need to add the requested lines. This information was rebutted by Jan Filip Boon who informed Mgr Heylen that it was indeed the Abbé Derselle who had written the work. Derselle had visited Boon's office, asking him to publish his text and, on hearing that he needed an imprimatur, he had refused to ask for one.[15] Moreover, Dr Charles Derselle abbreviated his name with the letters Ch. and thus not a single C. (as it read on the cover page).

Abbé Clement Derselle (of Halma, later curé of Our) and Dr Charles Derselle (from Silenrieux) were uncle and nephew and the latter seems to have accepted to be named the author. Camille-Jean Joset suggests that Dr Derselle might have done so because of family ties or conviction (he had been present at the apparition site on 3 January 1933). As for Abbé Derselle's motivations, it was rumoured in pro-Beauraing circles that he first asked Mother Théophile, the head of the school in whose garden the apparitions took place, to share communications about the apparitions only with him and promised to share the profits of the publication. He then took revenge when his plan failed. Others suggested that he did not want Beauraing to become more popular than Lourdes.[16] "Derselle" in fact mentioned his reasons for publishing in the introduction to his notorious book. He believed that if the authenticity of the apparitions could indeed be doubted, Catholics had to defend the Virgin's honour.[17] In a later publication he added that he had been tired that his Christian faith was being equated with the events of Beauraing and the type of religion it represented. He thought that people had the right to know that there was more to Beauraing than the official stories.[18]

Whatever the reasons behind the book, the identity question provoked reactions. On 29 January 1933, only a few days after the publication, the Redemptorist Gaston Maes finished his response entitled *Beauraing: Response to the Brochure "And What if It Was the Devil?" of C. Derselle* (*Beauraing: Réponse à la brochure "Et si c'était le diable?" de C. Derselle*). Referring to a letter of Jan Boon to Dr Maistriaux and two letters of the publisher Édition Universelle, Maes concluded that it was in fact Abbé Derselle who had written the book and not Dr Derselle.[19] Only a day after Maes' response, Roger Saussus addressed the same question in his *The Scandal of Beauraing. Response to "What if It Was the Devil?" of the Priest or Doctor Derselle* (*Le scandale de Beauraing. Réponse à "Si c'était le diable?" de M. l'abbé ou M. le docteur Derselle*). Still in doubt about who C. Derselle was, Saussus emphasized that the fact the author did not want to reveal himself pleaded against the book's credibility.[20] Likewise, on 29 January 1933, *De Standaard* included an article about the brochures on Beauraing, including a Dutch version of Derselle's work *Beauraing, Where Lies the Supernatural?* (*Beauraing, waar ligt het bovennatuurlijke?*). Calling it a "suspicious" work as it did not carry an imprimatur and had been linked to both Abbé Derselle and Dr Derselle, the author described it as arrogant, credulous, and full of mistakes – an anonymous slander.[21]

"Derselle" addressed the commotion in the introduction to a second brochure, *Beauraing, the Truth Rises Again* (*Beauraing. La vérité en marche du nouveau!*) – described as "a popular adaptation of the *Études Carmélitaines*."[22] The introduction narrated how it was primarily members of the clergy who had campaigned against his first book. But for every opponent, he added, there also had been a supporter of the book (among them Prof. De Greeff). Commenting on the personal attacks launched by Saussus in his *Scandale*, Derselle noted that there had been an agreement between him and the publisher of the first book that if there were any profits, those would be invested in the future chapel of Beauraing, should the apparitions be recognized. He noted in frustration: "Why have you stubbornly insisted on letting the debate be sidetracked to a question of identity?" and cited from the *Annales de Beauraing*: "What do these discussions on the identity of the author mean? … The identity of the author is nothing but a side question; what is important above all is what he has said."[23]

While trying to minimize the importance of the authorship, the second book clearly showed an awareness of the commotion "C. Derselle" had caused. The second cover read "Dr C. Derselle" and meant to leave no doubt about who had written the text. But was Dr Charles Derselle indeed the author of the two books? We find more information on the matter in the notes on the first diocesan commission of Namur. Questioned during session 37, on 29 November 1935, Abbé Clement admitted that he had indeed written the works, but the two brochures were not the result of his individual labour. In fact it seems to have been a sort of writers' collective and he had been helped by Dr Charles Derselle; Mr Norbert Collard (head of the school in Beauraing); Miss Van Schingen (the mayor of Beauraing, 1930–33); her brother, the registrar, Anatole Van Schingen; Mr Libert, "the tax collector of Beauraing"; the priest Turlot (from La Louvière); and Dr de Roeck (from Antwerp). As for the accusations concerning the morality of Albert Voisin that were published in his brochure and later picked up by De Greeff: Derselle had received information about the matter from Mr Collard.[24] Also in this case the threat of a lawsuit loomed large. A letter from Dr Derselle, written on 24 November 1933, was added to the report on this session indicating that he was willing to withdraw the brochures that were still in the bookstores and hand them over on the condition that he would receive a statement signed by the father of Voisin that he was cleared of this affair and he would no longer threaten him with juridical consequences. He added that no publicity was to be given to his letter.[25] No doubt he knew about the public retraction of De Greeff that had been published in the newspapers on 7 November 1933 and feared public defamation.[26]

Abbé Derselle stirred commotion by not using his full name. Other clerical authors, for example Pierre Debongnie, published under a pseudonym (Gustave Leurquin). They had good reasons to do so as publishing as a member of the clergy on these matters exposed them to specific criticism. Aloïs Janssens from the Congregation of the Immaculate Heart of Mary, for instance, contributed to the *Études Carmélitaines* under his own name. The commotion that followed his article and his interview in *Ons Land* (5 and 12 August 1933) had as much to do with his somewhat abrupt style as with him being a member of the clergy. Janssens' interview seems to have become notorious. In a letter of November 1933, George Colle, head of the college of Tielt, described how he could only get a hold of the text with great effort – promising to return it that same evening (to a stoneworker): "The interview was passed on here among the workers and the petit bourgeois from house to house, almost secretly, as a bad book, and, very curiously, not in order to accept what was in it, but 'to see what a Father dares to write about Beauraing.'"[27]

In a previous letter to George Colle, dated 4 November 1933, Aloïs Janssens had tried to explain his reasons for publishing on the events in Beauraing and commented on the context of the interview in *Ons Land*. He described how after the *Études Carmélitaines* were published in July 1933, a storm of protest arose against him and De Greeff who had both published in the volume. He received anonymous cards and letters calling him "haughty, insane" and an "opponent of God and religion." He had published expecting a response like this because he did not believe it was a rational thing to organize a pilgrimage to Beauraing on the authority of five children before the church's official pronouncement. When, shortly after the publication, Tilman Côme called for a pilgrimage on 5 August and reporters of *Ons Land* contacted Janssens, he saw an interview as an opportunity to warn the faithful. The final result disappointed him however. The reporters, who had hardly taken notes, had twisted his words: He had never commented on pilgrimages in general, only about those to Beauraing, especially if they were driven by curiosity. In spite of all the contempt and hatred his comments had attracted, he still believed that priests and theologians should not join in the blind enthusiasm of the popular masses, fed by daily publicity.[28] The negative response to the interview got Janssens' superiors worrying about its effect on the reputation of the congregation. They asked him not to publish on the series of apparitions without the approval of the superior general.[29]

In sum, the Belgian clergy, or at least some of them, did not hesitate to show publicly how they thought about the apparition series. Long before the official examination started, they wrote about them and travelled as pilgrims to the apparition sites. Their involvement confused the faithful, who thought of their presence as an approval of the site or criticized their stance as overly negative. The bishops' warning had not stopped the members of the clergy and their involvement in both sides of the discussion continued also during the next phase of the evaluation: the formal ecclesiastical examination.

## *Those in Charge? The Bishops.*

In September 1933, *De Standaard* published the following anecdote about the bishop of Ghent: "At the time of the commotion caused by the apparitions of Beauraing, His Excellence Mgr Coppieters, who in all his stern episcopal dignity is also a frank man with a sense for pure humour, said: 'Yes, Mgr Heylen what is that good bishop going to experience, a case of apparitions, that's trouble. Luckily it's in his diocese, and he is the most wise and eldest among us, luckily it's happening in his diocese and not in mine!' "[30]

By the time the anecdote was published, the events had already caught up with the Flemish bishop, and he was confronted with various apparition sites in his diocese as well. The wave of apparitions in fact covered the whole country and all bishops were confronted with strange phenomena and lay enthusiasts. A joint response was thus a logical step. The episcopal letter of autumn 1933 was the first collective action that the Belgian bishops took after the series of events started in the winter of 1932. When drafting the clerical guidelines included in the text, the bishops seem to have been well aware that these might leave an impression of rigidity, especially for those priests who had organized pilgrimages with the best intentions.[31] Even though the original letter was written in Latin and meant only for the clergy, translations soon circulated in newspapers and periodicals and laymen were well informed about the public stance taken by their bishops.

Before their collective statement, the individual actions of the bishops concerning the apparitions in their dioceses had been quite diverse. While some waited for the events to blow over and ordered new visionaries not to seek public attention, the bishop of Namur, Mgr Heylen, attended a rosary prayer at the apparition site in Beauraing on 16 June 1933 (the day of the confirmation) and allowed the dean to be present every evening.[32] Moreover, Mgr Heylen gave a papal blessing to Albert Voisin. Especially the latter action provoked comments and was seen by some as a public rejection of the accusations concerning the young seer's morality.[33]

The bishop of Ghent, Mgr Coppieters, was less enthusiast about the apparitions in his diocese and asked the archbishop's advice about how to act regarding the so-called apparitions reported in Onkerzele. Thousands of people went there, among them many religious. The Ghent bishop said he did not dare to interfere, for he feared he would not be obeyed; there were still too many good people convinced of the truth of what was happening. "Catalepsy, insensitivity, exaltation" were all phenomena that left "a terrible impression on simple people."[34] Van Roey agreed and told the Ghent bishop that as long as the events were still developing he could do nothing in public. Coppieters had to remain completely neutral and avoid every impression of approving what was happening. He could, however, ask the priests and religious to abstain from visiting the site.[35] Half a year later, new apparitions demanded episcopal action. On 3 July 1934, Mgr Coppieters, again contacted the archbishop and told him that he had been obliged to interfere in the events of Lokeren II and the related "blasphemies, disturbances, nonsensical manifestations." The girls had only a small number of supporters and by far the majority of the townspeople were fed up with the so-called supernatural phenomena and were "getting furious." The bishop had warned the faithful not to go to the apparition site but his intervention had not generated the desired effect.[36] After the severe riots in Lokeren late July, the bishop and Cardinal Van Roey together published a letter on 25 August 1934, in which they declared that the Lokeren events did not have a supernatural character and forbade the faithful and clergy to visit the site.[37]

The Belgian bishops had been discussing the formalization of the examination since July 1933. While a medical commission was created in December 1933,[38] the planned interdiocesan theological commission does not seem to have taken a more concrete form even though the various bishops did indeed propose candidates.[39] The communal action seemed to be off the table when, in November 1934, the medical commission submitted its report rejecting all the Flemish visionaries and leaving room only for a possible supernatural origin in Beauraing and Banneux. In the opinion of Mgr Kerkhofs, the bishop of Liège, there was thus no need for an interdiocesan theological commission covering the events in all the dioceses. In a letter to the bishop of Namur, he noted that the two of them, as ordinaries of the two remaining sites, were to take on the examination.[40] Beginning in January 1935, the bishops of Namur and Liège contacted the archbishop and pleaded for two separate diocesan commissions rather than a single multidiocesan one whose members would be spread all over the country and could not result in the kind of thorough and detailed study that the extensive dossiers on the apparitions required.[41] Van Roey agreed on the condition that the theological examinations be conducted discreetly.[42]

However, in early 1935, the Holy Office in Rome had already reached is own conclusions as to how the investigations were to take place and the Vatican solution was quite different from what the bishops of Namur and Liège asked for. The Belgian wave of apparitions caught the attention of the Supreme Congregation of the Holy Office in Rome even before Van Roey wrote to Rome in December 1933. One of the first to contact Rome was the discalced Carmelite Bruno de Jésus-Marie, director of the *Études Carmélitaines* in Paris. He complained about the menaces and intimidation the critics of the Beauraing apparitions faced (threats of defamation processes) and the public attacks on them (for instance in Rex's *Soirées*). In his opinion "salvation can only come from Rome in this affair which is taking on alarming proportions."[43] Bruno de Jésus-Marie provided the Holy Office with ample documentation and created his own more general report that the Holy Office could use in its evaluation.[44] While emphasizing Albert Voisin's central role in the events (he was the first to see the Virgin) and emphasizing that the miraculous cures in Beauraing were dubious, he also reflected on the comportment of Mgr Heylen. By kneeling down in front of the hawthorn, Bruno de Jésus-Marie noted, the bishop had set a precedent. "In the past, people have never knelt before the sacred hawthorn tree ... People prayed standing up. The whole of Beauraing was there towards the end of the rosary and the Bishop was greeted by endless ovations. That day was decisive, and consecrated, in the eyes of the people, the whole block: the visions of the children and the visions of Tilmant Côme."[45] Concern about the bishop's behaviour was also central in Archbishop Van Roey's correspondence with Rome in December 1933. He asked what could be done to prevent too hasty decisions by the ordinaries of the various apparition sites. They had already allowed a part of the cult; was there a way to ensure that they would first have to ask the permission of the Holy See before making an official statement about the apparitions?[46]

The reports pro (the Jesuit Jean-Baptiste Lenain also sent in a text[47]) and contra formed the basis of the *votum* that Giovanni Battista Frey, *qualificatore* of the Holy Office, wrote on the Belgian apparition series (with emphasis on Beauraing) in May 1934. He started his report with a brief statement about the public interest that the events had generated: "Much has already been written and continues to be written on the facts of Beauraing, and a discrete library could be constituted of all the publications made on the subject. Passionate debates have been and are still being raised for and against the supernatural origin of these facts; and not always have all the ecclesiastic personalities who had to intervene used all the necessary prudence in such a delicate matter."[48]

Still, "no official enquiry was made until now: journalists, doctors, publicists, secular and regular priests each wrote, each on his own account, what they had seen or heard, often with less than objective criteria, or at least with very incomplete information."[49]

Adopting in his examination the criteria that Benedict XIV had suggested in his *De Servorum Dei Beatificatione et Beatorum Canonizatione*, Frey believed that (1) the personality of the visionaries did not seem to plead in their favour: According to the parish priest's testimony: "they are ordinary, neither bad nor very good." Moreover Albert Voisin had the reputation of being a "corrupter" and some of the events had been reported even after the apparitions had started.[50] (2) As for the way in which the apparitions took place, no precautions were taken to avoid fraud and the child visionaries gathered every evening to go to the apparitions together. Furthermore, (3) the religious life of the seers did not seem to have changed: they did not have more piety nor did they pray more. As for the conversions and great religious fervour among the population – Frey believed that to be purely inferior phenomena. Conversions could also happen in the case of non-approved events (like in Tilly, Loublande, and Limpias).[51]

His conclusion was uncompromising: "I see no truly convincing positive argument in favor of the supernatural origin of the facts of

Beauraing. On the contrary, there are quite a few presumptions to the contrary." The case lacked the positive criteria "that are never lacking when God authenticates one of His revelations." There was nothing wrong with being strict in these matters: "Faith loses nothing in being strict and in demanding adequate criteria. On the other hand, one runs grave risks in being too willing to accept such facts with closed eyes." In his opinion therefore, the Holy Office should instruct the Belgian bishops (1) not to allow shrines or chapels to be erected at the sites of the apparitions, (2) nor that priests promote or conduct pilgrimages there nor do anything that could be seen as an approval (such as celebrating mass), and (3) the Belgian bishops should use the utmost circumspection in the matter and keep the Holy Office informed.[52]

The consultors of the Holy Office discussed Frey's votum during their meetings in June 1934. Because they were divided about how to proceed,[53] they decided to hear the nuncio to Belgium.[54] Mgr Micara's report to the Holy Office, submitted on 15 December, was critical of the diocesan response. The nuncio complained that the curia of Namur had not been up to the task: It lacked energy and had shown itself rather in favour of the assertions of the supernatural character of the apparitions.[55] Instead of taking charge of the matter, carrying out a serious investigation, and subjecting seers, witnesses, and their confidents to a thorough examination "and thus imposing silence and discretion on all," the curia had allowed it to be discussed in newspapers and watched how the child visionaries and nuns of Beauraing were interrogated "by anyone who wanted to do so – and how many did so without the slightest discretion – and their statements were then given to the public."[56] All of this gave rise to controversy. Those in favour of Beauraing adopted an intimidating tone, and it seemed as if one could not express "the slightest doubt on the subject without being heaped with insults."[57]

With this in mind he had suggested to Cardinal Van Roey that the whole episcopate should take the matter in hand. He believed this to be the right course of action since the Namur curia had done almost nothing up until then and the events seemed to affect all the dioceses in some way. The clergy, miraculés, and pilgrims came from all Belgian dioceses, and newspapers and magazines from all over the country polemized about the apparitions. Given that Mgr Heylen had already publicly shown his approval of the Beauraing apparitions, a Namur setting did not seem opportune.[58] Micara had similar concerns regarding the bishop of Liège since he had allowed the construction of a chapel at the site and authorized the brochure of Géradin on the apparitions. In his opinion there was no doubt about what the outcome would be if the two bishops (of Liège and Namur) were to organize the canonical investigations in their own dioceses. Both bishops had already made their opinion known. He wondered if there was a way to keep the evaluation in the hands of the cardinal.[59]

Heeding the warning, the Holy Office decided to give the Belgian archbishop the mandate to organize a canonical process in his archepiscopal curia about the apparitions and revelations reported in Belgium. Rome wanted to remain involved, however, and before the decision was made public it had to be sent to the Holy Office by the nuncio to receive its approval. Pilgrimages and publications on the apparitions were explicitly forbidden and the bishops had to make sure that their instructions of October 1933 – so far as they had not yet been revised – were observed.[60]

Even though the decisions were made in Rome in January and February 1935,[61] the guidelines of the Holy Office only reached the Belgian bishops on 26 March 1935 when nuncio Micara returned from the deathbed of his mother in Italy.[62] By then however, the bishops of Namur and Liège had already taken action, creating separate diocesan commissions in March 1935.[63] On hearing that an archdiocesan commission was to be created, the two bishops contacted the archbishop. Van Roey confirmed and defended Rome's decision. Calling it a heavy burden, he argued that it was not so strange that Rome had put him in charge of the investigations, for the phenomena had not been limited to one diocese, but had affected several and it could not be denied that the events had been of interest to religion throughout the country. Events reported in different dioceses showed undeniable resemblances; it was impossible to judge Banneux without taking into account Beauraing and Onkerzele as well. It was thus not opportune that each bishop should judge the events in his diocese separately. In order to observe the strictest objectivity in the examination, he promised to give the task to members of the secular and regular clergy who had not yet been involved.[64]

Mgr Kerkhofs was not convinced and decided to take matters into his own hands. He travelled to Rome to discuss the matter with Cardinal Sbaretti, secretary of the Supreme Congregation of the Holy Office. On 10 April 1935, he pleaded his cause based on two developments that could not have been known in Rome when the Holy Office discussed the Belgian apparitions: (1) the reports of the medical commission rejecting all the so-called apparitions with the exception of Beauraing and Banneux, and (2) the decision of the two bishops, as a response to this report, to create diocesan commissions.[65] Sbaretti told him that he saw no reason why the diocesan commissions had to be abolished; all they had to do was to define clearly the respective tasks of the archdiocesan and the diocesan commissions.[66] Kerkhofs and the archbishop agreed that the two diocesan commissions would conduct their examinations and afterward send their report to the archbishop.

Kerkhofs also took the opportunity to discuss another matter during his stay in Rome. He and Mgr Heylen opposed the prohibition of pilgrimages to the apparition sites and of publications about the apparitions. The bishops wanted to ease these restrictions. The decisions had not been made public yet, so they argued that there still was room for a minor revision. More in particular, the bishops asked for more tolerance: periodicals like *L'Officiel de Beauraing* and *Banneux Notre-Dame* were not polemic, only incited piety, and provided information. As for the pilgrimages, if they had the approval of the bishop of the place where they started and where they ended, could they not be tolerated? For in forbidding them, one would take away people's hope and means to say thank you and also make it difficult to examine the cases thoroughly, since the examinations were as much about the effect of the apparitions as about the apparitions themselves. As Fernand Toussaint and Camille-Jean Joset note in their study of the apparitions in Beauraing, the response to the bishops' request seems to have been positive and in the future communication with Rome the matter was no longer an issue.[67]

The Belgian apparitions were on the Roman agenda again in May 1935. By then, it had become clear that it was too late to stop the bishops from proceeding, and there was no doubt that the two bishops were in favour of the apparitions in their dioceses.[68] The question was to what extent the Holy Office needed to play a part in this matter. They decided to act similarly to what happened in the Lourdes case where the Holy See had not intervened and the bishop had been the one to gather a commission of theologians, doctors, and natural scientists.[69] During an audience with the pope on 21 May, the Belgian nuncio was informed that Rome was not going to become involved in the decision-making process. The cardinal of Malines had the final say.[70]

In sum, in designing the framework of the evaluation process, the public (lenient and supporting) stance of the two bishops played no small part. The bishops' public acts of approval, like praying at an apparition site, might not be of the same binding nature as an official verdict, but the laity and clergy certainly read them as an indication of what their decision was going to be. The discussions therefore focused not so much on whether or not the bishops had the right to pass judgment (everyone agreed they had the authority as ordinaries). Rather, the question was whether or not they could guarantee the objectivity of the examination. While the two bishops as ordinaries of the sites indeed had the authority to pronounce their verdicts, the scale of the Belgian apparition series left room to manoeuver. Since apparitions had been reported all over the country, the evaluation of the series could be conducted at the national level as well. Rather than singling out Beauraing and Banneux and having them evaluated solely by their bishops, their examination became the archbishop's responsibility.

## Official Church Investigations: the First Diocesan Commissions

### *The Final Say?*

After the slightly chaotic start of the official examinations, in May 1935 three commissions were officially sanctioned by the Belgian archbishop: (1) the diocesan commission of Liège for the apparitions in Banneux; (2) the diocesan commission of Namur for the apparitions in Beauraing; and (3) the archdiocesan commission of Malines for any other apparitions worthy of attention.[71] By then the results of the medical commission authorized by the Belgian bishops in December 1933 were already in. The final medical report left room only for a supernatural origin of the initial apparitions in Beauraing and Banneux. But its rejection of the Flemish visionaries and the Beauraing seer Tilman Côme did not preclude an examination of their cases by a diocesan commission. A number of Flemish sites and visionaries discarded by the medical commission were still on the agenda of the archdiocesan Malines commission.

Diocesan commissions like those in 1930s Belgium were not uncommon in cases of paramystical phenomena. Their roles and procedures could differ, however. The goal of a commission was not to formulate a final judgment on the apparitions, but to help prepare the judgment of the pontifical or episcopal authority.[72] The bishop could follow the verdict of the commission (voted by majority), or formulate a different opinion.[73] In cases of national importance, the national conference of bishops could intervene.[74] The Apostolic See could also get involved "if requested either by the ordinary himself, by a qualified group of the faithful, or even directly by reason of the universal jurisdiction of the Supreme Pontiff."[75] There were three possible outcomes of the investigation: the supernatural origin is "established," "not established," or "excluded." In more formal terms, possible outcomes were thus: (1) *Constare apparitiones et revelations quovis supernaturali penitus esse destitutas,* or *Constare de non-supernaturalitate apparitionum* – indicating that the events did not have a supernatural character; (2) *Non constare de supernaturalitate apparitionum,* indicating that there was no (sufficient) proof to declare the apparitions authentic; and (3) *Constare de supernaturalitate apparitionum,* confirming the supernatural origin and approving the apparitions.[76] The commission could also abstain from making a statement if its members were still in doubt.[77] The second outcome, *"non constare"* was in fact a rather problematic option. While it did not really reject the apparitions, the formulation did not approve of them either. As Laurentin and Sbalchiero remark, this dubitative and ambiguous formula "concludes nothing," especially since it was generally not accompanied by clarifying arguments.[78]

Diocesan commissions can comprise theologians, canonists, and medics and, if necessary, they can also call upon other experts. While the (then) Congregation for the Doctrine of Faith circulated a clear set of guidelines for such a "discernment" of apparitions and private revelations only in 1978, already in previous centuries investigations seem to have focused on what Yves Chiron calls a triple critique: historical (focusing on the witnesses: about the factual information on the apparitions), human (or psychological, focusing on the visionaries), and theological (focusing on the apparitions from the perspective of faith).[79]

Two aspects of the decision-making process (prior to May 2024) need to be emphasized here since we see examples thereof in the Belgian investigations. First of all, in the case of a positive outcome or indecision, the bishop could allow limited devotion at the site while further investigations were conducted.[80] So a devotion inspired by the apparitions could be officially recognized even before the apparitions themselves were. In fact, the devotion might even contribute to the recognition of the events as one of the criteria related to the spiritual fruits of the events.[81] Both in Banneux and Beauraing, the devotion at the site was approved years before the apparitions were recognized. Secondly, when the local bishop wrote an official evaluation and judgment in the final stage of the evaluation process, he did not need to accept the decision of the investigating commission.[82] In this respect, the decision-making processes were similar to that of canonization processes (with of course the major difference that the final decision is in the hands of the pope and not the bishop). As Birgit Emich has shown in her study on the procedures used in early modern canonization processes, there were two modes of decision-making: (1) the mode of the bureaucrats – the procedures involving the examination of written proof and historical-critical research (by members of the Congregation of Rites), and (2) "prayer, illumination, and the intervention of the Holy Spirit" (the pope). The congregation never made the final decision, but gave a recommendation that "the pope might or might not heed. Both outcomes occurred." He first recommended the matter to prayer and also prayed himself. The pope's indecision "was ultimately rooted in prayer and in divine assistance that notoriously defied human deadlines."[83] In Emich's opinion, it was the combination of the two decision-making processes that made them particularly impactful: "The legal, institutional Church alone would lack the legitimacy of (divine) inspiration; the spiritual dimension, conversely, lacks tested procedures capable of assembling the binding force of law."[84]

As we shall see, each of the three commissions created in 1935 had its own approach in examining the events and they differed in number and type of commission members and manner of investigation. Some of the diocesan commissions, in this phase of the evaluation and in the second evaluation in 1942, were composed as canonical commissions and included a *promotor fidei* and *postulator*. This was not a requirement for a commission on apparitions (contrary to those on canonization processes, for instance) and no "miracle" had to be attested and proven (as in cases of canonization). The main task of an apparition commission was "discernment" (for instance between good and bad, dishonesty and sincerity, the identification of the spiritual fruits of an event).[85]

In the evaluation of the 1930s Belgian apparitions, Rome created a hierarchical order in the evaluation process and the archbishop was given the final say. However, it was not his opinion about the apparitions in Beauraing and Banneux that was eventually made public in 1949. By then, the decision power on these cases was again in the hands of the ordinary. What happened? Would the future of Beauraing and Banneux have looked different in the hands of the archbishop? In the following pages, the dynamics and decision process of each of the commissions will be addressed separately. We first discuss the commissions on Banneux and Beauraing because they in turn had to send their reports and evaluation to the commission of Malines, which based its own judgment regarding these cases in part on the files of these two commissions. As both Micara's and Frey's reports on Beauraing described the intense public debate culture and mass press coverage as a loss of control over the situation, a special focus is on the effect the public character of the events had on the examination.

## THE DIOCESAN COMMISSION ON BANNEUX

The diocesan commission on Banneux, the first commission to be formed, examined apparitions that had remained in the shadow of the events in Beauraing. The series of eight apparitions reported by Mariette Béco in 1933 from 15 January until 2 March had, in comparison with Beauraing, attracted little attention during the events and stirred far less commotion. Banneux seemed a little suspect because of its temporal and geographical proximity to the Beauraing apparitions. Even the supporters of the site admitted that it seemed very unlikely that the Virgin would appear twice in such close vicinity. Nonetheless, support for the apparitions – praised for the simplicity of the content and physiology – increased substantially, and already in May 1933 the construction of a small chapel on the apparition site had begun. The bishop of Liège, Mgr Kerkhofs, not only approved of this construction but also gave other signs of his support for the cause before he formed a diocesan commission that was to examine the apparitions (and the miraculous cures that were linked to the site).

The commission the archbishop approved in May 1935 had been officially constituted on 20 March 1935, two years after the events in Banneux.[86] Its president was Mgr Eugène Leroux, head of the Great Seminar who had a PhD in theology. Other members were Lucien

Creusen, parish priest-dean of Seraing; the Jesuit René Rutten,[87] head of the house for retreats in Xhovémont who had a PhD in theology; and A. Martin, chaplain of Sart Tilman, who had a PhD in civil rights and who acted as notary of the commission.[88] The dean of Chênée, Eugène Ruyters, joined the commission only after the other members had already visited Banneux on 7 June 1935.[89]

During the commission sessions (fifty-six in total), the members heard seventy-three witnesses (of which twenty-seven had attended an apparition),[90] among them the visionary Mariette Béco,[91] her parents, teachers, and other people from Banneux, members of the clergy, and several doctors. The arguments for or against the authenticity of the apparitions were similar to the ones we discussed in our chapter on the lay response and medical perception. The discussions centred on the morality and character of the visionary, her physical features before, during, and after the apparitions, and the content of the messages she claimed to have received. Four topics re-occur regularly in the interrogations and the subsequent deliberations. (1) Mariette Béco was whispered to have read or still possess at the time of the apparitions a brochure on Lourdes. (2) The "identification" of the "Virgin" – rumour had it that this identification happened after Béco's mother suggested to her daughter that the lady she saw was in fact the Virgin. (3) The extent to which the priest, Louis Jamin, influenced Béco (as we have seen, his "mystical" nature had also been of interest to the medical commission). And (4) the financial profit the Béco family was said to have obtained from the events by selling memorabilia in their house.

By late 1936, the commission members had gathered sufficient information from the on-site visits and testimonies, and started discussing what they had learned. Commenting on the quality of the testimonies, they noted that they had the impression that all the witnesses had answered sincerely. However, since already two years had passed, the eyewitnesses could not always remember or relate precisely the exact circumstances. Furthermore, the commission members did not think it unlikely that some of the witnesses reconstructed some events in ways slightly different from what actually happened, and, in any case, they thought the reconstruction of the exact reality "morally impossible." In their note, they also commented on Mariette Béco, her parents, and the chaplain, Jamin. They described the visionary as "a good young girl, very ordinary, ignorant enough, with an open and good nature, but uncultivated and a rather personal character," and Jamin as certainly not gullible, but open to the supernatural, not a dreamer but practical, with organizational talent.[92]

The commission ended its activities on 18 February 1937 and since it was a rogatory commission, its members did not have to formulate a final judgment. Still, they decided to write a short report of their impression and gave that to the bishop. In their opinion, a natural explanation of the events was insufficient and Mariette Béco's sincerity could not be doubted. There were some contradictions but these were not due to a lack of honesty but rather to the fact that her memories had become less exact. Furthermore, because of repeated interrogations, the girl sometimes answered in order to be done with it. The commission discarded autosuggestion and suggestion, since in that case her parents or chaplain Jamin would have played a role. The parents were deemed incapable of such a scenario, and while the chaplain might have stimulated the continuation of the suggestion with his interrogations of Béco, this would not explain the start of the events, when she had been avoiding his catechism classes. Moreover the beauty and simplicity of the apparition message could not be explained if one followed the hypothesis of hallucination. The commission thus concluded: "taking into account the whole of the depositions, the members of the commission believe that the reality of the apparitions of the Holy Virgin to Mariette Béco is AT LEAST PROBABLE." They added that several aspects hindered them from taking a firmer stand on the matter. First of all, there was the confusing character of the visionary: Béco could not be called perfectly "normal," and the events did not have the effect on her piety that might have been expected. Secondly, the character of Abbé Jamin was problematic. His interest in Beauraing and hope for the reality of the Banneux apparitions were suspect. Even though he had abstained from attending the apparitions, the abbé had not conducted his examination with the necessary reserve. Finally, they called for caution since Mariette Béco was said to have had a brochure on Lourdes in her possession when the apparitions began.[93]

The commission's files and this short final report were sent to Malines for evaluation. Hoping for a positive outcome, the bishop did what he could, and approved of a prayer for the "good outcome of the canonical process" on 16 March 1937.[94] In the meantime, the examination of the neighbouring apparition site, Beauraing, had started as well.

## THE DIOCESAN COMMISSION ON BEAURAING

The Beauraing events started the whole Belgian series of apparitions. The five Voisin and Degeimbre children claimed thirty-two to thirty-five encounters with Mary between 29 November 1932 and 3 January 1933, although not all of them always saw her. As we have seen, medical professionals made ad hoc examinations, and doctors, members of the clergy, and laymen questioned the children. A more official examination followed two years after the initial events. The diocesan commission of Namur can be traced back to 21 April 1935 – but was officially constituted on 16 May.[95] According to Canon Arthur Monin, a member of the commission who later wrote a book on the Beauraing apparitions and its cult, its formation tamped down the polemics that surrounded the Beauraing series.[96] However, this 1935 commission seems not to have been the first commission examining the events in Beauraing. In an article about Mgr Heylen and the apparitions, Joset suggests that already in June 1933 the bishop confirmed in private letter to the journalist Jan Boon that a commission had been created and Father Lenain was in charge of the examination.[97] Is this a reference to the interdiocesan theological commission that was under discussion when the medical commission was created, and of which Lenain, together with Canon Blondiau, would have been a member on behalf of the Namur diocese? It seems unlikely, for this would imply that members of the commission were already gathering information before the medical commission had even been discussed or had filtered out the cases that were worthy of further investigation.

Nonetheless, Lenain was subsequently appointed member of the 1935 Namur diocesan commission. Canon Blondiau, the other candidate who the bishop Namur had suggested for the interdiocesan theological commission, was a member as well. As opposed to Blondiau, who became the president of the Beauraing examination, Lenain was linked to the commission only briefly. Convinced that he threatened the objective character of the commission's examination – he had already published a considerable amount on the Beauraing events[98] – he withdrew. Other sources suggest that he believed that two Jesuits in the commission might be too many: his fellow Jesuit Joseph Van de Walle[99] was also a member. Both Lenain and Van de Walle acted as "assessor judges," as did the Benedictine Cyrille Lambot,[100] while Canon Edouard Ranwez, professor at the seminar of Namur,[101] was "promotor of the faith," and Canon Joseph Henri Bouchat was the notary.[102] Arthur Monin, professor at the University of Louvain,[103] replaced Lenain and from 23 January 1936 on, the Archpriest Maximilien Demanet[104] replaced the ailing Blondiau, and Monin became president.[105]

As with to the Banneux commission, the commission on Beauraing focused only on the apparitions to the children and not on the cures linked to the site. The commission held seventy-three sessions between 17 May and 21 July 1936 and collected 109 testimonies.[106] The issues addressed during the various sessions touched upon the aspects also discussed in the monographic issue of the *Études Carmélitaines*: the children re-enacting the story of Jeanne d'Arc; their knowledge of Lourdes and other apparitions; the Albert Voisin matter (discussed in at least fifteen of the sessions); the corporeal aspects of the apparitions; and the role of Dr De Greeff and his thesis about the importance of fear in the children's behaviour.

The public controversies of the previous years had an impact on the examination process and not every witness agreed to appear. Among those who refused were the critics of the Beauraing case, Étienne De Greeff and Aloïs Janssens. These two men later consented to testify before the commission of Malines to whom the Namur files would be sent. Pierre Debongnie – "Gustave Leurquin" in the *Études Carmélitaines* issue – also refused to testify on two occasions. He was, however, as a member of the Belgian clergy, eventually forced take the stand before the commission of Namur on orders of the bishop. Clement Derselle, once also a centre of commotion, did appear before the commission even though some, he said, had told him not to because it consisted solely of pro-Beauraing members.[107] Derselle's testimony and the refusals of other witnesses left their marks in the files of the commission. In their final report, the commission members referred to what they called the "sabotage" of their activities[108] and complained that their examination had a certain unilateral character because of it: "In spite of the concern for the impartiality of the commission, the examination was continuously hindered by the attitude of certain scholars."[109]

Moreover, since the commission was created two years after the apparitions, numerous publications had already seen the light and stirred controversy. These polemics doubtless left an effect on the examination of the commission. Furthermore, the tardiness of the commission also had to be taken into account when evaluating the testimonies. It was not realistic to demand an accurate recall of details after all these years and it was impossible that the witnesses were not influenced by the publications and the polemics surrounding Beauraing. In the eyes of the commission members, this did not mean that the testimonies had no value, only that they had to be evaluated with prudence.[110]

Apart from the visionaries, who seemed sincere to them, the commission members differentiated between the Beauraing circle and the "anti-Beauraing upheaval." As for the first group, there were indeed some people who had gained a material profit from the apparitions, but there were also numerous Beauraing supporters who sincerely believed in the apparitions and whose conscience did not allow them to commit perjury. The commission found only limited evidence of the pressure and menaces the Beauraing circle had allegedly employed toward the opponents of the apparitions. Apart from the insinuations and evasive answers from some, only one real threat had been detected. Solely Beda O.F.M., had indeed been pressured (by mail and attempts to bribe him). Still, even in that case the threat was directed to his religious order in general and not to him personally.[111] In other instances it was not the opponents' negative opinion about the apparitions that the Beauraing circle responded to, but the tone and the media employed in their polemics. Cases like Derselle's were not caused by his skepticism about the apparitions, but by the unacceptable polemic devices he had employed. As for the rumour that the bishop of Namur had threatened to have De Greeff fired, the bishop had formally refuted the accusation. Furthermore, the commission members did not doubt the sincerity of some of the Beauraing opponents, but they did question the seriousness of their objections and their procedures. They noted that those who boasted about their scientific superiority often displayed an astonishing lack of equanimity, and their refusal to take the stand was based on hearsay. While it had been impossible to find instances of pressure and intimidation in the case of the Beauraing circle, these were not hard to find among the "anti-Beaurinois," who had dissuaded witnesses to appear and had threatened the visionaries by mail. The commission members thus added: "If we draw the attention to the actions of the 'anti-Beauraing' circles it does not mean that we forget our obligation to show to both parties the strictest impartiality. But we find it necessary to make clear that passion and the attitudes inspired by passion, are not, as the most disinterested public been led to believe … limited to those in favor of Beauraing.[112]

As for the testimonies of the child visionaries: In the eyes of the commission members there was no doubt that the children were convinced they had seen the Virgin. The testimonies of the individual children largely coincided, and where they differed, it was only in details. Moreover, their corporeal characteristics during the apparitions and their courage and perseverance afterwards seemed to confirm the children's statements. The objections against the reality of the apparitions and their supernatural origin (fraud, illusion, hallucination, hypnotism, and also diabolic intervention) could all be rejected. They could not draw a final conclusion however, for some matters remained unresolved due to lack of evidence and witnesses. Among these, was the issue of Albert Voisin's morality.

> Without doubt, we were able to check a number of the assertions uttered by those who refuse to admit the hypothesis of the divine supernatural in the events of Beauraing; the result of that control allows us to think that there is a large amount of "bluff," even blackmail, in the multiple allusions made by Dr De Greeff and others to mysterious documents whose mere disclosure would suffice, so they say, to convince those who believe in the supernatural origin of their error, but that they have systematically refused to let us see. Meanwhile, as long as there exists the menace of certain revelations capable of modifying our judgment, we cannot without imprudence, in a so grave and delicate matter, pretend to conclude the examination with firm conclusions.[113]
>
> [W]e tend towards the hypothesis of the divine supernatural, which does not exclude (as has been said in this report) a more or less considerable amount of human elements, – even diabolic, if one wishes – mingled with factors of divine origin … waiting for the future to confirm or invalidate our current opinion … we believe that nothing impedes the continuation or even the development of a Marian cult in Beauraing, even more since in the last four years, Beauraing has shown itself as a centre of Marian piety and a site of favours and blessing for a great number of faithful.… However, as long as the case of Albert V. has not received a favourable solution, we consider an episcopal approbation inopportune, for it would positively encourage the belief in the divine origin of the events that are under discussion.[114]

A month later, on 15 December 1936, Mgr Heylen received the final report.[115] Curiously, there was a half-year delay before he forwarded the report to Malines (on 13 September 1937) to be examined by the archdiocesan commission.[116] In the meantime he was also confronted with a new set of apparitions that started in March 1936 in Ham-sur-Sambre. It did not take him long to reach a decision on that case: already in March 1938 he publicly rejected them.[117]

## THE COMMISSION OF MALINES

The commission of Malines held its first session on 11 May 1935. While the commission in theory operated under the supervision of the archbishop, in practice it was led most of the time by its vice-president, Mgr Franciscus Tessens, vicar-general and president of the Great Seminary of Malines. There were four assistant judges: the Jesuit Edouard de Moreau, professor of ecclesiastical history at the theological college of the Jesuits in Louvain; Ernest Massaux, provincial of the Belgian Dominicans; Chérubin Vromans, professor of moral theology and former provincial of the Franciscans of Belgium; and Canon Aloïs Van Hove, professor of dogmatic theology of the Great Seminary. The promotor fidei was Canon Joseph Claes, licentiate in canon law and secretary of the archdiocese, and the notary was Canon Pierre Gillet, professor of canon law at the Great Seminary.[118]

During the first session, the cardinal reminded the commission members that the bishops of Namur and Liège were holding their own canonical examinations and would send in their reports, and the Malines commission was thus to focus on the events at other sites. Lists of these had been drawn up by the Belgian writer and journalist Louis Wilmet (of Genval) and Abbé Didion (of Bonneville). Among these events, only the cases of Etikhove, Onkerzele, Olsene, Lokeren, and Tubize seemed to be worthy of examination. It is thereby important to note that even though the bishop of Ghent and the archbishop had already publicly rejected the apparitions in Lokeren and Onkerzele II in the summer of 1934, the cases were still studied in detail by the members of the archdiocesan commission.

The way the commission reached its conclusion differed slightly from that of the two diocesan commissions. Whereas the Beauraing and Banneux commissions focused largely on oral testimonies, the Malines commission primarily collected testimonies that were written, which were read out loud during the sessions.[119] Apart from these, the commission members also discussed the files they separately compiled: Van Hove wrote reports on Lokeren, Onkerzele, and Etikhove; Moreau created one on Onkerzele, as did Massaux and Tessens. The only exception to this procedure was the case of Laure Dulière and her bleeding crucifixes. As these events took place while the commission members were still conducting their examination, they could go on a site visit and question witnesses. Their investigation left an unfavourable impression, and, in March 1936, they drafted a warning about the bleeding images (in Brussels, Antwerp, and other locations) indicating that the phenomena did not have a supernatural origin and were often the result of fraud.[120]

A month later, the Malines commission members finished their examination of the apparitions in Etikhove with a conclusion that was not as harsh as the one adopted for Lokeren and Onkerzele. They decided that, for Etikhove, it was more correct to indicate that nothing pointed in the direction of a supernatural origin, rather than stating that the supernatural origin was radically rejected. In this respect the conclusion was similar to that about Olsene.[121] In that same sixteenth session they ruled out a divine origin of the phenomena in Onkerzele and summed up their general opinion: (1) The events in Onkerzele and Lokeren did not contain any elements that pointed in the direction of a supernatural origin; (2) The events in Tubize, Olsene, and Etikhove did not hold elements that might give a positive argument for a supernatural origin; (3) The events at the other locations did not seem worthy of consideration. There was thus a slight difference in the evaluation of the apparition sites. Tubize, Olsene, and Etikhove were rejected with a more positive – or rather more "open" – formulation than the other sites.[122]

More than a year later, the commission members gathered again to commence their investigation of Banneux and Beauraing. By then the reports of the diocesan commissions had been received, and the Malines commission embarked on two followup examinations before formulating a final conclusion on the two apparition series. For Banneux, the archbishop asked the commission members to study the cult that developed at the site. They could not reach a unanimous conclusion. Some commission members tended to believe in the supernatural origin of the events, but others excluded a supernatural cause.[123] None of them was convinced that the supernatural origin could be stated without doubt.[124]

As for Beauraing, the commission studied the files of the diocesan commission of Namur, but also heard additional witnesses in March and April of 1938. During sessions 22 to 26 they listened to Étienne De Greeff, Aloïs Jan'ssens, Bruno de Jésus-Marie (of the *Études Carmélitaines* group), Dr Rouvroy (De Greeff's colleague), and to Norbert Collard, the head of the school where Albert Voisin had been accused of immoral acts. All these witnesses had refused to appear before the Namur commission. The result of these examinations was a firmer stand than the one they had taken on Banneux. According to the commission members (on 9 November 1938), the supernatural origin of the Beauraing apparitions could not be proven. They were aware that the Namur commission tended toward a supernatural explanation, but only if the accusations against Albert Voisin proved to be false. The members of Malines commission had investigated those events themselves, and believed them to be true. There was, however, no unanimity about how to evaluate the impact of this immorality.[125]

The general conclusion about Beauraing was thus "*non constat de supernaturali indole.*" Their decision was built on the rejection of the miraculous cures by the medical commission, on their own evaluation of the testimonies and examinations (they pointed for instance at the disagreement between "serious and Christian men"), and on the accusations against Albert Voisin.[126]

## *The One in Charge? The Archbishop.*

On 14 February 1939, the archbishop summarized the conclusions in a report for Rome and asked what had to be done about the cults in Beauraing and Banneux that had developed with the permission of the two bishops. Up until then they had attracted numerous pilgrims, so what should be announced? That after a careful examination the supernatural origin could not be ascertained? As for the cult of Our Lady in Beauraing and Banneux, could it be allowed, on the condition that it was not linked to the wonderful events from which it had originated?[127] The Holy Office answered that since the supernatural origin of the apparitions in Beauraing and Banneux could not be affirmed, he and the bishops of Liège and Namur had to stop pilgrimages to these sites, the chapel in Banneux had to be closed, and the Union Internationale de Prière was to be suppressed.[128]

In Belgium, the long silence from Malines and Rome seems to have caused some unease, especially among the bishops of Liège and Namur. In June 1939, the Holy Office informed Archbishop Van Roey that the bishop of Liège complained about not having been called to testify. He believed that before the decision was announced, he should at least be heard.[129] Two months later, Mgr Kerkhofs decided to take further action. He contacted the archbishop and sent him an elaborate report with his reasons for believing in the apparitions of Banneux (the character and circumstances of the events, exclusion of a pathological origin, the development and fruits of the cult).[130] Mgr Kerkhofs turned to Rome as well. He and the bishop of Namur both sent a personal report to Rome of why they believed the apparitions in their dioceses needed to be approved. They built their arguments on the nature of the apparitions (dignity and beauty), the favours that had been received (conversions and cures), but also stressed how much the faithful needed this approval. A positive message would be most welcome to the public "in the gravity of the hour" as nations were rising against one other.[131]

The letters seem to have generated some effect. On 13 December 1939, the Holy Office asked Van Roey to postpone his announcement of his decision because of new information about the case. Van Roey had indeed not made a public declaration yet. His delay had everything to do with the fact that he feared his decision would not be accepted by several parties, especially since the two bishops had publicly shown their approval and were counted among the supporters of Beauraing and Banneux. He asked the Holy Office to investigate everything and decide what had to be done.[132]

The Holy Office seems to have been open to this line of thinking and asked the archbishop in January 1940 for all the documents relating to the apparitions.[133] Van Roey sent the information and also included an extra note on the public reception of the apparitions. He remarked that the prescriptions of the Holy Office concerning the publications and the pilgrimages had not been observed, and that, on the contrary, all was organized in such a way (with the approval of the bishops) as if the supernatural origin was not to be doubted and the church had already recognized the events. Furthermore, while the apparitions in Beauraing and Banneux might contain nothing reprehensible, the subsequent national series of apparitions included elements of human fraud, and even the bad spirit ("*interventio mali spiritus*"). Since the apparition series was seen as a whole, the bishops who opposed apparitions (for instance, the Ghent bishop) were pitted against the ones who favoured them (for instance, Namur). The events in Beauraing and Banneux were connected and he could not see how Banneux could be declared of supernatural origin if Beauraing was not. Moreover, it was difficult to say in which of the cases the positive effects were better than the bad. While for some faithful their devotion to the Virgin increased, others started to doubt about religious matters. The matter created severe discussions among the laymen and the priests and religious. Van Roey wondered if it was not strange that the child-visionaries were from a socialist and liberal-socialist milieu? Their parents could hardly be called exemplary Catholics.[134]

The Holy Office subsequently ordered two reports, one on Beauraing and one on Banneux. The first one, building on an analysis of the nature, seers, and effect of the apparitions in Beauraing, concluded that the decision should be left to the archbishop of Malines and the verdict should be "non constare de supernaturalitate." Consequently, cults and religious movements that were based on these phenomena should not be promoted and devotions and religious exercises that already existed should be suppressed (but with care, as the two bishops had been involved in their promotion).[135] The second report, on Banneux, was milder. The votum was written by the Jesuit Creusen, professor at the Gregoriana and brother to the dean of Seraing who had been part of the commission of Liège.[136] Creusen knew the Banneux case intimately and stressed how important it was that those judging the case would not be far removed from the people and things they were examining – for those in Rome, these would always be dead documents. Creusen was inclined to believe in the supernatural character of the events. For him, the Banneux apparitions differed from all the other wondrous events because of their simplicity and the true piety shown (by the girl and pilgrims).[137] He saw two possible outcomes (of which he liked the second one better): either stating that "the supernatural nature of the facts (or of the apparitions and messages) cannot be established,"[138] or giving the ordinary the right to pronounce a verdict. The decision would then have a local and personal character. That was fitting for private apparitions and revelations as the worship was first purely local and its worldwide resonance would soon cease if it did not come from God. In that case, the bishop would have to explain to the faithful the nature and power of his decisions concerning the apparitions or cures.[139] While the members of the Holy Office seemed to be in agreement that the new cult could be allowed, they differed in opinion where the apparitions were concerned.[140]

In the meantime, the bishop of Liège once again asked permission to announce his own verdict as ordinary of the diocese.[141] This time, the pope, who knew about the indecisiveness of the commission of Malines, of the archbishop of Malines, and of the Holy Office, was willing to leave the decision to the bishop.[142] The Holy Office agreed and informed the archbishop on 2 January 1942 that while he remained in charge of the decision on Beauraing and could communicate the conclusion of the Malines commission, the Banneux apparitions became once again the responsibility of the bishop of Liège. The bishop was granted his wish to announce his judgment "with sole responsibility for the alleged extraordinary events."[143]

This was no small shift in the decision-making process. It was the first time in the examination of the wave of Marian apparitions in Belgium that the examination process of Beauraing and Banneux was differentiated. The decision on Beauraing remained in the hands of the archbishop of Malines, while that of Banneux was left to the bishop of Liège.

## Revising the Verdicts – Making Public Statements

In February 1939, when the reports were sent to Rome, the Belgian public knew almost nothing about what had been examined or decided. From the moment the Belgian commissions started their activities in 1935, the bishops had only taken a public stand on a small number of apparition sites and visionaries (Lokeren II, the Onkerzele visionaries, and Ham-sur-Sambre). The evaluation process took place behind closed doors and none of the decisions on the other events was communicated to the broader public. Nine years after the first apparitions had been reported, there were two verdicts (on the apparitions in other dioceses and on Beauraing), but these were not yet announced. The patience of the faithful was to be further tested.

## *First Step: Recognition of the Cults of Beauraing and Banneux*

The Belgian bishops seem to have known very little about what was going on in Rome. The information came to them through hearsay. In February 1941, Mgr Heylen, the bishop of Namur, heard from Mgr Millot, the vicar general of Paris, that the *Études Carmélitaines* group had not ceased its activities and a rejection of the apparitions by Rome was imminent.[144] Whether the rumour was true, Heylen never found out, for he died later that year and on 12 December 1941 was succeeded by André-Marie Charue.[145]

The Banneux apparitions had been on the agenda in Rome on 2 January 1942, but it took a month before the decision reached Liège and Malines on 6 February.[146] The Holy Office's decision was excellent news for the bishop of Liège,[147] but it put the newly appointed bishop of Namur, Mgr Charue, in a difficult position. The new bishop was confronted with the whole matter on the day of his ordination, when the bishop of Liège, surprised that he had not received a letter similar to his, advised him to write to Rome and request the same privilege.[148] In a letter following up on the day's events, Kerkhofs remarked to Charue that the "non constare" was not the same as a condemnation. Maybe that was something the archbishop could communicate to the faithful in the document he was planning to publish on the events?[149] Charue, who had not yet given the apparitions much thought, was forced to take immediate action. Observing the consternation among the few members of his clergy whom he had told about the news, he wrote the archbishop and asked him not to make any public statements before he had written to Rome. "[A]fter waiting nine years and since we are no longer in the fever of the beginning," he believed it was not against the spirit of Rome's decree to grant him that delay.[150] The archbishop agreed, on the condition that the bishop of Liège would not yet make a public statement either. Charue then wrote to Kerkhofs and asked him not to publish anything yet.[151]

In Liège, Kerkhofs had been considering his next move since he had received the good news from Rome. René Rutten, once a member of the Banneux commission, had contacted him on hearing about Rome's decision. He showed himself concerned about the close connection that existed between Beauraing and Banneux (metaphysically possible, but "morally" hard to accept). If Banneux was going to be approved, then all rules of caution had to be observed.[152] Kerkhofs seems to have taken this warning to heart, for when he wrote to the archbishop on 1 March 1942 (before Charue had contacted him), he indicated that he planned on convoking a second commission and agreed with the archbishop's proposal to delay all official communication about the Banneux apparitions.[153] In the meantime however, he wanted to authorize the cult of Our Lady of the Poor (of Banneux): "This, as an answer to the impatient wait of the faithful of Banneux, is a guarantee against the potential 'safety catch' that Rome might impose after your intervention and cannot augment the distress in Namur – as my pastoral letter of Lent has rendered the letter of the Holy Office public that authorized me to judge Banneux as ordinary, without compromising either Rome or Malines."[154]

On 19 March 1942, the bishop of Liège published a pastoral letter in which he gave his official permission to observe the cult of Our Lady of the Poor of Banneux. The cult had already existed for nine years, he observed, without displaying any bizarre elements, doctrinal novelties, or anything not in accordance with the ecclesiastical tradition.[155]

Kerkhofs' public statement forced Archbishop Van Roey to act. He wrote to Charue and asked him if he had already contacted Rome. If that was the case, he promised to wait with a statement about Beauraing. Charue had indeed written to Rome (again) a few days before. True to his word, the archbishop only mentioned in his pastoral letter on the Belgian apparitions of 25 March 1942 that he could not yet publish the conclusion of the examination of the Beauraing case.[156] The archbishop added that, in accordance with the wish of the Holy Office, the decision on the Banneux case was in the hands of the bishop of Liège who had already approved of the cult of Our Lady of Banneux. As for the other apparition sites and bleeding images, he confirmed and thereby also published the decisions made by the Malines commission.[157]

After the statements of Van Roey and Kerkhofs, the Beauraing apparitions were the only events whose evaluation seemed not to have progressed, despite the fact that the apparitions there were the first ones to be reported. Mgr Charue had not been idle since he had first heard about Rome's decision to grant Mgr Kerkhofs the permission to pronounce on the Banneux case. He had sent a report to Pope Pius XII about the evaluation process that the Beauraing apparitions had already gone through by the diocesan commission of Namur and the archdiocesan commission of Malines. He stressed the hesitance of the Namur commission to make a statement because the Albert Voisin issue was not clarified, the unwillingness of some witnesses to testify, and the lack of communication from the commission of Malines about what those witnesses had said.[158] He did not seem to know what the final verdict of the Malines commission was. He thought that commission had declared with regard to both Banneux and Beauraing that the supernatural character of the apparition was not proven. Since the bishop of Liège had been granted the prerogative to pronounce on the apparitions of Banneux, Charue requested the same right. He feared severe spiritual inconveniences if the two cases were treated differently, especially since, at the time, the Banneux apparitions were considered by many as a kind of secondary confirmation of the Beauraing apparitions. Nevertheless, if he could not be granted the same decision power, he requested at least a new examination.[159]

In his opinion, the circumstances were quite similar to those of Banneux: (1) The lack of unanimity about Banneux among the members of the commission of Malines was similar to the dissonance of opinion among the commission members in Beauraing's case, but here it was between the commissions of Namur and that of Malines. (2) The archbishop probably had the same doubts on judging Banneux as he had concerning Beauraing. (3) Rome did not have all the documents needed to make a fair judgment on the Beauraing case. (4) Similar to the bishop of Liege, Mgr Heylen had also petitioned the Holy Father (on 9 September 1939) to be allowed to utter his judgment as ordinary of the place. Charue himself had done likewise on 22 March.[160]

The Holy Office[161] agreed to examine the case of Beauraing again and demanded a full report of facts and arguments and, if he thought it necessary, new documents.[162] Charue immediately set to work and asked for the conclusion of the commission of Malines, or at least the text that had been transmitted. Archbishop Van Roey agreed to provide – confidentially – a copy of the complementary examinations and the conclusions of the commission of Malines.[163] The doctrinal commission of Namur resumed its activities early August 1942. The surviving members of the commission, Monin, Ranwez, and Lambot, studied the report and created a file on the decision-making process of the commission of Namur and the commission of Malines. Two elements were discussed in more detail: the case of doctor De Greeff and the accusations against Albert Voisin.[164]

The focus on these two cases seems almost self-evident: De Greeff's refusal to take the stand before the commission of Namur had left the work of the commission unfinished and had made it impossible for them to formulate a final conclusion. The members of the Malines commission had been obliged to hear the last witnesses on the Beauraing case themselves and based their final verdict on what they had heard. After the reports on these testimonies had been communicated to the Namur commission, this was one part of the decision-making process of Malines that the members of the Namur commission could now study themselves. They concluded with satisfaction that "Dr De Greeff did not produce in Malines any new argument or document that was not already known." Nonetheless, the commission members were well aware of the impact of De Greeff's opinions on the adversaries of Beauraing: "The adversaries of the reality, or at least the supernatural divine character of the 'Events of Beauraing,' have largely based themselves on the opinion of a witness who appeared to them so authorized, both because of his scientific titles, and his functions, and because of the scientific apparatus that he has given to his examination and publications."[165] They thus added some observations on the value of De Greeff's opinion. First, referring to a letter of a former colleague of his, De Greeff was described as a "systematical contradictor" who even doubted the reality of the apparitions in Lourdes. Secondly, De Greeff also seemed to have attached particular importance to his own "impressions," "direct perceptions," and "psychological evidence" – not necessarily shared by his colleagues who were also present at the site. Furthermore, as his acceptance of the rumour about a spiritual circle in Beauraing demonstrated, De Greeff had not been very critical about what he was told by others.[166]

As for the second point of emphasis, the conclusions of the diocesan commission of Namur had included a cautionary note concerning the Albert Voisin case ("as long as the case of Albert V. has not received a favorable solution, we consider an episcopal approbation inopportune"). The commission of Malines, on the other hand, believed the events to have been sufficiently proven; what they had not agreed upon, however, was the importance to be attached to them. For both commissions, then, the case had been an important factor in the evaluation of the

Beauraing apparitions. Could someone who had been singled out to witness a Marian apparition perform morally dubious actions even after he had seen the Virgin?[167] The commission members believed that the documents and testimonies that had been collected during the two examinations in fact also allowed to "mitigate the objective gravity of the deeds and words he has been reproached for, and also to create doubt about their subjective malice." After discussing whether or not Albert Voisin was a corrupted and corrupting child, and concluding that his immoral character had been exaggerated, the commission members discussed the "gravity" of the words and gestures he had been accused of. They noted that as far as his utterances were concerned, the accusations were at times based on hearsay while Voisin's gestures had only been part of childish play.[168]

Furthermore, apart from studying the extra documentation, the commission also gathered information about cures that could be considered exceptional and were linked to Our Lady of Beauraing. It was Dom Cyrille Lambot who contacted the members of the Comité Pro Maria and asked them for a file on the three to four most important cures "with the most possible precision and the appreciation of physicians. Let them be well-described cases, and indisputably extraordinary if not miraculous."[169] On 9 January 1943, the doctrinal commission on Beauraing sent in its second report, which included in its appendices the rejection of the theories of Bruno de Jésus-Marie, Aloïs Janssens, and Roland Dalbiez. After studying the additional documents and depositions, the commission members believed that they were in a position to make a firmer statement on the Beauraing apparitions than the one they had made in 1936. Referring to "remarkable cures" and conversions, the commission stated that "without pronouncing itself on the supernatural divine origin of the events, the diocesan authority of Namur can allow a public cult to Our Lady of Beauraing" insofar as the sovereign pontiff accepts it.[170] On receiving the report, Mgr Charue wrote a new letter to the Holy Office requesting the permission to make an announcement on the Beauraing apparitions. On 28 January 1943, he finally received word from Rome, where the matter had been discussed already in early December 1942, thus before his new letter and in response to his message of 17 June 1942. The Holy Office granted the new bishop his wish.[171] Four days later, Charue travelled to Beauraing to officially recognize the cult of Our Lady of Beauraing. His pastoral letter on the matter followed on 19 February 1943.[172]

So in early 1943, the intermediate result after ten years of waiting was the official approval of the cults that had developed in Banneux and Beauraing. The official recognition of the apparitions at the two sites required extra examinations, so new diocesan commissions set to work.

### *The Pressure of Rumours and a Precedent*

On 16 March 1942, three days before the bishop of Liège published his pastoral letter on the cult of Our Lady of Banneux, he set up a second diocesan commission to study the Banneux case. This time the commission was constituted in a manner similar to commissions in charge of canonisations.[173] Rutten was the "postulator" while Canon Kiselstein was the "promotor of the faith" and three other members acted as judges. Three of the commission members –Leroux, Ruyters, and Rutten – had participated in the first commission as well. Canon Clijsters was a surprising addition, for he was well-known for his critical stance toward the Banneux apparitions. The bishop however, was so convinced of the truth of the apparitions that he believed the truth would soon become apparent to this opponent as well.[174] Unfortunately, he was proven wrong, for when the commission handed in its report in February 1945, its conclusion was that "the supernatural character of the events does not appear certain to them, and not even probable."[175] Referring to the letter of the Belgian bishops of 30 October 1933, they indicated that one had to be quite careful in making statements about the supernatural character of events. In this case, one had to be especially careful, for it was rather doubtful that the Virgin would have appeared twice on such a short notice in almost the same corner of the small country. Investigating such events always leaves certain questions unsettled, but in this case, there was a whole number of objections that could not be counterbalanced by a real, truly firm, argument. Everything led to skepticism and distrust: the personality of the visionary (she had refused to submit to a medical exam); her behaviour and that of her family after the events (they had not become more devout); the mentality of Abbé Jamin (his tendency toward mysticism) and the way he had conducted the investigation (with guiding questions); the circumstances of the events (hallucination); and even the content of the message (asking for a chapel was a standard demand). As a document appended to the conclusion indicated, the fact that Mariette Béco might have had a brochure on the Lourdes apparitions on loan during her own series of apparitions did not generate confidence either.[176]

What had happened? And, more importantly, was the bishop obliged to take the new commission's decision into account? He had already approved the cult of Our Lady of Banneux, how was he to deal with the commission's rejection of the events that had led to this new cult? According to Léon Wuillaume, who studied the commission in his 1982 article, the first session already set the tone and examined the suggestion that Mariette Béco had been intrigued by the events in Beauraing, read a book on the Lourdes apparitions, and consequently had been susceptible to the phenomenon of hallucination. After that first session, the commission members continued to follow that hypothesis and, in the end, they dedicated more than 300 pages of their file to the question of the Lourdes brochure and pondered the "hysterical" constitution of Béco in six reports. The three judges did not wait for Rutten's answer, and signed their final conclusion.[177]

The bishop had heard rumours about the impending negative verdict even before he received the final report of the commission. Even though he immediately informed the Belgian bishops and nuncio,[178] he was not willing to accept the conclusion as final verdict. He asked Rutten whether he believed his work was completely finished. Did he not have to create a sort of last response to the report in question? "Might I not, if necessary, agree with your opinion rather than that of the judges?"[179] Moreover, there also seemed to be some formal grounds to question the validity of the report. The file was not dated, it did not carry the signature of the secretary of the commission, and the postulator Rutten had not – contrary to their 1937 file – given his consent. The moment the commission members handed in their conclusion, Rutten was still working on his response (the commission had already given him a delay of several extra months). As Jean Beyer remarked, they seem to have been convinced that his observations would not alter their opinion.[180]

While there had been no official statement, many people – especially clergy – seemed to know that the commission had formulated a negative conclusion.[181] Such rumours eventually forced the bishop to make a public statement, published in several periodicals, on 31 May 1945.

The bishop thereby warned against "fantasy" rumours that fraud had been proven and the competent authority was about to pronounce on the case. He confirmed again that the cult of Our Lady of Banneux remained authorized in his diocese, and he added that it was too soon to make a public statement on the apparitions.[182]

In the meantime, the bishop had asked the Jesuit Scheuer to study the commission's report. He concluded that the commission had not brought new information to light.[183] In view of the first commission's positive stance and the fact that Rome had granted the bishop permission to formulate his decision (in his opinion a sign of a favourable evaluation), the result of the examination of the 1942 commission could only be called "an assault" without moral or judicial value. It almost seemed, he added, that the commission had used the methods of Sherlock Holmes to reach the conclusion of hysteria. He could not call it a serene, impartial investigation: Every aspect favourable to Banneux had been neglected. He almost wished the document was published: It was a magnificent argument "*ad absurdem*" and he exclaimed, "May that precious document at least be guarded with care, as a precious stone, of great worth, in the archives of the Virgin of the Poor!" He also tried to explain how this negative tendency had taken hold of the commission members, and believed it to be due to an individual who had been an opponent of the Banneux apparitions from the start. Scheuer believed that this commission member had a tendency toward "a psychosis" that made it impossible to see clearly, or consider the arguments against his own fixed idea. The opinion of this commission member had been dominant, absolute, and contagious: He had been able to convince his colleagues and dragged them along. In short, the commission's report, according to Scheuer, should be ignored.[184]

The bishop, relieved on receiving Scheuer's file, nonetheless asked him to write a new version in June 1946. Kerkhofs wanted him to adopt a milder tone and to take into account the comments of Rutten on the document. In July, the new version was finished. Nevertheless, the bishop did not want to formulate a final conclusion before he could read the study that Rutten was still in the process of writing. He therefore suggested, in September 1948, to start with the typing of at least a part of the files Rutten had already drafted.[185] That same month, Scheuer suggested to the bishop that they might organize a confrontation of the two parties in a discussion session in the presence of the bishop.[186]

The commission members, however, refused to participate. Such a verbal discussion, so they believed, "would certainly remain sterile and would expose us to new injuries by Scheuer, even in the presence of Your Excellence … Even if the report of the father is profoundly injurious to us, it is in no way capable of altering our opinion." They had decided to answer Scheuer's attack with a short and substantial report, in which they would not oppose "insult to insult" and to which they would not give any publicity. To this written response they added a file listing a number of the insults Scheuer had addressed to them.[187]

Mgr Kerkhofs, whose own convictions about the matter had not changed on receiving the negative report of the commission, confirmed his position in a pastoral letter to the clergy of his diocese in December 1946. Still, he did not rush his conclusion and waited for Rutten to finish his work before publicly recognizing the authenticity of the events. He did, however, already confirm his approbation of the *cult* of Our Lady of Banneux (in 1942) in a pastoral letter of 19 March 1947. In that letter, he announced the creation of a shrine in Banneux and elaborated on his personal opinion on the apparitions: "In the same pastoral letter we have proposed the events of Banneux as sufficiently founded to be, at least within the limits of a serious possibility, worthy of human faith." After five years of studying the case, he believed that he could still stand by his former statement.[188] He nonetheless differentiated between his personal opinion and his role – and authority to judge – as ordinary of the site. For an official approval, more research was needed.[189]

Even after this public episcopal sign of support, the commission did not retract its conclusion. Instead, the members sent in their response to a new file created by Scheuer at the request of the bishop.[190] They rejected his allusions to a positive evaluation in Malines and Rome, questioned what he called the "perfection" of the apparitions, doubted the value of Mariette Béco as a visionary (she could not be called beyond all doubt), and emphasized that the *vox populi* could not be called upon as an argument in favour of the truth of the apparitions. They thus confirmed their initial conclusion and considered the supernatural character of the events of Banneux neither proven nor even probable.[191] Scheuer on the other hand encouraged Mgr Kerkhofs to make a definite statement. He was, after all, the final judge in the matter and the arguments of the commission had proven to be unworthy of consideration.[192] The bishop did not let himself be pressured, however. Only two years later, after consulting numerous *intimi* and observing the high number of miraculous cures at the site, did he make a public statement. On 22 August 1949, he affirmed "without any reservations" the reality of the eight apparitions to Mariette Béco in January to March 1933.[193] The results of the 1942 commission had caused a delay but not a rejection of the apparitions.

Imagine the surprise of the Holy Office: The last thing the congregation had heard about the apparitions in Banneux was the negative verdict of the second commission of Liège. On 21 February 1945, Mgr Kerkhofs had informed Micara about that decision and the nuncio had forwarded the letter to Marchetti-Selvaggiani, the secretary of the Holy Office. The bishop had, so the nuncio added, made an obedient impression writing about the rejection: "But the fact is there; the Good Lord has allowed it, I try to accept it with a generous abandonment to divine Providence." He did, however, mention that he was still waiting for the answer of Rutten.[194]

"Then there was no further news," so a note of the Holy Office recalled, "and it was thought that everything was finished; when, on 20 September 1949, the nuncio forwarded to the Holy Office the pastoral letter from the Bishop of Liège confirming his belief in the apparitions of Banneux."[195] This declaration, so the nuncio added, caused confusion among the faithful and scandal among the enemies of religion. The bishop, who was "appreciated everywhere for his piety, zeal and charity" hardly paid any attention to the decision of the diocesan commission and without actually possessing new positive elements to modify the conclusion, "only moved by his intimate persuasion and personal observations, recognizes 'malgré tout' … the authenticity of the apparitions of Banneux."[196]

Mgr Kerkhofs decided to travel to Rome to announce the news himself. On Wednesday 9 November, he first had a meeting with the pope. The bishop planned on building a large church in honour of Mary, Queen of Peace, at the site of the apparitions in Banneux and asked for a blessing. The pope however showed reservations and asked him to meet the assessor of the Holy Office who informed him that a document had been sent in to contest the reality of the apparitions.[197] So, for the time being, the Holy See could not in any form be involved in his building initiative "since the matter is, in many respects, still very controversial."[198]

The nuncio's note accompanying Mgr Kerkhofs' pastoral letter was indeed not the only critical comment that reached the Holy Office. The archives also hold an (anonymous) French document on Mgr Kerkhofs' public announcement of his approval and his letter to the clergy.[199] The text carefully analyzed the bishop's reasons for publicly appraising the apparitions. In his texts, the bishop stressed that the decision was "inspired by our intimate conviction" and that he, in comparison with the commission, took into account "the whole of the facts, their evolution, their fruits" and not just the testimonies of the witnesses as the commission did. The decision therefore lacked, so the author believed, "the canonical foundation wisely required for interventions of such gravity. The letter recognizes this quite clearly."[200] Moreover, so the document continued, the bishop did not hide that he was ignoring the opposition of the commission. Was all this haste in approving the apparitions not triggered by the fact that Beauraing's examination was almost finished and there was pressure for the cause of Banneux to move on as well? "All of this," so the note concluded, "causes many of the faithful to be troubled. A serious uneasiness has arisen, which threatens to lead to the conclusion that the Church's decisions in such serious matters as miracles and apparitions are light."[201]

Mgr Kerkhofs himself later declared that he made his announcement because the news about the negative evaluation was starting to circulate and he feared for its negative effect. He felt himself torn between saving Banneux – a source of Christian renewal as he believed – and the fear of going against a traditional procedure and of the criticism that such an intervention would provoke.[202] Nonetheless, he seems to have realized that it was an exceptional manoeuvre and the public needed clarification. He therefore ordered a book to be written on the topic. *Notre-Dame de Banneux. Études et documents* was compiled by Van Houtryve, O.S.B., Scheuer, S.J.; and Abbé Servais, doyen of Sprimont, but published anonymously under the responsibility of Mgr Kerkhofs in 1950. The bishop himself also set to work and started to write the report Mgr Ottaviani had asked him on the matter.[203]

In this document Kerkhofs commented on the evaluation process and his personal opinion about the matter. Among others he lauded the beauty, simplicity, and originality of the message and the scenario in which it featured, and also the ignorance of the uncultivated child who had been the messenger. He elaborated on the investigations and findings of the various commissions and noted that the medical commission had concluded that the events "have nothing to do with pathology." The first diocesan commission had finished its activities concluding that the "reality of the apparitions in Banneux was at least probable." As far as the commission of Malines was concerned, the members had pronounced themselves on certain cases, but not on Beauraing and Banneux. "His Eminence did not believe he could pronounce a judgment on the subject and deferred everything to the Holy Office." He himself had long ago made up his mind on seeing the large number of pilgrims, hearing the positive reports of the clergy, and reading the publications on the matter. The negative evaluation of the second commission had been particularly painful, but he had not hesitated to inform the other bishops and the nuncio about it. The bishop emphasized that the commission members had signed their conclusion even before they heard back from the postulator. Furthermore, their conclusion was diametrically opposed to the conclusion of the first commission, of which two of them had been members. His own opinion had not been changed, and when he officially recognized the apparitions in 1949, that announcement was well-received. Those who might have had objections had adopted a "respectful silence" and up until then, "I have had no indication of discontent and even less of criticism or overt opposition from their side."[204]

However self-confident the tone of his letter, the final paragraphs indicate the bishop was be well aware that his opinion and decision might not coincide with those of the Vatican. The few lines he added almost create the impression that he wanted to make sure the Holy Office would not interfere in the matter. He described it as a given that the Vatican never interferes:

> I know that Rome does not intervene directly in the official recognition of events of that genre. It can do so even less in the present case, which is about a cause recently recognized and in conditions somewhat in the margin of the usual procedure.
>
> The Holy Father in his prudence, after careful consideration, might examine whether, without appearing to recognize the events in question himself, he might facilitate the creation of the proposed Marian shrine, an homage of all the nations, symbol and centre of their piety, confidence, of their prayers to obtain through Mary, peace and well-being of the world.[205]

In comparison with the Banneux evaluation, the second part of the Beauraing process went rather smoothly. Two topics dominated the investigation: the question of morality and the miraculous cures that had been reported. While the second report of the diocesan commission had already mitigated the accusations against Albert Voisin, the matter still seems to have bothered the bishop. He himself wrote a ten-page report about it in November 1947 in which he investigated the moral constitution of Voisin during and after the apparitions and the role of the head of the school Voisin attended[206] and concluded that "the objections drawn as to the immorality of A.V. are no longer valid."[207] A collaborator of the bishop reached a similar conclusion. (No name mentioned, but according to Joset it was most probably Ranwez.) In April 1948, Charue also engaged two legal experts, Joseph Blanke, emeritus president of the tribunal of Namur, former judge in the juvenile court, and Henri Bribosia, former dean of the order of lawyers from the same tribunal. Both agreed that the accusations lacked a sufficient basis and had to be placed in the context of the semi-rural school where they took place.[208]

After one of the most important arguments against the authenticity of the apparitions had been rejected, Mgr Charue asked the members of the diocesan commission to investigate the cures that had been reported. The focus was on two cases: Maria Van Laer (Sister Pudentia in religion, whom we discussed in more detail in the previous section) and Mrs Maria-Magdalena Acar-Group. The diocesan commission now included two new members: Canon François Martens (a Flemish Norbertine active as chaplain for the Flemish pilgrims in Beauraing[209]) and Abbé Fernand Toussaint (doctor in canonical law). The role division was similar to what it had been in the previous examinations by the diocesan commission: There were three "*juges assesseurs*": Monin, Ranwez, and Martens; Lambot as postulator; Toussaint as promotor; and Bouchat as secretary.[210] For each of the cases, a core group of three investigators was appointed among the members of the commission.[211]

As we have seen, the commission members deemed the miraculous character of both cures convincing,[212] and on 2 July 1949, Charue officially affirmed that the Queen of Heavens appeared to the children of Beauraing in the winter of 1932–33 to show her maternal heart, and ask for prayer – especially for the conversion of sinners – through her mediation.[213] Belgium now had two new officially recognized apparition sites. The chaos had calmed down, discussions were buried in the archives. For the apparitions that were officially approved, Beauraing and Banneux, it is clear that the success of one site had put pressure on the development of the other – too much delay in taking a parallel step caused rumours.

## *Old Arguments, New Interpretations, and Public Statements*

The faithful looked upon members of the clergy – the religious authority of old – for some guidance and firm ground as they saw their country flooded with Marian apparitions. Many responded, even though the bishops tried to stop the clergy's involvement in pilgrimages to apparition sites and hinder them from publishing on the matter. Actions were as meaningful as words and the faithful read public acts like praying or kneeling at an apparition site as a statement. The bishops of Liège and Namur also gradually started to show such signs of support of the apparitions in Banneux and Beauraing. As we have seen, this had repercussions on the official examination. Their behaviour prior to the official investigation diminished their credibility as impartial judges and initially caused them to lose the right to pronounce their judgment on the apparitions. The rumours and slander campaigns targeting different types of experts likewise entered the commission's rooms. The battle might have quieted down, but its memory haunted the testimonies.

The voices we heard in the previous chapters, the evaluations of laymen, doctors, and members of the clergy, also reverberated during the sessions of these commissions. Whether these witnesses appeared in person or were heard or evaluated through written reports depended on the commission (and sometimes the witness). Each of the commissions had its own way of examining the events and attached different importance to, for instance, the recognition of the miraculous character of cures related to the sites (of central importance for the acceptance of Beauraing not for Banneux). Furthermore, the passage of time seems to have diminished the importance of some of the counterarguments. While the question of morality was critical for the first commission on Beauraing and the archdiocesan commission, the morality of the seers was judged more leniently in 1947.

It is clear that the final judgment for the two approved cases cannot be studied separately from one another. For both, the other site's success – especially when publicly announced – created pressure to take a similar step. Still, it is thereby important to keep in mind that the commissions worked independently from one another and the communication between them was not optimal. In 1947, Scheuer, for instance, ended the file he created about the Malines evaluation of Banneux with the following words:

> Officially, we know nothing about the commission of Malines. The last remnants of the opposition might abuse the universal ignorance to denigrate the honest work of the commission of Malines to the low level of the miserable verdict of the former commission of Liège.
>
> That is why I do not feel obliged to keep exclusively to myself the few facts that I alone possess, and that a witness "*omni exceptione maior*" has communicated to me as a defender of Banneux rather than as a friend.
>
> I deposit these confidential notes in the archives of Banneux, for any useful purpose, in the interest of Banneux, and for the honor of the commission of Malines.

In the pages he deposited he described how the fate of the Banneux apparitions would have been quite different if everything had depended on the Malines commission, whose members did not consider the supernatural character certain (1937). In his opinion, it would have meant the end of the devotion to Our Lady of the Poor. However, at this point providence had intervened: the Holy Office had taken over the investigation (1939). This had been just as unexpected as the restitution of the case to the hands of the bishop of Liège a few years later (1942).[214] Scheuer was well aware of the danger in a lack of transparency about the examinations, and in order to avoid any abuse of this silence, he consciously planted the file in the Banneux archives (1947). Three years after the official recognition of the Banneux apparitions (1949), he also drafted a note on the second commission of Banneux and explained why the bishop of Liège did not mention this commission in his *Études et documents* (1952).[215]

Scheuer's fear in 1950 about an abuse of silence was not so far-fetched as it may sound at a first reading. Taciturnity, rumours, and lack of transparency were a damaging mix – not just for the Banneux devotion, but for the Beauraing devotion as well. A year after the official recognition had been announced in a pastoral letter, the Belgian archbishop and the bishop of Namur made a joint statement about the relation between the Namur commission and the Malines commission. In a letter approved by Van Roey, Charue described how in fact the findings of both commissions had not differed that much. Given the phase that the investigations were in, the members of the Malines commission had only concluded that the supernatural character of the apparitions did not "constat"; but there had been no definitive rejection of the case. The Namur commission, in spite of its more favourable opinion of the events, had been just as hesitant in formulating a final opinion and stressed the importance of further investigations. In the following years, while the Malines commission suspended its activities, the Namur commission had continued its work, which resulted in the approval of the cult in 1943 and the recognition of the miraculous nature of two cures in 1949. The latter was also fundamental for the recognition of the reality of the apparitions. "Nothing in the stance of the commission of Malines excluded that outcome of the study of the case."[216] With this statement, the bishops responded to rumours that had been circulating due to the limited transparency about the examinations and commissions. Potential questions were also answered when one of the members of the diocesan commission, Canon Monin, published its files.[217] While his book included numerous copies of the letters and other source material studied by the commission on Beauraing, the author explicitly mentioned that he had left some of the material out, as it would be "pernicious to touch upon certain delicate points and risk recreating the excited atmosphere" of those first controversies. The commission believed that some details were not yet ready to be published.[218] What was known to some members of the clergy was not the same as what was proper for the "general public" to know. That was also the case for the Banneux apparitions, and when the bishop of Liège was contacted about a future publication in October 1949 he explicitly asked the author not to refer to the results of the second commission on Banneux.[219] The faithful, or more specifically the supporters of Beauraing and Banneux, believed they knew enough, as will be seen in the next chapters.

# 5

# Time

## The Aftermath of the Apparitions

In 1949, sixteen years after the apparitions of Beauraing and Banneux were reported, the bishops of Namur and Liège officially recognized their supernatural origin. The faithful had not waited so long to show their support. In fact, their unwavering enthusiasm for the apparitions and support of the new Marian cults were considered an argument in favour of the credibility of the apparitions. In October 1937, Abbé Jamin of Banneux noted how the continuing appeal of these sites showed how they had survived a first filtering: "The other foyers of the apparitions have seen their support drop, and now only Beauraing and Banneux remain as centers of prayers, graces and conversion. The cult has continued. The inevitable filtering has taken place. A human or diabolic fact does not have any resistance, after some time, fraud becomes apparent."[1]

Returning to the various apparition sites, we look at what remained of the initial enthusiasm after the series had ended. The following pages briefly summarize what happened during the long years before the official statement and examine the effect of the official approval and condemnation (of the cults and events). Did episcopal rejection mean the end of religious enthusiasm? Or did the faithful continue to publicly show their trust and invest in the site? In exploring these issues, we need to keep in mind that this was a national public series of apparitions: the development at one site could become the benchmark for another.

The evolution of the sites of apparitions and "apparitionettes"[2] – as the followup series was mockingly called – was, as might be expected, quite different. In an article on the vestiges of the Belgian apparitions,

Chris Maunder listed three possible outcomes for the sites: One was that when the apparitions gained approval, the sites would become an international place of pilgrimage (Beauraing and Banneux). Another was that even when the apparitions were not recognized by the church, devotees could still maintain the site (as at Onkerzele). The third was that after the rejection by the church, popular support died out and only vague remnants of the apparition past remained.[3] Maunder's differentiation certainly works from a present-day perspective but it is important to also point at the different paces and timing (before or after the approval or rejection) of development at the various sites. In exploring these cases we will be able to add a fourth scenario to Maunder's options that was not yet of relevance when his study appeared: the revival of an apparition site after decades of neglect. Let us first, however, direct our gaze at the approved sites.

## *Banneux*

In August 1934, a supporter of the Beauraing visionary Tilman Côme contacted the dean of Beauraing and complained that in comparison with Banneux, things were moving rather slowly in Beauraing. "All the supporters of Beauraing are indignant and incensed about the fact that Banneux, which took place after Beauraing, manages everything so well." They were counting on the dean to make sure that they could organise as soon as possible everything as it was done in Banneux.[4]

Banneux's development was indeed impressive and quick. Only six weeks after the last apparition, on 15 April 1933, the non-profit organization Pèlerinages de Banneux published its statutes in the official government gazette (*Staatsblad*). Several of its members had been trained in Lourdes in supervising pilgrimages and the goal of their new association was to monitor and shelter the pilgrims who came to Banneux. Changing its name to Caritas (in 1935), this group of laymen took on the task of building the chapel that the Virgin had asked for.[5] With the permission of the bishop, the chapel was built on the site of the first apparition and consecrated on 15 August 1933, the Assumption of Mary.[6] Given the fact that neither the cult nor the apparitions had been approved, the bishop's permission to build the chapel might appear unusual. However, as the Jesuit Creusen noted in his discussion of the bishop's 1933 guidelines: "If, in the aftermath of

Figure 5.1 Mariette Béco (with trowel) lays the foundational stone of the chapel in Banneux.

events of a non-suspected supernatural character, a cult develops that in all aspects conforms to the principles of faith and the practice of the Church, nothing hinders the ordinary from favoring the development." He added explicitly that this did "not entail an official declaration, or even an indirect one, of the supernatural character of the events that have provoked the outbreak of devotion."[7] The bishop of Liège also gave other indirect signs of approval such as an imprimatur for the Caritas periodical *Banneux Notre-Dame* and by joining the Union Internationale de Prière, a Banneux-centred prayer movement.[8]

The Banneux promoters were ambitious and wanted to turn the site into a shrine easily accessible for sick pilgrims. After all, the Virgin had announced "I come to relieve the sick. I come to relieve the suffering."[9] In December 1933 they bought the Castle of Fawes, only a kilometre away from the place of the apparitions and turned it into the Home de la Vierge des Pauvres where sick pilgrims could stay during their visit to Banneux.[10] In 1938–40, they added the Hospitalité.[11] In this care for the sick, the Lourdes shrine figured as an example, especially since the Banneux apparitions, similar to the Pyrenean ones, granted an important role to a local spring. As at Lourdes, in 1935 the Banneux

Figure 5.2 The chapel in Banneux and the Béco family home.

promoters installed baths in a small building near the spring. At the beginning, similar to Lourdes, patients were completely submerged in the "*baignoires*," but after a while patients only sprinkled or bathed the affected part after reciting (together with the nurse) an act of repentance.[12] Furthermore, Caritas also planned a medical bureau and a new series of baths near the new esplanade with taps where the pilgrims could obtain water. Its collaborators also circulated the spring water worldwide free of charge[13] and claimed that by 1937 they had already sent out 20,000 bottles.[14] The similarities between the development of the Banneux and the Lourdes shrines caught the attention of the commission of Liège. The question was explicitly addressed during extra sessions about the cult at Banneux held at the request of Malines in October 1937, subsequent to the conclusion of the Malines examinations. When asked whether the Caritas group did not tend to copy Lourdes and push the cult of Banneux in that direction, the dean of Sprimont answered that even though he believed that they benefitted from their experience in Lourdes (especially as far as the sick were concerned), he did not think that they "have gone beyond the events of Banneux in order to copy Lourdes."[15]

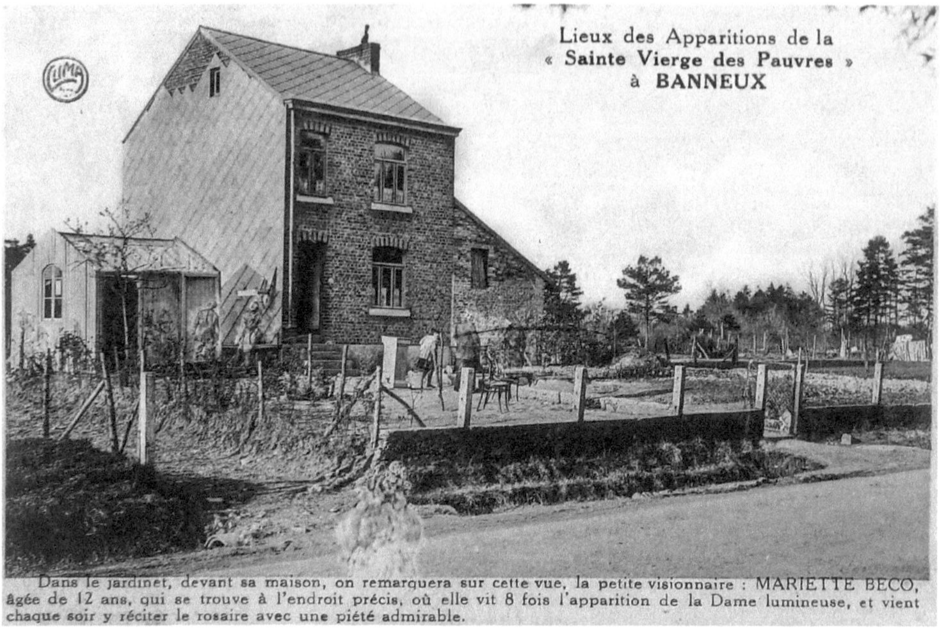


Figure 5.3 The little shed at the apparition site in Banneux.

While these were all lay initiatives, the clergy also came to help with the sick (among others, the Sisters of Charity from Gijzegem, the Annunciates from Heverlee, and the Franciscan Orantes of Maria Mediatrix). Nevertheless, when asked in October 1937 whether it was the laypersons or the clergy (and in particular Abbé Jamin) who had stimulated the growth of the cult of Banneux, the dean of Sprimont answered that the clergy had been reticent and it was primarily the work of the laity.[16] Abbé Jamin advised them on religious matters.[17] He saw it his duty to watch over the evolving cult and make sure it did not develop into bizarre and superstitious devotions, always a risk, so he believed, when laymen were left to their own devices.[18] The bishop knew about Jamin's involvement, for the chaplain had only started to attend the rosary at the apparition site in July 1933, after obtaining his permission. He was aware that his presence there created the impression of an approval and made the evening prayer a little more official.[19]

There are no statistics available on the number of pilgrims, but according to Jamin (in 1936), the number of pilgrims on summer days could be as high as 3,000. Pilgrims came from Wallonia, Flanders, and

Figure 5.4 The baths in Banneux.

from the neighbouring countries.[20] The site seems to have been particularly attractive to Belgian coal miners. Various groups, for instance from Waterschei and Liège, already came in pilgrimage in 1933, and often did so in their professional attire.[21]

So even though the material development of the site and the promotion of the cult started before there was an official recognition of the cult and the apparitions, devotees had indeed indirect indications that the episcopal authorities did not oppose the cult. Still, the official recognition remained high on the agenda of the supporters of the site, and they set up a visitor's book for those who visited Banneux and were eager for its official recognition. The signatures included devotees from Bulgaria, Italy, Rumania, Palestine, France, the Netherlands, and more.[22] Even the war with its concomitant difficulties in transport and the prohibitions did not temper the enthusiasm. When the official recognition of the cult (19 March 1942) was celebrated on 31 May, about 13,000 pilgrims were said have attended.[23]

As we have seen, the material development in Banneux conformed to "known" and approved apparition sites like Lourdes. All stayed within the limits of what was acceptable. For the Beauraing shrine, however, the situation was quite the reverse; almost nothing "grand" was created at the site before official approval of the cult and the apparitions.

## *Beauraing*

> In 1943, more than ten years after the apparitions of Our Lady, the courtyard was still in the same state as in 1933, a few lines of benches were placed there and that was all![24]
>
> Aurélien Pierroux

Aurélien Pierroux, secretary of the Beauraing committee Pro Maria reflected, years after the apparitions, on the evolution of the shrine in the period between the initial events and the recognition of the cult of Our Lady of Beauraing. Compared to Banneux, nothing much seems to have happened. Still, Pierroux noted, even though Beauraing did not have marble statues, one could not say that it was dead: You could feel the divine presence during the rosary.

Pierroux was a prime witness for he was the secretary of the Pro Maria committee, the lay association that took charge of the organization of the Beauraing pilgrimage and the development of the shrine. The group was not the immediate outcome of the lay interest in the apparitions of the child visionaries of winter 1932–33. The first initiatives of this committee can be traced back to the pilgrimage requested by Tilman Côme, a visionary later rejected. Pro Maria was created prior to 5 August 1933, when thousands of pilgrims were expected in Beauraing for the scheduled apparitions of Côme. The members of the committee (at the time known as Familia) wanted to be ready to receive and accommodate the masses. At first it was an improvised measure, but the laymen involved realized that a more permanent organization was needed. A few days later, they decided to take care of all matters concerning the Lourdes imitation grotto where the initial apparitions were said to have taken place, answer the numerous letters, organize pilgrimages, and build a chapel.[25] They received Mgr Heylen's permission for the association on 16 August. While it was a lay organization, its members had clerical guidance, and Dean Lambert of Beauraing became the honorary president. Another organization, the Association of Saint Martin (l'Association Saint Martin) developed that year as well. Consisting primarily of members of the clergy, this interparochial group was responsible for the organization and financial management of the shrine and was under direct control of the bishop. It delegated several tasks to Pro Maria, such as the organization of pilgrimages, the distribution of stretchers, the distribution of leaves from the apparition tree, and the publication of *La Voix de Beauraing*.[26]

As in Banneux, one of the first points of attention was the construction of a chapel requested by the Virgin during her apparition on 17 December 1932. All seemed set for a swift realization of that plan: The bishop of Namur had permitted its creation when he visited Beauraing on the occasion of the confirmation of the local youth in June 1933, and the funds were available since they had received the a donation of 2,500,000 francs from the winner of the colonial lottery in July 1933. However, once the diocese adopted a more cautious stance in October 1933, it postponed the chapel construction, though it continued to permit public services for pilgrims.[27] Even after the recognition of the cult of Beauraing in February 1943, it took several years before the chapel was completed. Delayed by the war, the first stone was laid in 1947 and the chapel was consecrated on 21–22 August 1954.[28] After the recognition of the cult, the boarding school of the Sisters of the Christian Doctrine, on whose grounds the apparition had taken place, was moved to a new location, and the school building was converted into a shelter for the sick.[29] There had been dreams of a basilica from the start in 1933, and land was purchased for that purpose, but, as in Banneux, these plans were eventually abandoned.[30]

The development of the Beauraing shrine only really started after the recognition of the cult of Our Lady with the Golden Heart. In 1946 the committee managed to buy the ruins and domains of a castle in the neighbourhood (later named Castle Sainte-Marie) where they could organize religious retreats and set up a way of the cross. In that same year, on 22 August, an official statue by Aurélien Pierroux was installed at the site of the apparitions. Prior to that, wooden panels with an image of the Virgin had marked the exact spot.[31]

While the material development of the site was somewhat slower, that does not mean religious activity there was minimal. The devotees from Belgium and abroad[32] showed their trust in Beauraing's Virgin by flocking to the garden and praying the rosary together with the child visionaries every evening at 6:30 p.m. In late June 1933, Mgr Heylen

Figure 5.5 The statue at the apparition site in Beauraing.

gave permission to the dean of Beauraing, Abbé Lambert, to be present at these prayers, and on 26 June the bishop himself attended. Mass could only be celebrated in the parish church, but sometimes – on days when a high number of pilgrims was expected – the bishop made an exception and permitted an open-air mass in the garden.[33] B. Delvaux, who studied the pilgrims in 1981, was quite critical about the value of the numbers preserved, but still believed they allowed some broad generalizations.[34] During the apparitions (November 1932 to January 1933), both curious and faithful found their way to Beauraing. The rest of that winter there were fewer people, with about 200–300 attending the rosary every evening. Even though there was a massive increase in August 1933, due to Tilman Côme's apparitions,[35] the numbers dropped in the following years.[36] People were losing interest, especially since the apparitions were not recognized and no ceremonies were allowed at the site. Things changed when Pro Maria, with the authorization of Mgr Heylen, organized pilgrimages to pray for world peace in 1939 and 1941.[37] It was only a brief revival, similar as the one linked to the solemn inauguration of the cult of Our Lady with the Golden Heart by the bishop (16 May 1943) that was attended by about 15,000–20,000 people. By 1944–45 the number of pilgrim groups was almost reduced to zero because of the wartime difficulties of communications and insecurity. After the war, things took a turn for the better. The numbers increased again in 1946, especially once the cult was recognized and grand ceremonies were allowed. The shrine continued to be upgraded, with inauguration of the Marian domain on 22 August 1946 and start of the construction of the chapel in 1947. In 1949, the year of the recognition of the supernatural character of the apparitions, a record number of pilgrim groups travelled to Beauraing.[38]

The pilgrims could stay in the Beauraing neighbourhood in one of the hotels carrying names such as Hotel of Our Lady of Beauraing, Hotel of the Hawthorn, or Hotel of the Grotto. They could purchase small religious items that were already for sale at the site in the 1930s or procure a small piece of the apparition tree, perceived as a "relic" by some and imbued with the powers often attributed to relics. These were free of charge and could be obtained from the Pro Maria committee and the Sisters of the Christian Doctrine.[39] After the inauguration of the official statue in August 1946, small replicas of that image were available as well.[40]

For Beauraing, the development of the Banneux apparition site was an important point of reference and stimulus. Shortly after the cult of Banneux was officially approved on 19 March 1942, Pro Maria engaged in a prayer campaign answering the call for prayers launched by Mgr Charue on 15 April.[41] There was a massive response. As letters in the Beauraing shrine archives indicate, there was much bewilderment over the fact that Banneux was approved before Beauraing.[42] Their efforts paid off and on hearing the news in late January 1943 that Beauraing was going to be recognized as well, the relief was immense: "What we felt was indescribable; an immense joy mixed with amazement; it was like a bright and unexpected sunshine dispelling the mists of the night; it was triumph after darkness, work and struggle. It was finally the possibility of proclaiming everywhere, without fear or constraint, our love and veneration for the Lady of our home."[43]

Summarizing the evolution of the two sites that were eventually approved, we can note a difference in their development. For Banneux, the importance of the official recognition was minimal; for Beauraing official recognitions were more important. Yet, it was not only the approval of the cult and apparitions of the Beauraing site, but also those of the neighbouring (and subsequent) apparition site at Banneux that stimulated the development at the Beauraing site.

## The "Apparitionettes"

In Beauraing and Banneux the events were eventually approved and the supporters of the sites were rewarded for their patience and fervour. What happened at the sites that were publicly rejected or ignored by the bishops? Did the official stance count for as much (or little) as it did in the cases of the two approved sites? Most of the sites reported during the wave of apparitions had soon ceased drawing public attention. The site in Etikhove, for instance, was abandoned a few months after the apparitions were reported there, and an article in the liberal newspaper *Het Laatste Nieuws* of March 1934 featured a photograph of the deserted site with empty benches and a neglected statue of the Virgin.[44] Likewise in June 1939, the parish priest of Onkerzele reported how one of the initiatives of the itinerant visionary Jules De Vuyst, a home for children, was now an empty building with three nurses and no children, except on the "grand days" of the visionaries when, according to the priest, it became the "foyer" of those opposed by the church – "much to the annoyance of the rural population, thank God still deeply Christian, who realised in time that only in loyalty to the church lies the path towards salvation and spiritual welfare."[45]

The public rejection by Cardinal Van Roey in March 1942 changed nothing and only confirmed what time had already demonstrated: these sites were not worthy of the devotees' attention. While some of the promoters of sites like Lokeren and Olsene continued to plead their case until the 1940s and even into the 1950s, they seemed to have gained almost no support and remained isolated voices.[46] The small chapel constructed in Olsene was an anomaly.[47] The Onkerzele apparitions, the Beauraing visionary Tilman Côme, and the apparitions in Ham-sur-Sambre are three major exceptions to this scenario of diminishing popular support. In the following pages the focus is on Onkerzele and Ham-sur-Sambre, two sites whose continuing popularity eventually triggered an episcopal response. In Onkerzele, enthusiasm centred on Leonie Van den Dijck, the first visionary reported at the site, and not on the visionaries of the second series (Berthonia Holtkamp and Henri Kempenaers). As noted, the latter were publicly rejected already in August 1934 and, apart from a small crowd of followers, attracted scant attention. The case of Leonie Van den Dijck, however, is quite different.

## *Onkerzele*

On 25 March 1942, the archbishop had published a statement that "the events of Onkerzele and Lokeren-Naastveld lacked all supernatural character," a formulation that left no doubt about the rejection of the case. Still, even today, years after her death in 1949, there exists a committee pleading Leonie "Nieke" Van den Dijck's case. The Komiteit voor de zaak Leonie Van den Dijck organizes pilgrimages and even runs a museum in her honour.[48] Moreover, every first Saturday of the month, pilgrims "from all over Flanders and the Netherlands" (in the words of the komiteit) meet in the parish church to pray, sing, and visit the place of the apparitions (a chapel near an imitation Lourdes grotto), the seven chapels of Our Lady of the Seven Sorrows (closely connected to the apparitions), and Leonie Van den Dijck's grave. A special celebration is held on 15 September, the feast of Our Lady of Sorrows.[49]

It is difficult to know how the enthusiasm for Van den Dijck, whose apparitions had been discarded, continued. Most information that we have on the period after the public renunciation of the apparitions comes from a hagiographic account written in 1953 and published in 1987 by one of Van den Dijck's fervent supporters, Gustaaf Schellinck.[50] Schellinck never witnessed the initial apparitions (which ended on 31 October 1933), but met the visionary when she had already entered what has been called her "second era." This phase ran from the start of 1934 until May 1940, and was a period of greater seclusion in comparison with her public apparitions in the first phase.[51] According to Schellinck, Van den Dijck remained rather popular at the beginning of this period because of her alleged predictions of the deaths of King Albert and Queen Astrid. Still, these stories also lost her some credit among her supporters. Louis Wilmet, author of *Beauraing, Banneux, Onkerzele,* wrote to his fellow enthusiast Princess de Croÿ that all kinds of stories were circulating, so "Nieke" was probably just inventing them. The fact that she made her predictions only public retroactively gave them – to say the least – a suspect character.[52] Van den Dijck's popularity gradually faltered and the number of visitors diminished to about fifty regular ones by May 1940.[53]

It did not help her cause when Van den Dijck also got caught up in the promotion of the devotion to the Sacred Head of Jesus.[54] As noted in the discussion about Berthonia/Veronica Holtkamp, this devotion was rejected by the ecclesiastical authorities in June 1938.[55] The faithful were warned at a more local level as well. The parish priest Duerinck of Onkerzele informed followers who contacted him that the documents for Van den Dijck's case were still in the rectory in Onkerzele, since Rome had never requested additional information. He thought it unlikely that Van den Dijck's case would ever be approved, since the authorities had not needed much time to decide that she was not to be taken seriously.[56] Hanging the official documents on the door of his church (though they were twice removed) was an effective strategy. Many of those who came to Onkerzele in good faith and were invited by the pilgrimage committee never returned. Still, the priest continued to receive anonymous cards and letters with insults directed at the diocesan authorities and himself. The most fervent Onkerzele promoters did not want to listen. While Duerinck could prevent them from entering his church on the days that they called "special," he could not forbid their activities near the chapel and grotto, as it was public land.[57]

The definitive rejection of Onkerzele followed, as noted, in March 1942. Van den Dijck's supporters were, of course, not unaware of the disapproval. In August 1943, Angeline G. wrote to the parish priest of Onkerzele and asked him what she should do. She had been disappointed on reading in the Hoogstraten newspaper that "Onkerzele lacked all supernatural character," but she had now received word from Van den Dijck that the seven chapels were going to be re-installed just like the Virgin requested. Angeline thus asked the priest if she was allowed to spread the devotion to Our Lady of Onkerzele and lend out books on that topic. She also wanted to know whether the rose leaves she had received from Mr Schellinck and in which she now spotted the child Jesus, a Sacred Heart, and Our Lady were, indeed, a gift from Van den Dijck and whether she was allowed to venerate them?[58]

The phenomena that were linked to Van den Dijck had indeed become more diverse than "apparitions" and, apart from the "magical" rose leaves, her supporters claimed that some of her tears had turned into pearls and that she could communicate with foreign stigmatics without ever leaving her house. Since Good Friday 1940 she also claimed to experience Christ's passion (the start of a "third era" in her life, 1940–43). Schellinck, her loyal secretary, reported that she bore the stigmata since September 1940.[59] Increasingly secluded, she became less and less mobile, and the few friends who tried to visit her were often sent away.[60]

Nevertheless, even after her death in 1949 her supporters pleaded her cause.[61] The Onkerzele committee even exhumed her body in June 1972. Since her remains displayed no signs of decay (as the visionary allegedly had predicted[62]), her followers saw it as another confirmation of Van den Dijck's exceptional status. The open mouth of her corpse was interpreted as her giving last warnings to mankind and inciting the people to do penance.[63] This action, and the media attention that went with it, led to a diocesan circular reminding the faithful of the decision of Cardinal Van Roey on 25 March 1942, that the events in Onkerzele lacked all supernatural character. They were unaware of "any reason that would lead us to deviate from this standpoint."[64]

The evolution of Onkerzele is thus quite different from that of Beauraing and Banneux. Whereas in the latter two locations the emphasis was on the apparitions and the sites of the events and less on the special status of the visionaries, in Onkerzele the focus was on the visionary. More than a "sacralization" of the site, Leonie Van den Dijck's story is about the sanctification of a (living) person. Even while she was still alive, Van den Dijck was asked to pray for the benefit of others and allegedly often did so successfully. Moreover, her personal belongings were collected as relics.[65] Schellinck's semi-hagiography of Van den Dijck is a textbook example of selection processes traced also at other apparition sites. There were only minimal references to the other Onkerzele visionaries in the final version,[66] and it was subject to significant revision, as with the predictions about the Belgian royalty that failed to come true, excised from later versions.[67] This selective memory might have something to do with the local committee's endeavours to obtain ecclesiastical approval of their veneration of Leonie Van den Dijck.

Still, we should pause for a moment and wonder why Onkerzele, where so many visionaries independently of one another claimed to see the Virgin and many claimed to have been cured, did not develop into a shrine centred on the apparition events as Beauraing and Banneux did. Is it because the site already had religious meaning as it consisted of a small chapel and a Lourdes grotto and there was no need for an apparition-loaded sacralization of the site? The only material changes at Onkerzele that can be linked to the apparition series are an improvement of the steps leading up to the chapel and the re-installation of the seven small chapels in honour of Our Lady's Seven Sorrows. While these chapels predated Leonie Van den Dijck's visions, their reinstallation was inspired by her messages. Only one chapel still existed when Van den Dijck's apparitions commenced, and the Virgin allegedly asked for a new series of seven. Since these chapels were in honour of a devotion that had been approved by the church, and the procession had received episcopal permission in the seventeenth century, the parish priest of Onkerzele saw no reason why the pilgrims' money should not be invested in this undertaking. The first three chapels were reinstalled during the Second World War.[68]

Leonie Van den Dijck's "cult" and the seven chapels of Our Lady of Sorrows that she pleaded for were eventually combined. On the first Saturdays of the month and 15 September her followers walk from one chapel to the next and end at Van den Dijck's grave, which is decorated

Figure 5.6 Chapel and grotto in Onkerzele.

with an image of Our Lady of Sorrows. A mix of approved and non-approved religious practices is apparent also in their information folders, which display a picture of Van den Dijck's preserved corpse and an announcement of a procession in honour of Our Lady of Seven Sorrows (explicitly mentioning the bishop's approval).[69]

### *Ham-sur-Sambre*

The apparitions at Ham-sur-Sambre took a slightly different course. The apparitions started in March 1936, hence after the episcopal commissions had been installed, and their examination followed a time path different from that of the rest of the Belgian series. Furthermore, while the apparition site in Ham-sur-Sambre, like Onkerzele, still draws followers today, the Walloon site was abandoned for decades and only recently started to appeal to pilgrims again. Nonetheless, in comparison with other rejected Belgian locations, in the first twenty years after the apparitions, the site flourished because the stubbornness and disobedience of the visionaries and promoters was far more outspoken than at other sites.

Ham-sur-Sambre has been repeatedly condemned by the episcopal authorities in Belgium and France. These rejections did not stop a group of supporters of believing in, and promoting, the apparitions near the tunnel. There were two groups of followers, one for each visionary. The first group, Virgo Virginum,[70] supported the original visionary, Emelda Scohy in Ham-sur-Sambre; the second one developed around Adeline Pietquin and her satellite apparition site in French Bouxières. Both in France and Belgium, the bishop tried (in vain) to stop the enthusiasm.

The apparition series in Ham-sur-Sambre continued for years and was problematic for several reasons: Emelda Scohy and her friends dressed as Mary and other saints, Adeline Pietquin's messages were tied up with the reconstruction of the Bourbon monarchy, and the followers of both visionaries willfully disobeyed their bishops.[71] After Mgr Heylen had been informed that a chapel and statue had been installed at the apparition site, he decided to make a public statement. He warned the clergy and faithful on 11 March 1938 that nothing indicated that anything supernatural had happened in Ham-sur-Sambre. The priests were advised not to go to the apparition site, not to participate in the organization of a pilgrimage to the "Poor Tunnel," and to ask the faithful to abstain as well.[72] The condemnation did not generate the desired effect, and the bishop had to repeat it two years later.[73]

The apparitions in Ham-sur-Sambre were not only a thorn in the side of Mgr Heylen. The archbishop of Malines on March also rejected them on 25 March 1942.[74] Mgr Charue, the successor of Mgr Heylen, likewise took a firm stance against them. On 25 April 1943, he declared that "the alleged messages and revelations form a sacrilegious profanation" and that "[t]hose who are known to be the organizers, if they persist in their harmful attitude, must be considered as revolting against the Church and cannot have access to the sacraments."[75] The faithful should better invest their fervor in the devotion to the Virgin and in other religious practices approved by the church.[76] While Emelda Scohy seems to have repented as a response to this statement and even signed a formal submission, she quickly resumed her ways.[77]

Why did the episcopal condemnations fail to have an impact on these movements? While we should be wary of making generalizations, looking at the attitude and opinions of one of them can help us see the promoters' side of the story. We are well informed about the opinion of Vital Brachot, one of the main promoters of the cult, since Abbé Edmond Phillippart, curé-doyen at Gosselies, elaborately reported about it to his bishop, Mgr Rasneur, in Tournai. Vital Brachot, so the curé wrote, believed he was living in some sort of "theocracy" with Jesus the Good Shepherd and the Virgin of Virgins at the top together. These divine figures made the decisions and communicated them by Emelda Scohy. The bishop was, however, not elected by the Holy Spirit, but through intervention of the archbishop, king, and the chapter.[78] So, whatever judgment or decision the bishop made about the apparitions, it always had a "human" element. Consequently, whenever Vital Brachot believed the bishop's decisions to be in contradiction with the will of Jesus or the Virgin, he preferred to obey them instead.[79] His behaviour had repercussions however and he was excluded from the holy communion. While this was painful for Brachot, he stressed this exclusion was not going to change his mind: "I have indeed received three affronts in three different churches, and I am now somewhat steeled, as I have been prepared for a long time and by personal experience. It is not that which will weaken my resistance."[80]

The Ham-sur-Sambre visions were also condemned in France. This had to do with a satellite apparition site. The second visionary, Adeline

Pietquin, frequently visited French Bouxières-aux-Dames and even stayed there for more than a year during the war.[81] Her host, the parish priest Lucien Césard,[82] began informing his parishioners about her visions and celestial messages in 1938, a year after her arrival.[83] When the bishop of Nancy and Toul, Mgr Fleury, asked him to stop announcing these, Césard circulated the messages in private. The start of the war and the death of two of his collaborators put a temporary stop to this circulation, but the distribution restarted in 1941. The texts were a mixture of a call for prayers and penitence, apocalyptic prophecies, and the repeated call for the construction of chapel similar to the one of Our Lady of the Poor Tunnel in Ham-sur-Sambre. In spite of the bishop's prohibition, a chapel was created in 1942.[84]

As in the other "branch" of the Ham-sur-Sambre movement, the decisions of the episcopal authorities did not seem to have had much effect. Abbé Césard's attitude was similar to that of Vital Brachot. Like Brachot, he believed he was obeying a greater power than the bishop as he was following the orders of the Holy Virgin.[85] On 21 September 1943 the bishop declared that all priests who participated in the pious exercises that Abbé Lucien Césard organized would be punished with the *suspens a divinis* that prohibited them from celebrating mass and administering the sacraments.[86]

The condemnation seems to have had little effect on the enthusiasm of Césard and his followers. So in October 1946, Mgr Fleury went one step further. In a letter to the parishioners of Bouxières-aux-Dames he explained how Abbé Césard had repeatedly disobeyed formal orders and therefore had been removed. Since Césard had refused to leave, the bishop had to impose the "suspense."[87] Abbé Césard sought the support from the Holy Office but was ordered to submit to the authority of his bishop.[88]

As Césard still did not show any signs of departing, Mgr Fleury announced on 20 July 1947, that "conform the decrees of the Holy See and in particular the Code of Canonic Law (canons 1326 and 1399)" Abbé Césard had been forbidden "any manifestation related to those messages or events of Bouxières, as these concern private revelations that have not been approved by the Church."[89] He reminded everyone that every priest who participated in a collective pious manifestation there would be subjected to the suspens a divinis and that the faithful who did so would not be allowed to receive the eucharist.[90] A few months later little had changed. Césard was still planning pilgrimages to Ham-sur-Sambre.[91] Eventually, the police intervened: On 25 June 1948 they stormed the building and removed Césard and his followers.[92] Abbé Césard went to live with his family and only submitted to his bishop in 1950.[93]

Abbé Césard's downfall does not seem to have ended the apparition movement surrounding Adeline Pietquin. In August 1948, mere months after the police stormed the presbytery, two prominent members of the network travelled to Rome to have a private audience with the pope and seek his approval of the Ham-sur-Sambre apparitions. The same pair discussed Pietquin's apparitions with the bishop of Namur in December 1950. They tried to convince him that the seer had ruptured the ties with Abbé Césard and promised to Abbé Brigou, the curé of Ham-sur-Sambre, to abstain from all propaganda relating to her apparitions. The bishop responded that as long as Adeline Pietquin indeed obeyed the rules, she no longer fit the description of 25 May 1946 and was allowed access to the sacraments again.[94]

Imagine the parishioners in Ham-sur-Sambre. After years of turmoil and discussions they saw Adeline Pietquin receiving the communion again, yet they did not get more information about the changing circumstances that allowed the problematic visionary access.[95] The diocese therefore had to send an explanation informing the parishioners that since the members of one of the apparition groups had given assurances that they would abstain from all propaganda, they no longer had to be subjected to the exclusion from the sacraments. "In fact," so the message emphasized, "the authority has not changed its original position in any way, but acknowledges the change of attitude which has occurred in the members of one of the two groups."[96]

Once again, however, the promises made were not made to be kept. The curé reported in May 1952 that Pietquin continued to receive many foreign visitors.[97] The situation deteriorated and on 20 August 1954 the parish priest of Ham-sur-Sambre warned the bishop of Namur that the pilgrimages to the apparition site could involve "a thousand people." The propaganda had intensified beyond Ham-sur-Sambre in the last two years, especially through the activities of Vital Brachot from Thuin who circulated translations of the messages in Flanders.[98]

Emelda Scohy once more seemed to make her peace with the diocese in April 1958 when she wanted to get married and have a Catholic service. It was, however, a repetition of the previous scenario: While she formally submitted to the diocesan guidelines,[99] she continued to receive visitors, made prophecies, handed out tokens that were to protect people from misfortune, and accepted money. She does, however, seem to have stayed away from the apparition site.[100] She appears to have spread her dire prophecies primarily in Germany.[101] On 26 September 1958, the bishop of Namur therefore announced anew that none of the condemnations (of 1938, 1942, 1943, and 1946) had ever been revoked so those spreading the message of Ham-sur-Sambre or staging religious ceremonies at the apparition site, "should be considered in rebellion against the Church and should not be admitted to the Blessed Sacrament."[102]

Still, in spite of the stubbornness of the visionaries and their devotees, the enthusiasm did diminish, and in the 1960s the two visionaries no longer had revelations and disappeared from public view.[103] It was not the end of the affair however. While the apparition site lay abandoned for decades and vegetation reconquered the domain,[104] a new initiative to clean the site started in 2018. The group taking care of the site seems to be the present-day version of the Confrérie Virgo Virginum that dissolved in 1958. Also known as Confrérie des soldats de Jésus Bon Pasteur et enfants de la Vierge des Vierges, the confraternity has a private status, not a canonical one. On their website, the confraternity members explain why they invested in cleaning up the site: "This place is part of the local history! The apparitions that took place here (they are not recognized by the ecclesiastical authorities, the domain – private – cannot therefore be considered as a work of the Catholic Church) are in the past, but nevertheless belong to the history of the place. One either believes in it or not: it is up to one's conscience."[105]

In sum, Ham-sur-Sambre was publicly rejected early on and the bishops involved held the same opinion. Still in spite of this unanimity, with the bishops supporting each other's decisions and referring to them in their own statements, the members of the apparition movements persisted in their disobedience as they thought Mary's and Jesus' authority to be higher than the bishop's.

## Time Will Tell?

As this short overview of the evolution of the apparition sites and devotions has shown, looking at the chronology of the development can provide important new insights about the impact of the public approval or rejection of the sites and devotions. However, as the case of Banneux makes abundantly clear, while the official approval was a moment the devotees longed for, the faithful did not pin the bishop's approval down to that one solemn occasion. His allowing the building of a chapel and the creation of site-specific devotional cards were read as indications of what his judgment would be. Still, the Banneux scenario was not the only option. We have seen a more cautious stance in Beauraing, where the material development was more limited in comparison with Banneux, and in Onkerzele, where the money raised by the devotees was invested in approved devotions: the statue of the Lourdes grotto was replaced and the chapels in honour of Our Lady of Sorrows were reinstalled.

Moreover, the official rejection by the bishops did not always have the effect we would expect it to have. In Ham-sur-Sambre the supporters of the two visionaries believed they took their orders directly from divine beings such as the Virgin Mary and preferred to obey her and not their bishops. They thus continued to support the visionary and promoted the devotion as they had done before the rejection. Nonetheless, such an official condemnation did have an effect on the other faithful, on those who were not involved in the apparition movements. They could see their fellow parishioners excluded from going to communion and hence also from their Catholic community.

For some of the disobedient faithful, like those of Ham-sur-Sambre or Onkerzele, time was a means to an end. Negative memories could fade and they could show their true dedication to the cause. They believed that if they waited long enough, the "truth" about the apparitions would eventually come out. In the case of the Onkerzele supporters, their moment came when the visionary Leonie Van den Dijck was publicly exhumed in June 1972. With the press and numerous people present, the Onkerzele supporters unearthed what they believed to be an incorrupt body. Using this as "proof" of the authenticity of the deceased visionary, the supporters rekindled the religious enthusiasm for Leonie Van den Dijck, forcing the diocesan authorities to intervene and remind the faithful of the rejection of the apparitions by Cardinal Van Roey on 25 March 1942.[106] In Ham-sur-Sambre, time seems to have erased some of the negative connotations of the apparition site. After years of abandonment, the site is once again the location of religious fervour.

Finally, the passing of time also had a filter effect, erasing some sites added to the credibility of others. Less credible apparitions were segregated from the cause the faithful wanted to promote. In Beauraing, supporters of the site emphasized in *La Voix de Beauraing* the difference between the initial two cases, Beauraing and Banneux, and the "cycle" of apparitions following them. In 1935, they noted that while time had drawn the curtain over certain sites, the continuity of such "troubling" and "strange" events had an effect on the perception of the initial sites as well. Some people rejected all sites, and others seemed to accept every case without any distinction.[107] It was, however, not the first time such exuberant sequels had followed an initial, sober event. The same had happened in Lourdes where frightening things had been reported in the aftermath of Bernadette Soubirous' visions.[108] So while such an exuberant aftermath was certainly not a novelty, and in fact added to the credibility of the original Beauraing apparitions as it allowed comparison with Lourdes, it was important to filter and differentiate. Beauraing and Banneux were the ones that had survived the test of time and became a point of reference.[109]

# Conclusion

## On Silence and Public Attention

In January 2009, various newspapers and internet sites reported that Pope Benedict XVI had asked the Congregation (now Dicastery) for the Doctrine of Faith to compose a new vademecum for Marian apparitions. The planned guidelines sounded similar to what we have seen in the previous chapters and referred to examining the mental health of the visionary, investigating whether they had benefitted economically from the apparition claims, and if the messages conformed with the gospel and the doctrine of the church. However, one of the new rules did sound completely new: The faithful were to be asked to not seek public attention for their apparitions until they had been examined by a diocesan commission of psychiatrists, psychologists, theologians, and educators. A visionary craving attention, so the articles noted, was an indication that something was amiss. "Therefore," so the Italian Petrus-site summarized, "one who will not remain silent but causes the news of these alleged apparitions to circulate freely, attracting around themselves the presence of the curious, journalists and the faithful in search of a particular grace will have already given a sign that shows the falseness of their mysticism."[1] Newspapers headlined: "Catholics ordered to keep quiet over Virgin visions" and "Who sees Mary, needs to keep the vision a secret."[2]

This new vademecum and its rule on the visionary's silence never materialized. In fact, they were never even on the agenda of the congregation. After a few days of commotion, one of the websites that had covered the initial story informed its readers that an anonymous member of the Congregation for the Doctrine of Faith denied that he and his colleagues were working on new guidelines.[3] So why mention this here? Given our discussions in the previous chapters, it is intriguing that remaining silent about one's visionary experience and not drawing too much attention became the main takeaway of the 2009 imaginary new set of rules. Its prominent place in the news coverage suggests that the public attention that Marian apparitions had been attracting was not unproblematic.

The new rules that the Dicastery of Faith did promulgate in May 2024 confirm this preoccupation with public attention and the effect media coverage has on religious enthusiasm.[4] As we have seen in the previous chapters, this is not a new feature. The Belgian wave of apparitions of the 1930s was public and well covered in the press. Moreover, just like the phenomena described in the 2024 document, the religious fervour triggered by the events surpassed the boundaries of a single diocese.[5]

Throughout the chapters we have seen various attempts to control this religious enthusiasm. At the same time, however, some of the bishops pleaded against a complete suppression and argued for the cultivation of an orderly enthusiasm that could function as a pro argument in the discussions on the credibility of (some of) the apparitions. Spiritual fruits of the events, like conversions (and other graces), according to the bishops of Namur and Liège, had to be weighed in the evaluation process. They therefore protested vehemently against the Holy Office's decision to forbid the pilgrimages and publications. Other authorities, like the qualificatore to the Holy Office Giovanni Battista Frey and the members of the second commission of Liège thought of religious fervour as an inferior phenomenon or not as an argument in favour of the truth of the apparitions. The massive interest that the reports on the apparitions inspired and the thousands of faithful and curious travelling to the sites created unease. Almost from the onset, the diocesan authorities tried to contain the enthusiasm by controlling the press coverage and other publications in a directive of 20 October 1933. This initiative seems have had hardly any effect, and Nuncio Micara indicated in his report to the Holy Office in December 1934 that the guidelines had largely remained "lettera morta."[6] Interestingly, in that same public statement of October 1933, the Belgian bishops stressed that it was up to the ecclesiastical authority to judge these matters, not to the public opinion.[7]

Public apparitions called for public action. However, as the previous chapters have shown, we should not limit the effect of this setting and reception of the events on the evaluation as merely the public warnings and the announcement of the results of the evaluations. If we are to take the modern format of this apparition series seriously, we need to include at least two other consequences of their public character: a first reception layer of lay discernment of the events and the effects the public setting had also on the more formal investigations by medical experts and ecclesiastical authorities. It is somewhat surprising that this public element has not drawn much attention yet since the cautious words of the Belgian bishops in October 1933 clearly indicate that they were already struggling with some of the issues that inspired the new approach of 2024. The members of the Namur commission, for instance, thought it impossible that the publications and polemics did not influence the witnesses they called to the stand. Likewise, when Mgr Kerkhofs made the decision to save Banneux he was well aware that he was going against the established procedure. He, however, feared the impact of the rumours of the rejection and felt the pressure of the pending public approval of Beauraing.

Furthermore, the evaluation of the Belgian wave of apparitions did not start with the official examinations by the diocesan commissions behind closed doors. Medical experts, the clergy, journalists, and laymen had been commenting on the series and showing rejection or approval long before the first sessions of the commissions took place. These initial responses, often quite public, affected also the official examination. Could a bishop be entrusted with presiding the committee if he had already shown his approval by allowing the construction of a chapel, the installation of ex-votos, the publication of booklets and devotional cards, and had kneeled at the apparition site? Were members of the clergy or medical experts who had spoken up at meetings and published their opinions in newspapers the right ones to engage in the examination? As we have seen in the previous chapters, these questions were all raised during the official examinations.

Acknowledging the public character of the events and studying also the lay discernment processes allowed us to compare and reflect on the different knowledge systems at play in the evaluation of alleged supernatural events in modern Catholicism.[8] Rather than addressing the different settings of the evaluations separately and focusing solely on one of them (for instance, the reception of the devotees as Apolito did so effectively, or at the diocesan level like Joachim Bouflet[9]), I adopted an integrated approach and studied them together.

This allowed me to show that the evaluation – and filtering out – worked by different decision-making processes and epistemologies. Expanding our scope has offered a more complex image than that of the formal decision imposed on the rest of the faithful. Lay Catholics were well informed through press coverage and site visits (allowing them to experience for themselves) and compared their own findings to what they had heard about other apparitions. Furthermore, as we have seen in the chapter on medical expertise, the devotees could be quite critical about what type of knowledge, and what level of expertise, had to be called upon in the evaluation. While the need for a medical examination was never questioned, the general public did voice criticism of the doctors' competence and comportment, as did their colleagues. Moreover, hearing the bishop's public condemnation of an apparition did not necessarily change the devotees' minds. In the opinion of some of the apparition supporters, obeying the Virgin and God was more important than listening to their bishop. The bishops seemed to have been well aware that their words only had limited effect. Worrying about the "terrible impression" phenomena like exaltation and insensitivity made on "simple people" the bishop of Ghent – as we have seen – initially hesitated to intervene at the Onkerzele site for fear that he would not be obeyed.[10] For the lay Catholics, hierarchy did not necessarily trump eye-witnessing.

So did the difference in opinion between the devotees and ecclesiastical authorities mirror a difference in criteria? As noted, there were no fixed rules for discernment in interwar Belgium. The (then named) Congregation for the Doctrine of Faith only issued the *Norms Regarding the Manner of Proceeding in the Discernment of Presumed Apparitions and Revelations* in 1978 and had them translated and made public in 2011. However, some promoters, like Louis Wilmet, did seem to know about the criteria Pope Benedict XIV formulated in 1744. These criteria related to the behaviour of the visionary, miracles, and the persistence of popular enthusiasm. Other devotees did not refer to these formal criteria, but compared what they heard or saw at the apparition sites to what they knew about famous (international) sites like Lourdes and Ezquioga. Their testimonies inform us that they likewise paid much attention to the character and behaviour of the visionary and were keen on hearing about miraculous cures as these were "testable," unlike other graces like conversions or winning the lottery. This interest in corporeal signs also shows in their descriptions of the altered state of the visionaries (enhanced beauty, ecstasy) and of the bystanders own sensations (like smelling sweet odours or witnessing miracles of the sun). Their evaluation thus often built on their own perceptions. In this regard their decision making differed from that of the commission members and of the medical experts who (most often) had to rely on testimonies of others (challenged by fading memories) and other sources.

As for the criteria and procedures at the more formal level of the investigation and evaluation: at the diocesan level the procedure was not fixed, the criteriology was still developing, and the various commissions all had different formats. Moreover, the hierarchical order of the decision making went through some changes at the start of the official ecclesiastical examination. While in the end the final decision on Beauraing and Banneux was in the hands of the ordinaries, they might have easily ended up as the responsibility of the archbishop of Malines. Our study of the Belgian wave of Marian apparitions therefore shows how this nationwide scale of alleged supernatural events and their very public character challenged the adequacy of an evaluation system that was tailored to events on a diocesan scale.[11] The results of the recalibration were ad-hoc solutions in which the new scale and the impact of the public reception of the apparition series were factored in. Because of their novelty, the new structures of the decision process could be questioned and, as we have seen, this happened in both the case of Beauraing and Banneux. In other words, studying the public side of the evaluation of the 1930s series of apparitions has not only allowed us to show how different knowledge systems functioned in parallel, but also how the decision-making procedures of those in charge within the highly hierarchically organized Catholic Church were questioned and rethought.

While this book focused primarily on the impact of the public character of the apparition series on the evaluation, I hope the previous chapters have also shown that in order to understand the effect of this public side, one also needs to look at what happened behind closed doors (for instance on the level of the diocesan commissions) and in silence (for instance the unmasking of imposters like Benito Peligri that did not lead to a public statement), and what was not supposed to become public (for instance Dr Derselle's willingness to retract his booklet on Beauraing as long as his letter was not made public). We have seen the strategic silence of the bishops of Namur and Liège who did not want to publish (some of the material of) the second diocesan commission (as not to stir new commotions), and the gradual forgetting of apparition sites that ceased to attract devotees. Most importantly, we have come across instances where the contemporaries consciously planted sources in the archives for future historians so that certain episodes or parts of the story would not be forgotten. I have tried to do all of them justice.

# Notes

## Abbreviations

| | |
|---|---|
| AAM | Archives of the Archdiocese of Malines |
| ADDF | Archives of the Dicastery for the Doctrine of the Faith |
| ADG | Archives of the Diocese of Ghent |
| ADL | Archives of the Diocese of Liège |
| ADN | Archives of the Diocese of Namur |
| ADT | Archives of the Diocese of Tournai |
| ASBG | Archives of the Shrine of Beauraing |
| ASBX | Archives of the Shrine of Banneux |
| CAL | City Archives Lokeren |
| DAG | Decanal Archive of Geraardsbergen |

## Introduction

1 “Le triomphe sera d’ailleurs plus beau pour nos successeurs que pour nous: nous avons trop connu les petits côtés, les vilénies, la ‘cuisine’ des idées et de la lutte, au point que nous sommes revenus sur bien des causes, notamment sur la valeur de la sincérité des gens, sur la légèreté de jugement chez maints arbitres de l’esprit, chez maints ‘savants’ conducteurs des idées … cela a été pénible et nous emportons des grosses désillusions. Nos successeurs, en cas de reconnaissance, ne verrons plus que le beau côté, comme à Lourdes. Tout comme les soldats restés sous l’impression de l’horreur de la bataille, conservant des souvenirs autres que ceux qui n’ont vu que la victoire.” ADN, L.5 bis, Louis Wilmet to Abbé Didion, 17 September 1936.

2 Louis Wilmet was a painter, journalist, essayist, and novelist (1881–1965). He wrote for *Revue Générale*, *Le XXe siècle*, and *La Libre Belgique* among others. Hanlet, *Les écrivains*, 811–15.

3 A quotation of Benedict XVI's Post-Synodal Apostolic Exhortation *Verbum Domini. On the word of God in the life and mission of the Church*, 30 September 2010, cited in William Card. Levada, preface to the 2011 translation of the 1978 *Normae de modo procedendi in diudicandis praesumptis apparitionibus ac revelationibus*, (www.vatican.va/roman_curia/congregations/cfaith/documents/rc_con_cfaith_doc_20111214_prefazione-levada_en.html). See also Laurentin, "Introduction," 20–1.

4 Pius X, *Pascendi Dominici Gregis. Encyclical of Pope Pius X on the Doctrines of the Modernists*, September 8, 1907, consulted 25 November 2019, http://www.vatican.va/content/pius-x/en/encyclicals/documents/hf_p-x_enc_19070908_pascendi-dominici-gregis.html.

5 Chiron, *Enquête*, 28.

6 Porte, *Pontmain*, 14; Klimek, *Medjugorje*, 46; Petri, "Marienerscheinungen," 55.

7 Dicastery for the Doctrine of Faith, *Norms for the Proceeding in the Discernment of Alleged Supernatural Phenomena*, 17 May 2024, consulted 28 June 2024, https://www.vatican.va/roman_curia/congregations/cfaith/documents/rc_ddf_doc_20240517_norme-fenomeni-soprannaturali_en.html.

8 An era prior also to the first public norms of 25 February 1978: Sacred Congregation for the Doctrine of Faith, *Norms Regarding the Manner of Proceedings in the Discernment of Presumed Apparitions or Revelations*. In these rules the verdict still referred to the phenomena and their supernatural origin (or not) and not to the bishop's adequate response.

9 Kselman, "How Abundant," 140.

10 Ventresca, "The Virgin"; Blackbourn, *Marpingen*.

11 Chiron, *Enquête*; Zimdars-Swarts, *Encountering Mary*.

12 A small selection: Badone, "Echoes"; Blackbourn, *Marpingen*; Halemba, *Negotiating*; Claverie, *Les guerres,* Harris, *Lourdes*; Kaufman, *Consuming visions*; Klein, "The Virgin"; Kotulla, "*Nach Lourdes!*"; Porte, *Pontmain*; Scheer, *Rosenkranz* and "Verspielte Frömmigkeit"; Ventresca, "The Virgin"; Zimdars-Swartz, *Encountering Mary*; Zumholz, *Volksfrömmigkeit*.

13 Hermkens, Jansen, and Notermans, "Introduction"; Kotulla, "*Nach Lourdes!*"; Kaufman, *Consuming Visions*.

14 Geppert and Kössler, *Wunder*; Black, *A Demon-haunted Land*; and O'Sullivan, *Disruptive power*.

15 Bitel, "Introduction"; Christian and Klaniczay, *The "Vision Thing."*

16 Laurentin, "Introduction"; 41; Henryot and Chantin, "Apparitions," 40. Sara Horsfall ("The Experience," 375–6) mentions 21,000 cases since the fourth century (of which more than 200 were between 1928 and 1975.) Boniface ("La dévotion mariale," 51) refers to sixty-five between 1917 and 1945.

17 University of Dayton, "Marion Library," consulted 13 July 2022, https://udayton.edu/marianlibrary/index.php.

18 I have removed Amsterdam (1945) from the list given the recent decision of the Dicastery for the Doctrine of Faith (2020). Louchez, "Mariophanie," 1136. In five cases, there was an approval by the Coptic Church (all in Egypt: Zeitun, 1968; Edfu, 1982; Shoubra, 1986; Assiut, 2000; and Warraq-el-Hadar, 2009).

19 Christian, *Visionaries*; Blackbourn, *Marpingen*; Zumholz, *Volksfrömmigkeit.*

20 Horsfall, "The Experience," 379; Zimdars-Swartz, *Encountering Mary*, 5; Porte, *Pontmain*, 13.

21 Jeffrey Bennett (*When the Sun*, 147) suggested that the takeoff in terms of crowd attraction in Fátima happened the moment the newspaper started to cover the apparitions. Andreas Kotulla ("Lourdes," 143) likewise pointed at the importance of the medial appraisal for the appeal of the Pyrenean apparition site.

22 For instance, Bernadette Soubirous saw the Virgin eighteen times in Lourdes. Her series of apparitions were followed by those of other seers. Harris, *Lourdes*, 83–109.

23 Christian, *Visionaries*, 6.

24 Zimdars-Swartz, *Encountering Mary*, 8.

25 Christian, "Afterword," 158.

26 Harris, *Lourdes*, 67.

27 Bitel, "Looking," 88, see also 70.

28 On the development, see: Sarasin, "Was ist Wissensgeschichte?"; Burke, *What is the History of Knowledge*; Östling, Larsson Heidenblad, and Hammar, "Introduction," 17; Mulsow "History"; Sarasin, "More than Just Another Specialty"; Lässig, "The History."

29 "What was held to be knowledge at the time," Mulsow, "History," 161. See also Brilkman, "Confessional Knowledge," 31; Lässig, "The History," 39: "What people in the past understood by the idea of knowledge and what they defined or accepted as knowledge." This broad approach has been narrowed down by scholars such as Lorraine Daston ("Comment," 176) to systematized knowledge (allowing reflections on epistemological hierarchy – whose knowledge is valued by whom and why).

30 Not all scholars agree that religion and belief systems should be part of the endeavour since, as a knowledge system, they are, just like art, quite different from rational knowledge. Sarasin, "Was ist Wissensgeschichte?" 165. Sarasin, "More than Just Another Specialty," 4 (our understanding of knowledge as a basic "garden variety" form of rationality, evidence, and arguments. He however stresses that the distinction is historically highly volatile and not clear-cut).

31 Lässig, "The History," 39 and 48. Or, as Kajsa Brilkman and Anna Nilson Hammar ("Religion as Knowledge") stressed, "Religions produce doctrine, theories, room for action, models for interaction and practice, for self-fashioning etc., all part of the interwoven production and circulation of knowledge in a given historical context."
32 Kajsa Brilkman prefers to use the term confessional knowledge rather than religious knowledge ("Confessional Knowledge," 29) as this better captures "knowledge production for the specific variant of Christianity that occurred after the Reformation" ("Confessional Knowledge," 31).
33 Lässig, "The History," 48.
34 – "The History," 39. She discusses (50) for instance the Jewish debates surrounding circumcision: "claims to authority for bodies of knowledge that rested on entirely different structures and legitimations."
35 Mulsow, "History," 160.
36 – "History," 79, thereby responded to a suggestion from Loraine Daston ("Comment," 176).
37 Boute, Badea, Cavarzere, and Vanden Broecke, "A Product's Glamour," 10.
38 Zimdars-Swartz, *Encountering Mary*, 11 and 19. Cited also in Badone, "Echoes," 456.
39 Christian, "Six Hundred Years," 107; Park, "The Negotiation"; Harris, *Lourdes*, 9–10, 56; Badone, "Echoes," 453 and 467; Hynes, *Knock*, 173.
40 Badone, "Echoes," 468.
41 Christian, *Visionaries*, 8.
42 Blackbourn, *Marpingen*, 48, 17; "Die von Gottheit überaus bevorzugten Mägdlein," 172. Christian, "Six Hundred Years," 107, 16, and 118. On the importance of the media in the creation of a typical "stigmatic," see Van Osselaer e.a., *Between Saints*.
43 Halemba, *Negotiating*, 39 and 43. She refers to Zimdars-Swartz and Margry ("Global Network").
44 Bouflet, "Institution"; Sbalchiero, *Enquête*; Klimek, *Medjugorje*.
45 On the evolution of the discerning process, see Porte, *Pontmain*, 15; Bouflet, *Faussaires*, 70; Barnay, *Les apparitions*, 72; Bouflet and Boutry, *Un signe*, 11.
46 Porte, *Pontmain*, 15. The new rules of May 2024 make the involvement of the Dicastery of the Doctrine of Faith obligatory.
47 Smith Foster, "Canonical Considerations,"131.
48 – "Canonical Considerations," 133.
49 Schneider, "Ein 'deutsches Lourdes,'"194. See also Jelly, "Discerning," 46; Louchez, "Mariophanie," 1132.
50 For the guidelines, see *Norms Regarding the Manner of Proceeding in the Discernment of Presumed Apparitions or Revelations*, Cardinal Šeper, 25 February 1978, consulted on September 15, 2015, http://www.vatican.va/roman_curia/congregations/cfaith/documents/rc_con_cfaith_

doc_19780225_norme-apparizioni_en.html. It was a private document for bishops examining mystical phenomena and only in 2011 did the Vatican make the norms publicly available. For a discussion of these criteria, see Jelly, "Discerning"; Klimek, *Medjugorje,* 53.

51 Schneider, "Ein 'deutsches Lourdes,'" 195.

52 The faithful were expected to obey their bishops in these matters. Smith Foster, "Canonical Considerations," 144.

53 Grasmück, *Eine Marienerscheinung,* 58.

54 Park, "The Negotiation," 19.

55 Zumholz, *Volksfrömmigkeit*, 29; "Die Resistenz," 251.

56 Laycock, *The Seer,* 11.

57 Taves, *Fits,* 4.

58 Bitel, "Looking," 70, 81.

59 Zimdars-Swartz, "Popular Devotion," 138.

60 Apolito, *Apparitions*, 82; Harris, *Lourdes*, 55, 61, 71, and 80.

61 Bitel, "Looking," 83–4, 88. On the importance of studying the "rhetorics of evidence" (reference to Richard B. Gregg) and not seeing evidence as "raw material" (that everyone thinks of in the same way): Rice, *Awful Archives*, 4.

62 Taves, *Religious Experience*, xiii.

63 The following pages use "authority" in the way Laura Feldt describes the concept: as relational, fragile, and different from power. "Authority," so she states, "suggests an uneven relation of influence, the power to motivate and gain obedience, or an ascribed prestige, recognition, or status." Feldt, "Reframing Authority," 185; Feldt, "Marginality," 8. Consequently it is relevant in our discussions about the scientific authority (of medical experts) as in those on the "authority of office." On the difference between *auctoritas*/authority (counterpart: trust) and *potestas* (counterpart: obedience) see Krieger, "The Idea."

64 Bitel, "Looking," 70–88.

65 Preserved in the archives of the diocese of Ghent.

66 Preserved in the archives of the diocese of Namur.

67 I anonymized the names of the visionaries and miraculés who were not mentioned in the press at the time.

68 Porte, *Pontmain*, 154.

## Chapter One

1 Van Osselaer, *The Pious Sex*, 23. On the development of the so-called "Catholic pillar," see also: De Maeyer and Hellemans, "Katholiek reveil," 195; Deneckere, "Nieuwe geschiedenis," 579; Gerard, "Grondlijnen," 150–1; Hellemans, *Strijd.*

2 Leclercq, "La vie religieuse," 220–1.

3 Pasture, "Kerk," 19–20.
4 Conway, "Building," 119.
5 Like Queen of Heaven or Seat of Wisdom. On Mary as a polymorphous figure in Catholicism, see Delfosse, "De maagd Maria," 78.
6 The text of this 1910 song was written by the priest August Cuppens (1862–1924) with music by Lodewijk de Vocht (1887–1977).
7 Van Haver, *Voor U*, 150.
8 Heimann, "Catholic Revivalism," 78; Gibson, *A Social History*, 151; De Maeyer, "De wending," 152.
9 Harris, *Lourdes*; Kaufman, *Consuming Visions*, 2; D'Hertefelt, "Analyse," 13–15.
10 Kotulla, "Lourdes," 154. The railroads were important. In 1867 twelve trains brought about a thousand pilgrims each to Lourdes. D'Hertefelt, "Analyse," 16, 31.
11 Kotulla, "*Nach Lourdes!*" 149 and footnote 421. Every year in the spring and autumn several pilgrimages were organized at the city level. The May pilgrimage developed into a national pilgrimage in 1894. That year 600 Belgian pilgrims travelled together with sixty sick persons to Lourdes. A year later more than a thousand pilgrims and one hundred sick participated. Boissarie, *Les grandes guérisons*, 488.
12 D'Hertefelt, "Analyse," 39 and 63. Similarly for Germany: Kotulla, "Lourdes," 144; Kotulla, "*Nach Lourdes!*" 143.
13 Kaufman, *Consuming Visions*, 25.
14 That periodical had a section on the "Flemish Lourdes," Oostakker. "Aanbevelingen en dankzeggingen," *De Bode van het Heilig Hart* 28 (1896): 214–15. See also Boissarie, *Les grandes guérisons*, 162–83.
15 D'Hertefelt, "Analyse," 39.
16 Meulenkamp and De Nijs, *Buiten de kerk*, 46–9; Geeraerts, "Gewijde geschiedenis" (on the specialized ateliers).
17 The Onkerzele, Wielsbeke, and Eeklo apparitions also took place near a Lourdes grotto.
18 ASBG, dossiers Aurélien Pierroux (Pierroux), 1934–35, 79. S.d. Sclayn.
19 See overviews in: Ernst, *Lexikon*, 135, and Laurentin and Sbalchiero, *Dictionnaire*.
20 There are some indications that the Belgian apparition series also enhanced the knowledge about the other apparition sites. For instance, the widow Jusnot sold booklets on the Fátima apparitions at the Beauraing site. ADDF, Dev. Var., 1933.2 Beauraing, box 4: report of the first Namur commission, session 68 (16 April 1936).
21 ASBG, Pierroux, 1932–33: "Reflexions au sujet de l'article de Mr Leurquin dans les *Études Carmelitaines*"; ADDF, Dev. Var., 1933.2 Beauraing, box 4: report of the first Namur commission, session 12 (5 July 1935).

22 Zimdars-Swartz, *Encountering Mary*, 190. Interest in the apocalyptic messages increased after World War II as they were rescripted and linked to anti-communism and an anti-Soviet campaign. Margry, "Marian Interventions," 246 and *Cold War Mary*.

23 On the series, see Christian, *Visionaries*.

24 Bouflet and Boutry, *Un signe*.

25 Laurentin and Sbalchiero, *Dictionnaire*; Bouflet, *Faussaires*; Chiron, *Enquête*; Delfosse, "De maagd Maria"; Louchez, "Mariophanie," 1179–91. An exception is Chris Maunder's chapter on the Belgian series in his book on Marian apparitions in twentieth-century Europe (Maunder, *Our Lady of the Nations*) and his article on the remnants of the apparition wave (Maunder, "The Footprints").

26 Camille-Jean Joset (*Dossiers de Beauraing*) published a series of volumes on the Beauraing apparitions: (1) on the response of Mgr Heylen the bishop of Namur, (2) on his successor Mgr Charue, (3) on the message of Beauraing, (4) unpublished sources, (5) on the official examinations, and a more general overview (Toussaint and Joset, *Beauraing*); Rutten (*Histoire critique*) wrote a Catholic introduction to Banneux; Jean-Pierre Delville has worked on the apparitions in Banneux and studied their political and economic context (Delville, "Marie") as well as on the apparitions to a rabbi (hidden at the site) in 1942 (Delville, "Le choc"). Furthermore, Agnes Desmazières' research on Catholic psychoanalysis also touches upon the apparitions in Beauraing (Desmazières, "Psychology"). More local studies: Cock, "Mijn gezegend oord" (Onkerzele); Gosseye, "De verschijningen" (Olsene); De Merlier, "Omer" (Etikhove).

27 See figure 1.2, the initial sites are marked with a triangle.

28 Both by Catholics and non-Catholics. Epidemic terminology is used in DAG, Onkerzele, 239: letter from parish priest Duerinck to Minister Sap, 27 June 1939 ("Verschijningen-epidemie") in s.n., "Een epidemie van verschijningen!" *Vooruit*, 4 November 1933, 3 ("epidemie van verschijningen") and in s.n., "O.L. Vrouw acht zich voor niets te gemeen!" *Vooruit*, 15 November 1933, 3. Fever terminology can be found in M. De Ceulener, "Het uitzicht van Beauraing, het verschijningsoord," *Het Laatste Nieuws*, 6 August 1934; 3 ("Verschijningskoorts"). Wave references can be found in M. De Ceulener, "Het verlaten kapelletje te Etichove," *Het Laatste Nieuws*, 22 March 1934, 9 ("golf").

29 ADG, Vermeire, 50: letter from Vandekerckhove-Baert, 11 July 1935.

30 ADG, Apparitions, 77: report on the apparitions to Jules October–November 1936, 14 November 1936.

31 DAG, Onkerzele, 60: report on Kempenaer's vision of 4 February 1934.

32 ASBG, Pierroux, 1934–35, 1935, 123: anonymous letter to the dean, 11 November 1935.

33 DAG, Onkerzele, 13: letter from Vandekerckhove about the visions of Gerard Cardoen on 8 December 1934, dated 11 December 1934.

34 DAG, Onkerzele, 14: about the visions of Mr De Langhe.

35 AAM, Van Roey, Apparitions, 21: diverse apparitions, Onkerzele, letter from Alfons Theys to the archbishop, 12 July 1935.

36 ADN, L. 42–3, Wilmet III: circular letter to the collaborators of the *Annales* 2.

37 Christian, *Moving Crucifixes*; Ventresca, "The Virgin"; Reynolds, "The Templemore Miracles."

38 ADG, Apparitions, 72: reports on the apparitions to Jules, 1 August 1935–September 1935.

39 ASBG, Archives doyen Léon Lambert (Lambert), 66: diverse visions, newspaper cut about the visionary of Melen.

40 AAM, Van Roey, Apparitions, 24. Processus, BXII2: letter from parish priest Vander Maeren to Mgr Coppieters, 28 October 1934.

41 This becomes clear when one takes a closer look at the paintings that depict Henri Kempenaers' visions. ADG, Onkerzele, Vermeire, 55: letter from Vandekerckhove, 27 May 1935.

42 ADG, Vermeire, 21: letter from L. Sebruyns-Desmet, 19 September 1940. They read on 1 September 1940 the predictions Elisabeth Cornelis had fomulated on 24 June 1934 and that were only to be opened after her death.

43 DAG, Onkerzele, 13: letter from Vandekerckhove with declaration of Gerard Cardoen about 28 October 1934.

44 ADG, Vermeire, 51: declaration of Leonie Van den Dijck on 27 September 1935.

45 AAM, Van Roey, Apparitions, 24. Processus, BIXA1: letter from Van Winkel, 31 March 1934.

46 AAM, Van Roey, Apparitions, 23. Processus, BII: report of Louis Wilmet about Lokeren, 24 August 1934.

47 See the letter and testimony of Mary Pousset-Dodémont. ASBG, 44: diverse healings and favours, report about 4 September 1933 (cure of Henri G.).

48 Maunder, "Marian Visionaries," 293.

49 Not the "Sacred Face," that devotion *did* exist. References to the Sacred Head can also be found in the reports on the "mystic" Teresa Higginson. They sometimes equated the latter devotion with the devotion to the Sacred Head of Jesus (as a seat of wisdom) to mislead public and clerical authorities in order to obtain permission for their pilgrimages and ceremonies.

50 AAM, Van Roey, Apparitions, 21: diverse apparitions, Onkerzele, letter from Mr Peeters to the editor-in-chief of *De Gazet van Antwerpen*, post 25 August 1934; ADG, Apparitions, 136: letter from parish priest Vander Maeren to Mgr Coppieters, 2 June 1938; 138: idem, 26 June 1938.)

51 DAG, Onkerzele, 20: report from Boon about the visionary Jules De Vuyst on 27 June 1935.

52 So the visionaries at these sites already had visionary experiences at other sites. Their testimonies were, however, the first reports of an apparition in Antwerp, Berchem, Edegem, Pontaury, Sint-Niklaas, Turnhout, and Wilrijk.

53 Kortrijk and Ledeberg.

54 These numbers are not absolute: They depend on the names I could retrieve from the documents preserved in the various archives; most probably, far more people claimed to have experienced something extraordinary. Moreover, the documents include more general descriptions, such as "200 persons."

55 Based on the population count of 1910. Duvosquel, Hasquin, Van Uytven, *Gemeenten.*

56 "Les autres auront lieu dans des lieux identiques." AAM, Van Roey, Apparitions, 25. Processus, BXII6a: Didion, additions to his previous research, 1 December 1935, 10.

57 Ladon, *Une* épidémie *mentale*, 63.

58 ASBG, Lambert, 66: diverse visions, Verviers, s.n., "Un 'fait troublant' au cimetière de Verviers," *Courrier du Soir*, 12 November 1933 (newspaper cutting s.p.).

59 Blackbourn, *Marpingen*, 17–18. For the changing features of the prototypical visionary in Spain, see: Christian, "Six Hundred Years."

60 Three other names might belong to either a young girl or an adult woman, and three are unspecified children. Nine seers are mentioned only by surname and the documents include also more general references such as "hundreds of people" and nicknames. This was, for example, the case in Saint-Stevens Woluwe where the visionary was only referred to as "The Beard," or the "hermit from Marcourt." ASBG, 66: diverse visions, cutting of s.n., "Autour des apparitions de Rendeux," *La Wallonie*, 25 January 1933.

61 Christian, *Visionaries,* 250. The numbers are based on the reports of Wilmet and Didion and additional source material found in various archives and published sources.

62 A (factory) chauffeur (2), waffle maker (1), worker (6), agricultural worker (3), mason (unemployed) (1), weaver (5), (lumber) seller (2), innkeeper (2), painter (1), leather dyer (1), shoemaker (1).

63 On Tilman Côme's financial difficulties and unemployment – ADN, L.42–3, Wilmet I: letter from the wife of Tilman Côme to Princess de Croÿ, 26 February 1934 and letter from Tilman Côme to Princess de Croÿ, 6 January 1935. On Henri Kempenaers and the financial aid he got from his supporters – ADG, Vermeire, 113: letter from Kempenaers to "Dear friend," 13 October 1934. Apart from these, we also have the testimonies of two doctors, an engineer, an editor-in-chief, a tax collector and a functionary.

But none of these male visionaries ever started a site, they only claimed to have experienced a divine intervention at sites where other visionaries had already reported Mary's presence. The same holds true for the members of the clergy who testified that they had experienced a divine encounter. There were two chaplains, a parish priest, a canon, and a curate/assistant priest who claimed visions. These findings differ from Van Osselaer, "Sensitive," as they are based on not just the lists of Wilmet and Didion, discussed in that article, but also include other sources as well.

64 For example, Leonie Van den Dijck (Onkerzele)/Elisabeth Cornelis (Lokeren)/Laure Dulière (Beauraing, Brussels e.a.).

65 AAM, Van Roey, Apparitions, 24. Processus, BIXA2: letters from parish priest Vander Maeren, 30 January 1934, 18 July 1934.

66 "Vooruit willen komen en doen aan vrouwelijke aanstallerij in de lijn van zulke lage volksvrouwen." AAM, Van Roey, Apparitions, 24. Processus, BXII2: letter from parish priest Vander Maeren to Mgr Coppieters, 24 December 1934.

67 Wilmet, *Beauraing,* 226. The devotion to Our Lady of Beauraing was not permitted yet, so the priest dedicated the masses to Our Lady of Snow.

68 A copy of a letter (with heading "Monsieur N") in the Beauraing shrine archives, summed up some of the relations. The writer noted that Our Lady of Herzele sent her visionary to Onkerzele, and that a visionary from Onkerzele confirmed her own status in Lokeren when she claimed to have visions there as well. Moreover, the Virgin's message in Etikhove was almost literally the same as that of the Sacred Heart and Virgin in Onkerzele. ASBG, Pierroux, 1932–33: letter about Onkerzele 12 April 1934, see also DAG, Onkerzele, 69: reports on 25 March 1934; ADN, L.42–3, Wilmet I: letter from Tilman Côme to Princess de Croÿ, 27 March 1934.

69 DAG, Onkerzele, 68: report from Jan Filip Boon, 23 March 1934; 78: texts of Berthonia Holtkamp's visions, 25 January–1 February 1936; AAM, Van Roey, Apparitions, 24. Processus, BVII.b1: letter from Maistriaux to "Monsieur" about Holtkamp, 7 May 1934 and letter from Berthonia Holtkamp to Maistriaux about her vision on 25 March 1933, 9 August 1933; ADG, Coppieters, 9.5 Apparitions: letter from Georges Van den Broecke, 5 November 1937 about Berthonia Holtkamp.

70 ASBG, Lambert, 3: unpublished manuscripts, report of Pierroux 1932–43.

71 AAM, Van Roey, Apparitions, 21: diverse apparitions, Onkerzele, letter from Sr. Marie Régine to Mgr Van Roey, 31 December 1933.

72 ASBG, Lambert, 3: unpublished manuscripts, report of Pierroux 1932–43.

73 ADG, Apparitions, 46: reports on Jules' visions March 1935; DAG, Onkerzele, 21: reports on Jules' visions 1–31 July 1935.

74 In the case of Gerard C., this was voiced even explicitly by a local commentator. AAM, Van Roey, Apparitions, 24. Processus, BXII2e: De Saegher to "Excellence," 12 February 1935.

75 ADG, Apparitions, 223: letters from parish priest Vander Maeren, 21 and 23 April 1938; Apparitions, 218: letter from Vander Maeren about Fontenoy, 26 May 1936. Visits to other sites did not always lead to apparitions there; sometimes the visits only served to demonstrate belief and interest. AAM, Van Roey, Apparitions, 24. Processus, BIXA1: reports by Louis Wilmet, 21November 1933, 28 December 1933.

76 DAG, Onkerzele, 40: Boon to parish priest Vander Maeren, 6 October 1935 (Laure had a vision indicating that Van den Dijck was plagued by jealousy); ADG, Coppieters, 9.5 Apparitions: letter from Sr. Marie Régine to the bishop, 6 March 1935 (Jules from Herzele saw her in his visions); AAM, Van Roey, Apparitions, 24. Processus, BXI2: letter from Magain including a document "Why Mariette Béco does not believe in Onkerzele" ("Pourquoi Mariette Béco ne croit pas à Onkerzele").

77 AAM, Van Roey, Apparitions, 25. Processus, BXII6a: Didion, additions to his previous research, 6 December 1935.

78 Christian, *Visionaries,* 6.

79 Ventresca, "The Virgin," 447.

80 S.n., "À la Congrégation des Rites. La Bienheureuse Bernadette," *Vers l'Avenir,* 4 March 1932, 1; S.n., "De gelukzalige Bernadette Soubirous," *Het Nieuws van de Dag,* 30 November 1932, 1; S.n., "De eerbiedwaardige Bernadette Soubirous," *De Standaard,* 7 December 1932, 2; S.n., "La canonisation de Bernadette Soubirous?" *Le Vingtième Siècle,* 7 December 1932, 1.

81 Toussaint and Joset, *Beauraing,* 39, 64, and 66.

82 Maistriaux, *Wat gebeurt er,* 10.

83 Toussaint and Joset, *Beauraing,* 23–32; Lourtie, *Les apparitions,* 27–8.

84 "Comme des lampes électriques dans la tête." ADDF, Dev. Var., 1933.2 Beauraing: les faits de Beauraing, brèves remarques, 24 March 1933 (8 pages, s.n.), 6.

85 "Pour qu'on vienne ici en pèlerinage." Toussaint and Joset, *Beauraing,* 70; Lourtie, *Les apparitions,* 35.

86 "Je convertirai les pécheurs," Toussaint and Joset, *Beauraing,* 84–8; Lourtie, *Les apparitions,* 43–5.

87 Toussaint and Joset, *Beauraing,* 84–5 and 94.

88 – *Beauraing,* 84.

89 A first inventory of these polemical publications can be found in Decelle, "Le scandale."

90 On 1 March 1933, Mgr Heylen, the bishop of Namur, permitted the faithful to install ex-votos on the walls of the grotto. Toussaint and Joset, *Beauraing*, 96.

91 Sbalchiero, "Banneux" in Laurentin and Sbalchiero, *Dictionnaire*, 111–15.

92 Etienne, Pirotte, and Bauwens, *Gids*, 103.

93 J[an] B[oon], "Banneux," *De Standaard*, 28 March 1933, 2.

94 "Cette source est réservée pour moi." Delville, "Marie," 87.

95 "Je suis la Vierge des pauvres," "Cette source est réservée pour toutes les nations, pour soulager les malades," "Je désirais une petite chapelle." Delville, "Marie," 87–8.

96 – "Marie," 88. "Je viens soulager la souffrance."

97 Stéphany, *Les années 20–30*, 63. In March 1933 twenty-five cures had been reported. J[an] B[oon], "Verschijningen van O.L. Vrouw te Banneux in het bisdom Luik," *De Standaard*, 23 March 1933, 1–2; S.n., "Nog Maria-wonderen in ons land? Bij mevrouw Goethals-De Deene te Antwerpen," *De Standaard*, 28 June 1933, 3.

98 J[an] B[oon], "Verschijningen van O.L. Vrouw te Banneux in het bisdom Luik," *De Standaard*, 23 March 1933, 1–2.

99 S.n., "Banneux," *De Standaard*, 28 March 1933, 2.

100 "Een devotie tot Onze Lieve Vrouw der Armen, de werklieden bekeerend welke van de kerk zijn afgedwaald." J[an] B[oon], "Verschijningen van O.L. Vrouw te Banneux in het bisdom Luik," *De Standaard*, 23 March 1933, 1–2, 1.

101 Van den Steen, "Tilman Côme," 23 and 28.

102 – "Tilman Côme," 28–9. " À demain." "Je suis venue pour la gloire de la Belgique et pour préserver cette terre de l'envahisseur … Hâtez-vous!"

103 – "Tilman Côme," 29. Van den Steen cites a newspaper article spelling it as Böring and not Bôring, for the Bôring spelling see also page 270 endnote 197 and Wilmet, *Beauraing*, 22.

104 – "Tilman Côme," 30–1."Montrez-vous parmi le monde. Vos vœux seront exaucés. Priez."

105 – "Tilman Côme," 32, 34.

106 See comments some weeks before in s.n., "Du nouveau à Beauraing," *Le Peuple*, 18 June 1933, 1.

107 S.n., "Kroniek van Beauraing. Het geval Tilman Côme – Een wonderbaarlijke genezing en twee nieuwe verschijningen?" *De Standaard*, 14 June 1933, 3.

108 Sindic, *Tilman Côme*; Burnon, *Vrai visage;* Gerard, *Hâtez-vous*.

109 "Er zijn veel socialisten, zoowel hardnekkige, die met sociale eischen begaan zijn als gematigde die zich eenvoudig voor stoffelijke belangen bezorgd maken. Een derde van de aanhangers van de 'Werkliedenpartij' gaat naar

de kerk … Overigens sterven zij allen in den schoot van de Kerk." Wilmet, *Beauraing*, 221.

110 S.n., "Wat is er gaande te Onkerzele?" *De Standaard*, 10 September 1933, 3; Cock, "Mijn gezegend oord."

111 "Ik ben gekomen om de zondaars te bekeeren en de godslasteringen te doen ophouden." Wilmet, *Beauraing*, 228.

112 – *Beauraing*, 238, 232. "Ik zal uw land beschermen!"

113 – *Beauraing*, 242, 240, 250.

114 – *Beauraing*, 237. For similar numbers, see s.n., "Te Onkerzele," *De Standaard*, 24 September 1933, 3 (each night about 3,000 people pray at the site).

115 "Om te Onkerzele vol te houden dat ge Onze Lieve Vrouw ziet, is er op zichzelf al meer dan een buitengewone dosis moed en gemoedssterkte noodig." S.n., "Wat is er gaande te Onkerzele?" *De Standaard*, 10 September 1933, 3.

116 Mar. De Rijcke, "De Maagd verschijnt ook te Onkerzele (bij Geeraardsbergen)," *De Vooruit*, 6 September 1933, 3.

117 M. De Ceulener, "De volkstoeloop te Onkerzele," *Het Laatste Nieuws*, 15 October 1933, 9; S.n. "Bij de verschijningen in Zuid-Vlaanderen. Een Vlaamsch Beauraing?" *Het Laatste Nieuws*, 11 September 1933, 3.

118 As at other apparition sites, miraculous cures were reported in Onkerzele. Jacobs, *De zienster*, 13: Van Saelen from Antwerp was, for instance, cured of osteomyelitis (inflammation bone marrow).

119 Jean Marèze, "La Vierge apparaîtra-t-elle de nouveau, ce soir au petit mécano de Chaineux?" *Paris-Soir*, 18 October 1933, 3.

120 On the doubts about the authenticity, see s.n., "Te Etikhove," *De Standaard*, 1–2 November 1933, 3.

121 Several of the sources have been made digitally available by Arvia (Centre de Conservation et de diffusion des archives médiatiques de la ville de Herve et ses villages), consulted 20 July 2022, https://www.arvia.be/archive/chaineux-houlteau-1933-apparitions-de-la-vierge-a-chaineux/#media-10256-3.

122 For more information on Antoinism, see Scaillet, "La religion populaire," 135. The cult was created by Louis Antoine (1846–1912), a metallurgy worker from Liège, in 1910 when a temple was installed in Jemeppe-sur-Meuse. The cult was particularly successful in the worker milieu in the Liège region and in certain French cities. In 1993 there were still thirty-six Antoinist temples in Wallonia.

123 Lecloux, *Les Apparitions*, 7.

124 Zeyen, "La Vierge," 15.

125 "Les 'apparitions' de Chaineux," 21 October 1933, 3. Clipping on the Arvia website, consulted 3 January 2025, https://www.arvia.be/

archive/?fwp_evenements=1933-apparition-de-la-vierge-a-houlteau-chaineux. The title of the newspaper is not mentioned.

126 "De Maagd is op tournée in Vlaanderen." M.D.R., "Etikhove is nu ook een verschijningsoord der Maagd. Geloovigen komen in verzet," *De Vooruit*, 18 October 1933, 2.

127 S.n., "Te Onkerzele en te Etikhove," *De Standaard*, 29 October 1933, 5.

128 S.n., "Onderzoek te Etikhove," *De Standaard*, 21 October 1933, 3.

129 "Sa femme lui crie: 'Se sont tes demis que tu vois.'" DAG, Onkerzele, 42: E. Marroyen (Forest-Bruxelles), "Voyage à Etichove samedi 21 octobre 1933."

130 De Merlier, "Omer," 19.

131 S.n., "Te Onkerzele en elders," *De Standaard*, 15 October 1933, 5; M. De Ceulener, "De volkstoeloop te Onkerzele," *Het Laatste Nieuws*, 15 October 1933, 9. De Merlier ("Omer," 18) mentions 1,500 people since 12 October.

132 "Er dient te worden opgemerkt dat onder de menigte volk deugnieten waren die spotten, vloekten, kleeren van biddenden scheurden, enz. Maar daarbuiten ook duizendenden die prachtig ingetogen, ongestoord voortgaan met zang, gebed en litanie." S.n., "Maria-verschijningen in Vlaanderen?" *De Standaard*, 19 October 1933, 4.

133 De Merlier ("Omer," 20) spells it as Reckegem.

134 S.n., "Te Etikhove," *De Standaard*, 28 October 1933, 5.

135 M. De Ceulener, "De belangstelling te Etichove," *Het Laatste Nieuws*, 31 October 1933, 3; De Merlier, "Omer," 24.

136 "Komen de eenen er uit nieuwsgierigheid en de anderen uit overtuiging," s.n., "De 'Verschijningen'. Belangstelling in verschillende plaatsen," *Het Laatste Nieuws*, 8 November 1933, 2.

137 Reported together with, for instance, Wielsbeke and Olsene. S.n., "De 'Verschijningen'. Belangstelling in verschillende plaatsen," *Het Laatste Nieuws*, 8 November 1933, 2.

138 S.n., "De 'Verschijningen' te Lokeren," *Het Laatste Nieuws*, 16 November 1933, 2.

139 ADG, Coppieters, 9.5 Apparitions, 15: Levensschets van Maurits Van den Broecke Olsene (12 typed pages by H. Blondeel, 1943).

140 Gosseye "De verschijningen," 110. AAM, Van Roey, Apparitions, 24. Processus, BVII2: litterae R.D. Lejour, parochi in Olsene, 18 June 1935.

141 "Onze Lieve Vrouw Bovenal." Gosseye, "De verschijningen," 114.

142 ADG, Coppieters, 9.5 Apparitions, 15: Levensschets van Maurits Van den Broecke Olsene (12 typed pages by H. Blondeel, Mont St Guibert 1943).

143 AAM, Van Roey, Apparitions, 24. Processus, BVIIa: documenta ex Curia Gandavensi circa facta in Olsene, 3; report by Magain, 12 December 1933.

144 DAG: liber memorialis 1815–1949, notes by Pastor Vander Maeren.

145 AAM, Van Roey, Apparitions, 24. Processus, BIXA1: documenta GII, 1 (19 October–28 December 1933), biography of Holtkamp (by Boon).

146 DAG, Onkerzele, 46: report on the apparitions; idem. 9: Interviews *De Standaard.*

147 AAM, Van Roey, Apparitions, 24. Processus, BIXA1: documenta GII, 1 (19 October–28 December 1933); report about Onkerzele by Louis Wilmet about 21 November 1933.

148 "Lieve Vrouw van het Heilig Aanschijn." AAM, Van Roey, Apparitions, 24. Processus, BIXA1: documenta GII, 1 (19 October–28 December 1933), biography of Holtkamp (by Boon).

149 AAM, Van Roey, Apparitions, 24. Processus, BIXA1, documenta GII: 1 (19 October–28 December 1933), letter from Magain about 18 December 1933, report of the questioning of the visionaries by Boon (for Vander Maeren) 28 December 1933, letter from Vander Maeren to Mgr Coppieters 25 December 1933, report by Boon 25 December 1933.

150 AAM, Van Roey, Apparitions, 24. Processus, BIXA1.1: letter from Louis Wilmet (23 December 1933) with a report on the solar phenomena in Onkerzele on 18 December 1933.

151 Van Osselaer, "Uit de lucht," 292–3.

152 Christian, *Visionaries.*

153 "Het tweede Ezkioga." AAM, Van Roey, Apparitions, 23. Processus, BIVb: letter to "Monseigneur," 14 July 1934.

154 CAL, XL.1031: apparitions near Naastveld (1933–4), report of the policemen De Nul and Vervaet about 1 July 1934, report by van Eetveld (23 July 1934).

155 S.n., "Lokeren. Langs om zonderlinger," *De Vrije Waaslander,* 2 September 1934, 2.

156 "Ellendelingen, de straf wacht U." "Opgehitst." CAL, XL.1031: report about 24 July 1934.

157 CAL, XL.1031: report of the adjunct police commissioner (about 29 July 1934 and 31 July 1934).

158 CAL, III.12: city council reports (year IV–1976): session of 2 August 1934.

159 L.S., "De verschijningen te Lokeren," *Het Laatste Nieuws,* 22 August 1934, 13. S.n. "Lokeren. Langs om zonderlinger," *De Vrije Waaslander,* 2 September 1934, 2.

160 Among others published in *De Standaard,* 30 August 1934. AAM, Van Roey, Apparitions, 23. Processus, BIVb: letter to the faithful by Mgr Van Roey.

161 On this transnational aspect, see the unpublished MA thesis of Jens Wouters ("Transnationale spanningen").

162 In reality this was a small culvert excavated in a hill (on which the old Charbonnage railway used to be) to bring water to the village.

163 "Quelqu'un illuminé d'un rayon de lumière." AAM, Van Roey, Apparitions, 27: nonapproved apparitions and predictions/Ham-sur-Sambre (1938–51), Sondervorst, "Eenige beschouwingen bij de verschijningen van Ham-aan-Samber" (15 May 1939).

164 Wouters, "Transnationale spanningen," 11. See also L.O., "Les 'Apparitions' de Ham-sur-Sambre," *La Gazette de Charleroi*, 31 March 1936, 2; Marnix, "Le paradis s'ouvre devant les yeux fiévreux d'une fillette à Ham-sur-Sambre," *Journal de Charleroi*, 5 April 1936, 3.

165 Wouters, "Transnationale spanningen," 11 and 14.

166 *La Gazette de Charleroi* called its series of articles "à l'instar de Beauraing." L.O., "Les 'Apparitions' de Ham-sur-Sambre," *La Gazette de Charleroi*, 31 March 1936, 2.

167 Marnix, "Le paradis s'ouvre devant les yeux fiévreux d'une fillette à Ham-sur-Sambre," *Journal de Charleroi*, 5 April 1936, 3.

168 Wouters, "Transnationale spanningen," 13–14.

169 Bouflet, "Institution," 272.

170 S.n., "Een hernieuwing van het Lourdes-wonder?" *De Standaard*, 10 December 1932, 1–2.

171 "Als nieuwe Bernadettes." S.n., "De wonderbare verschijningen te Beauraing," *De Standaard*, 30 December 1932, 1.

172 "Als in een Vlaamsch Beauraing." M. De Ceulener, "Een nieuw bedevaartsoord," *Het Laatste Nieuws*, 11 September 1933, 3.

173 See introduction. Christian, "Afterword," 156 and 162.

174 Scheer, "What She Looks Like."

175 J[an] B[oon], "Verschijningen van O.L. Vrouw te Banneux in het bisdom Luik," *De Standaard*, 23 March 1933, 1–2, 2.

176 S.n. "Kroniek van Beauraing," *De Standaard*, 1 July 1933, 2 (the article mentions pilgrims from the Netherlands, Germany, France, and Luxembourg as well). See for instance the testimony of Mrs Borras at the thirty-third session of the commission investigating Banneux (21 February 1936). She indicated that she had visited, Banneux, Melen, Onkerzele, and Beauraing. ADL, Kerkhofs, D/IV. Marian cult, 28: canonical examination of the events of Banneux. See also De Jongh, *Het mirakel*, 9.

177 S.n., "De bedevaart naar Etichove," *Het Laatste Nieuws*, 31 October 1933, 1.

178 "Exaltés." "Les circulaires distribuées à la foule en faveur du 'Rosaire vivante' avec l'affiche en agrandi placée sur … (je m'excuse de devoir vous le dire!) le ventre du bonhomme distributeur manquait totalement de bon sens et de gout." ASBG, Pierroux, 1935, 85: complaint against the *exaltés* (29 May 1935).

179 DAG, Onkerzele, 8: testimony of Leonie Van den Dijck to Jan Boon, 13 July 1934; ADN, L.42–3, Wilmet I: letter from Tilman Côme to Princess of Croÿ, 14 March 1934.

180 E.g., reports in *The Universe* (5 August 1933), *De Tijd*, and *De Maasbode* were referred to in *De Standaard*, 24 August, 1933 and 6 September 1933; for Germany: Scheer, *Rosenkranz*, 88, footnote 46.

181 Christian, *Visionaries*, 152.

182 I consulted *De Standaard* (created in 1914, first edition in 1918, the paper had a Catholic orientation), *Het Laatste Nieuws* (created in 1888, had a Flemish liberal undercurrent), *Le Peuple* (created in 1885, linked to the Belgian Workers' Party), and *De Vooruit* (Flemish, created by a Socialist co-operative in 1884).

183 Creusen, "Les faits 'merveilleux,'" 275. For the journalistic activities at the sites, see Van Osselaer, "Mystics."

184 "Den journalistieken kant der voorkomende feiten (het voor den gewonen toeschouwer zichtbare en hoorbare), zooals ons is voorgeschreven." S.n., "Te Onkerzele," *De Standaard*, 10 December 1933, 3. See also AAM, Van Roey, Apparitions, 24. Processus, BIXA2: letter from van Cauwenberg (28 January 1934) requesting *De Standaard* to stop covering the series.

185 AAM, Van Roey, Apparitions, 24. Processus, BIXA2: G. De Myttenaere (*Nieuws van de Dag*) to Taelman, 8 February 1934.

186 For instance, J. Wiser wrote a poem about Onkerzele and wanted to distribute a thousand copies. AAM, Van Roey, Apparitions, 21: diverse apparitions, Onkerzele, letter from Wiser to Mgr Van Roey, 24 March 1934.

187 Sources on Boon's book: Kadoc, Jan Boon, 5.2.5.1: correspondence about articles in *De Standaard* and the publication of the book, 1933–34; letter to Mgr Tessens, 23 May 1934; letter to Mgr Van Roey, 16 June 1934. For Boon's manuscript see AAM, Van Roey, Apparitions, 36: Beauraing–Banneux. Sources on Magain's book: DAG, Onkerzele, 266: letters of Alfred Magain to parish priest Vander Maeren, 16 November 1933, 3 May 1934; AAM, Van Roey, Apparitions, 24. Processus, BXII3: documenta G varia, letter of Magain to Mgr Van Roey, 18 November 1933, response on 3 December 1933; GIV: letter of Magain, 28 April 1934 (the Flemish booklet was removed from circulation after a process of defamation; the husband of the visionary protested against his description).

188 ADG, Coppieters, 9.5: apparitions, sub secreto St. Officii, letterae S.Off. rel. ad. apparitione. Beauraing–Banneux et alias.

189 Preface of Lenain in Wilmet's book, *Beauraing, Banneux en Onkerzele* (1935).

190 J[an] B[oon], "Inzake Beauraing. Om legendevorming in Nederland tegen te gaan," *De Standaard*, 6 September 1933, 1–2.

191 "De uitgaven 'Rex' hebben de meest volledige en de meest doeltreffende bewijsstukken uitgegeven over de 'Verschijningen' te Beauraing en te Banneux." S.n., *De verschijningen*, s.p.

192 Maistriaux, *Que se passe-t-il à Beauraing?* (1932); *Les dernières apparitions de Beauraing* (1933); Géradin, *Des apparitions à Banneux* (1933).

193 *De verschijningen van Beauraing en Banneux* (1933); Magain, *Onze Lieve Vrouw bij de Vlamingen: de verschijningen van Onkerzele*; Sindic, *Des*

*apparitions en Flandre*; Sindic, *Tilman Côme, est-il un imposteur?* (1933); *Les apparitions de Belgique* (1933); Johanns, *Die Ereignisse* (1933).

194 S.n., "Que s'est-il passé à Chaineux?" *Soirées* 108, 27 October 1933, s.p.

195 Charlier, *Léon Degrelle,* 76; Van den Steen, "Les apparitions"; Narvaez, *Degrelle,* 103. Dannau (*Zo sprak,* 63) mentions that Hoyois from the ACJB said that Rex sold in total more than two million copies of the first booklet erasing all debts at once. On the different numbers, see footnote in Christian, *Visionaries,* 434, endnote 76.

196 Tihon, "Les mouvements"; Vos, "Het dubbelspoor," 30–1.

197 There were two types of Catholic Action organizations: one following a centralized model, organized at the national level and under control of the clerical hierarchy, and another organized on the basis of class and profession. In Belgium the two types developed. Gerard, "Cardijn," 124; Tihon, "Association."

198 Rosart and Zelis, "Formation," 304.

199 Van den Heede, "Les maisons d'édition," 593; Van den Steen, "Les apparitions," 51; Conway, "Building," 141; De Bens, *De Belgische dagbladpers,* 243; and Fincoeur, "Le 'réseau rexiste,'" 226.

200 "Les gens rigolent souvent de ces histoires, moi pas: nous ne connaissons à peu près rien encore des forces spirituelles." Charlier, *Léon Degrelle,* 75 (a series of interviews for the French television).

201 Van den Steen, "Les apparitions," 55. Léon Degrelle is mentioned as witness of the questioning of the child visionaries of Beauraing on 1 January 1933. Joset, *Dossiers de Beauraing,* vol. 4, 99.

202 Van den Steen ("Les apparitions," 55) refers to the testimony of the Belgian writer Pierre Daye.

203 "Dat is de oplossing! Wij gaan heel volkse uitgaven bezorgen en die verkopen in al de katholieke scholen, bij de kwezels, van Aarlen tot Oostende." Dannau, *Zo sprak,* 54.

204 "Het is trouwens heel typisch hoe de mensen zich met duizenden naar de grot in de hof van de Zusters haastten, enkel op basis van verklaringen, die trouwens vrij onnozel waren. Onze-Lieve-Vrouw verscheen iedere dag. Ik heb mij dikwijls afgevraagd of het hele zaakje geen mooie fopperij is geweest met dia's. Hoe dan ook, wij hebben er heel wat geld aan gewonnen. Te Beauraing greep in elk geval het mirakel van Rex plaats." Dannau, *Zo sprak,* 59.

205 Fincoeur, "Le 'réseau rexiste,'" 244.

206 De Vroylande, *Quand Rex,* 60.

207 – *Quand Rex,* 62. They were sold for three francs, which was a lot of money at the time. Van den Steen, "Les apparitions," 55.

208 William Christian suggest that this might have been through the articles in the French photo magazine *VU*. Christian, *Visionaries,* 152.

209 "Leur reportage sera la plus fantastique enquête qui ait jamais paru au monde, puisqu'elle rassemble à la fois l'horreur des plus épouvantables prédictions et le tableau déchirant de centaines de visions incontestablement surnaturelles." Léon Degrelle, "Les 2/3 des hommes vont mourir," *Soirées* 103 (22 September 1933): s.p.

210 "Un objet de discussion et de dosage." Louis Picard, "Pas de reportage sur Ezkioga," *Soirées* 105 (6 October 1933): s.p.

211 ADDF, Dev. Var., Beauraing 1933.2, 6: Bruno de Jésus-Marie o.c.d. to Mgr Canali (assesseur du Saint-Office, 15 October 1933). For the letter from the bishop, see: Christian, *Visionaries,* 153; see also xiii–xv and 159.

212 AAM, Van Roey, Apparitions, 24. Processus, BIXA1, documenta GII: letter from Magain to Mgr Coppieters, 4 November 1933.

213 "Les sages prescriptions des Evêques et Archevêque ont balayé les imprudences, le mercantilisme, les débordements hystériques. Il fallait ce grand calme pour qu'on put étudier d'une part, prier et espérer de l'autre." Léon Degrelle, "Beauraing revoit à nouveau des foules," *Soirées* 142 (22 June 1934): s.p.

214 Christian, "Afterword," 156, 162.

215 – "Afterword," 162.

216 Thurston, *The War and the Prophets,* 1; Bromley and Bobbit, "Visions," 8; Zimdars-Swartz, "Popular Devotion," 126; Bennett, *When the Sun,* 140; Scheer, *Rosenkranz,* 14, 29; Maunder, *Our Lady of the Nations,* 3. General overviews of Marian apparitions show that in the early 1930s, the late 1940s, and mid-1950s the reports peaked. See for instance Billet, "Le fait," 10; Blackbourn, *Marpingen,* 361–2; and Chiron, *Enquête.*

217 At the parliament elections on 27 November 1932, Catholics did better than they did at the local elections of 9 October 1932 (when the Catholics had lost seats to Liberals and BWP). On 17 December 1932 the new De Broqueville cabinet started. Gerard, "De democratie," 1049–50.

218 ASBG, Pierroux, 1932–33: conférence donnée à Bruxelles le 25 janvier 1933 par Monsieur Louis Wilmet sur Beauraing, après La Salette, Lourdes, Fátima.

219 Perry and Echeverria, *Under the Heel,* 199; Blackbourn, *Marpingen,* 361; Delvaux, "Naissance," 16.

220 Gerard, "De democratie," 1043, 1048–9; Gerard, *De schaduw,* 197; Plavsic, *Le Cardinal Van Roey,* 59.

221 "Schone ziel van het kind." Gerard, "De democratie," 1049.

222 "Marie apparaît donc au moment le plus tragique de la crise en Belgique." Delville, "Marie," 92.

223 Gerard, "De democratie," 1052, 1070.

224 – "De democratie," 1077.

225 Conway, *Collaboratie,* 9; Van den Heede, "Les maisons d'édition," 594.

226 Gerard, "De democratie," 1077.
227 Gevers, "Voor God," 45; Conway, "Building," 125–9, 149–50; Gerard, "De democratie," 1064, 1075–7; Gerard, "Grondlijnen," 150–1; Plavsic, *Le Cardinal Van Roey*, 65.
228 Conway, "Building," 143–5; Conway, *Collaboratie*, 10, 12. The Catholic party was left with sixty-three seats. Gerard, "De democratie," 1079, 1077.
229 Gevers, "Voor God," 48–9.
230 Conway, *Collaboratie*, 13; Gerard, "De democratie," 1089, 1091.
231 Conway, *Collaboratie*, 13–14; Gerard, "De democratie," 1092–4; Plavsic, *Le Cardinal Van Roey*, 68; De Bens, *De Belgische dagbladpers*, 246.
232 In May 1937 the partnership with the VNV ended as well. Gevers, "Voor God," 49.
233 Conway, *Collaboratie*, 3, 14.
234 Van den Steen, "Les apparitions," 55.
235 S.n., "Après la condamnation de Rex," *Annales de Beauraing et de Banneux* 106 (15 May 1937): 4.
236 ADN, L.5 bis, Louis Wilmet: typed copy of *Judex* 8 (13 May 1936); L.42–3, Wilmet III: "Beauraing 18 mai 1936" (s.n., s.d.).
237 S.n., "Après la condemnation de Rex," *Les Annales de Beauraing et Banneux* 106 (15 May 1937): 4.
238 For the term linear narrative, see Orsi, "Abundant History," 14.
239 "In dezen tijd van radio en electriciteit, van vliegtuigbouw en andere wetenschappelijke verwezenlijkingen." M. De Ceuleneer, "Een nieuw bedevaartsoord," *Het Laatste Nieuws*, 11 September 1933, 2.
240 "Leven in een atmosfeer alsof de mirakels elken dag in de lucht hangen en de verschijningen elk oogenblik zich kunnen voordoen." M. De Ceulener, "De volkstoeloop te Onkerzele," *Het Laatste Nieuws*, 12 September 1933, 3. For a more extensive discussion of the newspaper war, see: Van Osselaer, "Mystics."
241 Blackbourn, *Marpingen*, 30.
242 "The workers are starving," so a booklet titled the *Scandal of Beauraing* (*Het schandaal van Beauraing*) read. "Beauraing is just an anaesthetic to let the workers perish slowly and without pain." "Beauraing is slechts een verdoovingsmiddel omde arbeiders langzaam en zonder pijn te laten omkomen." The author accused, among others, the Jesuits, nuns, and Christian worker movements of plotting this distraction. Vervoort, *Het schandaal*, 22.
243 DAG, Onkerzele, 167: letter from Hélène N. (Bruges), 18 March 1934.
244 "Onkerzeele! Terre de Flandres! Serais-tu jalousie de ta soeur Wallonie?" AAM, Van Roey, Apparitions, 27: nonapproved apparitions and predictions, letter from Richard Berce. See also AAM, Van Roey, Apparitions, 26.

Processus, D.1, litterae de apparitionibus in genere (2 December 1938 and 28 November 1938): a letter from "un humble enfant de Marie" to Mgr Van Roey.

245 AAM, Van Roey, Apparitions, 23. Processus, BIVb: letter with cutting "De 'Verschijningen' te Lokeren" of *Het Laatste Nieuws* (16 November 1933), letter to Monseigneur, dated 29 November 1933.

246 DAG, Onkerzele, 86: notes of the parish priest Vander Maeren on the apparitions of 4 August–23 September 1933.

247 "Mijnheeren, In naam van al de verontwaardigde stadsgenooten vraag ik u ernstig en vriendelijk de volksopruiers die oorzaak zijn van de al te droevige gebeurtenissen op de wijk Naastveld, op de komende demonstratie huiswaarts te zenden ofwel aan te houden, zooniet gelast ik me ze ter plaatse neer te schieten. Met hoogachting gegroet." CAL, XL.1031: apparitions in Naastveld, anonymous note to Mayor and aldermen.

248 "Fanatieke kwezel," "geldafzetterij." S.n., "Hoe lang gaat dat nog duren?" *Vrije Waaslander,* 8 July 1934, 2; S.n., "Lokeren. Bij de feiten," *Voor Allen. Socialistisch Weekblad voor Vlaamsch België,* 8 July 1934, 7.

249 "Van af rond 21 uur stelden wij een gisting onder de menigte vast, welke niet te beteugelen scheen: het volk drong zich immer meer- en meer-vooruit, vijandelijke kreten gingen uit de menigte op, er kon elk oogenblik eene overrompeling van den ordedienst, met bestorming op de bidders, plaats grijpen, en toen op een zeker oogenblik de drie zoogezegde ziensters van uit de dreef tot dicht bij den openbaren weg waren gekomen en tot het volk spraken (men verzekerde mij nadien dat zij beleedigende verwijten tot het volk hadden gericht) dan was het slechts door een uiterst krachtdadig optreden dat den ordedienst kon worden gehandhaafd, waardoor zeker geweldige gebeurtenissen werden vermeden." CAL, XL.1031: report of the adjunct police commissar about 29 July 1934.

250 CAL, XL.1031: report of the adjunct police commissar about 31 July 1934.

251 "Moordzuchtige menigte." AAM, Van Roey, Apparitions, 23. Processus, BIVb: report of Jan Filip Boon about 31 July 1934.

252 CAL, XX: Police, 413/2, charges, 135–7 and 157–9; AAM, Van Roey, Apparitions, 23. Processus, BIVb: copy of the letter from the Mayor Raemdonck (1 August 1934) to Mr Mistler and Mistler's note to others.

253 The letter from Mgr Coppieters was, a.o., published in *De Standaard,* 30 August 1934. AAM, Van Roey, Apparitions, 23. Processus, BIVb: letter to the faithful by Mgr Van Roey.

254 S.n., "Ordonnances episcopales," *Les Annales de Beauraing et de Banneux,* 15 September 1934, 3.

255 Maunder, *Our Lady of the Nations,* 86.

256 Thurston, *Beauraing,* 35.

257 Deneweth, *Kroniek*, 25–6.
258 On the political content, see Christian, *Visionaries*, 7; Scheer, *Rosenkranz*, 20, 22; O'Sullivan, *Disruptive Power*; Matter, "Apparitions," 128. For instance for Mary's anti-communist stance and the Cold War, see Margry, *Cold War Mary*; Maunder, *Our Lady of the Nations*, 122–36; Di Stefano and Ramón Solan, "Introduction," 14.
259 Blackbourn, "The Catholic Church," 788.
260 Zimdars-Swartz, "Religious Experience," 37.
261 "Je préserverai ce pays des envahisseurs." Thurston, *Beauraing*, 27.
262 ASBG, Lambert, 37, apparitions in the diocese of Namur (apparitions Namur), E.2; Tilman Côme: letter from Guibert Naniot (Maredsous), 12 December 1942; ADL, Kerkhofs D/IV. Marian cult, 30. Banneux: letter from Leon Van Winkel, 1940; idem, text 1961; Van Osselaer, "The Changing Face."
263 "De man der boosheid, de scheiding der volkeren, de overweldiger," AAM, Van Roey, Apparitions, 27: nonapproved apparitions and predictions, report on the apparitions to Jules De Vuyst in July 1935. In an accompanying letter, dated 2 November 1939, Louis Wilmet suggests to Van Roey that the report was written by Jan Boon.
264 "Ik zal uw Belgenland bevrijden en bestieren," ADG, Apparitions, 79: report on Jules De Vuyst, 11 June 1937, 8.
265 ADN, L.42–3, Wilmet III: circular letter to the collaborators of the *Annales* (July 1934); Maunder, *Our Lady of the Nations*, 93.
266 ADG, Apparitions, 192: letter from Mlle Fontenoy to Hitler and one to Chamberlain, 4 September 1940.

## Chapter Two

1 "J'ai pensé cependant que ces notes pourraient aussi intéresser l'historien futur qui, après notre génération, entreprendrait de retracer les origines du culte de Notre-Dame de Beauraing. Il pourrait y trouver quelques détails inédits et surtout voir comment on a apparu les débuts de Beauraing à un observateur contemporain, d'autant plus libre de dire ce qu'il sait, qu'il ne songe pas à publier sa relation.... Avant d'écrire ce chapitre, il faudrait pouvoir visiter les archives des évêchés de Namur, Liège, Malines et celle du Saint Office. Mais elles sont bien gardées et le secret qui les couvre ne sera pas levé de sitôt." ASBG, Lambert, 11: papers of Gaston Maes II, 13; Dossier Planque "Souvenirs de Beauraing," (3 January 1950), 17.
2 See Christian, "The Eyes."
3 I thus agree with Paolo Apolito that people's reasoning, argumentation tells us something about the world they live in. Apolito, *Apparitions*, 91.
4 "Vertrauen wird allgemein als konstitutives Element v. Einstellungen, Haltungen und Handlungen verstanden, in denen man auf die

Verlässlichkeit v. Dingen, Personen u. Ereignissen baut (V. zu Dasein, Welt, sich selbst, Menschen, Dingen, Institutionen, Zukunft, Gott). V. ist mit Risiko u. Wagnis verbunden, aber auch v. der Überzeugung getragen dass das worauf man vertraut, das V. rechtfertigt u. somit vertrauenswürdig ist." Ernst, "Vertrauen," 745.

5 "Une atteinte pleine de sécurité," "une espérance plus ferme." Noble, "Confiance," 1406.

6 As Welskopp describes his praxis-oriented approach to trust. Welskopp, "Vertrauen," 49.

7 Hosking, *Trust*, 3; Frevert, "Über Vertrauen," 48; Frevert, *Vertrauensfragen*, 13, 24.

8 A caveat here is that, as Chris Maunder has remarked, in the account of the original apparitions in Beauraing to the children, there was no reference "to suffering or threat, at least not in the received tradition of visionary messages established at the shrine." Maunder, *Our Lady of the Nations*, 85. Maunder does see the effect of a crisis context however (84).

9 Eade and Sallnow, "Introduction," 6.

10 "En ces moments d'agitation mondiale, devant les menaces de guerre, qui nous jettent dans l'angoisse de la reconnaissance de Beauraing et de Banneux donneront un élan de piété et de confiance qui réconforterait les coeurs et ferait espérer l'intervention de la T.S. Vierge, qui à Banneux a déclaré venir pour toutes les nations. C'est d'ailleurs la conviction de notre saint évêque qui m'a communiqué lui-même sa conviction à ce sujet." ASBX, 2 C 3 XV 4: démarches à Rome, lettres diverses, Mgr L. De Gruyter, Liège, to Mgr Eras, Dutch college in Rome (18 November 1939).

11 "Avec tant d'amour et de confiance à Onkerzele pour implorer sa guérison … Il trouve que Lokeren ressemble à Ezquioga." AAM, Van Roey, Apparitions, 23. Processus, BII: report on Lokeren (Louis Wilmet) Louis Wilmet to Mgr Van Roey, 24 August 1934.

12 "Les faveurs d'ordre temporal, notamment les guérisons ont été fort nombreuses. Une partie en est enregistrée avec grand soin. Les bénéficiaires en témoignent une grande reconnaissance à la Vierge des Pauvres, et l'on constate que c'est là l'explication du mouvement des pèlerinages à Banneux et de la croissante confiance dans des affaires de plus en plus étendues." ADDF, Dev. Var., 1934.11 Banneux, 6: letter from the bishop of Liège (23 December 1934) to Mgr Micara.

13 "Au pied du talus, au sommet auquel je me trouve, se jouent des scènes du plus haut comique; des hommes, des femmes, la plupart en belles toilettes, essaient de monter de la chaussée jusqu'au sommet du remblai pour mieux voir ce qui se passe vis-à-vis, à la chapelle; mais la terre, glaiseuse et boueuse, glisse et cède sous leurs pieds; les uns s'affalent de tout leur long; les autres font des efforts surhumains pour tenir en équilibre, mais

finissent par s'étaler, eux et leurs beaux habits, dans la vase, aux éclats de rire des gens qui les regardent d'en haut, narquois et impuissants à les aider dans leur ascension périlleuse. D'aucuns s'abattirent ainsi à plat ventre, et glissèrent ensuite jusqu'au bas du talus, tandis que leurs petites valises à provisions de bouche s'ouvraient, répandant sur le sol boueux les victuailles désormais inmangeables. C'était un spectacle pitoyable, dont on riait pour ne pas en pleurer; les rires étaient d'ailleurs plutôt des rires nerveux de gens inoccupés et impatients que des moqueries déplacées." AAM, Van Roey, Apparitions, 24. Processus, BIXA1: report of Wilmet, 28 December 1933.

14 AAM, Van Roey, Apparitions, 24. Processus, BIXA1: report of Louis Wilmet, 28 December 1933.

15 See Cock's article, "Mijn gezegend oord," 276–87.

16 "Où nous reconnaissons maints fervents des autres lieux d'apparitions." Wilmet himself reported on Beauraing, but also Onkerzele, Lokeren, Etikhove, Herzele, Chaineux, and Melen. AAM, Van Roey, Apparitions, 23. Processus, BII: report on Lokeren, 21 August 1934 added to a letter of 24 August 1934.

17 DAG, Onkerzele, 40: letter from Boon to parish priest, 6 October 1935.

18 From the de Croÿ family of Rumillies (1897–1957). She organized a pilgrimage in memory of the apparitions to Tilman Côme in Beauraing each year.

19 Germaine De Smet (1888–1969) was a writer (poetry, novels, and plays), editor of the Catholic newspaper *La Métropole* (Antwerp), and a correspondent for, among others, *Les Annales de Beauraing et de Banneux, Banneux Notre-Dame*. CAL, XL.1031: apparitions near Naastveld, visiting cards of Germaine. Daniël van Ryssel, *55 Vergeten Gentse schrijvers*, s.p.

20 In two cases, the promoters inform us about their motives for getting involved. Jan Boon, for instance ascribed his son's healing to a visit to Beauraing and was rumoured (and acknowledged) to have experienced a Marian apparition himself on 31 July 1934. AAM, Van Roey, Apparitions, 24. Processus, BIXA1: notes of Jan Filip Boon about 15 November 1933. See also DAG, Onkerzele, 192: letter from Jan Boon to parish priest Vander Maeren, 19 September 1934. Germaine De Smet, on the other hand, claimed that her thumb had healed miraculously thanks to Mary's intervention. She solemnly swore that she would dedicate her talent to the promotion of the Virgin's cause out of gratitude. AAM, Van Roey, Apparitions, 24. Processus, BIXA1: letter from Germaine De Smet to Mgr Coppieters, 18 December 1933.

21 Badone, "Echoes," 465, on how the testimony of certain categories of people is accorded greater or lesser credibility.

22 – "Echoes," 453.

23 See also Van Osselaer, "Mystics," 1172.

24 ASBG, Pierroux, 1935, 121: letter to the dean from the diocese of Namur informing after Les Amis de Beauraing, 5 November 1935. See also Lambert, 11: papers of Gaston Maes II, 13; and Dossier Planque "Souvenirs de Beauraing," 17–23. For the original association, Familia and the later primarily clerical Association Saint-Martin (responsible for the financial side), see Delvaux, "Naissance," 32.

25 ASBG, Lambert, 37. Apparitions Namur: letter from Lambert to Excellence, propaganda letter.

26 Originally named Pèlerinages de Banneux (in 1933) renamed in 1935. ADDF, Dev. Var., 1934.11 Banneux: letter from miraculé Philipp B. (Cologne) to Pope Pius XI, 26 September 1934.

27 Wilmet (*Beauraing*, 255) claims the committee was erected (11 October 1933) with the approval of the bishop of Ghent. On Lokeren, see ADN, L.42–3, Wilmet III: document s.n., s.t., on Lokeren ("Résulte des documents").

28 AAM, Van Roey, Apparitions, 21: diverse apparitions, Onkerzele, letter from Gaston Gevaert to Mgr Coppieters and Canon Gheysels of Audenaerde, 7 November 1933.

29 Circulaires of the *Annales*, nr.2. ADN, L.42–3, Wilmet III. On Ham-sur-Sambre's Virgo Virginum, see L.7/2, HSS, apparitions 1943–51: articles of the association, 22 March 1946.

30 AAM, Van Roey, Apparitions, 23. Processus, A2XII: report of Van Hove, 23 November 1935 for the interdiocesan commission (11 December 1935); BIXB1: letter from Van Hoeymisse (2 November 1935).

31 ADG, Vermeire, 62: letter from E. Cappelle to "friend and family" (Vermeire), 26 September 1934.

32 The *Cenacle* gathered in Brussels on every second and fourth Sunday to inform its members on visions, bleedings, and predictions. The Penitent Servants of Mary (Les Serviteurs Pénitents de Marie), a Brussels-based association with ramifications in Flanders (Antwerp, Opwijk, Sint Niklaas, and Lokeren), went on a pilgrimage to Beauraing every third Sunday of the month and to Banneux on the first. There were about 200 to 250 members. AAM, Van Roey, Apparitions, 24. Processus, BIXB2: cénacle de N.D. Médiatrice, Reine de la Paix, Circulaire 2, 19 June 1935; BIXB: letter from Van Hoeymisse to the bishop, 12 September 1935.

33 Coleman and Eade, "Introduction," 3. Movement to and movement at the sites "in certain cases trace the ways in which mobile performances can help to construct – however temporarily – apparently sacredly charged places."

34 ADG, Apparitions, 99: letter from parish priest Vander Maeren, 16 February 1936. There are fewer pilgrims, but they still come. Primarily on days dedicated to the Virgin.

35 ASBG, Lambert, 37. Apparitions Namur, E.2. Tilman Côme: letter to Princess de Croÿ, 16 April 1943, and a letter from Princess de Croÿ to Monseigneur, 23 April 1943.

36 Van den Steen, "Tilman Côme."

37 One of them, Martha M., even got a free seat on the bus since the driver called her good for business. AAM, Van Roey, Apparitions, 24. Processus, BIXA2: documenta GII1, relata in documento annexo IX, 2 (6 January–31 March 1934), M. Vanneste (White Fathers Antwerp), 24 January 1934, sends a copy of a letter from Martha M. (19 January 1934).

38 In the 1930s sources there are also references to a prayer union that focused on the apparitions to Tilman Côme. ADN, L.42–3, Wilmet I: letter from Michel Declaye from Siège, to Princess de Croÿ, 22 November 1936.

39 ASBG, Pierroux, 1934–35, 34: letter from Adolphe Poyot, 22 October 1935, on the conflict between the two associations Serviteurs Pénitents de Marie, and their spinoff, Pèlerins Serviteurs Pénitents de Marie.

40 Eade, "Order," 51.

41 A "divinely ordained site." Halter, "Field Notes," 111. On the "possibility of breaking through to the realm of the transcendent," see Eade and Sallnow, "Introduction," 6.

42 See the reports in the liberal newspaper. M. De Ceulener, "De belangstelling te Etichove," *Het Laatste Nieuws*, 31 October 1933, 3.

43 Letter from the *Annales*, nr.2 (ADN, L.42–3, Wilmet III): The visionary Mathieu L. was building the chapel requested by Mary, pilgrims donated 800 francs but he needed 16,000.

44 For instance, the Committee of Lokeren tried to create a place of prayer and shelter: ADG, Apparitions, 32: letter from Mistler to Mgr Coppieters, 24 February 1939.

45 In Onkerzele this sponsoring went wrong the moment that one of the financers, Mme Van de Walle, tried to take back the money she had donated for the renovation of the seven chapels of Our Lady's Sorrows and the expansion of the chapel, since she no longer believed the visionary. AAM, Van Roey, Apparitions, 24. Processus, BXII3: documenta G Varia, correspondence between Vander Maeren and Van de Walle (typed version, 19 May 1934), manuscript; BXI2: documenta GIV, letter from Vander Maeren to Van de Walle.

46 ADN, L.42–3, Wilmet I: letter from Wilmet to Princess de Croÿ, 1934. He had a visit from Maurice's spiritual leader who told him that the site for the chapel had already been donated but that the mayor and bishop were opposed to the plans. ADG, Apparitions, 99: letter from Vander Maeren, 16 February 1936: to "His Excellence." In it, he described how the committee from Brussels had purchased seventeen acres of the land behind

the church and churchyard and donated it to Jules De Vuyst who has to give it to the parish in order to put up the seven chapels.

47 The visionary Jules De Vuyst even "helped" the architect who drew these plans, claiming Mary informed him as to the exact location and measurements. ADG, Apparitions, 96: report of Jan Boon about 26 February 1935.

48 "Weet wel dat ik meermaals eene lange reis ondernam, liever dan eenen brief achter te laten, 'k doe tegenwoordig gansch het tegenovergestelde. Ik beoog dat 'schrijven zouden blijven.' Ik weet waarom." ADG, Vermeire, 88: letter from Léon Sebruyns-Desmet to Honoré Vermeire, 12 February 1936.

49 "La reine des voyants." ASBG, Pierroux, 1932–33: A letter about Onkerzele, 12 April 1934.

50 AAM, Van Roey, Apparitions, 24. Processus, BXI2: Alfred Magain, 13 April 1934.

51 DAG, Onkerzele, 4: text of Jan Boon about Berthonia Holtkamp's religious life, 1 December 1933.

52 AAM, Van Roey, Apparitions, 24. Processus, BXII3: testimony, Father Valveke 28 November 1933.

53 "Ereboetsters," AAM, Van Roey, Apparitions, 24. Processus, BXI2: report of Jan Boon, 27 June 1934.

54 AAM, Van Roey, Apparitions, 24. Processus, BXII4c: letter from Thyssen to his Eminence 21 March 1935; BXII4b: Testimony of Thyssen, parish priest of Saint Joris, Antwerp, 8 April 1935; ADG, Vermeire, 76: letter from "Maria Veronica," 27 February 1936.

55 AAM, Van Roey, Apparitions, 23. Processus, BIVb: letter from Mgr Van Roey to the faithful.

56 ADG, Apparitions, 179: Hubert Peeters to Mgr Coppieters, 28 April 1936, answers to dioceses of Ghent and Bruges, letter to Holtkamp and Quatannens, 29 April 1936; 67: Poppe (vicar-general Ghent) 11 May 1936 to Holtkamp and Quatannens. Holtkamp's messages about the Sacred Head of Jesus showed remarkable resemblances to what Teresa Higginson, a nineteenth-century English schoolteacher, had claimed. DAG: Onkerzele, 59: report of the questioning of Holtkamp in the parsonage, 3 February 1934. For Higginson, see Heimann, "Mysticism."

57 ADG, Apparitions, 118: visions of Maria Veronica, 7 March 1936.

58 ADG, Apparitions, 4: note with negative judgment devotion to the Sacred Head; "Brief van Z.H. Exc. Mgr. den Bisschop aan de gelovigen der deekenij van Geerardsbergen," *Godsdienstige week van het bisdom Gent* 27 (1 July 1938): 1. After a time in Anzegem, they seem to have moved back to Onkerzele and turned it into an international pilgrimage centre. Berthonia Holtkamp seems to have reported visions until 1953. Speleers, "Verschijningen," 39. Quatannens died in 1970.

59 "Anversois," AAM, Van Roey, Apparitions, 24. Processus, BXI2: letter from Alfred Magain, 28 April 1934; 23. Processus, BIXA2: documentation on the fallout between Holtkamp and Magain (at the beginning of February 1934).

60 ADN, L.42–3, Wilmet III: letter from Louis Wilmet to "Reverend father," 24 August 1933.

61 "Maintenant que … je connais les dangers du silence … et de la parole." ADN, L.42–3, Wilmet III. That same month Abbé Francot advised him to postpone the publication of his book. ADN, L.42–3, documents of Louis Wilmet III: letter from Francot, 23 August 1933.

62 ADL, Kerkhofs, D/IV Marian cult, 30. Banneux, II. Tilman Côme: manuscript, post 1943.

63 There was a similar call for reports on cures to be published in *Les Echos d'Onkerzele* 1, no. 2, a typed periodical that seems to have been put together by "Sr" Marie Régine, ADG, Apparitions 192–3.

64 Jan Van Saelen, a miraculé from Onkerzele, left his crutches there in a public ceremony and Henri Kempenaers left an ex-voto. AAM, Van Roey, Apparitions, 24. Processus, BIXA1: report of Sebruyns on 16 February 1934 in a letter of 17 February 1934; BIXA2: letter from parish priest Vander Maeren, 17 February 1934; AAM, Van Roey, Apparitions, 21: diverse apparitions, Onkerzele, letter from Richard B. (9 July 1936) about his trip to Onkerzele, 16 February 1936.

65 AAM, Van Roey, Apparitions, 24. Processus, BXII2: letter from parish priest Vander Maeren to Mgr Coppieters and a draft version of his answer, 22 October 1934.

66 "Examiner et croire, c'est deux. Et il faut commencer par examiner, avec sympathie certes, mais avec défiance, oui, avec méfiance, sachant que le diable est le maitre du monde et qu'il a même tenté le Christ et l'histoire abonde en preuves de sa force. Ici, on croit d'abord, on veut que le surnaturel existe à tout prix et on s'égare dans le domaine le plus délicat du monde et le plus périlleux." ADN, L.42–3, Wilmet III: letter from Louis Wilmet to Princess Madeleine de Croÿ, 14 August 1934.

67 "Mais j'ai simplement voulu montrer qu'il est dangereux de se fier à ce que l'on croit un 'critère' parce que alors on explique tout en fonction de l'idée que l'on croit devoir défendre." ADN, L.42–3, Wilmet I: letter from Wilmet to Abbé Didion, 17 September 1936.

68 On the long tradition of such discernment and the importance of the singularity of each apparition, see Ziegenaus, "Kriterien," 167.

69 Lenain, Jean-Baptiste, "Les faits de Beauraing au point de vue théologique," *Saint-Luc Médicale*, 11.4 (1933), 147–9, 148.

70 Christian, "The Eyes," 79.

71 Blackbourn, "Die von Gottheit überaus bevorzugten Mägdlein," 172.

72 The vision content was subject to filtering as well. Messages were summarized and adjusted "until they resembled what people expected or wanted to hear." Christian, "Six Hundred Years," 116, 118.

73 "C'est un simple paysan, d'intelligence inculte, d'instruction et d'éducation rudimentaires, ne parlant qu'un fruste patois flamand; il est ainsi au niveau de la plupart des visionnaires, choisi presque toujours parmi les plus humbles et les plus insignifiants, parce qu'ils sont incapables de tirer d'eux-mêmes ou d'études antérieures les messages qu'ils apportent." AAM, Van Roey, Apparitions, 27: nonapproved apparitions and predictions, reports on Jules De Vuyst by Constant Van der Meer, 8 January 1944.

74 On the male visionaries, see Van Osselaer, "Sensitive."

75 "Ouvrier apôtre." ASBG, Pierroux, 1932–33: letter from Hamont, 14 July 1933.

76 Van Osselaer, "Sensitive," 135.

77 ASBG, Pierroux, 1934–5, 1935.4: the ideas of C. from Jemelle, 10 January 1935.

78 AAM, Van Roey, Apparitions, 24. Processus, BIXA2: letter from A. Martin to secretary of the bishop of Ghent, 31 January 1934.

79 AAM, Van Roey, Apparitions, 24. Processus, BIXA1: report of the questioning of the visionaries, 21 November 1933, letter from parish priest Vander Maeren to Mgr Coppieters, 21 November 1933.

80 For the narrative of the converted visionary, see Van Osselaer, "Sensitive."

81 ADDF, Dev. Var., 1933.2 Beauraing, 57: letter from an "obeying and devoted Belgian" ("une Belge obéissante et dévoué") to the Holy Father (29 January 1939) noting that the Beauraing children had these last six years continued to pray at the site of the apparitions. Conversely, Théodore Weemaes, who had been called as a witness for the commission in Malines, noted that he could not believe that Omer Eneman had experienced a Marian apparition since he had not become more pious since the events. AAM, Van Roey, Apparitions, 23. Processus, A3, copia actorum: testimony of Théodore Weemaes, fifth session of the commission of Malines, 13 June 1935.

82 ADN, L.42–3, Wilmet II: letter from Magain to Wilmet, post 28 August.

83 "The instrument of the Germans," ("L'instrument des Allemands") L. De Hulster, "Une Enquête. Le mystère de Beauraing," *Le Peuple*, 26 July 1933, 2.

84 The Voisin children of the Beauraing series also faced comments on their family's morality. ASBG, Pierroux, 1932–33: Georges Lejeune, "Les visionnaires de Beauraing. Fernande, Gilberte et Albert Voisin." s.d.; AAM, Van Roey, Apparitions, 40: Beauraing and Banneux, document on the morality of the visionaries and their family.

85 "'t zijn menschen," DAG, Onkerzele, 211: letter from Louis Wilmet to parish priest, February 1934.

86 "La vague de grande confiance et de foi en Banneux est alimentée sans cesse par tous les bienfaits attribués à la prière envers Marie, Vierge des Pauvres." ADDF, Dev. Ver., 1934.11 Banneux, 13: *Banneux Notre-Dame – bilan des faveurs*, 1934.

87 Kempenaers had visions in, among other places, Beauraing and Onkerzele.

88 DAG, Onkerzele, 46: interviews conducted by H. De Kelver for *De Standaard*, 19 October 1933; 5: visionaries, information on Kempenaers, 1 December 1933 re: consumption ("longtering") since 1929.

89 "Alles langzaam en statig, geen enkele krampachtige beweging – met zeer secuur gebaar bijvoorbeeld knopje van zijn col losmakend … armen lichtjes open boven zijn hoofd (als in kruis) niet horizontaal maar schuinsch nogal breedopen naar omhoog gesloten oogen tong in den mond – bittere uitdrukking." AAM, Van Roey, Apparitions, 24. Processus, BIXA1: report of 25 December 1933 by Jan Boon.

90 S.n., "Te Onkerzele," *De Standaard*, 30 December 1933, 3.

91 "Toen heb ik het volgende gezien aan mijn handen: deze waren precies hol geworden van binnen, alsof het slechts maar een vel meer was langs den palm en een vel op den rug. Als ik er op drukte scheen er geen vleesch meer in. Er was een groote roode (licht roode, een lichter kleur dan bloed) vlek op den binnenkant der handen ongeveer dezelfde vlek in beide handen, er waren teekens zoals van iets dat vaneengescheurd is en waar het vleesch is in stukken getrokken." AAM, Van Roey, Apparitions, 24. Processus, BXI2: letter from Boon about Kempenaers, 25–8 June 1934.

92 Kane, "'She Offered,'" 107. See the Stigmatics database, accessed 8 August 2024, mediahaven-stigmatics.uantwerpen.be/, and Van Osselaer, Graus, Rossi and Smeyers, 2020.

93 AAM, Van Roey, Apparitions, 23. Processus, BIVb: letter from Roland to the bishop of Ghent, 2 August 1934.

94 Van Osselaer, "Uit de lucht;" AAM, Van Roey, Apparitions, 23. Processus, BIIIa: letter from C. Borromaeus Vandewalle, 20 February 1935; BIV: a letter from Borromaeus Vandewalle, 29 May 1935

95 At least eleven cures were reported in Onkerzele between September 1933 and February 1940, but they were no match for the cures reported in connection to the two recognized sites. An overview of the Banneux cures of 1934 lists at least 238 instances (both improvements and general cures). ADDF, Dev. Var., 1934.11 Banneux, 13: booklet *Banneux Notre-Dame: Overview of Cures 1934*. For the miraculous cures reported in Onkerzele, see Jacobs, *De zienster*, 13: Van Saelen from Antwerp was, for instance, cured of osteomyelitis (inflammation bone marrow).

96 ADN, L.42–3, Wilmet III: circular letter to the collaborators of the *Annales* 2.

97 ADDF, Dev. Var., 1933.2 Beauraing, 22: texts of the *Annales de Beauraing et de Banneux*, "circulaire aux collaborateurs des Annales. Strictement confidentielle."

98 ADN, L.42–3, Wilmet III: letter from Wilmet to Lenain, 28 August 1933.

99 Signori, "Die Wunderheilung," 82–3.

100 ASBG, Pierroux, 1934–5, 1935: twenty-four documents on the cure of Sr R. of Mons, 29 August 1935.

101 S.n., "Kroniek van Beauraing. De genezing van H. De Wolf van Turnhout," *De Standaard*, 24 June 1933, 2.

102 ASBG, Lambert, 44: various cures and favours, documents on the cure of Hermine P.

103 ADDF, Dev. Ver., 1934.11 Banneux, 13: *Banneux Notre-Dame – bilan des faveurs*, 1934.

104 Kaufman, *Consuming Visions*, 96.

105 For a description of Holtkamp as hysterical, see ADL, Kerkhofs, D/IV Marian cult, 30. Banneux: documents on Tilman Côme II, M. De Croÿ to abbé, s.d. See also AAM, Van Roey, Apparitions, 24. Processus, BXII3: letter from Tharcisius Valvekens to Mgr, 23 November 1933. For a similar comment on Martha M. see DAG, Onkerzele, 242: report of Wilmet 24 February 1934; idem, 6: anonymous letter to Wilmet, s.d.

106 ASBG, Lambert, 3: unpublished manuscripts, text of A. Pierroux about 1932–43.

107 Boon, *Getuigenis*, 76.

108 See, for instance, these two sources on Kempenaers: AAM, Van Roey, Apparitions, 24. Processus, BXII3: letter Dewinter to Mgr about Kempenaers, 7 December 1933; and DAG, Onkerzele, 63: report on the apparitions in Onkerzele, 23 February 1934.

109 AAM, Van Roey, Apparitions, 24. Processus, BVIIb1: report on the apparitions by Vander Maeren, 4 August 23 – September 1933; similar: s.n., "Te Onkerzele," *De Standaard*, 24 September 1933, 3.

110 AAM, Van Roey, Apparitions, 24. Processus, BIXA1: report of Magain on 21 November 1933.

111 AAM, Van Roey, Apparitions, 23. Processus, BIVb: letter from Emma Veldeman to Mgr 21 June 1934.

112 AAM, Van Roey, Apparitions, 25. Processus, C3h: letter from parish priest of Stockel, 14 April 1934 (on a visionary "overstrained because of his nocturnal work," "overspannen door nachtwerk").

113 "Ils invoquent si facilement la suggestion, hallucination, hystérie, hypnotisme … Les médecins sont tous un peu … matérialistes. On consulte trop la science médicale que Dieu ou la Sainte Vierge viennent précisément bouleverser." ASBG, Pierroux, 1932–33: letter from Hamont, 14 July 1933.

114 "La Ste vierge peut même se servir d'un 'fou' aux yeux du monde; d'un hystérique prouvé par la science pour confondre cette science humaine." ASBG, Pierroux, 1932–33: letter from Hamont, 14 July 1933.

115 ADN, L.2: commission for the recognition of the apparitions in Beauraing, opposition, notes of Pierroux, reflections on De Greeff, 13 March 1936.

116 DAG, Onkerzele, 57: letter from Commandeure Faure de l'Ordre du Saint-Sépulcre, report about 21 January 1934 ("it is a sudden joy," "c'est une joie subite"); S.n., "Wat is er gaande te Onkerzele?," *De Standaard*, 11 September 1933, 3 (happiness on Van den Dijck's face); AAM, Van Roey, Apparitions, 24. Processus, BIXA1: report of Jan Boon on Kempenaers' reembodiment of Christ's passion on 25 December 1933 ("a tender glow on his face," "teedere glans op het gelaat").

117 AAM, Van Roey, Apparitions, 24. Processus, BXII2: letter from parish priest Vander Maeren to Mgr Coppieters, 28 October 1934.

118 "Je note que durant les prières devant l'arbre, j'ai difficilement distingué l'état d'extase de celui de non-extase. Seule sa fixité des regards me renseignait, car la physionomie gardait son aspect normal sans expression particulière. Le sourire était doux, les gestes étaient très lentes, aucune pâleur, pas d'émotions vives, pas de transfiguration." AAM, Van Roey, Apparitions, 24. Processus, BIXA1: report about Onkerzele by Louis Wilmet, 21 November 1933.

119 "Comme toujours elle est très belle." AAM, Van Roey, Apparitions, 24. Processus, BIXA2. "Impression d'au-delà," report of Germaine De Smet, 6 January 1934.

120 "Frisch en engelachtig," s.n., "Te Onkerzele," *De Standaard*, 20 November 1933, 3; AAM, Van Roey, Apparitions, 24. Processus, BIXA1: report on Onkerzele by Magain about 21 November 1933, 89.

121 DAG, Onkerzele, 40: letter from Jan Boon to the local parish priest, 6 October 1935.

122 AAM, Van Roey, Apparitions, 24. Processus, BIXA1: report of Louis Wilmet, 21 November 1933. Leurquin emphasized the subjectivity in such descriptions noting that he saw nothing supernatural in Berthonia Holtkamp's smile. He added that similar descriptions of the angelic smile of Martha M. had been published, whereas at the time he was writing his comment no one still had confidence in her. AAM, Van Roey, Apparitions, 24. Processus, BIXA2: report Leurquin (Auderghem), 6 February 1934.

123 ASBG, Pierroux, 1934, 163: letter from Watteyne to the dean of Beauraing, 24 October 1934. Louis Wilmet noted that whereas some called Tilman Côme's features fearful, he would rather call them "pensive." ADN, L.42–3, Wilmet I: letter from Wilmet to Didion, 17 September 1936.

124 On emotions and mysticism, see Van Osselaer, "Sensitive." ADG, Vermeire, 17: description of the apparitions to Omer Eneman, 14–17 October

1933 (Enemans is crying and praying); AAM, Van Roey, Apparitions, 24. Processus, BIXA1: report of Louis Wilmet, 21 November 1933 (Kempenaers expresses his emotion through crying).

125 "Gevoelig," "sentimenteel," AAM, Van Roey, Apparitions, 24. Processus, BIXA1: Boon on the life of Berthonia Holtkamp.

126 AAM, Van Roey, Apparitions, Van Roey, Apparitions, 23. Processus, A3: Copia actorum, testimony of Wilmet on the fifth session, 13 June 1935 (on the theatrical, even grotesque movements of Elisabeth Cornelis); idem, 24. Processus, BIXA1: letter from Wilmet to Mgr Coppieters (19 February 1934) including notes on a letter from de Croÿ to Wilmet, 6 January 1934 (when Martha M. is in ecstasy her arm movements make a displeasing impression).

127 ADN, L.42–3, Wilmet I: document "Chez abbé Aneuse," 6 January 1934 (pencil notes). Similarly, another eye witness of the Beauraing events testified that he believed in them because he was very moved when the apparitions took place. ASBG, Lambert, notebook Gilles Carlsbourg, August 1934, 1.

128 AAM, Van Roey, Apparitions, 23. Processus, BII: Wilmet's report on Lokeren 25 July 1934.

129 S.n., "Te Onkerzele," *De Standaard*, 30 December 1934, 3.

130 DAG, Onkerzele, 46: interviews for De Standaard about 29 October 1933; AAM, Van Roey, Apparitions, 24. Processus, BIXA1: report of Magain, 28 December 1933; A2: report of Sebruyns-Desmet, 23 February 1934 and 3 March 1934.

131 AAM, Van Roey, Apparitions, 24. Processus, BIXA1: report from Wilmet about Onkerzele, 21 November 1933.

132 "Papier d'Armenie," AAM, Van Roey, Apparitions, 24. Processus, BIXA1: questioning by Jan Boon of Berthonia Holtkamp, 15 November 1933.

133 "Balsemgeur," ADG, Apparitions, 69: letter from Germaine De Smet, 27 December 1934.

134 Davis and Boles, "Pilgrim Apparition Work," 376.

135 On the importance of photography for the promotion of the cases, see Christian, *The Stranger*, 58: "A critical change from the early modern episodes is that photography, film and video have become the key means of demonstrating reality, replacing in the popular mind sworn testimony … In the twentieth century, photographs and films became evidence in the deliberative process both for Church authorities and for public opinion."

136 Christian, "L'œil de l'esprit."

137 Their model might have been the Ezquioga photos in *Soirées* (8 September, 22 September, 6 October 1933, see 51) or the Belgian-based Ezquioga newspaper *L'Enigme d'Ezkioga* published occasionally by Fernand Remisch (Dorola) from December 1933 until 1936.

138 See the photographs and photo albums preserved in the archives of the diocese of Ghent. William Christian has worked on the selection of photographs of the Ezquioga site. Christian, "L'œil de l'esprit."

139 Davis and Boles, "Pilgrim Apparition Work," 389 and 395.

140 Beauraing: 3 January 1933, 6 August 1933; Onkerzele: 18 December 1933, 6 January 1934, and Lokeren; 25 July 1934.

141 ADN, L.42–3, Wilmet III: letter from Tielemans to Wilmet, 13 August 1933 and son Arnold Tieleman to Wilmet 13 August 1933.

142 Bennett, *When the Sun,* 161. S.n., "Kroniek van Beauraing," *De Standaard* 17 August 1933, 2–3.

143 According to Didion, 5,000 people saw the phenomenon in Onkerzele. AAM, Van Roey, Apparitions, 24. Processus, BIXA1: letter from Louis Wilmet, 23 December 1933, and a report on the solar phenomenon of Onkerzele, 18 December 1933.

144 AAM, Van Roey, Apparitions, 24. Processus, BIXA1: letter from Louis Wilmet, 23 December 1933, and a report on the solar phenomenon of Onkerzele, 18 December 1933.

145 AAM, Van Roey, Apparitions, 24. Processus, BIXA1: report of Tielemans. Louis Wilmet even called it a pity that what had happened in Onkerzele was compared to Fátima. In his opinion the dubious character of the Onkerzele events rubbed off on Fátima's reputation. Ibid.: report of Wilmet about Onkerzele, 28 December 1933.

146 ADN, L.5bis: "Lourdes et Beauraing" (with the stamp of Hubert Simons).

147 AAM, Van Roey, Apparitions, 40: Beauraing and Banneux, letter from Watteyne, 27 July 1934. Similarities with more positively evaluated phenomena also caused doubts. Abbé Didion was convinced that the devil knew about these previous cases and could easily imitate them. ADN, L.42–3, Wilmet I: letter from Didion to Wilmet, 16 September 1936.

148 ADN, L.42–3, Wilmet II: letter from Princess de Croÿ to Wilmet, 20 July 1934, 93; DAG, Onkerzele, 201: letter from J. Sobrie, July 1934.

149 AAM, Van Roey, Apparitions, 23. Processus, BIVb: letter to Mgr, 14 July 1934. Others believed that the decision about Ezquioga would soon be revoked and, as the Spanish site would be approved, so would Lokeren. Idem, BII: Wilmet's report about Lokeren, 25 July 1934.

150 According to Jamin, the parish priest of Banneux, the Verviers apparitions were a practical joke, and no one had taken them seriously. Still, even as late as February 1934, the Verviers apparitions were on the mind of Leurquin, who then questioned the Onkerzele visionary, Berthonia Holtkamp, about their authenticity. ADDF, Dev. Var., 1934.11 Banneux, 21: extraits divers concernant l'attitude du P. Bruno et du Dr De Greeff by Jamin, 3 October 1936; AAM, Van Roey, Apparitions, 24. Processus, BIXA2: report of Leurquin from Auderghem, 6 February 1934.

151 ADN, L.42–3, Wilmet III: anonymous note, probably around November 1933.

152 "Wij zijn niet in een land van lichtgeloovigen, noch van menschen die zich gemakkelijk appelen voor citroenen laten in de hand stoppen, de Vlamingen vooral zien dit alles aan met nuchter verstand." S.n., "Te Onkerzele en elders," *De Standaard,* 15 October 1933, 5.

153 S.n., "Les prétendues apparitions de la Vierge à Rochefort," *La Libre Belgique*, 2 September 1933, 3.

154 "Nous constaterons en terminant que la presse catholique fait une publicité exceptionnelle en faveur de Beauraing et reste muette quand il s'agit de Rochefort." Pardaf II, "Celle dont la presse cléricale ne parle pas: La Vierge de Rochefort," *Le Peuple*, 31 August 1933, 2.

155 First reports: Pardaf II, "Espérant pour Rochefort," *Le Peuple*, 26 August 1933, 1, 3.

156 S.n., "Te Onkerzele en elders," *De Standaard,* 15 October 1933, 5.

157 S.n., "Les mystérieuses apparitions de Rochefort. L'explication du phénomène," *Le Peuple*, 5 September 1933.

158 S.n., "Les prétendues apparitions de la Vierge à Rochefort," *La Libre Belgique*, 2 September 1933, 3.

159 Raphael Sindic, "Que s'est-il passé à Chaineux?," *Soirées*, 27 October 1933, s.p. and 3 November 1933, s.p.; S.n., "Des apparitions de la Vierge à Chaineux?" *La Libre Belgique*, 12 October 1933, 3.

160 ADL, Kerkhofs, D/IV Marian cult, 28: enquête canonique sur "les faits de Banneux," session 14 (9 October 1935) R.P. Dom Boniface del Marmol, OSB of Maredsous; idem, session 17 (23 October 1935): Mademoiselle Madeleine del Marmol.

161 Albert Bouckaert, "Les 'Apparitions' de Chaineux," *Le Soir*, 14 November 1933, cutting preserved in ASBG, Lambert, 66. Diverse visions.

162 ADN, L.42–3, Wilmet III: circulation letter (typed), reference to a letter from Verviers, 3 February 1934.

163 ADN, L.42–3, Wilmet III: note probably circa November 1933.

164 S.n., "De vizioenenzwendel houdt aan en de H. Maagd laat niet af!" *De Vooruit,* 7 September 1934, 5; Geache, "Les miracles continuent! Notre-Dame de Woluwe," *L'Étoile Belge*, 14 September 1934: cutting preserved in ASBG, 66. Diverse visions.

165 S.n., "Autour des apparitions de Rendeux," *La Wallonie*, 25 January 1933, newspaper cutting preserved in ASBG, Lambert 66. Diverse visions.

166 S.n., "Nog nieuwe verschijningen. Verklaringen van een vrouw te Uitkerke," *Het Laatste Nieuws*, 7 November 1933, 2.

167 ADN, L.42–3, Wilmet III: note probably circa November 1933.

168 Frevert, *Vertrauensfragen*, 8.

169 "Ziehier mijn arm, genees hem, toon dat gij werkelijke de Lieve Vrouw der Armen zijt. Ik ben van zo ver gekomen, opdat Gij mij genezen zoudt!" –

"Genoeg gebeden, riep hij, ik ben genezen!" A. Magain, "De verschijningen van Onkerzele," *Gazet van Audenaerde*, 30 September 1933, 1. Press clipping in ADN, L.42–3, Wilmet II: documents on "Pellegri and Banneux."

170 ADN, L.42–3, Wilmet II: letter from Wilmet 28 August 1934 with reference to *Gazet d'Audenaerde*; press clipping of *Gazet van Audenaerde*, 30 September 1933, 7; idem 40: text by A. Magain. His name is spelled in different ways: Benito Pellegri, Pelegri, and Pelegri-Garcia.

171 ADN, L.42–3, Wilmet III: letter from Wilmet to "Cher et Révérend Père," 13 September 1933, circular letter to the collaborators of the *Annales* (s.d.); M.D.R., "De verschijning der Maagd te Onkerzele. Haar boodschap aan de bevolking," *De Vooruit*, 22 September 1933, 3; AAM, Van Roey, Apparitions, 24. Processus, BIXA2: letter from A. Martin (Auderghem) to secretary of bishop of Ghent.

172 ADN, L.42–3, Wilmet II: documents on "Pellegri and Banneux," report of the conversation with Mgr Coppieters on 7 December 1933.

173 AAM, Van Roey, Apparitions, 40: Beauraing and Banneux, letters of the faithful, pro and contra, letter from Octave Dive, parish priest of Onhaye, 6 June 1934.

174 See for instance Princess de Croÿ's warning of M. Verbeke in Onkerzele, AAM, Van Roey, Apparitions, 24. Processus, BIXA1: Wilmet to Mgr Coppieters, 19 February 1934.

175 ADN, L.42–3, Wilmet II: documents on "Pellegri and Banneux," report of the conversation with Mgr Coppieters on 7 December 1933.

176 "C'est un Espagnol, ils exagèrent et inventent tous." ADN, L.42–3, Wilmet II: documents on "Pellegri and Banneux," letter from Princess de Croÿ to Louis Wilmet, 18 June 1934.

177 ADN, L.42–3, Wilmet II: documents on "Pellegri and Banneux," early July 1934; letter to the bishop of Liège by Princess de Croÿ; letter from bishop of Liège to "Madame," 13 July 1934. The princess had also contacted the chaplain of Banneux and in response to one of her letters, his secretary indicated that Jamin would rather file a complaint with the office of the public prosecutor as this would respond more discreetly than the gendarmes; ibid.: letter from Princess de Croÿ to Abbé Jamin, 10 July 1934; letters of Ivan Radzitsky d'Ostrowick to Princess de Croÿ, 8 July 1934 and 12 July 1934.

178 ADN, L.42–3, Wilmet II: dossier on "Pellegri and Banneux," letter from Chr. de Croÿ to Wilmet, 25 August 1934; letter from Wilmet, 18 August 1934; letter from the Spanish Jesuits from Barcelona, 4 August 1934 (on Dr Trueta); letter from Forges-lez-Chimay (Trappist order), 20 June 1934; reports of Elise Jadin on Benito (statements dated 30 and 31 August 1934).

179 ADN, L.42–3, Wilmet II: letter from the princess to Louis Wilmet, 22 September 1934.

180 ADN, L.42–3, Wilmet II: dossier on "Pellegri and Banneux," letter from Wilmet to the princess, 1934, day of the Onkerzele pilgrimage; letter of Wilmet, 28 August 1934.

181 AAM, Van Roey, Apparitions, 40: Beauraing and Banneux, letters from the faithful pro and contra, letter from the retired parish priest from Gooreind-Wuustwezel, 10 October 1934.

182 ADG, Apparitions, 5: cutting: "Goede vangst te Marbais. Italiaanse oplichter geklist," 23 December 1934. The name of the newspaper is not mentioned.

183 ADG, Apparitions, 5: cutting: "Italiaanse bedrieger in het gevang van Nijvel," 28 December 1934. The name of the newspaper is not mentioned.

184 S.n., "Italiaanse bedrieger voor de rechtbank in Nijvel," *De Standaard*, 6 May 1935, 4.

185 The word "foyer" sometimes refers to the people creating the bleeding crucifixes and sometimes to the places where there is attention for these bleeding objects.

186 Christian, *Moving Crucifixes*, 6–7.

187 – *The Stranger*, 29–64; Ventresca, "The Virgin." The bleeding images reported in Ireland in August–September 1920 were soon proven to be false. Reynolds, "The Templemore Miracles."

188 "Un foyer est constitué par une seule personne. Il n'est pas requis, que cette personne soit actuellement, corporellement, physiquement présente pour faire saigner les croix; encore moins qu'elle ait touché aux objets, que des étrangers apportent et déposent chez la personne en question. Il n'est pas nécessaire non plus, que ces objets quittent les mains de leurs propriétaires, quittent les cartons, l'emballage, les cadres dans lesquels ils sont enfermés." AAM, Van Roey, Apparitions, 25. Processus, C4: report by Oswald Royen (10 February 1936).

189 The first bleeding crucifixes were signalled in the home of the family Van den Plas (Kiel-Antwerpen) in October 1934, followed by those of Jules De Vuyst (14 November 1934). The initial reports of the other foyers are difficult to date exactly. ADG, Vermeire, 10: letter from Father Oswald (Royen) to Honoré Vermeire, 19 April 1936.

190 AAM, Van Roey, Apparitions, 25. Processus, C4: letter from Oswald Royen, 15 April 1935.

191 Laure Dulière was born on 17 November 1884 in Jumet. She married and had a daughter, Suzanne, who was born in Liège in 1913. ASBG, Lambert, 37. Apparitions Namur, E4: Laure Dulière, documents provided by Jan Boon (L.D.).

192 AAM, Van Roey, Apparitions, 25. Processus, C4: letter from Jan Boon to Canon Caemerlynck, parish priest-dean of Courtrai, 4 November 1935.

193 Testimony of André Watteyne in ASBG, Lambert, 37. Apparitions Namur, E4. L.D.: appendix on Laure Dulière.

194 Her husband's name was Radineau, Radinot, or Radino.
195 She came after the five child visionaries and Tilman Côme.
196 ASBG, Lambert, 37. Apparitions Namur, E4. L.D.: appendix on Laure Dulière by Jan Boon; Pierroux, 1934, 165; a letter written by Laure Dulière (15 October 1934) in which she asks the dean to intervene in the behaviour of the Mother Superior.
197 ASBG, Pierroux, 1934: letter from A. Watteyne to the dean of Beauraing, 24 October 1934. See for instance AAM, Van Roey, Apparitions, 24. Processus, BXII5b: report of Father Bols (Institute de Parnasse, Ixelles), 23 November 1935. Laure Dulière's messages in fact confirmed those of Tilman Côme, who claimed that Mary requested a basilica in Beauraing, preferred the spelling Bôring to Beauraing, and promised to keep Belgium safe from invaders. ASBG, Lambert, 37. Apparitions Namur, E4. L.D.: report of Boon on a visit to Laure Dulière (24 May 1935).
198 Empress Zita, the former empress of Austria, who had been staying in Belgium near Brussels since 1929, seems to have been involved in the affair, as was Princess Stéphanie. ASBG, 37. Apparitions Namur, E4. L.D.: documents of Jan Boon sent to Mgr Heylen, 31 July 1935, on Laure Dulière's communication with the Virgin on 31 October 1934.
199 de Beauffort, "Miracle," s.p. See also the reference to the museum in the report of the Redemptorist Van Hoeymisse for the archdiocesan commission "this religious craze is taking a sad extension." ("cette folie religieuse prend une triste extension.") AAM, Van Roey, Apparitions, 24. Processus, BIXB1: letter from Van Hoeymisse to the bishop, s.d. (post 12 September 1935).
200 AAM, Van Roey, Apparitions, 24. Processus, BIXB2: letter from Jan Boon to Mgr Van Roey, 12 October 1935.
201 de Beauffort, "Miracle."
202 AAM, Van Roey, Apparitions, 25. Processus, BXV1: letter from Mrs Doyen to auxiliary bishop Mgr Carton de Wiart, 22 February 1936; BXV2: letter from Mrs Doyen, report on 25 November 1935; ASBG, Lambert, 37. Apparitions Namur, E4. L.D.: Laure Dulière's (Beauraing) thirty-third and last apparition; "Some documentary notes on the bleedings of the crosses" (1935) testimony of André Loones (Boschvoorde); letter from M. Cassiers to Jan Boon, 5 September 1935. At least one conversion seems to have been stimulated by the bleeding crucifixes. Mrs Doyen indicated in February 1935 that Mrs van Z. had been converted by all that was happening in Laure Dulière's presence and was preparing to be baptized. AAM, Van Roey, Apparitions, 23. Processus, BV1: letter from Mrs Doyen to the auxiliary bishop Carton de Wiart (Malines), 22 February 1936.
203 AAM, Van Roey, Apparitions, 25. Processus, C4: letter from Watteyne to the auxiliary bishop Mgr Carton de Wiart, 11 December 1935.

204 ASBG, Lambert, 37. Apparitions Namur, E4. L.D.: Laure Dulière (Beauraing) 28 July 1935; report on 5 September 1935 dated 17 September 1935. Jan Boon, editor-in-chief of the Catholic journal *De Standaard* at the time, took care of the dispatch and later also sent Dulière's rosary to the imperial couple of Ethiopia (allegedly at the request of the Virgin). ASBG, Lambert, 37. Apparitions Namur, E4. L.D.: report on 2 October 1935; 6 October 1935.

205 Christian, *Moving Crucifixes,* 7.

206 On these authority claims of visionaries, see Ventresca, "The Virgin," 447.

207 AAM, Van Roey, Apparitions, 25. Processus, C4: anonymous letter to Mr Sebruyns, 1935, and report on the bleeding crucifixes with no name mentioned on it, it was added to a letter from Jan Boon (4 November 1935 to the dean-parish priest of Courtai, Canon Caemerlynck); BXV1: letter from Mrs Doyen to the auxiliary bishop of Malines Mgr Carton de Wiart, 22 February 1936.

208 AAM, Van Roey, Apparitions, 25. Processus, C4: results of the tests run in the laboratories in Douai on 3 November 1935 added to a letter from Mr and Mrs Legland to Mgr Lamiroy, the bishop of Bruges, 28 November 1935. William Christian (*The Stranger*, 58) notes that the ameliorated chemical tests stimulated the increasing importance of this kind of proof.

209 "De simplicité naïve et de fraîcheur dans cette pauvre femme maintenant pourchassée partout et injustement. Malgré ses 51 ans elle est restée avec un âme d'enfant et un esprit très pur au milieu d'une nature fruste." AAM, Van Roey, Apparitions, 25. Processus, C4: letter from André Watteyne, an architect from Brussels, to Mgr Carton de Wiart, 11 December 1935. Nonetheless, Father Oswald Royen (10 February 1936) apparently did not think that the personality of Laure Dulière and her colleagues had to be given so much weight in the evaluation of the events. Discussing the various foyers and their central characters he noted "These persons are far from being saints." ("Ces personnes sont loin d'être des saints ou saintes.") AAM, Van Roey, Apparitions, 25. Processus, C4: report by Oswald Royen, 10 February 1936.

210 Statement of Watteyne cited in ASBG, Lambert, 37. Apparitions Namur, E4. L.D.: "Appendix" on Laure Dulière's person.

211 AAM, Van Roey, Apparitions, 25. Processus, C4: letter from Baroness Emmanuel d'Oultremont to the auxiliary bishop Carton de Wiart, 17 March 1936.

212 S.n., "Des Christs qui saignent à Bruxelles?" *Nation Belge,* 3 October 1935; Nicole, "Les Crucifix sanglants," *Indépendence*, 4 October 1935.

213 S.n., "Une affaire de 'christs saignants' à Bruxelles," *La Libre Belgique,* 5 October 1935. AAM, Van Roey, Apparitions, 24. Processus, BIXB1: letter from Van Hoeymisse, 2 November 1935, including a newspaper clipping of *The Universe*, 11 October 1935.

214 AAM, Van Roey, Apparitions, 24. Processus, BXII5d: letter from Mme de la Croix to Eminence, 23 November 1935, including a report of what had happened in Courtrai.

215 AAM, Van Roey, Apparitions, 25. Processus, C4: report by Camerlynck and Muyle.

216 Session 10 (18 November 1935), session 11 (20 November 1935), session 12 (11 December 1935), session 13 (18 December 1935), session 14 (19 February 1936), session 15 (11 March 1936), session 17 (12 June 1936), session 18 (23 June 1936).

217 AAM, Van Roey, Apparitions, 23. Processus, A2X1: interrogation of Roland; X2: interrogation of Prelle de la Nieppe; XIII1: interrogation of de Beauffort; XIV: interrogation of H. Jacques.

218 See AAM, Van Roey, Apparitions, 23. Processus, A3: report of session 18 (23 June 1936), including a letter from Jan Boon (18 June 1936) with Laure Dulière's confession, 82–6; C4: letter from Bilcke, 11 June 1936.

219 "La présence d'un véritable atelier de confection d'images et d'objets 'saignants' (flacons de teinture d'iode, d'éther, de glycerine, de bistre, pinceaux, images et objets, les uns déjà teintés, les autres, prêts à l'être, morceaux de soie portant des empreintes que Laure faisait passer pour surnaturelles et qu'elle fabriquait au moyen des médaillons et figures en relief retrouvés dans sa chambre, dont elle se servait comme de matrices pour faire ces empreintes, ainsi que la comparaison des unes et des autres l'établit à l'évidence." AAM, Van Roey, Apparitions, 23. Processus, A3: report of the investigation in Kortenberg added to the report of session 18 (23 June 1936), 81.

220 AAM, Van Roey, Apparitions, 23. Processus, A3: letter from Jan Boon (18 June 1936) and the confession of Laure Dulière, added to the report of session 18 (23 June 1936), 82–6.

221 ASBG, Pierroux, 1936–37: letter from Jan Boon to Dean Lambert, 23 June 1936.

222 AAM, Van Roey, Apparitions, 23. Processus, A3: report of the session 18 (23 June 36), 85.

223 ADG, Apparitions, 9: letter from Mgr Van Roey 25 March 1942.

224 "Il y a beaucoup de supercherie dans l'affaire des Christs saignants ou pleurants; l'affaire de Courtrai était une vulgaire tromperie." S.n., "Mises au point au sujet de quelques cas discutés et discutables," *Les Annales de Beauraing et de Banneux* 90 (15 September 1936): 1–2. Comparing the text with the correspondence preserved in the archives of the diocese of Ghent, it turns out to be a quotation from a letter from H. Philippe, the secretary of the bishop of Ghent, to Fr. Prins. ADG, Apparitions, 182: letter from H. Philippe, 27 June 1936.

225 ADG, Apparitions, 31: copy of a letter from Lager Lohfelden (forced labour camp), 25 April 1944.

226 "Ijselijke dood" ADG, Apparitions, 78: report by Jan Boon on pilgrimage 18 May 1937 (11 August 1937); day of death: extract from the death registers of the city of Liège (n°95). There is no mentioning of her death in the local newspapers *La Meuse, Gazette de Liège* and *Journal de Liège.*

227 "Il manque aux simples fidèles – doctes ou ignorants – cette assistance particulière que le S. esprit accorde aux pasteurs et, quelles que soient leurs conclusions, ils n'ont jamais que leur crédit personnel pour les imposer." S.n., "Les faits merveilleux de Belgique," *Banneux-Tancrémont* 10 (February 1934): 240–8, 243.

228 Taves, *Religious Experience*, 31–2.

229 We will study this differentiation more elaborately in our discussion of the aftermath of the apparitions.

230 "En dehors de la Révélation chrétienne, toutes nos vérités demandent à être conquises. L'intuition, le hasard, l'inspiration … ne peuvent inspirer confiance s'ils sont seuls mis en œuvre … Nous vivons sous le règne du spécialiste." F. Dorola (pseudonym of Fernand Remisch), *Les mystères*, 137 and 138.

231 Dorola, *Les mystères*, 141–2.

## Chapter Three

1 "Medicale of andere wetenschappelijke observatie is erin 't geheel niet." – "De katholieke geneesheren achten het schijnbaar niet de moeite zich te derangeren: a priori en op verren afstand weten zij dat het 'geestesstoornis' is, zonder zich de moeite te getroosten de feiten na te gaan noch de houding der vrouw te observeren." S.n., "Te Onkerzele," *De Standaard*, 24 September 1933, 3.

2 Szabo, "Seeing is Believing," 211; Desmazières, "Psychology," 1192 ("the medical intrusion in a field traditionally controlled by theology"). See also Amiotte-Suchet, "Tous égaux," 246; Van Osselaer, De Smaele, and Wils, *Sign*.

3 This was not a "secular" diagnosis. Various definitions of the term were mentioned in Christian texts long before the nineteenth century. On the evolution of the term "hysteria," see Micale, *Approaching Hysteria*; Falleyn, "Hysterie," 25, 38. On the "hysterization" of mystical phenomena, see Goldstein, "The Hysteria Diagnosis," 210; Velle, "De geneeskunde," 11; Edelman, *Les metamorphoses*, 208; Van Osselaer and Smeyers, "Divine Hysteria."

4 Szabo, "Seeing is Believing," 211; Micale, *Approaching Hysteria*, 270.

5 Also referred to in newspaper articles on the 1930s series of apparitions: s.n., "De wondere gebeurtenissen te Beauraing." *De Standaard*, 22 December 1932, 2; Falleyn, "Hysterie," 75–8; Lachapelle, "Between Miracle"; Klaniczay, "Louise Lateau"; Van Osselaer, "The Affair."
6 Duffin, *Medical Miracles*, 35.
7 Edelman, *Les metamorphoses*, 215; Maître, "De Bourneville," 772.
8 Bouflet and Boutry, *Un signe*, 13–14; Lachapelle, "Between Miracle," 87.
9 Duffin, *Medical Miracles*, 73–4.
10 Zumholz, "Die Resistenz," 223; Chiron, *Enquête*, 20–2.
11 Szabo, "Seeing is Believing," 224; Harris, *Lourdes*, 355, on science and religion: "both gave some ground and neither remained untouched by the other."
12 Agnes Desmazières indicates that in the *Dictionnaire de théologie catholique* and the *Dictionnaire de spiritualité*, both published in 1937, there were suggestions that apparitions could be linked to hallucinations. Desmazières, "Psychology," 1192–3.
13 Desmazières, "Psychology," 1194. She notes (1196) how, since the end of the nineteenth century, Catholic scientists had shown an increasing interest in psychology and a "new psychology" emerged. In her opinion, this "[p]sychology of religion can be considered as a result of experimental psychology and, more broadly, of the emancipation of human sciences: religious studies were no longer the privilege of theology and philosophy, but had also to deal with the emerging human sciences, such as psychology."
14 Lachapelle, "Between Miracle," 88, see also her footnote 21.
15 Falleyn, "Hysterie," 81 and 112.
16 The studies on "hysteria" of the Belgian psychiatrists and neurologists had an anticlerical potential: Velle, "De geneeskunde," 1, 13.
17 – "De geneeskunde," 14. On the Catholic doctors, see for instance Vandendriessche and Van Osselaer ("Religion") and Gijbels ("Medical Compromise").
18 Velle, "De geneeskunde," 15; Velle, "Het verenigingsleven," 105: in 1935 the Belgian movement had about 1,200 members. Vander Hulst and Vandendriessche ("Physician-apostles," 134) noted that it had a double goal: "Offering a site for the study of medical issues in relation to Catholic doctrine and of spreading Christian morality in the medical corps."
19 Original title: *Bulletin de la Société Médicale belge de Saint-Luc*. The title changed in 1930. At the end of 1934 the periodical had more than 12,000 subscribers. Velle, "De geneeskunde," 15.
20 Toussaint and Joset, *Beauraing*, 98.
21 ASBG, Pierroux, 1932–33: conference given in Brussels on 25 January 1933 by Louis Wilmet about Beauraing.

22 See for example the mentioning of doctors during the first series of apparitions in Lokeren. S.n., "De verschijningen te Lokeren," *Het Laatste Nieuws*, 16 November 1933, 2.

23 S.n., "Te Onkerzele en elders," *De Standaard*, 15 October 1933, 5; Merlier, "Omer."

24 Drs De Feyter (Ronse), Van der Donck (Oudenaarde), Maes (Etikhove), Vindevogel (Eine).

25 Articles in *De Standaard*, for instance: s.n., "Nog Maria-verschijningen in Vlaanderen?" *De Standaard*, 16 October 1933, 2–3; S.n., "Maria-verschijningen in Vlaanderen? Te Onkerzele," *De Standaard*, 17 October 1933, 2.

26 "Ik zou willen dat ik door groote doktoors onderzocht werd. Wie weet, heb ik soms geen ziekte, die mij zoo doet handelen en zien. Vermits de ziener het zelf wenscht, ware zulk onderzoek door psychiaters en andere specialisten zeker niet misplaatst. Die man heeft recht op zulk onderzoek, ook in 't belang van onzen heiligen godsdienst. We ondervonden trouwens zelf dat hij tamelijk vatbaar is voor suggestie." S.n., "Onderzoek te Etikhove," *De Standaard*, 21 October 1933, 3.

27 That is what the remark of Father Borromeaus Vandewalle seems to suggest. He noted about the Lokeren site (second series) that Dr Van Son attended all the episodes not realizing that by being there he boosted the case with his authority and compromised himself. AAM, Van Roey, Apparitions, 23. Processus, BIIIa: letter from Borromaeus Vandewalle, 20 February 1935.

28 Maistriaux, *Dernières apparitions*, 23–43.

29 Joset, *Dossiers de Beauraing*, vol. 4, 162–8.

30 E.g. a miraculée leaves her initials at the site. ADN, L.42–3, Wilmet III: circulaires of the *Annales*, nr.2.

31 On this continuity with the Lourdes apparitions, see Desmazières, "Psychology," 1191.

32 AAM, Van Roey, Apparitions, 23. Processus, BIIb3: letter from Jan Boon (20 August 1934) to Mgr Van Roey.

33 There are references to Maistriaux' collection up until the 1940s. When the supporters of the Beauraing sites were looking for documents on the miraculous cures on which they wanted to build their case for the approval of Beauraing (a second diocesan commission had just been created), they had to search for several days before locating them (Maistriaux had been arrested by the Germans). ASBG, Lambert, 3: unpublished manuscripts, report of A. Pierroux, 1932–43.

34 On the use of the citation as a tactic for belief/mistrust, see: De Certeau, *The Practice*, 188.

35 Bijker, Bal, and Hendriks, *The Paradox*.

36 See Van Osselaer, “A question.”

37 “Ce n’est pas au médecin à prouver le surnaturel, pas plus que ce n’est son rôle de s’y opposer. Il n’a aucune compétence en la question. Mais, pour secondaire qu’elle soit, son influence peut être énorme. On sait que dans des événements comme ceux de Beauraing il y a place pour beaucoup d’hypothèses; le seul but qu’un médecin catholique puisse avoir en s’occupant de cette chose c’est de rechercher si l’on peut trouver une explication naturelle à ces faits, et laquelle, et d’éclairer ainsi, du point de vue scientifique, l’ensemble examiné. Plus il aura été difficile dans le choix des preuves, rigoureux dans ses recherches, impitoyable pour les facteurs parasites dénués d’importance, et plus ses conclusions seraient utiles si elles venaient dire: on ne peut rendre compte de cela au point de vue naturel.” De Greeff, “Notes,” 31.

38 “L’intervention du médecin a pour seul objectif de démontrer que la guérison est ou n’est pas naturelle, qu’elle est survenue en marge des causes biologiques ou en opposition avec elles, enfin qu’elle ne peut être expliquée par l’action d’un traitement ou par une cause psychologique.” Vervaeck, *Le rôle*, 1. It is interesting to note that one of the decrees of the fifth council of Malines mentioned that in the case of apparitions and miracles, doctors should not be overly skeptical but should display a correct scientific posture. Salsmans, S.J., “Uit de decreten van de Ve Mechelse Concilie,” *Saint-Luc Médical* 17, no. 1 (1939): 45–51.

39 Thurston, *Beauraing*, 14, 22.

40 ADN, L.42–3, Wilmet III: letter from Wilmet to “Reverend Father,” 23 September 1933.

41 ADN, L.42–3, Wilmet IV: dossier Côme, sent to Mgr Heylen post 5 December 1934.

42 The apparition series also attracted attention abroad: See the studies of Herbert Thurston, *Beauraing*, and Pascal Brotteaux, *Hallucinations*.

43 “Le médecin est souvent comme Saint Thomas, il ne croit que ce qui tombe sous le sens; l’intuition pascalienne s’oppose à son esprit géométrique.” Gailly, “À propos des événements de Beauraing,” 193–205.

44 “Compte rendu de la Séance d’étude du 23 février.” *Saint-Luc Médical* 11, no. 4 (1933): 136–9.

45 Fransen, “Autour des faits,” 159.

46 Chiron, *Enquête*, 255; ADDF, Dev. Var., 1933.2 Beauraing, box 4: report of the first Namur commission, session 32 (15 November 1935); AAM, Van Roey, Apparitions, 24. Processus, BIXA1: report of Wilmet about 28 December 1933; report of Vermeire on 8 December 1933, 6 January 1934, and on 9 February 1934; BIXA2: report of Magain about 6 January 1934 and report of Sebruyns-Desmet about 30 March 1934.

47 De Greeff, "Notes," 60.
48 See the lists of the doctors present in: Joset, *Dossiers de Beauraing*, vol. 4, 162–8.
49 Desmazières, "Psychology," 1202.
50 Bossant, "Het dossier," 29.
51 Toussaint and Joset, *Beauraing*, 99.
52 ADDF, Dev. Var., 1933.2 Beauraing, box 4: report of the first Namur commission, session 68 (16 April 1936): questioning of Dr Rondelet – in his opinion Dr De Greeff questioned the children with very specific questions, not brutally, but rather rudely; on the discussion about the type of question between Jan Filip Boon and Dr Van Acker, see DAG, Onkerzele, 57: stenographic report of the questioning, 21 January 1934.
53 When De Greeff participated in the questioning in Beauraing on 17 December 1932, he remarked that none of the others involved were taking notes – he was the only one to do so. De Greeff, "Notes," 66.
54 "Il faut qu'il ait un certain développement intellectuel, car il ne doit pas seulement être un instrument enregistreur; à certains moments, l'enquêteur doit être actif; il pénètre dans la conscience de l'examiné, il le surveille, l'épie, le suggestionne, le maîtrise. S'il n'est pas au moins aussi intelligent que le sujet examiné, c'est celui-ci qui mène l'examen sans qu'il s'en aperçoive." De Greeff, "Vers une explication," 138–9.
55 Vervaeck, *Le rôle*, 3 and 7–18.
56 On the celebrity status of miraculés, see Kaufman "Les miraculées."
57 Thurston, *Beauraing*, 31.
58 This is discussed more elaborately in the next chapter.
59 During the Belgian series of apparitions, Dr Ladon also commented on the events in Beauraing (he witnessed one 3 January 1933) and called them the result of an illusion (initially individual and later collective). Albert Bouckaert, "Les 'apparitions' de Beauraing: la 'Vierge' a dit adieu aux enfants," *Le Soir*, 6 January 1933, 1–2.
60 Ladon, "Over de psychologie," 38.
61 "Zoo sterk was de indruk van kollektieven geest, dat het voor den buiten-massa individu tot een zeer onaangenaam, physisch gevoel van onvereenigbaarheid en misschien latente hostiliteit kwam." Ladon, "Over de psychologie," 36.
62 "Echte, waarachtige godvruchtigheid was de dominante trek der toegestroomde massa's, en dat religieus karakter was zoo ernstig uitgesproken, dat menige aanhangers van het bovennatuurlijke der feiten, het als beste argument voor hun thesis konden inroepen." Ladon, "Over de psychologie," 28.
63 "Paroxystische emotiviteit." Ladon, "Over de psychologie," 38.

64 "Die erbarmelijke individualiteiten die als zieners optraden." Ladon, "Over de psychologie," 35.

65 Ladon, *Une épidémie mentale*, 71 and 64: "Désarroi général qui pèse sur le monde; liquidation tardive des angoisses de la guerre; aspirations vers un équilibre spirituel, au sein de ce renversement des valeurs auquel on doit l'instabilité actuelle"; 66: "Atavisme mystique, perpétuelle présence du merveilleux dans la vie quotidienne."

66 "Il n'a pas de valeur scientifique. Toutes ces élucubrations pour défendre sa thèse, je les ai gratifiées en sa présence de roman scientifique devant 60 médecins à St. Luc. Je ne retire rien, sauf peut-être que le mot 'scientifique' m'apparait vraiment superflu." Fragment of a letter by Dr Gailly (11 December 1934) sent to the Vatican by Bonhomme. Rome, ADDF, Dev. Var., 1933.2 Beauraing, 20: fragments from a letter from Bonhomme, 19 November 1936.

67 On this association see the previous chapter. As we learn from an issue of this periodical on the Belgian series of apparitions, the local Saint-Luc groups held discussion meetings on the series on 21 February 1933 and 31 May 1933 in Brussels, on 23 February 1933 in Mons, on 17 May 1933 in Antwerp, and on 21 May 1933 in Charleroi. *Saint-Luc Médical* 11, no. 4 (1933). Lenain also published on the apparitions in *La Nouvelle Revue Théologique* 4 (1933): "Les événements de Beauraing" (327–56); "Beauraing. La controverse récente" (696–724).

68 Velle, "Het verenigingsleven," 104.

69 "La science medical ne peut expliquer … la clarté française devant les nuages de la science allemande" ADN, L.42–3, Wilmet III: response of Lenain to Wilmet's article "Actuellement à Beauraing" in *Les Annales de Beauraing and Banneux* 12 (15 June 1933): 2; (letter dated before 27 June 1933).

70 Van Acker, "Beauraing."

71 At the Journées de Psychologie Religieuse (Avon-Fontainebleau, 26–28 April). Ladon, *Une épidémie mentale*, 1; the text was also published in *L'Hygiene Mentale* 30 (1935): 205–45.

72 "La Société de Saint-Luc a toujours estimé que pour étudier une question avec un véritable esprit critique et selon une méthode vraiment scientifique, il est indispensable de pouvoir examiner sans parti pris et sans passion, tous les avis et toutes les solutions proposées." S.n., [Introduction], *Saint-Luc Médical* 11, no. 4 (1933): 123–4.

73 The journal was founded in 1911. Desmazières, "Psychology," 1204.

74 de Jésus-Marie, De Greeff, Janssens, Van Gehuchten, "Avertissement," 8, and de Jésus-Marie, "Introduction," 22.

75 See for instance, Van Acker, "Beauraing."

76 See for instance J[an] B[oon], "De kinderen van Beauraing. Uitputting van natuurlijke opheldering der feiten," *De Standaard*, 12 January 1933, 1.

77 Desmazières, "Psychology," 1202. S.n., "Nog wat over de gebeurtenissen te Beauraing," *De Standaard*, 20 December 1932, 2; S.n., "Beauraing," *Vers l'Avenir*, 19 December 1932, 4; Toussaint and Joset, *Beauraing*, 100; S.n. "De wondere gebeurtenissen te Beauraing," *De Standaard*, 22 December 1932, 4; S.n., "Beauraing," *Vers l'Avenir*, 21 December 1932, 3.

78 "En het zijn juist collega's die niets van psychologie en psychiatrie afweten die het geval in handen hebben. Het onderzoek is erbarmelijk ... Beauraing toch is door absoluut onbevoegden geobserveerd geweest en behalve bedroevend onwetenschappelijk is de den psychiaters verstrekte observatie ook nog bedroevend onvolledig." Van Acker, "Beauraing," 448. See also his letter of 9 December 1936, included in the testimony of Bruno de Jésus-Marie of the commission of Malines (session 26, 18 May 1938): "I think that those who conducted the interrogations in Beauraing lacked the necessary competence: they knew nothing about the psychology of testimony and the psycho-pathology of childhood."( 'J'estime enfin que ceux qui conduisent les interrogations à Beauraing n'avaient pas la compétence voulue: ils ignoraient tout de psychologie du témoignage et de la psycho-pathologie de l'enfance.")

79 ASBG, Lambert, Beauraing, (no number): diverse correspondences and commission, text of Dr Maistriaux: "What I reprove, in general, in the doctors who have spoken at St-Luc or have written in the newspapers, the periodicals." ("Ce que je reproche, en general, aux médecins qui ont parlé à St. Luc ou écrit dans les journaux, les revues.") s.d.

80 V.A. "Boekbespreking. Jan F. Boon, Getuigenis omtrent Beauraing," *Vlaamsch Geneeskundig Tijdschrift* 14, no. 49 (9 December 1933): 972–3.

81 "La première loi de l'histoire est de ne pas oser mentir; la seconde de ne pas craindre de dire vrai. Léon XIII," de Jésus-Marie, De Greeff, Janssens, and Van Gehuchten, "Avertissement," 7.

82 Toussaint and Joset, *Beauraing*, 110.

83 Chiron, *Enquête*, 256.

84 ADDF, Dev. Var., 1933.2 Beauraing, 6: letter from Bruno de Jésus-Marie to Mgr Canali, 15 October 1933.

85 La Rédaction, "Notre Réponse: Avant-propos," *Études Carmélitaines* 19, no. 2 (1934): 255–60, with contributions of Étienne De Greeff, Gustave Leurquin, and Roland Dalbiez. ADDF, Dev. Var., 1933.2 Beauraing, 26: letter from Bruno de Jésus-Marie to Mgr Canali, 17 January 1935, Casselman, *Etienne De Greeff*, 77.

86 Casselman, "Greeff, Etienne," 394.

87 De Greeff, "Notes," 31.

88 Casselman, *Etienne De Greeff*, 72.

89 "Depuis des 'apparitions,' certains faits se sont passés à Beauraing que, par délicatesse, nous pensions garder sous silence, espérant que les

autorités compétentes en seraient informées. … Je ne suis pas le seul à posséder au sujet de cette triste affaire des documents très graves. Il est infiniment probable que nombre d'incroyants les possèdent également et qu'il ne manqueraient pas de s'en server à l'heure opportune." De Greeff, "Rectifications," 128.

90 De Greeff, "Beauraing," *Saint-Luc* 11, no. 4 (1933): 214.

91 Mgr Joseph Schyrgens (1856–1937) was a priest, teacher, journalist, and a domestic prelate of the pope. He published his comments in *Revue Catholique des Idées et des Faits*, in the literary supplement to the *XXme Siècle* and in *Soirées*. Rome, ADDF, Dev. Var., 1933.2 Beauraing, 14. XIX: letter from De Greeff to Mgr Van Roey, 2 October 1933.

92 ADDF, Dev. Var., 1933.2 Beauraing, 14. XIX: letter from De Greeff to Mgr Van Roey, 2 October 1933. Documents in the archives of the archdiocese of Malines indicate that the cardinal contacted the bishop of Namur concerning this matter, informing him that no good would come of a trial and warning him not to make too hasty a decision. AAM, Van Roey, Apparitions, 40: Beauraing and Banneux, correspondence among the Belgian bishops, letter from Mgr Van Roey to Mgr Heylen, 14 October 1933. In his answer Mgr Heylen noted that a trial would probably not take place as De Greeff has promised to retract his statements publicly.

93 "Il m'est signalé de source digne de foi qu'une enquête sérieuse met à néant certaines accusations dirigées contre le petit Albert Voisin et que j'avais, après d'autres, relevées dans certains de mes articles: 'Faits mystérieux de Beauraing' et 'Saint-Luc médical.' En présence de ce témoignage contradictoire, je désire ne pas laisser subsister dans mes publications cette question touchant l'honorabilité d'Albert. Je tiens à déclarer aussi que je n'ai jamais rien voulu insinuer à propos des autres enfants." De Greeff, "À propos de Beauraing," *Vers l'Avenir*, 7 November 1933, 1.

94 They started to correspond after Dom Bodart had written a series of articles about the similarities between Lourdes and Beauraing for *L'Avenir* and sent a copy of them to De Greeff. ADN, diocesan commission for the recognition of the events of Beauraing: opposition, copies of the correspondence between Dom Bodart and De Greeff, September–November 1933; and ASBG, Lambert, 5: monks of Maredsous, copies of Bodart's correspondence with De Greeff.

95 "En diffamant Albert, j'avais commis un péché mortel dont l'absolution ne pouvait m'être donnée qu'après réparation intégrale." "Je vous dis cela au même titre qu'un confesseur." ADDF, Dev. Var., 1933.2 Beauraing, 14. XX: letter from De Greeff to Mgr Van Roey, 12 November 1933 (original: AAM, Van Roey, Apparitions, 25. Processus, C.6) and copies of the two telegrams he sent (XXI and XXII). The next day (13 November 1933) he,

Aloïs Janssens, and Bruno de Jésus-Marie had gone to Beauraing to collect more evidence about Albert Voisin's immorality. ADDF, Dev. Var., 1933.2 Beauraing, 13: letter from Alöis Janssens, 7 December 1933.

96 ADN, L.2: copies of the Bodart–De Greeff correspondence, letter from Bodart to De Greeff, 14 September 1933.

97 ADN, L.2: letter from De Greeff, 16 September 1933. He did not want to discuss other apparition sites, Beauraing was the only one that could be commented upon as it involved five visionaries who claimed to see the Virgin at the same time.

98 De Greeff, "Notes," 38, 40, and 42.

99 De Greeff, "Beauraing," 213.

100 ADN, L.2: copies of the Bodart–De Greeff correspondence, letter from Bodart 9 September 1933, annex.

101 ADN, L.2: copies of the Bodart–De Greeff correspondence, letter from De Greeff 16 September 1933, annex.

102 ADN, L.2: copies of the Bodart–De Greeff correspondence, letter from Bodart to De Greeff, 26 September1933.

103 ADN, L.2: copies of the Bodart–De Greeff correspondence, letter from De Greeff to Bodart, October 1933 (before 5 October 1933).

104 Newspapers primarily published portrait photographs. M. De Ceulener, "De gebeurtenissen te Beauraing," *Het Laatste Nieuws*, 10 January 1933, 3. At least one "doctor" (Van Son) photographed what he saw at the Flemish sites ("doctor" is a title he ascribed to himself without obtaining the necessary diploma.) AAM, Van Roey, Apparitions, 23. Processus, BIIIa: letter from Borromaeus Vandewalle, 20 February 1935. Berthonia Holtkamp seems to have protested against her picture being taken while she was in ecstasy. AAM, Van Roey, Apparitions, 24. Processus, BIXA1: report of Vermeire on 21 January 1934. On the use of photographs: Charcot's photoiconography and Lourdes adaptation of the practice, see Szabo, "Seeing is Believing," 217.

105 "C'est si difficile à mener un interrogatoire d'enfants … Et puis permettez-moi de vous dire que vous ne pouvez tout de même prétendre détenir le monopole en cette manière ni vouloir imposer vos critères et vos témoignages comme étant les seuls authentiques, les seuls admissibles. Il y a eu, dites-vous, des erreurs de jugement, des lacunes, des vices de méthodes dans les enquêtes; c'est possible, mais remarquez que c'est précisément ce même reproche que je vous adresse aussi." ADN, L.2: copies of the Bodart–De Greeff correspondence, letter from Bodart to De Greeff, 26 September 1933.

106 ADN, L.2: copies of the Bodart–De Greeff correspondence, letter from De Greeff to Bodart, 16 September 1933.

107 "Un gangster du surnaturel," statement of De Greeff in *L'Avant Garde*, 24 February 1934 cited by Bodart: ADN, L.2: copies of the Bodart–De Greeff correspondence, 36.

108 "Procédés de gangsters," De Greeff, "Conclusions," 265. In his article De Greeff does not discuss the Albert Voisin matter in detail, instead he focuses on Maes' criticism on his thesis and confirms the thesis he proposed in his previous publications.

109 De Greeff, "Conclusions," 269.

110 ASBG, Pierroux, 1934–5: letter from Bodart to the dean of Beauraing, 19 November 1934.

111 ADDF, Dev. Var., 1933.2 Beauraing, box 4: report of the first Namur commission, testimony of the Redemptorist Debongnie (session 45, 17 January 1936). Toussaint and Joset, *Beauraing*, 111.

112 Casselman, *Etienne De Greeff*, 78. See however the next chapter for the bishop's formal denial of having threatened to have De Greeff fired.

113 ADN, L.5 bis: "Science ou chantage." s.d. L.G. – probably Dr L. Goedseels from Brussels, who wrote the article ("La question de Beauraing et les médecins Catholiques") included just before this statement (that was included in "Remarques sur quelques faits nouveaux." 247–8).

114 ADDF, Dev. Var., 1934.11 Banneux, 15: testimony of the Dominican Pie Bonhomme, 3 May 1935.

115 "Il est donc indispensable, dans l'intérêt du fait de Beauraing lui-même, dans l'intérêt supérieur de l'Eglise Catholique, que ces guérisons soient nettement établies, contrôlées, et ne soient retenues, comme au bureau des Constatations de Lourdes, que lorsqu'elles portent les signes évidents d'une intervention surnaturelle. Cette manière de faire, seule, dissipera chez les sceptiques toute velléité d'opposition, et donnera aux amis de Beauraing une raison fondamentale d'étayer leur opinion et piété." ADDF, Dev. Var., 1933.2 Beauraing, 24a: letter from Cawet to Excellence, 14 September 1934; 24b: letter from Dr Wibo to Mgr Heylen, 22 September 1933.

116 Letter from Mgr Van Roey, cited in Lindemans, "Jan-Frans Fransen," 100, footnote 2. It is not clear on whose initiative the commission was created: There is a note on an Episcopal gathering of 24–5 July 1933 indicating that a medical commission about Beauraing and Banneux will be constituted that consists of members of Saint-Luc. AAM, reports of the meetings of the bishops, 24–5 July 1933. On the other hand there is also a letter from Dr Wibo, head of Saint-Luc, sent to Mgr Heylen on 22 September 1933 in which he remarks that it is absolutely necessary to examine the healings just as it is done in Lourdes. ADDF, Dev. Var., 1933.2 Beauraing, 24: a letter from Cawet to "Excellence," in a report sent to Mgr Micara, nuncio in Brussels. There are references to the creation of this commission in an

article of the *Osservatore Romano* on 20 December 1933 (4), but as a letter in the archives of the diocese of Namur indicates, there seems to have been no official statement for there was some discussion on whether this commission really existed and the *Osservatore* did not mistake the Saint-Luc sessions for a commission. ADN, L.5 bis: "À propos d'un article de l'Osservatore Romano" (stamp of Hubert Simons).

117 ADN, L.42–3, Wilmet IV: answer from Lenain to Wilmet, 8 August 1934.

118 Jan Frans Fransen (1886–1975) taught psychology and youth psychology at the University of Ghent, the Catholic School of Antwerp, and the Social School of Heverlee. Lindemans, "Fransen;" Elaut, "Professor Fransen," 36–8.

119 Born on 21 December 1889.

120 AAM, Van Roey, Apparitions, 23. Processus, A3: Copia actorum, session 9 (12 November 1935) of the commission of Malines. Louis Wilmet mentions other members of the commission in his confidential note on the commission (indicating also the date of its creation on 2 December 1933): Dr Sebrechts (Bruges), Dr Goedseels, and Dr Wibo (president) and others he does not know. ADN, L.42–3, Wilmet III: confidential note on the medical commission.

121 ADN, L.42–3, Wilmet III: letter from Lenain to Wilmet, s.d.

122 Van Gehuchten, "Un témoignage," "Une lettre," and "Quelques réflexions."

123 See his testimony for the diocesan commission of Namur (session 56, 21 February 1936) ADDF, Dev. Var., 1933.2 Beauraing, box 4: report of the first Namur commission.

124 "Le roman scientifique," "Voilà un fait qui s'explique par des exigences et surtout des habitudes intellectuelles qu'entraîne une formation spécialisée dans un certain domain scientifique." Gailly, "Les apparitions," 139–47.

125 Fransen, "Autour des faits," 184.

126 ADDF, Dev. Var., 1933.2 Beauraing, 9: note on the apparitions in Beauraing for use of the Sacred Congregation of the Holy Office, s.n., stamp: 28 November 1933, "sub secreto"; 26: letter from Bruno de Jésus-Marie to Mgr Canali, 17 January 1935 (thus after the commission had sent in its first findings).

127 "Van Gehuchten a fourni trop de preuves de son impressionnabilité et de sa superficialité pour que son opinion ait une valeur quelconque aux yeux de ceux qui n'ont pas le fétichisme du nom." ADN, L.42–3, Wilmet III: letter from Wilmet to Lenain, 6 January 1934.

128 ASBG, Lambert, 39: healing of Van Laer, miraculous cures, report on a meeting with Dr Gailly ("Commission médicale de S.-Luc." s.d.)

129 For instance, Prof. Fransen contacted Dr Verschueren about Onkerzele. AAM, Van Roey, Apparitions, 24. Processus, BXI2: documenta GIV, letter from Vander Maeren to Mgr Coppieters, 16 April 1934.

130 For instance, Dr Grypdonck, the assistant of Prof. Fransen, went with him to Onkerzele on 8 December 1933. His specific task was to observe and note the changing expressions and their duration. Lindemans, "Jan-Frans Fransen," 100.

131 DAG, Onkerzele, 57: stenographic report of the questioning 21 January 1934.

132 For instance, according to Jan Filip Boon, Dr Fransen was present in Onkerzele only three to four times for part of a day, although the visions took place over six months. AAM, Van Roey, Apparitions, 23. Processus, BIVb: letter from Jan Boon to Canon Barette, 27 August 1934.

133 ADN, L.42–3, Wilmet III: Louis Wilmet, "Beauraing. État actuel de la question" (post January 1935).

134 "Beroepsdeformatie," DAG, Onkerzele, 181: letter to the parish priest from Father Oswald Royen (Ghent), before 2 February 1934.

135 AAM, Van Roey, Apparitions, 24. Processus, BIXA2: report of Magain on 21 January 1934.

136 Jan Boon sent a text about Tilman Côme to Dr Fransen. Kadoc, Jan Boon, 5.2.5: letter from Jan Boon, 16 June 1934 to Dr Fransen.

137 "Ostéomyélite Générale," DAG, Onkerzele, 180. Jan Van Saelen, report on his cure by Magain (16 May 1934).

138 "Ik lees regelmatig het 'Bulletin de l'Association Médicale Internationale de N.D. de Lourdes' en bestatig dat in geval van Saele te Lourdes was genezen hij reeds lang zou aanvaard geweest zijn." DAG, Onkerzele, 180. Jan Van Saelen: report on his cure by Magain (16 May 1934), letter from Dr Vrints (10 October 1934). On 31 January 1936 Dr Vrints confirmed that Van Saelen had not relapsed.

139 Kerkhofs, *Wat gebeurde er*, 110–11.

140 "Pour chacun d'eux, dans la mesure où nous avons pû recueillir des renseignements suffisants, nous avons développé des commentaires et des conclusions. Pour certains d'entre eux, nous avons pû établir le diagnostic et montré que la guérison ne présentait rien d'extraordinaire. Pour d'autres, faute de renseignements précis, nous n'avons pû faire que des hypothèses. Dans aucun, il ne nous a paru être en présence des faits inexplicables pour la science médicale." ADDF, Dev. Var., 1933.2 Beauraing, 24b. Letter from Wibo, 4 November 1934, including the report of the medical commission. See also AAM, Van Roey, Apparitions, 23. Processus, B1: report of the medical commission. On the decision-making process in cases of "miraculous" cures, see Amiotte-Suchet, "Tous égaux," 246.

141 ADDF, Dev. Var., 1933.2 Beauraing, 24b: letter from Wibo, 4 November 1934, including the report of the medical commission; AAM, Van Roey, Apparitions, 23. Processus, B1: report on the examination May–June 1934 by Dr Van Gehuchten and Dr Gailly.

142 "Explication naturelle, pathologique pour les trois; imitation simulée de Beauraing et d'Ezkioga." AAM, Van Roey, Apparitions, 21: diverse apparitions, examination of the visionaries of Flanders; 23. Processus, Bib.: medical report on the healings of Banneux and on the "events" of Onkerzele and Etikhove. Kerkhofs, *Wat gebeurde er*, 110–46.

143 See for instance the comments of Louis Wilmet, supporter of Tilman Côme: ADN, L.42–3, Wilmet IV: dossier Côme, sent to Mgr Heylen post 5 December 1934.

144 Drs Dimanche (session 23, 26 July 1935, from Beauraing), François Questiaux (session 24, 27 September 1935; from Beauraing), Antoine Goethals (session 28, 11 October 1935, from Hastière), Leopold Falmagne (session 30, 11 October 1935, from Namur), Jean Calozet (session 31, 25 October 1935, from Franière), Raymond Leurquin (session 32, 15 November 1935, from Houyet), Joseph St. Viteux (session 33, 15 November 1935, from Laroche), Henri Gailly (session 56, 21 February 1936, from Charleroi), Fernand Maistriaux (session 58, 28 February 1936, from Beauraing), Jules Havet (session 66, 3 April 1936, professor of the medical faculty of Louvain), Albert Rondelet (session 68, 16 April 1936, from Bertrix).

145 See letter from De Greeff to the commission, 17 March 1936 (read at session 62, 20 March 1936).

146 As noted, Dr Gailly was a member of the medical commission responsible for the Beauraing examination.

147 ADDF, Dev. Var., 1933.2 Beauraing, box 4: report of the first Namur commission.

148 "Medicolatrie," ASBX, 2C3 XV 2: actions in Rome, letter to Bonhomme of 4 February 1938.

149 AAM, Van Roey, Apparitions, 23. Processus, A2IX2: testimony of Moreau, references to the findings of drs Fransen, Van Acker, Careels, and Keysenaer. See also the references to the medical commission in the Malines commission's final conclusions.

150 AAM, Van Roey, Apparitions, 23. Processus, A2XXII1: interrogation of De Greeff; A3: Copia actorum, session 22 (25 March 1938); C6: Beauraing, letter from De Greeff to Canon Gillet (17 March 1938); see also the note on his personal state when conducting the examinations (a firm belief in Lourdes), 27 March 1938, and medical notes (of drs De Greeff and Rouvroy obtained from other doctors, 5 April 1938). Bodart sent his correspondence with De Greeff to Malines, 29 July 1935: AAM, Van Roey, Apparitions, 25. Processus, C6.

151 AAM, Van Roey, Apparitions, 23. Processus, A2XXII2: note from De Greeff on Beauraing (23 March 1938).

152 "Lorsqu'on a une certaine habitude d'étudier ces phénomènes, les réactions des individus, les déformations, etc., notre examen ne constituait nullement un tour de force, mais une interrogation vraiment banale, entraînant aussi banalement que possible la conviction qu'il ne s'était rien passé." AAM, Van Roey, Apparitions, 23. Processus, A2XXII1: interrogation of De Greeff; A3: copia actorum, session 22 (25 March 1938).

153 See previous chapter.

154 "Nourrie, poussée et finalement exploitée par des adultes," AAM, Van Roey, Apparitions, 23. Processus, A2XXII1: interrogation of De Greeff; A3: copia actorum, session 22 (25 March 1938).

155 AAM, Van Roey, Apparitions, 23. Processus, A3: copia actorum, session 23 (1 April 1938).

156 The Namur commission contacted at least two of the doctors involved in the medical commission: drs Gailly and Van Gehuchten. In late March they asked Dr Gailly, who had a rather positive impression of Albert Voisin, whether he would allow them to include his findings in their reports. ASBG, Lambert, 39: cure of Van Laer, letter to Gailly on 30 March 1949 and his positive response on 1 April 1949. The second diocesan commission of Liège, created in 1942, also questioned the medical reports that the first commission had worked with (for instance the note of Gailly on Mariette).

157 ASBG, Lambert, 39: cure of Van Laer, report on a meeting of Toussaint with Van Gehuchten, 27 April 1949.

158 ASBG, Lambert, 39: cure of Van Laer, report of the diocesan commission, 4 April 1949.

159 "Fut atteinte d'une maladie infectieuse grave de nature tuberculeuse ou staphylocoxique, probablement d'ostéomyélite," ASBG, Lambert, 39: cure of Van Laer, report of Picard and Robaux, 27 March 1949.

160 "À supposer que les experts en aient eu connaissance, le fait qu'ils ne l'ont pas admis n'est pas un précédent dont la Commission de Namur doive se préoccuper. Les experts avouent eux-mêmes qu'ils ont examiné les cas qui leur paraissaient les plus intéressants. Mais cette première appréciation n'a qu'une valeur relative; elle dépend en particulier de l'état dans lequel ils ont trouvé la documentation et des possibilités d'enquête. La commission de Namur n'a pas à se soucier de ce que purent être leurs impressions au sujet du cas Van Laer, maintenant que sa documentation comporte assez d'éléments objectifs pour permettre d'établir tant la nature de la maladie que les circonstances de la guérison." ASBG, Lambert, 39: cure of Miss Van Laer, report of the doctrinal commission of Beauraing on the case of Maria Van Laer: plaidorie, 3 April 1949, conclusion, 4 April 1949.

161 ASBG, Lambert, 39: cure of Miss Van Laer, report of the doctrinal commission of Beauraing on the case of Maria Van Laer, 3 April 1949.

162 ASBG, Lambert, 39.

163 "Elles ont été guéries subitement, parfaitement et définitivement," ASBG, Lambert, 39: cure of Van Laer, decree of Mgr Charue on the cures of Van Laer and Acar, 2 July 1949.

## Chapter Four

1 On his return from France, the bishop, Mgr Heylen, publicly confirmed the guideline.
2 ADDF, Dev. Var., 1933.2 Beauraing, 24a: report of Cawet to the nuncio Micara, 14 September 1934 (sent to Rome by Mgr Micara); ASBG, Pierroux, 1932–33: M. Questiaux, "Dernières nouvelles," 7 December 1932.
3 AAM, Van Roey, I.37 bis: handwritten reports meetings of the deans, 3 May 1933.
4 "Car qu'il le veuille ou non, le prêtre donne à toutes ses interventions publiques une apparence d'approbation." Creusen, "Les faits 'merveilleux,'" 7–8.
5 "Bisschoppelijke Onderrichting omtrent de zaak der Verschijningen in ons land," *De Godsdienstige Week van het Bisdom Gent* 6, no. 48 (1 December 1933): 193; "À propos des faits de Beauraing et ailleurs," *L'Ami du clergé*, no. 50 (14 December 1933): 818.
6 For instance: AAM, Van Roey, Apparitions, 24. Processus, BXII3: letter to Monseigneur, 19 November 1933.
7 ADDF, Dev. Var., Beauraing 1933.2, 24: letter from Mgr Micara to Mgr Canali, 15 December 1934.
8 The parish priest Lejour, who was faced with the apparitions in Olsene, reported to the commission investigating the events that he never attended any of the events and had not examined the case. At that late hour, he added, everyone "sees." AAM, Van Roey, Apparitions, 25. Processus, C3b: parish priest Lejour to Gillet, 17 July 1935.
9 For instance in Lokeren: AAM, Van Roey, Apparitions, 23. Processus, BIVb: letter from Boon to Mgr Coppieters, 2 August 1934. The Dutch Abbé Kwakman, however, and a missionary from Scheut were listed among the supporters of the events. AAM, Van Roey, Apparitions, 23. Processus, BII: report of Louis Wilmet about 15 July 1934.
10 AAM, Van Roey, Apparitions, 24. Processus, BXII6b: invitation letter to presentation of Abbé Didion, 15 January 1934.
11 See for instance April 1933 issues of *L'Ami du clergé* and the series of articles published by Mgr Schyrgens in *Revue Catholique des Idées et des Faits* since March 1933.
12 ADDF, Dev. Var., 1933.2 Beauraing, 24: letter from Mgr Micara to Mgr Canali, 15 December 1934.
13 The Redemptorist Pierre Debongnie, who contributed among others to

*Études Carmélitaines*, did not sign with his own name but preferred to use "Gustave Leurquin." Toussaint and Joset, *Beauraing*, 113.

14 "Étude objective, faite par M. l'abbé Derselle, après une enquête impartiale."

15 Joset, *Dossiers de Beauraing*, vol. 4, 305–6.

16 – 304–6; Toussaint and Joset, *Beauraing*, 106–7, 109.

17 Derselle, *Et si c'était le diable*, 7.

18 Derselle, *Beauraing*, 9.

19 Maes, *Beauraing. Réponse*, 4–5.

20 Saussus, *Le scandale*, 10–12.

21 J[an] B[oon], "Beauraing. Brochuren over Beauraing. C. Derselle: Beauraing: Waar ligt het bovennatuurlijke?" *De Standaard*, 29 January 1933, 2.

22 Derselle, *Beauraing*.

23 "Pourquoi vous êtes entêtés à faire dévier le débat et à réduire celui-ci à une question de personnes? Comme l'écrivaient très judicieusement les Annales de Beauraing, (n°4): 'que signifient ces discussions à propos de l'identité de l'auteur?' (Je cite de mémoire). 'L'identité de l'auteur n'est que question accessoire; ce qui importe avant tout, c'est ce qu'il a dit.'" Derselle, *Beauraing*, 8.

24 "Le receveur des contributions de Beauraing." ADDF, Dev. Var., 1933.2 Beauraing, box 4: report of the first Namur commission, session 37 (29 November 1935); Toussaint and Joset, *Beauraing*, 109.

25 ADDF, Dev. Var., 1933.2 Beauraing, box 4: report of the first Namur commission, session 34 (22 November 1935).

26 See the chapter on De Greeff.

27 "Het interview werd hier onder de werklieden en in de kleine burgerij van huis tot huis overgegeven, bijna in den duik, als een slecht boek, en, zeer curieus, niet om te aanvaarden wat er in stond, maar om 'eens te zien wat een Pater durft te schrijven over Beauraing.'" Kadoc, Congregation of the Immaculate Heart of Mary (Scheut), Aloïs Janssens (Janssens), 40. Letter from George Colle to Aloïs Janssens, 5 November 1933.

28 "Hoovaardige, een waanzinnige, een bestrijder van God en godsdienst." Kadoc, Scheut, Janssens, 40. Letter from Aloïs Janssens to George Colle, 4 November 1933.

29 Kadoc, Scheut, Janssens, 40. Letters from Daems dated 16 August 1933 and 16 October 1933; 37. Notebook of Aloïs Janssens, 2 December 1933: this prohibition was eventually lifted in December 1933.

30 "Ten tijd der opschudding veroorzaakt door de verschijningen van Beauraing, zeide Z. Excellentie Mgr. Coppieters die in al zijn strenge bisschoppelijke waardigheid toch een gul man is met zin voor zuiveren humor: 'Ja Monseigneur Heylen wat gaat die brave bisschop nog beleven,

een verschijningszaak dat is erg. Wat een geluk dat het in zijn bisdom is, hij is de meest wijze en de oudste onder ons, wat een geluk dat het in zijn bisdom voorvalt en niet in het mijne!" S.n., "Wat is er te Onkerzele," *De Standaard*, 18 September 1933, 2.

31 The letter is dated 30 October 1933, but comments on the text were sent in by the various bishops early November, see for instance the comments by the bishop of Ghent (2 November 1933), Namur and Liège (4 November 1933) about the effect it might have on the priests. AAM, Van Roey, Apparitions, 40: Beauraing and Banneux, correspondence among the Belgian bishops. An accompanying note with which Mgr Van Roey sent the letter was dated 6 November 1933. Kadoc, Scheut, Janssens, 39: letter to the clergy of the diocese of Malines, 6 November 1933.

32 ADN, L.2: apparitions of Beauraing from 29 November 1933 to 3 January 1933, chronological overview of the apparitions and their aftermath. On the more reserved stance of the bishop of Liège refusing to visit the site of Banneux in January 1934, see Beyer, "Le procès," 210.

33 ADDF, Dev. Var., 1933.2 Beauraing, 6: letter from Bruno de Jésus-Marie to Mgr Canali, 15 October 1933; 9: note on the apparitions of Beauraing for the use of the Sacred Congregation of the Holy Office, 28 November 1933.

34 AAM, Van Roey, Apparitions, 24. Processus, BXII4c: letter from Mgr Coppieters, 10 January 1934.

35 AAM, Van Roey, Apparitions, 24. Processus, BIXA2: letter from Mgr Van Roey to Mgr Coppieters, 11 January 1934.

36 "Godslasteringen, opstooten, onzinnige manifestaties." "Het volk wordt razend." AAM, Van Roey, Apparitions, 25. Processus, C3: letter from Mgr Coppieters, 3 July 1934.

37 The letter from Mgr Van Roey and Mgr Coppieters was read out loud in the churches on 2 September 1934 and was published in *De Standaard*. S.n., "Een schrijven van Z.E. Kard. Van Roey, aartsbisschop," *De Standaard*, 28 August 1934, 3. AAM, Van Roey, Apparitions, 23. Processus, BIVb: letter from Mgr Van Roey.

38 See the chapter on the medical commission. Beyer, "Le procès," 211 – the two commissions were discussed since July 1933. ADDF, Dev. Var., 1933.2 Beauraing, 20: report on the events in Beauraing (8 January 1934), sent by Mgr Heylen; AAM: reports of the meetings of the bishops, 24–5 July 1933.

39 AAM: reports of the meetings of the bishops, 24–5 July 1933; AAM, Van Roey, Apparitions, 40: Beauraing and Banneux, correspondence among the Belgian bishops, letter from Mgr Heylen, 15 November 1933; Toussaint and Joset, *Beauraing*, 124.

40 ADN, L.2: apparitions of Beauraing from 29 November 1933 to 3 January 1933, chronological overview of the events and their aftermath.

41 AAM, Van Roey, Apparitions, 40: Beauraing and Banneux, correspondence among the Belgian bishops, letter from the bishop of Liège, 3 January 1935.

42 ADN, L.2: apparitions of Beauraing from 29 November 1933 to 3 January 1933, chronological overview of the apparitions and their aftermath; Toussaint and Joset, *Beauraing*, 135.

43 "Il est évident que le salut ne peut venir que de Rome dans cette affaire qui prend des proportions alarmantes," ADDF, Dev. Var., 1933.2 Beauraing, 6: letter from Bruno de Jésus-Marie, 15 October 1933, to Mgr Canali, assessor of the Holy Office.

44 ADDF, Dev. Var., 1933.2 Beauraing, 12: letter from Bruno de Jésus-Marie, 24 November 1933, to Mgr Canali.

45 "Alors que jusqu'ici on ne s'était jamais agenouillé devant ce lieu. On priait debout. Tout Beauraing était là vers la fin du chapelet et l'Evêque fut salué par des ovations interminables. Ce jour fut décisif et consacra, aux yeux du peuple, tout le bloc: visions des enfants et visions de Tilmant Côme." ADDF, Dev. Var., 1933.2 Beauraing, 9: note on the apparitions of Beauraing for the use of the Sacred Congregation of the Holy Office (stamped 28 November 1933); Bruno de Jésus-Marie continued to report: for instance ADDF, Dev. Var., 1933.2 Beauraing, 26: letter from Bruno de Jésus-Marie, 17 January 1935, to Mgr Canali.

46 ADDF, Dev. Var., 1933.2 Beauraing, 16: note from Mgr Van Roey on the apparitions (stamped 12 December 1933); Banneux 1934.11, 38: relazione (dicembre 41), 2.

47 He pointed out that not all medical experts involved had a training in psychiatry, and rejected De Greeff's research as aprioristic and anecdotal. ADDF, Dev. Var., 1933.2 Beauraing, 20: les évènements de Beauraing (Lenain), submitted January 1934.

48 "Molto si è già scritto e si continua a scrivere sui fatti di Beauraing, e si potrebbe costituire una discreta biblioteca con tutte la pubblicazioni fatte sulla materia. Discussioni appassionate furono sollevate e sono ancora in corso pro e contra l'origine soprannaturale di questi fatti; e non sempre tutti i personaggi ecclesiastici che ebbero da intervenirvi usarono di tutta la prudenza necessaria in materia così delicata." ADDF, Dev. Var., 1933.2 Beauraing, 19: suprema sacra congregazione de S.Offizio, maggio 1934 n° 794/33, I fatti di Beauraing, 13 maggio 1934 relazione e voto del Rev. mo P. Giov. Batt. Frey, Qualificatore, 1.

49 "Epperò nessuna inchiesta officiale fu fatta fin adesso: giornalisti, medici, pubblicisti, sacerdoti secolari e regolari scrissero, ognuno per conto suo, quello che avevano visto o sentito, spesso con criteri poco oggettivi, o almeno con informazioni molto complete." ADDF, Dev. Var., 1933.2 Beauraing, 19: suprema sacra congregazione de S.Offizio, maggio 1934

n° 794/33, I fatti di Beauraing, 13 maggio 1934 relazione e voto del Rev. mo P. Giov. Batt. Frey, Qualificatore, 2.

50 "Essi sono ordinari, né cattivi né molto buoni," ADDF, Dev. Var., 1933.2 Beauraing, 19: suprema sacra congregazione de S.Offizio, maggio 1934 n° 794/33, I fatti di Beauraing, 13 maggio 1934 relazione e voto del Rev. mo P. Giov. Batt. Frey, Qualificatore, 10; he discussed the accusations more extensively, 13.

51 ADDF, Dev. Var., 1933.2 Beauraing, 19: suprema sacra congregazione de S.Offizio, maggio 1934 n° 794/33, I fatti di Beauraing, 13 maggio 1934 relazione e voto del Rev.mo P. Giov. Batt. Frey, Qualificatore, 13.

52 "Non vedo *nessun argomento positivo veramente convincente* in favore dell'origine soprannaturale dei fatti di Beauraing. Invece esistono *non poche presunzioni in senso contrario* ... mancano nel caso i criteri positivi che non difettano mai quando Dio vuole autenticate una sua rivelazione ... La fede non perde niente nel mostrarsi severa e nell'esigere criteri adeguati. Si corrono invece rischi gravissime nel mostrarsi troppo proclive ad accettare ad occhi chiusi fatti simili." ADDF, Dev. Var., 1933.2 Beauraing, 19: suprema sacra congregazione de S.Offizio, maggio 1934 n° 794/33, I fatti di Beauraing, 13 maggio 1934 relazione e voto del Rev.mo P. Giov. Batt. Frey, Qualificatore, 14–16.

53 ADDF, Dev. Var., 1933.2 Beauraing, 19: suprema sacra congregazione de S.Offizio, report of Feria II, 11 June 1934.

54 "Audiatur Nuntius Apostolicus" (Feria IV, 20 June 1934). ADDF, Dev. Var., 1934.11 Banneux, 38: relazione (December 1941: "Namur-Liège-Beauraing-Banneux"), 2.

55 He added a report by Mgr Cawet, auxiliary bishop and vicar general of Namur (who inclined toward the affirmative) and a report by the medical commission organized by the Association of St-Luke. ADDF, Dev. Var., Banneux 1934.11, 38: relazione (December 1941: "Namur-Liège-Beauraing-Banneux"), 2–3.

56 "E di imporre quindi a tutti silenzio e discrezione ... fossero interrogati da chiunque voleva farlo – e quanti lo hanno fatto senza la minima discrezione – e lo loro dichiarazioni fossero date quindi alla pubblicità." ADDF, Dev. Var., 1933.2 Beauraing, 24: letter from Mgr Micara to Mgr Canali, assessor of the S. Offizio, 15 December 1934, 2.

57 "A che non sembra lecito esprimere il minimo dubbio in proposito senza sentirsi ricoperti di ingiurie." ADDF, Dev. Var., Beauraing 1933.2, 24: letter from Mgr Micara to Mgr Canali, assessor of the S. Offizio, 15 December 1934, 2.

58 ADDF, 1933.2 Beauraing, 24: letter from Mgr Micara to Mgr Canali, 15 December 1934, 4–5.

59 ADDF, Dev. Var., 1934.11 Banneux, 5: letter from Mgr Micara to Mgr Canali, 29 January 1935, and 6, report of the bishop of Liège, 23 December 1934.

60 ADDF, 1933.2 Beauraing, 28: letter from Mgr Micara to Mgr Van Roey, 26 March 1935; Toussaint and Joset, *Beauraing*, 137.

61 The pope approved the solution for Banneux at the audience of 7 February 1935, after being informed about the report the nuncio had sent in on 29 January. The solution for the Beauraing apparition site had already been discussed at a meeting of the S.O. on 9 January 1935. In later communication about this solution, only 9 January 1935 is mentioned as the date. ADDF, Dev. Var., Banneux 1934.11, 38: relazione (December 1941: "Namur-Liège-Beauraing-Banneux"), 2.

62 The added report is dated 25 March 1935.

63 ADDF, 1933.2 Beauraing, 28: letter from Mgr Micara to Mgr Van Roey, 26 March 1935. Toussaint and Joset, *Beauraing*, 135, 137.

64 "La plus stricte objectivité," AAM, Van Roey, Apparitions, 40: Beauraing and Banneux, correspondence among the Belgian bishops, letter from Mgr Van Roey, 5 April 1935.

65 Beyer, "Le procès," 220.

66 ADN, L.2: apparitions of Beauraing from 29 November 1933 to 3 January 1933, chronological overview of the apparitions and their aftermath; AAM, Van Roey, Apparitions, 40: Beauraing and Banneux, correspondence among the Belgian bishops, letter from Mgr Heylen, 13 April 1935; ADL, Kerkhofs, D/IV. Marian cult, 30. Banneux: copy of Mgr Kerkhofs' letter to the pope, 4 September 1939.

67 ADDF, Dev. Var., 1934.11 Banneux, 11: notes on the decision of the Holy Office of 9 January 1935 by the bishops of Liège and Namur, 16 April 1935; Toussaint and Joset, *Beauraing*, 139.

68 ADDF, Dev. Var., 1933.2 Beauraing, 37 and 38: reports on the discussions of 2, 4, 8, and 9 May.

69 ADDF, Dev. Var., 1933.2 Beauraing, 37: report on the meeting of 2 May 1935 (Feria V).

70 "Egli non deve dire di essere stato delegato; e la sentenza, qualunque essa sia, deve essere presa personalmente dal Cardinale." "He cannot say that he has the status of a delegate; and the verdict, whatever it may be, must be personally taken by the Cardinal." ADDF, Dev. Var., 1933.2 Beauraing, 39: report on the decisions of 21 May 1935.

71 As noted in the previous chapters, the first two commissions had already been created in March 1935 but after Rome's intervention and the discussion on the decision power and the procedure to follow, the archbishop had to authorize their formation.

72 Laurentin and Sbalchiero, *Dictionnaire*, 201; Collinet, "Le rôle de la commission," 309.
73 Chiron, *Enquête*, 44–7.
74 Porte, *Pontmain*, 15; Smith Foster, "Canonical Considerations," 131.
75 See the 2011 translation of the 1978 *Normae de modo procedendi in diudicandis praesumptis apparitionibus ac revelationibus*, consulted on 15 September 2015, http://www.vatican.va/roman_curia/congregations/cfaith/documents/rc_con_cfaith_doc_19780225_norme-apparizioni_en.html. For instance in the case of Medjugorgje the Apostolic See decreed that the apparitions needed to be examined anew by the conference of bishops. Smith Foster, "Canonical considerations," 131. In this respect the new May 2024 rules introduced an important change: now the Dicastery of the Doctrine of Faith always gets publicly involved.
76 Chiron, *Enquête*, 48.
77 AAM, Van Roey, Apparitions, 23. Processus, A3: copia actorum, report on the first session, 11 May 1935.
78 Laurentin, "Introduction," 37.
79 Chiron, *Enquête*, 44–7. On this use of experts, see also Laurentin, "Introduction," 37; Laurentin and Sbalchiero, *Dictionnaire*, 197 and 199; Bouflet, *Faussaires*, 68; Tonquédoc, "Apparitions," 806–8.
80 Porte, *Pontmain*, 15.
81 Jelly, "Discerning," 53.
82 Porte, *Pontmain*, 15.
83 Emich, "The production," 167, 172–3.
84 –167.
85 Laurentin and Sbalchiero, *Dictionnaire* 198–9, 249 and 254.
86 ADL, Kerkhofs, D/IV. Marian cult, 28. Canonical examination of the events of Banneux, report on the first session, 20 March 1935.
87 René Rutten (1878–1948) studied philosophy at the junior seminary of Saint-Trond and theology at the Gregoriana University of Rome where he obtained his PhD in 1902 after his ordination in 1901. He studied sociology at the Leo XIII seminary in Louvain and became professor in philosophy at Saint-Trond. In 1907 he became the head of the college of Saint-Quirin in Huy. In 1912 he entered the novitiate of the Jesuits in Arlon. From 1916 onward he worked in the house for retreats Xhovémont and later, in 1935, in Charleroi. From 1942 up until his death he was part of the community of the college Saint-Servais (Liège) as postulator of the Banneux cause. Wuillaume, "Introduction," IX. His book *Histoire critique des apparitions de Banneux* was published after his death, in 1985.
88 Eugène Leroux (1880–1964) studied theology in Louvain and was ordained in 1904. He was a teacher at the junior seminary of St Roch in 1907 and

the great seminary in Liège in 1908. He was the head of the seminar from 1927–45. Dean and titular canon of the chapter of the Cathedral of Liège since 1931, he became a domestic prelate of His Holiness in 1932. Lucien Creusen (1873–1962) was vicar in Dolhain (1896), priest in Bilstain (1910), Hodimont (1917), and dean of Seraing (1927). He became vicar-general in 1942 and in 1957 apostolic protonotary. Beyer, "Le procès," 217–18. ADL, Kerkhofs, D/IV. Marian cult, 28: canonical examination of the events of Banneux, report on the first session, 20 March 1935.

89 On 15 June 1935, Eugène Ruyters (1885–1956), ordained in 1908, was vicar of St Jacques in Liège (1909), military chaplain (1914–19), priest of St Walburga in Liège (1925), and dean of Chênée (1931). He became a canon of the cathedral of Liège in 1943. Beyer, "Le procès," 222.

90 Wuillaume, "La reconnaissance," 302.

91 She was interrogated on 18 and 19 July 1935, in sessions that the bishop attended as well. Beyer, "Le procès," 222.

92 "Moralement impossible de reconstituer l'exacte réalité," "une jeune bonne fille très ordinaire, assez ignorante, d'une nature franche et bonne, mais inculte et d'un caractère assez personnel." ADL, Kerkhofs, D/IV. Marian cult, 28: canonical examination of the events of Banneux, report on session 56 (17 December 1936).

93 "Cela étant, et tenant compte de l'ensemble des depositions, les membres de la Commission estiment que la réalité des apparitions de la Sainte Vierge à Mariette Béco est AU MOINS PROBABLE." ASBX, 2C 3 XIII 2: first commission, letter from the commission members Leroux, Creusen, Rutten, and Ruyters, 18 February 1937; Beyer, "Le procès," 223.

94 "L'heureuse issue du procès canonique" Kerkhofs, *Notre-Dame,* vol. 3, 18.

95 Joset, "Monseigneur Th.-L. Heylen," 233. ADN, L.2. Commission on Beauraing, chronological overview of the events and the activities of the commissions.

96 Monin, *Onze Lieve Vrouw,* 106.

97 Joset, "Monseigneur Th.-L. Heylen," 227. Similar references to a committee created by the bishop in *July* 1933 in a letter from Paul Haese to Mr Vervoort. ASBG, Pierroux, 1932–33: letter from Paul Haese to Vervoort, 27 July 1936.

98 For instance in *Nouvelle Revue Théologique*, "Les événements de Beauraing" (April 1933), "La controverse" (October 1933), and "Encore Beauraing" (April 1935).

99 Joseph Van de Walle (1868–1940) entered the Jesuit order at eighteen. A speech impediment hindered him from entering the teaching profession, and after a short detour as historian he became treasurer ("économe") in Namur and a well-respected confessor. Joset, *Dossiers de Beauraing,* vol. 5, 30.

100 Cyrille Lambot (1900–1968) entered the novitiate in Maredsous, earned a PhD in theology in Louvain, and after two years at the University of Strasbourg returned to Maredsous in 1930 where he continued his academic career. Joset, *Dossiers de Beauraing*, vol. 5, 30–1.

101 Edouard Ranwez (1883–1980) was ordained in 1906, earned a PhD in philosophy and theology at the Gregoriana University, and was a professor of the seminar of Namur. From 1908 to 1910 he was vicar in Gembloux. From 1910–21 he taught philosophy in Floreffe. From 1921–56 he taught morals and ascetic theology at the seminar of Namur. Joset, *Dossiers de Beauraing*, vol. 5, 29.

102 Joseph Henri Bouchat (1873–1953) had already taken on a similar role in commissions created to introduce a cause in Rome. He became the secretary of the diocese of Namur in 1895 and held that position for fifty years. Joset, *Dossiers de Beauraing*, vol. 5, 34.

103 Arthur Monin (1881–1954) studied philosophy in Floreffe and theology in Namur where he was ordained in 1903. After a year of teaching in Bastogne, he became a professor at the American College and professor of canon law at the University of Louvain in 1911. Joset, *Dossiers de Beauraing*, vol. 5, 37–8.

104 Maximilien Demanet (1873–1940) was ordained in 1896 after a decade of teaching, became a parish priest. He became titulary canon and archpriest of the cathedral in 1919. Joset, *Dossiers de Beauraing*, vol. 5, 38.

105 Monin took the oath on 3 June 1935. ADDF, Dev. Var., 1933.2 Beauraing, box 4: report of the first Namur commission, information added to report on session 9 (14 June 1935); Joset, "Monseigneur Th.-L. Heylen," 233.

106 Joset, *Dossiers de Beauraing*, vol. 5, 42–6. Mgr Heylen did not attend the sessions, but he was informed of its activities by Van de Walle, who was his confessor, and by the reports of Canon Bouchat. Joset, "Monseigneur Th.-L. Heylen," 234.

107 ADDF, Dev. Var, 1933.2 Beauraing, box 4: Report of the first Namur commission, session 37 (29 November 1935).

108 Joset, *Dossiers de Beauraing*, vol. 5, 78.

109 "Malgré le souci de l'impartialité de la Commission, l'enquête fut continuellement entravée par l'attitude de certains savants." ADDF, Dev. Var, 1933.2 Beauraing, box 4: extra file with a reflection on the activities of the commission of Namur.

110 ADDF, Dev. Var., 1933.2 Beauraing, box 4: extra file with the questions of the commission of Namur and a reflection on its activities.

111 He testified about these threats during session 52 (7 February 1936) and also mentioned that someone who was financially interested in Beauraing had tried to buy his silence. ADDF, Dev. Var., 1933.2 Beauraing, box 4: report of the first Namur commission.

112 "Si nous relevons ces agissements des cercles 'anti-beaurinois' ce n'est pas que nous perdions de vue l'obligation qui nous incombe de témoigner aux deux parties la plus stricte impartialité. Mais nous estimons nécessaire de faire voir comment la passion et les attitudes inspirées par elle, ne sont pas, comme on l'a fait croire au public le plus désintéressé … le fait des seuls pro-beaurinois." ADDF, Dev. Var., 1933.2 Beauraing, box 4: extra file with the questions of the Namur commission and a reflection on its activities

113 "Sans doute, nous avons pu exercer notre contrôle sur nombre d'assertions émises par ceux qui refusent d'admettre l'hypothèse du surnaturel divin dans les Faits de Beauraing; et le résultat de ce contrôle nous permet de penser qu'il y a une bonne part de 'bluff,' voire de chantage, dans les multiples allusions faites par Mr. le Dr De Greeff et d'autres à des documents mystérieux dont la production suffira, dit-on, à convaincre d'erreur les tenants d'hypothèse du Surnaturel divin, mais qu'on s'est systématiquement refuse à nous faire connaître. Cependant, aussi longtemps que pèsera sur nous la menace de certaines révélations capable peut-être, de modifier notre appréciation, nous ne pouvons sans témérité, en matière si grave et si délicate, prétendre clore l'enquête par des conclusions fermes." ADDF, Dev. Var., 1933.2 Beauraing, box 4: extra file with the questions of the Namur commission and a reflection on its activities.

114 "Nous inclinons vers l'hypothèse du surnaturel divin, laquelle d'ailleurs (comme il a été dit dans le rapport) n'exclut aucunement une dose plus ou moins considérable d'éléments humains – voire diaboliques, si l'on veut – mêlés aux facteurs d'origine divine … en attendant que l'avenir confirme ou infirme notre opinion actuelle … nous estimons que rien n'empêche la continuation, ni même le développement d'un culte marial à Beauraing, d'autant plus qu'au cours de ces quatre dernières années, Beauraing est apparu comme un centre de piété mariale et un lieu de faveurs et de bénédictions pour un grand nombre de fidèles … Toutefois, aussi longtemps que le cas Albert V. n'aura pas reçu une solution favorable, nous croyons inopportune une approbation épiscopale qui encouragerait positivement la croyance à l'origine divine des faits en cause." ADDF, Dev. Var., 1933.2 Beauraing, box 4: extra file with the questions of the Namur commission and a reflection on its activities.

115 ADN, L.2: commission on Beauraing, chronological overview of the events and the activities of the commissions.

116 Joset, *Dossiers de Beauraing*, vol. 5, 75.

117 ADN, L.7/2, HSS: announcement of the diocese, 11 March 1938; S.n., "Les frénésies de Ham-sur-Sambre," *La Libre Belgique*, 15 March 1940, 2.

118 ADDF, Dev. Var., 1934.11 Banneux, 27: the archdiocesan commission about the extraordinary events in Belgium, general report on its activities, 10 February 1939.

119 They did hear some testimonies, for instance, of Louis Wilmet and the parish priest of Etikhove. AAM, Van Roey, Apparitions, 23. Processus, A3: copia actorum, session 5 (13 June 1935, 13).
120 See the discussion of Laure Dulière; AAM, Van Roey, Apparitions, 23. Processus, A3: session 15 (11 March 1936).
121 AAM, Van Roey, Apparitions, 23. Processus, A3: copia actorum, session 16 (1 April 1936, 74).
122 AAM, Van Roey, Apparitions, 23. Processus, A3: copia actorum, session 16 (1 April 1936, 71–80). About the differences in formulation: Chiron, *Enquête*, 304–5.
123 There were reports from Tessens, Vromans, Van Hove, De Moreau, Massaux, and Gillet about the events in Banneux. AAM, Van Roey, Apparitions, 23. Processus, A3: copia actorum, session 20 (22 November 1937, 87–8).
124 ADDF, Dev. Var., 1934.11 Banneux, 28 bis: letter from Mgr Van Roey to Rome about the commission of Malines, 14 February 1939.
125 ADDF, Dev. Var., 1934.11 Banneux, 28 and 28bis. Letter from Mgr Van Roey to Rome about the commission of Malines, 14 February 1939 and a report dated 10 February 1939.
126 "Hommes sérieux et chrétiens," AAM, Van Roey, Apparitions, 23. Processus, A3: copia actorum, session 28 (23 November 1938, 164–5).
127 ADDF, Dev. Var., 1934.11 Banneux, 28bis: letter from Mgr Van Roey 14 February 1939.
128 ADDF, Dev. Var., 1934.11 Banneux, 30: note by Viglio Dalpiaz, 26 February 1939; 34: Votum Creusen (October 1941).
129 AAM, Van Roey, Apparitions, 21: diverse apparitions, letters of the nuncio and Holy Office, letter from Mgr Marchetti-Selvaggiani to Mgr Van Roey, 16 June 1939.
130 ASBX, 2 C3XV6: démarches à Rome. Avis de Mgr. Kerkhofs adressé au Cardinal de Malines, 19 August 1939.
131 "La gravité de l'heure." ADL, Kerkhofs, D/IV. Marian cult, 30: Banneux, copy of the letter from Mgr Kerkhofs to the pope, 4 September 1939. See also the reference to "the tragical hour" in Mgr Heylen's letter; ADDF, Dev. Var., 1933.2 Beauraing, 63: letters from Namur, 8 September 1939 (the chronological overview preserved in the archives of the diocese of Namur suggests it was 9 September 1939); ADN, L.2: apparitions of Beauraing from 29 November 1932 to 3 January1933: chronological overview.
132 AAM, Van Roey, Apparitions, 21: diverse apparitions, letters of the nuncio and Holy Office, letters to Mgr Van Roey, 13 December 1939 and 28 December 1939.
133 AAM, Van Roey, Apparitions, 21: diverse apparitions, letters of the nuncio and Holy Office, letter from the Holy Office (Mgr Marchetti-Selvaggiani) to Mgr Van Roey, 30 January 1940.

134 ADDF, Dev. Var., 1933.2 Beauraing, 69: letter from Mgr Van Roey to Mgr Marchetti-Selvaggiani, "Supremae S. Congregationis Sancti Officii Secretario," 20 February 1940.

135 ADDF, Dev. Var., 1933.2 Beauraing, 74 and 75: documents on the transfer of the findings between de Guibert and Hürth, 18 May 1940 and 20 May 1940; 77, transcript of the report.

136 "Le T.R. Père Creusen, S.J. professeur à la Grégoriana, ancien professeur de Louvain, connait certainement aussi la cause. Son frère, le T.R. Doyen de Seraing fut parmi les théologiens de la commission d'enquête de Liège." ADDF, Dev. Var., 1933.2 Beauraing, 63: letters from Namur, letter from Mgr L. De Gruyter, curé de St Christophe, 18 November 1939 (unclear to whom).

137 ADDF, Dev. Var., 1934.11 Banneux, 34: votum October 1941.

138 "Sedula inquisitione expleta, non certo constat de indole supernaturali factorum (vel apparitionum et verborum)." ADDF, Dev. Var., 1934.11 Banneux, 34: votum October 1941, 19. This judgment did not forbid the devotion to the Virgin of the Poor.

139 ADDF, Dev. Var., 1934.11 Banneux, 34: votum October 1941, 19.

140 ADDF, Dev. Var., 1934.11 Banneux, 35–6: notes on discussions and vote (discussed in October and November 1941); 38: relazione (December 1941), 11–12.

141 Since (1) it had already been nine years, (2) it was normally the ordinary who judges such facts, (3) Rome's intervention was a source of complaints, and (4) the judgment of the bishop of Liège would neither compromise the Holy See nor the Belgian ecclesiastical province, he asked to be given the right to announce his judgment. ADDF, Dev. Var., 1934.11 Banneux, 37: letter from the bishop of Liège, 12 November 1941.

142 After hearing the opinion of secretary and other members of the Holy Office. They discussed it at their meeting (Feria IV) of 17 December 1941. ADDF, Dev. Var., 1934.11 Banneux, 38: relazione (December 1941), 12.

143 "Sede nè l'Eminenza Vostra incaricata dalla S.Sede per l'inchiesta, dia un giudizio con la sola su responsabilità su gli asseriti fatti straordinari." ADDF, Dev. Var., 1934.11 Banneux, 38: Relazione (December 1941), 12; 43: letter to Mgr Kerkhofs, 2 January 1942. Beyer, "Le procès," 230; Joset, *Dossiers de Beauraing*, vol. 2, 59.

144 Joset, "Monseigneur Th.-L. Heylen," 235.

145 On 28 October 1941 according to the chronological overview preserved in the archives of the diocese of Namur, L.2, apparitions of Beauraing from 29 November 1932 to 3 January 1933: chronological overview.

146 ADDF, Dev. Var., 1934.11 Banneux, 44: letter from Mgr Kerkhofs to "très sainte Père," 14 February 1942.

147 See for instance his letters on the matter: ADDF, Dev. Var., 1934.11 Banneux, 44: letter from Mgr Kerkhofs to "très sainte Père," 14 February 1942 and to "Eminence," 13 February 1942.
148 Joset, *Dossiers de Beauraing*, vol. 2, 31.
149 Letter from Mgr Kerkhofs to Mgr Charue, 12 February 1942 cited in Joset, *Dossiers de Beauraing*, vol. 2, 31–2.
150 "Après avoir attendu neuf ans et alors qu'on n'est plus dans la fièvre des débuts," AAM, Van Roey, Apparitions, 40: Beauraing and Banneux, correspondence of the Belgian bishops letter from Mgr Charue, 28 February 1942.
151 ADN, L.2: apparitions of Beauraing from 29 November 1932 to 3 January 1933 (chronological overview), references to letter from the archbishop, 2 March 1942, and letter to Mgr Kerkhofs, 3 March 1942.
152 Letter from Rutten (9 February 1942) cited in Wuillaume, "La reconnaissance," 303.
153 Beyer, "Le procès," 226. ASBX, 2C 3 XV 1: démarches à Rome, lettres importantes, letter from Mgr Kerkhofs to the archbishop, 1 March 1942.
154 "Ceci, répondant à une attente impatiente des fidèles de Banneux, est une garantie contre un éventuel 'cran d'arrêt' que Rome pourrait poser à la suite de votre intervention et ne pourra guère augmenter l'émoi de Namur – d'autant que ma Lettre Pastorale de Carême a rendu publique la lettre du S. Office m'autorisant à juger Banneux à titre d'Ordinaire et sans compromettre ni Rome, ni Malines." Letter from Mgr Kerkhofs to Mgr Charue, 7 March 1942, cited in Joset, *Dossiers de Beauraing*, vol. 2, 42–5. See also his letter a few days earlier, 4 March 1942 (cited in Joset, *Dossiers de Beauraing*, vol. 2, 41).
155 Kerkhofs, *Notre-Dame*, vol. 3, 42–5.
156 ADN, L.2: apparitions of Beauraing from 29 November 1932 to 3 January 1933: chronological overview, reference to letter from the archbishop, 24 March 1942.
157 A short note at the end of the letter indicated that it was not to be read out loud from the pulpit. "N.B. Cette lettre n'est pas destinée à être lue en chaire." Pastoral letter from Mgr Van Roey, 25 March 1942 (on the Feast of the Annunciation of the Holy Virgin) cited in Joset, *Dossiers de Beauraing*, vol. 2, 57–60.
158 "Enfin, en considération d'une affaire spéciale, relative à un seul enfant, ils estimèrent moins opportune de soutenir catégoriquement la cause aussi longtemps que l'expérience n'aurait pas démontré que cette affaire ne présentait plus d'obstacles à la reconnaissance officielle." Letter from Mgr Charue, 22 March 1942, to Pius XII, cited in Joset, *Dossiers de Beauraing*, vol. 2, 55.

159 Letter from Mgr Charue to Pius XI, 22 March 1942. He sent a similar request on 17 June 1942. Joset, *Dossiers de Beauraing*, vol. 2, 53–6, 71.

160 ADDF, Dev. Var., 1933.2 Beauraing, 86: letter from Mgr Charue, 7 June 1942.

161 The Holy Office discussed the matter in April and May. ADDF, Dev. Var., 1933.2 Beauraing, 83: report of April 1942 "Namur-Liegi-Beauraing-Banneux"; Banneux 1934.11, 38: Aggiunta alla relazione (April 1942), 4.

162 AAM, Van Roey, Apparitions, 40: Beauraing and Banneux, correspondence among the Belgian bishops, letter from Mgr Marchetti-Selvaggiani, secretary of the Holy Office, to Mgr Charue, 30 May 1942 (Latin version). ASBG, Pierroux: letter from Mgr Charue to the vicar, 3 July 1942.

163 Letter from Mgr Van Roey, 8 July 1942, cited in Joset, *Dossiers de Beauraing*, vol. 2, 73.

164 ADN, L.2: second report of the diocesan commission of Namur, written by Canon Monin and with annexes by Canon Ranwez, 9 January 1943. The document is included in Joset, *Dossiers de Beauraing*, vol. 5, 85–152. See also Toussaint and Joset, *Beauraing*, 157. Demanet and Van de Walle had both died in July 1940.

165 "M. le Dr De Greeff n'a produit à Malines aucun argument nouveau, aucun document qui ne fût déjà connu." "Les adversaires de la réalité, ou du moins du caractère surnaturel divin des 'Faits de Beauraing,' ont tout naturellement fait grand état de l'avis d'un témoin qui leur a paru si autorisé, et par ses titres scientifiques, et par ses fonctions, et par l'apparat scientifique qu'il a donné à son enquête et à ses publications." Report of the doctrinal commission of 1942, cited in Joset, *Dossiers de Beauraing*, vol. 5, 110.

166 "Un contradicteur systématique," "impressions," "perceptions directes," and "évidences psychologiques," report of the doctrinal commission of 1942, cited in Joset, *Dossiers de Beauraing*, vol. 5, 111, 114.

167 Report of the doctrinal commission of 1942, cited in Joset, *Dossiers de Beauraing*, vol. 5, 135.

168 ADDF, Dev. Var., 1933.2 Beauraing, 10: the case of Albert Voisin according to the documents I to VIII (stamp 28 November 1933); see also the depositions in AAM, Van Roey, Apparitions, 23. Processus, A3: copia actorum, session 25 (5 May 1938, 153–4).

169 "Avec le plus des précisions possibles et l'appréciation des médecins. Que ce soit des cas bien caractérisés, et indiscutables du point de vue extraordinaire sinon miraculeux." ASBG, Pierroux, 1942, 221: letter from C. Lambot, 18 November 1942. See also 226 (response to his letter, 22 November 1942); and 227–8, 236, 238–9, 248–55, 257, 264–7.

170 "Sans se prononcer sur la réalité et le caractère surnaturel divin des faits, l'autorité diocésaine de Namur pourrait permettre un culte public à

N.D. de Beauraing pour autant que le Souverain Pontife l'agrée." Joset, *Dossiers de Beauraing*, vol. 5, 141; Toussaint and Joset, *Beauraing*, 160.

171 Joset, *Dossiers de Beauraing*, vol. 2, 80–1.

172 Decree of Mgr Charue authorizing the cult of Our Lady of Beaurang, 2 February 1943, published on 19 February with his pastoral letter, cited in Joset, *Dossiers de Beauraing*, vol. 2, 98–109.

173 Beyer, "Le procès," 232.

174 Wuillaume, "La reconnaissance," 304.

175 "Le caractère surnaturel des faits de Banneux ne leur apparaît pas ni certain ni même simplement probable." Wuillaume, "La reconnaissance," 304.

176 ADL, Kerkhofs, D/IV Marian cult, 27: "Jugement du tribunal constitué par Mgr. l'évêque." The commission wrote twenty-five reports. The annex on the Lourdes brochure was not considered part of the conclusion, see Beyer, "Le procès," 234, 237.

177 "Supposons Mariette prédisposée au phénomène d'hallucination." Wuillaume, "La reconnaissance," 305–6.

178 Beyer, "Le procès," 237.

179 "Et ne puis-je éventuellement me rallier à votre sentiment plutôt qu'à celui des juges?" ASBX, 2D 1 XVI/5: letter from Mgr Kerkhofs, 22 December 1944.

180 Beyer, "Le procès," 236–7.

181 ASBX, 2 C 3 XV 1: letter from Mgr Kerkhofs to Mgr Ottaviani, 9–10 November 1949.

182 Beyer, "Le procès," 239.

183 ADL, Kerkhos, D/IV Marian cult, 28: cause de Banneux, the report of Scheuer. The opinion of the professor of ecclesiastic history Édouard de Moreau was also of central importance. Beyer, "Le procès," 244–5.

184 "Un attentat commis," "par l'absurde," "Que du moins le précieux document soit gardé jalousement, comme une gemme, de grand prix, dans les archives de la Vierge des Pauvres!" ADL, Kerkhofs, D/IV Marian cult, 28: cause de Banneux, copy of the report of Scheuer.

185 Beyer, "Le procès," 240–1.

186 Wuillaume, "La reconnaissance," 307 and Beyer, "Le procès," 241.

187 "L'outrage à l'outrage," "serait certainement stérile et qui nous exposerait à de nouvelles injures du P. Scheuer, en présence même de Votre Excellence … Cependant, si le rapport du père est profondément blessant pour nous, il n'est nullement de nature à modifier notre conviction." ASBX, 2D1 XVI/7 2e Commission: letter from E. Leroux, 12 October 1946.

188 Wuillaume, "La reconnaissance," 307; Beyer, "Le procès," 243.

189 "Dans la même Pastorale nous avons proposé les faits de Banneux comme assez fondés pour être, au moins dans les limites d'une sérieuse probabilité, dignes d'une foi humaine." Kerkhofs, *Notre-Dame*, vol. 3, 69.

190 Beyer, "Le procès," 242.

191 ADL, Kerkhofs, D/IV. Marian cult, 28: canonical examination of the events of Banneux, response to Scheuer's report, s.d.

192 Beyer, "Le procès," 245–6.

193 Kerkhofs, *Notre-Dame,* vol. 3, 83–7.

194 "Mais le fait est là; le Bon Dieu l'a permis, je tâche de l'accepter avec un généreux abandon à la divine Providence." ADDF, Dev. Var., 1934.11 Banneux, 46: letter from Mgr Micara to Mgr Marchetti-Selvaggiani, 1 March 1945 (including a copy of the letter Mgr Kerkhofs wrote him on 21 February 1945).

195 ADDF, Dev. Var., 1934.11 Banneux, 58a: relazione (November 1949), 1–2.

196 "Quel venerando Vescovo, ovunque apprezzato per la sua pietà, zelo e carittà, quasi non curando le conclusioni delle Commissioni Diocesane e senza possedere nuovi positivi elementi che modificassero tali conclusioni, ma unicamente mosso da una sua intima persuasione e da osservazioni personali, riconosce 'malgré tout' (sono sue parole), l'autenticità delle apparizioni di Banneux." ADDF, Dev. Var., 1934.11 Banneux, 49: letter from the nuncio to Mgr Marchetti-Selvaggiani, 20 September 1949.

197 Beyer, "Le procès," 249. Beyer refers to a personal note he received about this from Mgr Kerkhofs.

198 "Dato che la cosa è, sotto parecchi aspetti, ancora molto controversa." ADDF, Dev. Var., 1934.11 Banneux, 54: report of the visit of Mgr Kerkhofs to the Holy Office, 9 November 1949; 55: letter to Fernando Cento, nuncio in Brussels, 15 November 1949.

199 ADDF, Dev. Var., 1934.11 Banneux, 51: note sur la lettre de S.E. Mgr Kerkhofs.

200 "Inspirée par notre conviction intime," "qu'il y manque le fondement canonique sagement requis pour des interventions d'une telle gravité. La Lettre le reconnaît d'ailleurs assez clairement." ADDF, Dev. Var., 1934.11 Banneux, 51: note on the letter from S.E. Mgr Kerkhofs, 1.

201 "Tout cela fait que de nombreux fidèles sont troublés. Un malaise grave s'ensuit, qui menace de faire conclure à la légèreté des décisions de l'Eglise en matière aussi grave que les miracles et les apparitions. Devant Dieu, il paraît qu'il y a là une situation funeste et qu'une mise au point serait nécessaire." ADDF, Dev. Var., 1934.11 Banneux, 51: note on the letter of S.E. Mgr Kerkhofs, 3.

202 ADDF, Dev. Var., 1934.11 Banneux, 56: letter from Mgr Kerkhofs, 13 November 1949: he sends in the requested report and his notes ("Notes sur les faits de Banneux et sur la reconnaissance de leur caractère surnaturel," 16 November 1949).

203 Beyer, "Le procès," 249.

204 "N'a rien à voir avec la pathologie," "Son Eminence ne crut pas pouvoir

prononcer de jugement à leur sujet, et déféra le tout au St.-Office," "silence révérencieux," "je n'ai nul indice de mécontentement, moins encore de critique ou d'opposition ouverte, de leur part." ASBX, 2 C 3 XV 1: letter from Mgr Kerkhofs to Mgr Ottaviani, 9–10 November 1949.

205 "Je sais que Rome n'intervient pas directement dans la reconnaissance officielle de faits de ce genre. Moins encore peut-elle le faire dans cas présent, où il s'agit d'une cause reconnue récemment et dans les conditions quelque peu en marge de la procédure habituelle. Le Saint-Père, dans sa prudence, et tout bien pesé, pourra examiner si, sans apparence de reconnaissance par Lui-même des faits en question, Il pourrait nous faciliter l'érection du Sanctuaire marial projeté, hommage de toutes les nations, symbole et centre de leur piété, de leur confiance, de leurs prières pour obtenir, par Marie, la paix et le salut du monde." ASBX, 2 C 3 XV 1: letter from Mgr Kerkhofs to Mgr Ottaviani, 9–10 November 1949.

206 We know something about the opinion of the bishop of Namur on Collard through a letter he wrote in December 1943: While he had not been a practising Catholic and sometimes even been anticlerical, he had converted just before his death in a cell in Louvain that he shared with a supporter of the apparitions of Beauraing. AAM, Van Roey, Apparitions, 40: Beauraing and Banneux, letters of the bishops and reactions, letter from the bishop of Namur, 1 December 1943.

207 "Dès lors l'objection tirée de l'immoralité d'A.V. deviant caduque." Report of Mgr Charue cited in Joset, *Dossiers de Beauraing*, vol. 5, 153.

208 – *Dossiers de Beauraing*, vol. 5, 153–4.

209 The inclusion of Martens in the diocesan commission certainly facilitated communication between the Flemish witnesses and the predominantly Walloon commission. ASBG, Lambert, 38: cure of Mrs Acar, letter from Mrs Acar to Martens, 23 December 1948.

210 ASBG, Lambert, 38: cure of Mrs Acar.

211 For the Van Laer case, the report carries the names of Cyrille Lambot and F. Toussaint – no third name is mentioned. However, the interrogations seem to have taken place in the presence of Lambot, Toussaint, and Martens. ASBG, Lambert, 39: cure of Van Laer, questioning of the sister of Maria Van Laer and her aunt.

212 ASBG, Lambert, 38: cure of Mrs Acar, final conclusion of the diocesan commission, 26 May 1949.

213 ASBG, Lambert, 38: cure of Mrs Acar, letter from Mgr Charue to the clergy and his decree, 2 July 1949. See Monin, *Onze Lieve Vrouw*, 167–273 and Joset, *Dossiers de Beauraing*, vol. 2, 135–7.

214 "Officiellement nous ne savons rien de la Commission de Malines. Les derniers restes de l'opposition pourraient abuser de l'ignorance universelle pour rabaisser le probe travail de la Commission de Malines à l'infime

niveau du misérable verdict de l'ex-Commission de Liège. C'est pourquoi je ne me crois pas obligé à garder pour moi seul les quelques renseignements que j'étais seul à posséder; et qu'un témoin omni exceptione maior a communiqués au défenseur de Banneux bien plus qu'à l'ami. Je dépose ces notes confidentielles dans les archives de Banneux, à tout fin utile, pour les intérêts de Banneux et pour l'honneur de la Commission de Malines." ASBX, 2D 1 XVI/7 2e Commission: notes on the work and the conclusion of the commission, Banneux et la Commission de Malines (29 June 1947), two copies of the text (one signed by Scheuer).

215 Scheuer noted that the commission did not have the mandate to examine the reality of the apparitions, that the commission members did not wait for the response of the postulator Rutten, and that two commission members had been part of the first commission and at that time formulated a more positive conclusion. Moreover, there were no transcripts of the commission, there were doubts about whether they were ever drafted, or the bishop ever saw them. As for the commission members, he attached little importance to their opinion. He uses very colourful terms in his 1952 evaluation. ADL, Kerkhofs, D/IV. Marian cult, 27: observations on the conclusions of the second commission.

216 "Rien dans l'attitude de la Commission de Malines n'excluait cet aboutissement de l'étude de la cause." Letter from Mgr Charue, 9 April 1950, co-signed by Mgr Van Roey, cited in Joset, *Dossiers de Beauraing*, vol. 5, 82–3.

217 AAM, Van Roey, Apparitions, 36.I: Beauraing and Banneux, letter from André Marie, bishop of Namur, 22 May 1948; ASBG, Lambert, 38: cure of Mrs Acar, letter from Mgr Charue to the clergy and his decree, 2 July 1949; Beyer, "Le procès," 248–9.

218 "Het zou overigens nadelig zijn bepaalde tere punten aan te raken en zo gevaar te lopen terug die opgewonden atmosfeer te scheppen waardoor de eerste controverses gestoord werden." Monin, *Onze Lieve Vrouw*, 60.

219 ADL, Fonds Kerkhofs, D/IV. Marian cult, 30: Banneux, letter from Mgr Kerkhofs to Mr le Professeur, 27 October 1949. As there were still rumours circulating that the French Carmelite Bruno de Jésus-Marie had information that could put the evaluation into question, he was eventually summoned to appear before the church officials in Paris (19 October 1950). He testified that he had deposited all his information in Malines and Rome and refused to reveal his sources. His testimony and his unwillingness to reveal new information tied up the last loose ends for the Beauraing commission, according to Toussaint and Joset (*Beauraing*, 171).

## Chapter Five

1 "Les autres foyers d'apparitions ont vu leur faveur tomber, et à présent c'est seulement Beauraing et Banneux qui sont demeurés des centres de prières, de grâces et de conversion. Le culte s'est maintenu. Le triage inéluctable s'est opéré. Un fait humain ou diabolique n'a pas de résistance, après quelque temps, la fraude apparait." ADL, Kerkhofs, D/IV. Marian cult, 32: Banneux, notes on the cult of Banneux by Abbé Jamin, 12 October 1937: annex nr.3.

2 J.A., "Les fausses apparitions," *La Voix de Beauraing* 6, no. 23 (1 December 1939): 10.

3 Maunder, "The Footprints," 13–14.

4 "Tous les ferventes de Beauraing sont indignés et révoltés de ce que Banneux qui est arrivée après Beauraing organise tout si bien … Tous nous comptons sur votre dévouement, monsieur le doyen, pour arriver al plus vite possible à organiser les choses comme à Banneux." ASBG, Pierroux, 1934–35, 143: letter of E. Jadin to the dean, 7 August 1934.

5 See for example the back of the May 1933 issue of *Banneux-Tancrémont* with a pricelist of images of the Virgin of the Poor. Deneweth, *Kroniek*, 27 and 35. Raising money for the basilica: s.n., "La basilique," *Banneux Notre-Dame* 4, no. 4 (August 1936): 152.

6 ADL, Kerkhofs, D/IV. Marian cult, 32: notes on the cult of Banneux by Abbé Jamin, 12 October 1937. The ground was purchased from Mariette Béco's father. S.n., "Évenements majeurs post apparitions," 1. On this tolerance, see also ADDF, Dev. Var., 1934.11 Banneux, 6: letter of the bishop of Liège, 21–3 December 1934.

7 "Mais si, à la suite des faits au caractère surnaturel desquels rien ne paraît s'opposer, se développe un culte de tous points conforme aux données de la foi et à la pratique de l'Église, rien n'empêche l'Ordinaire d'en favoriser le développement, sans qu'on puisse conclure à une déclaration officielle, même indirecte, du caractère surnaturel des événements qui en ont provoqué l'éclosion." Creusen, "Les faits merveilleux de Belgique," *Banneux Notre-Dame* 1, no. 10 (February 1934): 240–8, 244–5.

8 "Notice explicative de l'Union Internationale," *Banneux Notre-Dame*, 2, no. 6 (October 1934): 182–4. They prayed for the poor, suffering, and sick.

9 Caritas, "L'Œuvre de la Vierge des Pauvres," *Banneux-Tancrémont*, September 1, no. 5 (1933): 104–6; J.B., "Notre bilan et notre appel," *Banneux Notre-Dame* 1, no. 9 (January 1934): 215–44, 221.

10 L.J., "Avec la Vierge, soulageons les maladies," *Banneux Notre-Dame* 6, no. 11 (March 1939): 471–81, 474.

11 Deneweth, *Kroniek*, 26–8, 38.

12 Initially (in August 1933) there was only a humble shelter. On the baths and the rituals, see the testimony of Abbé Jamin before the commission of Liège (performing the examination at the request of the commission of Malines): AAM, Processus, A3: copia actorum, files attached to session 21 (questioning on 18 October 1937, 167). S.n., "L'Œuvre de la Vierge des Pauvres," *Banneux Notre-Dame* 3, no. 2 (June 1935): 75–7; S.n., "Chronique des faits." 3, no. 3 (July 1935): 106–9; Deneweth, *Kroniek*, 24.

13 L.J., "Avec la Vierge, soulageons les maladies," *Banneux Notre-Dame* 6, no. 11 (March 1939): 471–81, 478. The baths were used until about 1970. By then they were decrepit and were abandoned. Deneweth, *Kroniek*, 38.

14 AAM, Processus, A3: copia actorum, files attached to session 21 (questioning on 20 October 1937, 167).

15 "Aient dépassé les faits de Banneux pour copier Lourdes," AAM, Processus, A3: copia actorum, files attached to session 21 (questioning on 18 October 1937, 167). However, as a memorial book written by the pilgrims from Bruges indicates, the pilgrims seem to have experienced the baths as a hasty copy of Lourdes. Deneweth, *Kroniek*, 25.

16 AAM, Processus, A3: copia actorum, files attached to session 21 (questioning on 18 October 1937, 167).

17 Such as the evening rosary, the ablution and invocations near the spring, a prayer in front of the cross near the baths, and the ablution of the sick in the baths. ADL, Kerkhofs, D/IV. Marian cult, 32: Banneux, notes on the cult of Banneux by Abbé Jamin, 12 October 1937, annex: "the rites of Banneux." S.n., "Programme de visite à Banneux-Notre-Dame," *Banneux Notre-Dame* 3, no. 2 (June 1935): 44–56, 45.

18 ADL, Kerkhofs, D/IV. Marian cult, 32: notes on the cult of Banneux by Abbé Jamin, 12 October 1937.

19 AAM, Processus, A3: copia actorum, files attached to session 21 (questioning on 20 October 1937, 167).

20 Deneweth, *Kroniek*, 23; AAM, Van Roey, Apparitions, 23. Processus, A3: copia actorum, report added to session 21: questioning of Abbé Jamin on 20 October 1937; ADL, Kerkhofs, D/IV. Marian cult, 32: notes on the cult of Banneux, 12 October 1937. The Gestapo forbade German pilgrimages there in 1936. One of the German promoters of Banneux seems to have been sent to a concentration camp for spreading documentation on Banneux. O'Sullivan, "West German Miracles," 4.

21 S.n., "Chronique des faits," *Banneux-Tancrémont* 1, no. 4 (August 1933): 71; S.n., "Chronique des faits," *Banneux Notre-Dame* 3, no. 6 (October 1935): 244–5 and 4, no. 6 (October 1936): 256–9, 257.

22 ASBX: book "Signatures pour la cause de Banneux Notre-Dame," s.a.

23 S.n., "Banneux Notre-Dame pendant la guerre," *Banneux Notre-Dame* 8, no. 2 (July–August 1945): 3–10, 3.

24 "En 1943, plus de 10 ans après les apparitions de Notre-Dame; la cour se trouvait toujours dans le même état qu'en 1933, quelques rangées de bancs y furent placés et ce fut tout!" ASBG, Lambert, 3: unpublished manuscripts, e. report of Pierroux, 1932–43. On the lack of initiatives to change the site before the official recognition, see also: Delvaux, "Naissance," 36.

25 Joset suggests that it was eventually the consecration of the Banneux chapel on 15 August 1933 that made Beauraing supporters feel the need for their own permanent committee. Joset, *Dossiers de Beauraing*, vol. 3, 43.

26 ASBG, Lambert, 3: unpublished manuscripts, e. report of Pierroux, 1932–43; Joset, *Dossiers de Beauraing*, vol. 3, 44; Delvaux, "Naissance," 32.

27 ASBG, Lambert, 3: unpublished manuscripts, e. report of Pierroux, 1932–43; Joset, *Dossiers de Beauraing*, vol. 3, 16–17 and 19. On the various plans for a shrine and their location: Kevers, "L'organisation," 35.

28 Special issue of *La Voix de Beauring* in August 1947; Joset, *Dossiers de Beauraing*, vol. 3, 19; Toussaint and Joset, *Beauraing*, 172.

29 Joset, *Dossiers de Beauraing*, vol. 3, 36; Delvaux, "Naissance," 33.

30 S.n., "Souscription pour l'érection d'une basilique," *L'Officiel de Beauraing* 1, no. 1 (15 October 1933): 1; Nicaise-Vermer, "Où faut-il construire la basilique," *L'Officiel de Beauraing* 1, no. 2 (1 November 1933): 4; Joset, *Dossiers de Beauraing*, vol. 3, 44.

31 Delvaux, "Naissance," 35–7.

32 Foreign groups from Germany, the Netherlands, France, and Luxembourg had already visited Beauraing before any official recognition was announced. As for the origin of the Belgian pilgrim groups Delvaux studied: in 1933, 71 per cent of the pilgrims came from Flanders, whereas only 19.5 per cent were Walloon. In the years of little enthusiasm (1933–9) there seems to have been a balance between the two parts of Belgium and between 1943 and 1949 Wallonia dominated (with 50.3 per cent to 20.9 per cent Flemish groups). Delvaux studied the number of pilgrim groups; the number of individual pilgrims might have differed as Walloon pilgrims most probably did not have to call upon the group transport of pilgrimages to visit the site. Delvaux, "Naissance," 69, 78, 80, 90, 105, 107–17 and 186; Joset, *Dossiers de Beauraing*, vol. 3, 57.

33 Joset, *Dossiers de Beauraing*, vol. 3, 45–7; Monin, *Onze Lieve Vrouw*, 44.

34 The study examined the numbers reported in *L'Officiel de Beauraing* and the later *Voix de Beauraing* and information provided by other witnesses. The focus was on the period between the first events and the official recognition of the supernatural character of the apparitions (in 1949).

Delvaux, "Naissance." *La Voix* suspended publication during the war, so we do not have a continuity of numbers. ASBG, Lambert, 3: unpublished manuscripts, e. report of Pierroux, 1932–43.

35 Apparently no fewer than fifty-eight trains arrived on 5 August 1933 (according to the information of the Beauraing train station). Delvaux, "Naissance," 63.

36 ASBG, Lambert, 11: papers of Gaston Maes II; 13: Dossier Planque "Souvenirs de Beauraing." Only day trippers visited and prayed a rosary at the site. With the exception of certain days, the domain was left abandoned.

37 See the announcement and articles in *La Voix de Beauraing*: s.n., "A Beauraing … Le Pèlerinage pour la Paix," *La Voix de Beauraing* 6, no. 18 (15 September 1939): 4; S.n., "29 Novembre 1939," *La Voix de Beauraing* 6, no. 24 (15 December 1939): 7. See also ASBG, Pierroux, 1940, 94: circular letter for the committee members concerning 13 May; 3: unpublished manuscripts, e. report of Pierroux, 1932–43; Delvaux, "Naissance," 66.

38 ASBG, Lambert, 3: unpublished manuscripts, e. report of Pierroux, 1932–43; Delvaux, "Naissance," 68, 105; Toussaint and Joset, *Beauraing*, 173.

39 Van Osselaer, "Op eigen houtje."

40 Delvaux, "Naissance," 40.

41 Mgr Charue asked his clergy to pray that whatever the decisions of the ecclesiastical authority should be, it would contribute to the greater glory of Our Lady. Letter from Mgr Charue to the clergy of his diocese, 15 April 1942, cited in: Joset, *Dossiers de Beauraing*, vol. 2, 68–9. On the prayer campaign and local Beauraing iniatives, see ASBG, Lambert, 3: unpublished manuscripts, e. report of Pierroux, 1932–43.

42 ASBG, Pierroux, 1942, 28: Pierroux' call 25 March 1942 and responses, for instance from J. Van Seynhaeve, 5 April 1942; J. Van Campenhout, 7 April 1942; and Lacroix Laval, 12 April 1942. 3: Unpublished manuscripts, e. report of Pierroux, 1932–43.

43 "Ce que nous ressentîmes est indescriptible; une immense joie mêlée de stupeur; c'était comme un soleil éclatant et inattendu dissipant les brumes de la nuit; c'était le triomphe après l'obscurité, le travail et la lutte. C'était enfin la possibilité de clamer à tous les échos, sans peur et sans contrainte, notre amour et notre vénération à la Dame de chez nous." ASBG, Lambert, 3: unpublished manuscripts, e. report of Pierroux, 1932–43.

44 M. De Ceulener, "Het verlaten kapelletje te Etichove," *Het Laatste Nieuws*, 22 March 1934, 9.

45 "Alléén in trouw aan de Kerk den weg van zaligheid en heil kan vinden." DAG, Onkerzele, 239: letter from the parish priest Omer Duerinck to Minister G. Sap, July 1939.

46 See for instance the attempts of H. Blondeel to promote the apparitions in Olsene (ADG, Coppieters, 9.5 Apparitions: letter from Blondeel to Mgr Coppieters, 17 April 1944) or the letter from Watteyne to Mgr Calewaert in July 1952 that several of Jules' predictions had come true (ADG, Apparitions, 208: letter of Watteyne, 18 July 1952).

47 Gosseye, "De verschijningen," 117.

48 Cock, "Mijn gezegend oord," 271.

49 There are also special "ommegangs" on 23 June, the day she died, and 15 September, the feast of Our Lady of Sorrows. Schellinck, *Het wonderbare leven,* 5.

50 Cock, "Mijn gezegend oord," 288–9.

51 Jacobs, *De zienster,* 19–27.

52 ADN, L.42–3, Wilmet III: letters of Louis Wilmet, 9 November 1934 and 28 August 1934.

53 Schellinck, *Het wonderbare leven,* 93, 103, and 113: She claimed that some of the people of the Belgian royal court consulted her in various matters.

54 Schellinck's book refers to the devotion to the "Sacred Face," a devotion that had been approved, but not the devotion that the supporters of Onkerzele tried to promote in the 1930s. Schellinck, *Het wonderbare leven,*135.

55 DAG, Onkerzele, 221: episcopal warnings in the *Godsdienstige Week van het Bisdom Gent,* 24 June 1938, 1, and a confirmation of these guidelines in the issue of 22 July 1938, 1. Likewise, warnings were read out from the pulpit: ADG, Apparitions, 82: correspondence between the bishop and the parish priest of Balgerhoeke, 16 December 1938.

56 DAG, Onkerzele, 237: correspondence between Duerinck and Edith B., 20 August 1941 and 11 September 1941.

57 DAG, Onkerzele, 242: report of Duerinck for Mgr Coppieters, 29 October 1941 and the answer of the bishop.

58 DAG, Onkerzele, 196: letter of Angeline G. to the parish priest, 9 August 1943. Schellinck, *Het wonderbare leven,* 127, 152.

59 Schellinck, *Het wonderbare leven,* 128, 197, and 236. For her special "tears," see also DAG, Onkerzele, 260: examination by J. Planté, 1 April 1939.

60 Jacobs, *De zienster,* 19–27; Schellinck, *Het wonderbare leven,* 283, 293, 300.

61 ADG, Apparitions, 214: letter of Benoit Willems, 22 November 1951.

62 Jacobs, *De zienster,* 5.

63 Schellinck, *Het wonderbare leven,* 321.

64 "Er is ons geen enkele reden bekend dat zou toelaten van dit standpunt af te wijken." DAG Onkerzele, 269: exhumation of Leonie Van den Dijck, parish priest Willem Houtman about the events between 9 June and 1 July. Her body was exhumed again in 1982 when her son died. DAG, Onkerzele, 270–2: newspaper cuttings and letters.

65 Schellinck, *Het wonderbare leven,* 329, 246 and DAG, Onkerzele, 8: Leonia Van den Dijck.
66 See footnote in Jacobs (*De zienster,* 19) where they are called "false visionaries" who tried to steal Leonie Van den Dijck's thunder in a "demonic" countermove.
67 See Cock, "Mijn gezegend oord," 288; Badone, "Echoes," 454.
68 Schellinck, *Het wonderbare leven,* 127, 152, and 325. DAG, Onkerzele, 243–52: Omer Duerinck the restoration of the chapels of Our Lady of Sorrows.
69 DAG, Onkerzele, 119: information folder of the committee.
70 See its "articles of association" ("statuten") of 22 March 1946, ADN, L.7/2, HSS: file apparitions 1943–51.
71 Wouters, "Transnationale spanningen," 19.
72 ADN, L.7/2, HSS: announcement of the diocese, 11 March 1938.
73 On 3 March 1940, the diocese warned the clergy through the *Semaine Religieuse* (Bulletin du Diocèse de Namur) see reference in: "Mise en garde!" 21 April 1940, *La Croix de Belgique,* cutting in ADN, L7/2, HSS.
74 ADN, L.7/2, HSS, Apparitions 1951–61: letter by Mgr Charue, 26 September 1958; see also Apparitions 1943–51: letter to "excellence Révérendissime," 13 November 1950, from the bishop of Namur.
75 "Que les prétendus messages et révélations dont on parle constituent une profanation sacrilège … Ceux qui sont connus comme étant les organisateurs, s'ils persistent dans leur attitude néfaste, doivent être considérés, comme révoltés contre l'Église et ne peuvent avoir accès aux sacrements." Letter of Mgr Charue to the dean (doyen), 25 April 1943. ADN, L.7/2, HSS, Apparitions 1943–51.
76 ADN, L.7/2, HSS, Apparitions 1943–51: letter from Mgr Charue to the dean 25 April 1943.
77 ADN, L.7/2, HSS, Apparitions 1943–51: letters from Emelda Scohy to the bishop of Namur, 30 April 1943 and 20 June 1943; letter from Mgr Charue to his colleagues, 23 February 1947.
78 Moreover, he stressed that the bishop of Namur was not his bishop. ADT, Revelations – Apparitions, Apparitions de Ham-sur-Sambre (HSS): letter from Abbé Edmond-Philippart to "Monseigneur," 31 December 1946.
79 ADT, Revelations – Apparitions, HSS: letter from Abbé Edmond-Philippart to "Monseigneur," 31 December 1946.
80 "J'en ai en effet reçu 3 affronts dans trois églises différentes et je suis maintenant un peu cuirasse, étant, préparé de longue date et par expérience personnelle. Ce n'est pas encore cela qui fera fléchir ma résistance." ADT, Revelations – Apparitions, HSS: letter from Vital Brachot (27 December 1946) added to the letter from Abbé Edmond-Philippart to "Monseigneur," 31 December 1946.

81 Letter from Delbart to Mgr Charue, s.d. (ADN, L.7/2, HSS, Apparitions 1943–51).

82 Abbé Césard first got involved in the Ham-sur Sambre affair on 5 February 1937 (first trip there). That same year he published a booklet "My reasons for believing" ("Mes raisons de croire").

83 Bouflet, "Institution," 272.

84 In August 1942: prohibition of all propaganda. Referred to in letter from the bishop of Nancy and Toul, 12 August 1945. ADN, L7/2, HSS.

85 After he celebrated mass in the presence of 200 to 300 followers in his garden, the bishop intervened. He imposed a retreat of twenty days at a religious house and forbade all priests from elsewhere to celebrate mass in the Bouxières parish without his special permission. Letter from the bishop of Nancy and Toul (12 August 1945) to "cher et venerė Seigneur," but since there is a mention of "Excellence" and "your diocese" may be the bishop of Namur, ADN, L7/2, HSS.

86 Bouflet, "Institution," 272.

87 ADN, L.7/2, HSS: letter of the bishop of Namur and Toul to the parishioners of Bouxières-aux-Dames, 19 October 1946; Wouters, "Transnationale spanningen," 23.

88 Bouflet, "Institution," 272. They confirmed this twice: 15 June 1946 and 13 March 1947. See ADN, L.7/2, HSS: a copy of the letter of the Holy Office, 15 June 1946.

89 "En conformité avec les décrets du Saint-Siège et en particulier avec le Code de Droit Canonique (canons 1326 et 1399), nous avons interdit à M. l'Abbé Césard toute manifestation s'appuyant sur ces messages ou ces faits de Bouxières, puisqu'il s'agissait là de révélations privées non approuvées par l'Église," ADN, L.7/2, HSS, Apparitions 1943–51: "Communiqué de Monseigneur l'Évêque relatif aux faits dits de Bouxières-aux-Dames," *La Semaine Religieuse du Diocèse de Nancy et de Toul* 84, nr. 29 (20 July 1947): 218–9. Abbé Césard seems to have written a booklet *Les apparitions de Notre-Dame de Bouxières, au "Tunnel" et dans le Sanctuaire de l'Eglise* as a response to this condemnation.

90 Bouflet, "Institution," 274.

91 ADN, L.7/2, HSS: a letter from Jules Delbart to Mgr Charue, 26 April 1948.

92 Wouters, "Transnationale spanningen," 24.

93 Bouflet, "Institution," 274–5.

94 ADN, L.7/2, HSS, Apparitions 1943–51: letter from the bishop of Namur to the Holy Office (13 November 1950); response of the Holy Office dated 5 January 1951; text of the decision to end the actions (of 25 May 1946) against Adéline Pietquin by the bishop of Namur (12 December 1950); Wouters, "Transnationale spanningen," 20.

95 ADN, L.7/2, HSS, Apparitions 1943–51: letter of Henri Brigou, the curé of the parish of Adéline Pietquin, to the bishop.

96 "En fait donc l'autorité n'a changé en rien sa position primitive, mais elle reconnait le changement d'attitude survenu chez les membres d'un des deux groupes." ADN, L.7/2 HSS, Apparitions 1943–51: letter to the curé of Ham-sur-Sambre, 19 December 1950.

97 ADN, L.7/2, HSS, Apparitions 1951–61: letter of the parish priest (Henri Brigou curé) of Ham-sur-Sambre, 7 May 1952 and answer from the diocese of Namur (9 May 1952).

98 "Un millier de personnes" ADN, L.7/2, HSS, Apparitions 1951–61: letter of Abbé Henri Brigou from Ham-sur-Sambre to the bishop of Namur, 20 August 1954.

99 ADN, L.7/2, HSS, Apparitions 1951–61: note from the diocese, 19 May 1958, and resignation of Emelda Scohy, 21 April 1958.

100 ADN, L.7/2, HSS, Apparitions 1951–61: letter by Abbé Henri Brigou, curé of Ham-sur-Sambre, to the vicar general of Namur Mgr Musty, 15 October 1958. Copy of the dissolution of Virgo Virginum, from the *Moniteur Belge*, 31 May 1958, 765; letter from the vicar general Mgr Musty to A.R.S. in Munich, 13 September 1958.

101 ADN, L.7/2, HSS, Apparitions 1951–61: letter from the vicar general Mgr Musty to Paul Hoffmeister in Hagen, 27 January 1959; letter to the diocese of Namur and Tournai from Prof. Dr Hermann Lais, Dillingen a.d. Donau, 15 March 1961. See also the number of letters the Auxiliary Bishop Musty wrote to German devotees confirming that the diocese of Namur did not approve of the apparitions (2 March 1959, 8 October 1958, 19 May 1958, 14 August 1958, 13 September 1958, 27 January 1959, and 9 February 1959).

102 "Beschouwd moeten worden als in opstand tegen de Kerk en niet mogen worden toegelaten tot de hl. Sacramenten." ADN, L.7/2, HSS, Apparitions 1951–61: letter by Mgr Charue, 26 September 1958.

103 Bouflet, "Institution," 274–5.

104 See for instance the description and pictures in Lourtie, *Les apparitions,* 123.

105 "Ce lieu fait partie de l'histoire locale! Les apparitions qui ont eu lieu ici (non reconnues par les autorités ecclésiastiques, le domaine – privé – ne peut donc être considéré comme une œuvre de l'Église catholique) sont un fait passé, mais qui appartient néanmoins à l'histoire du lieu. On y croit ou on n'y croit pas: c'est selon la conscience de chacun." Domaine Marial Notre Dame du Pauvre Tunnel, consulted 24 October 2022, http://www.notredamedupauvretunnel.be/le-domaine-marial/reamenagement-du-site.

106 DAG, Onkerzele, 272: exhumation of Leonie Van den Dijck, note of the diocese of Ghent.

107 J.A., "Épidémie," *La Voix de Beauraing* 3, no. 12 (15 June 1936): 1; J.A., "Les fausses apparitions de Lourdes," *La Voix de Beauraing* 3, no. 9 (1 May 1936): 5–6; J.A., "Les fausses apparitions," *La Voix de Beauraing* 6, no. 23 (1 December 1939): 10.

108 They discussed the whole Lourdes series elaborately in a series of articles throughout the following year. For instance: J.A., "Fausses visions et faux miracles au temps de Sainte Bernadette," *La Voix de Beauraing* 2, no. 22 (15 November 1935): 1.

109 For instance to foreign apparitions as those of Heede in Germany.

## Conclusion

1 See the English translation (by Fr. Philip Pavich O.F.M.) of the original Italian article in the online magazine *Petrus*, "Does Pope Benedict XVI Plan to Issue a 'Vademecum' on Apparitions?" This English version on the Catholic culture website mentions explicitly that the Congregation for the Doctrine of Faith denies this: "Note: According to the National Catholic Register, this story has been denied by the Congregation for the Doctrine of the Faith. See our document description for details." Catholic Culture, consulted 27 December 2022, https://www.catholicculture.org/culture/library/view.cfm?recnum=8688.

2 See for instance Jerome Taylor and Simon Caldwell, "Catholics Ordered to Keep Quiet over Virgin Visions," *The Independent*, 13 January 2009, consulted 27 December 2022, https://www.independent.co.uk/news/world/europe/catholics-ordered-to-keep-quiet-over-virgin-visions-1332016.html; Lode Delputte, "Vaticaan: wie Maria ziet verschijnen, moet visioen geheimhouden," *De Morgen*, 14 January 2009, 15.

3 Jeff Mirus, "The Petrus Rumor: Hot News or Hoax?" 19 January 2009, Catholic Culture, consulted 27 December 2022, https://www.catholicculture.org/commentary/petrus-rumor-hot-news-or-hoax/. A few years later, in 2011, they did, however, publish translations in several languages of the 1978 rules *Normae de modo procedendi in diudicandis praesumptis apparitionibus ac revelationibus.* Before that date, these rules had never been officially published and a Latin version had only been sent to the bishops for their information. Vatican.va, consulted 28 December 2022, https://www.vatican.va/roman_curia/congregations/cfaith/documents/rc_con_cfaith_doc_20111214_prefazione-levada_en.html.

4 In the preface, the prefect Cardinal Víctor Manuel Fernández noted that the revision started in 2019, so ten years after the rumours on a forthcoming revision in 2009. Dicastery for the Doctrine of Faith, *Norms for the Proceeding in the Discernment of Alleged Supernatural Phenomena*

(17 May 2024) ("Norms"), Vatican.va, consulted 28 June 2024, https://www.vatican.va/roman_curia/congregations/cfaith/documents/rc_ddf_doc_20240517_norme-fenomeni-soprannaturali_en.html.

5 "With the development of modern means of communication and the increase of pilgrimages, these phenomena are taking on national and even global proportions, meaning that a decision made in one Diocese has consequences also elsewhere." Dicastery for the Doctrine of Faith, 2024, "Norms," Introduction, art. 7.

6 ADDF, Dev. Var., 1933.2 Beauraing, 24: letter from Mgr Micara to Mgr Canali, 15 December 1934.

7 "Vermits echter het oordeel over die feiten aan de Kerkelijke Overheid toekomt, niet aan de openbare meening, is het te wenschen dat wie iets merkwaardigs zou kennen, dit aan de Kerkelijke Overheid zou bekend maken liever dan het door schrijven openbaar te maken." S.n., "Bisschoppelijke onderrichting omtrent de zaak der verschijningen in ons land," *De godsdienstige week van het bisdom Gent* 6, no. 48 (1 December 1933): 193.

8 On the need to address this interaction of different types of knowledge systems: Lässig, "The History," 39; Mulsow, "History," 160.

9 Apolito, *Apparitions*; Bouflet, "Institution."

10 AAM, Van Roey, Apparitions, 24. Processus, BXII4c: letter of Mgr Coppieters, 10 January 1934.

11 Already in 1974 at the Plenary Assembly of the (then) Congregation for the Doctrine of Faith, the members already acknowledged that "an event of alleged supernatural origin often 'inevitably extends beyond the limits of a Diocese and even of a Nation.'" Cited in the preface to the new rules of May 2024. Dicastery for the Doctrine of Faith, "Norms." Vatican.va, consulted 28 June 2024, https://www.vatican.va/roman_curia/congregations/cfaith/documents/rc_ddf_doc_20240517_norme-fenomeni-soprannaturali_en.html.

# Bibliography

## Unpublished sources


| | |
|---|---|
| Banneux | Archives of the shrine of Banneux |
| Beauraing | Archives of the shrine of Beauraing<br>– Archives doyen Léon Lambert (Lambert)<br>– Dossiers Aurélien Pierroux (Pierroux) |
| Geraardsbergen | Decanal archive of Geraardsbergen:<br>Parish archives Onkerzele |
| Ghent | Archives of the Diocese of Ghent<br>– Archives of the apparitions (apparitions)<br>– Archives of the apparitions, fund Honoré Vermeire (Vermeire)<br>– H. Coppieters, 9.5 Apparitions in Banneux, Beauraing, Olsene, Lokeren |
| Liège | Archives of the diocese of Liège, Kerkhofs,<br>D/IV. Marian cult, 26–33 Banneux |
| Louvain | Kadoc<br>– Jan Boon-M. Ceulemans, 5.2.5. Getuigenis omtrent Beauraing<br>– Congregation of the Immaculate Heart of Mary (Scheut), Aloïs Janssens, |
| Lokeren | City archives of Lokeren<br>– XL: Non-recognised cults, 1031: Naastveld apparitions<br>– XX: Police |
| Malines | Archives of the archdiocese of Malines<br>– Reports of the meetings of the bishops<br>– Van Roey, Apparitions<br>– I.37. bis: Handwritten reports, meetings with the deans<br>– 21: Apparitions |

| | |
|---|---|
| | – 23–26: Processus circa assertas apparitions et revelations BMV in Belgio, 1935–38 (Processus) |
| | – 27: Nonapproved apparitions and predictions/ Ham-sur-Sambre |
| | – 36–40: Beauraing and Banneux |
| Namur | Archives of the diocese of Namur |
| | – L. Le vicariat judiciare, 1–5bis: Supernatural events and apparitions |
| | – L.7/2 and 7/3: Apparitions de Ham/Sambre |
| | – L.42–43: Louis Wilmet (Wilmet) |
| Rome | Archives of the Dicastery for the Doctrine of the Faith, Devotiones Variae |
| | – Beauraing 1933.2 (794/1933) |
| | – Banneux 1934.11 (3467/1934) |
| | – Bruges-Malines 1943.15 (00128/1943) |
| Tournai | Archives of the diocese of Tournai, Revelations – Apparitions: apparitions de Ham-sur-Sambre, 1947–48 |

## Published sources

### *Newspapers*

*De Standaard*
*Het Laatste Nieuws*
*La Libre Belgique*
*Vooruit*

### *Periodicals*

*Les Annales de Beauraing*
*Banneux-Tancrémont*
*Les Études Carmélitaines*
*Saint-Luc Médicale (1932–1940)*
*La Voix de Beauraing/L'Officiel de Beauraing*

### *Books and Articles*

Amiotte-Suchet, Laurent. "Tous égaux devant Dieu? Réflexions sur les logiques d'éligibilité des miraculés." *Social Compass* 52, no. 2 (2005): 241–54.

Apolito, Paolo. *Apparitions of the Madonna at Oliveto Citra. Local Visions and Cosmic Drama.* Pennsylvania: Pennsylvania State University Press, 1998.

Badone, Ellen. "Echoes from Kerizinen: Pilgrimage, Narrative, and the Construction of Sacred History at a Marian Shrine in Northwestern France." *Journal of the Royal Anthropological Institute* 13 (2007): 453–70.

Barnay, Sylvie. *Les apparitions de la Vierge.* Paris: Cerf, 1992.

Bennett, Jeffrey. *When the Sun Danced. Myth, Miracles, and Modernity in Early Twentieth-century Portugal.* Charlottesville/London: University of Virginia Press, 2012.

Beyer, Jean. "Le procès canonique de Banneux Notre-Dame." In *Les faits de Banneux Notre-Dame. Études*, edited by Jean Beyer, René Carpentier, Joseph Heuschen. Liège: Dessain, 1959, 205–51.

Bijker, Wiebe, Roland Bal, and Ruud Hendriks. *The Paradox of Scientific Authority. The Role of Scientific Advice in Democracies.* Cambridge: MIT Press, 2009.

Billet, Bernard. "Le fait des apparitions non reconnues par l'Église." In *Vraies et fausses apparitions dans l'Église*, edited by Bernard Billet, Joaquin-Maria Alonso, Boris Bobrinskoy, Marc Oraison. Paris: P. Lethielleux, 1976, 5–54.

Bitel, Lisa. "Introduction: Visualising the Invisible: Visionary Technologies in Religious and Cultural Contexts." *Visual Resources* 25 (2009): 3–5.

– "Looking the wrong way: Authenticity and Proof of Religious Vision." *Visual Resources* 25 (2009): 69–92.

Black, Monica. *A Demon-Haunted Land. Witches, Wonder Doctors, and the Ghosts of the Past in Post-WWII Germany.* New York: Metropolitan Books (Henry Holt), 2020.

Blackbourn, David. "The Catholic Church in Europe since the French Revolution." *Comparative Studies in Society and History* 33, no. 4 (1991): 778–90.

– "Die von Gottheit überaus bevorzugten Mägdlein-Marienerscheinungen im Bismarkreich." In *Wunderbare Erscheinungen. Frauen und katholische Frömmigkeit im 19. und 20. Jahrhundert,* edited by Irmtraud Götz von Olenhusen. Paderborn: Schöningh, 1995, 171–201.

– *Marpingen. Apparitions of the Virgin Mary in Bismarkian Germany.* Oxford: Clarendon, 1993.

Boissarie, Prosper-Gustave. *Les grandes guérisons de Lourdes.* Paris: Téqui, 1900.

Boniface, Xavier. "La dévotion mariale au XXe siècle." In *La dévotion mariale de l'an mil à nos jours*, edited by Bruno Béthouart and Alain Lottin. Arras: Artois Presse Université, 2005, 51–65.

Boon, Jan Filip. *Getuigenis omtrent Beauraing: ervaringen van een journalist 15-12-32 tot 30-9-33*. Courtrai: Vermaut, 1933.

Bossant, Els. "Het dossier van de verschijningen te Beauraing: een psychologische analyse en evaluatie." Unpublished master's thesis, University of Louvain, 1992.

Bouflet, Joachim. *Faussaires de Dieu. Enquête.* Paris: Presse de la Renaissance, 2000.

– "Institution et charisme dans l'Église de 1846 à nos jours: La question du jugement épiscopal sur les apparitions mariales modernes et contemporaines." PhD diss., Université Michel de Montaigne Bordeaux 3, 2014.

Bouflet, Joachim, and Philippe Boutry. *Un signe dans le ciel: les apparitions de la Vierge*. Paris: Grasset, 1997

Boute, Bruno, Andreea Badea, Marco Cavarzere, and Steven Vanden Broecke. "A Product's Glamour. Credibility, or the Manufacture and Administration of Truth in Early Modern Catholicism." In *Making Truth in Early Modern Catholicism*, edited by Bruno Boute, Andreea Badea, Marco Cavarzere, and Steven Vanden Broecke. Amsterdam: Amsterdam University Press, 2021, 7–38.

Brilkman, Kajsa. "Confessional Knowledge. How Might the History of Knowledge and the History of Confessional Europe Influence each other?" In *Forms of Knowledge. Developing the History of Knowledge*, edited by Johan Östling, David Larsson Heidenblad, Anna Nilsson Hammar. Lund: Nordic Academic Press, 2020, 29–46.

Brilkman, Kajsa, and Anna Nilsson Hammar. "Religion as Knowledge." Blog New History of Knowledge, 24 April 2019, https://newhistoryofknowledge.com/2019/04/24/religion-as-knowledge/ (consulted 10 July 2024).

Bromley, David and Rachel Bobbit. "Visions of the Virgin Mary. The Organizational Development of Marian Apparitional Movements." *Nova Religio: the Journal of Alternative and Emergent Religions* 14, no. 3 (2011): 5–41.

Brotteaux, Pascal. *Hallucinations ou miracles?… Les apparitions d'Ezquioga et de Beauraing. La prophétie du Moine de Padue*. Paris: Les éditions Véga, 1934.

Burke, Peter. *What is the History of Knowledge?* Cambridge: Polity, 2016.

Burnon, Pierre. *Le vrai visage de Tilman Côme. La réponse aux injures et aux attaques*. Genval: Robin, 1933.

Casselman, Joris. *Etienne De Greeff, 1898–1961. Psychiater, criminoloog en romanschrijver. Leven, werk en huidige betekenis*. Antwerp/Apeldoorn: Maklu, 2010.

– "Greeff, Etienne de." *Nationaal Biografisch Woordenboek*, vol. 20. Brussels: Koninklijke Academiën van België, 2011, 392–9.

Charlier, Jean Michel (ed.). *Léon Degrelle persiste et signe. Interviews recueillies pour la télévision française par Jean-Michel Charlier*. Paris: Éditions Jean Picollec, 1985.

Chiron, Yves. *Enquête sur les apparitions de la Vierge*. Paris: Perrin, 1997.

Christian, William A., Jr. "Afterword: Islands in the Sea: the Public and Private Distribution of Knowledge of Religious Visions." *Visual Resources* 25, no. 1–2 (2009): 153–65.

– "L'œil de l'esprit. Les visionnaires basques en transe, 1931." *Terrain* 30 (1998): 5–22.

– "The Eyes of the Beholders: Systematic Variation in Visions of the Christ of Limpias in Northern Spain, 1919–1936." In *The "Vision Thing": Studying Divine Intervention*, edited by William Christian and Gábor Klaniczay. Budapest: Collegium Budapest, 2009, 65–81.

– *Moving Crucifixes in Modern Spain*. Princeton: Princeton University Press, 1992.

– "Six Hundred Years of Visionaries in Spain: those Believed and those Ignored." In *Challenging Authority. The Historical Study of Contentious Politics*, edited by Michael Hanagan, Leslie Page Moch and Wayne te Brake. Minneapolis/London: University of Minnesota Press, 1998, 107–19.

– *The Stranger, the Tears, the Photograph, the Touch. Divine Presence in Spain and Europe since 1500*. Budapest: Central European University Press, 2017.

– *Visionaries. The Spanish Republic and the Reign of Christ*. Berkeley/Los Angeles/London: University of California Press, 1996.

Christian, William A., Jr, and Gábor Klaniczay (eds.). *The "Vision Thing": Studying Divine Intervention*. Budapest: Collegium Budapest, 2009.

Claverie, Élisabeth. *Les guerres de la Vierge. Une anthropologie des apparitions*. Paris: Gallimard, 2003.

Cock, Marcel. "Mijn gezegend oord Onkerzele.' Religieuze verschijningen in België, inzonderheid in Onkerzele, tijdens het interbellum (Deel 1)." *Het Land van Aalst* 66, no. 4 (2014): 269–92.

Coleman, Simon and John Eade. "Introduction: Reframing Pilgrimage." In *Reframing Pilgrimage. Cultures in Motion*, edited by Simon Coleman and John Eade. London/Abingdon: Routledge, 2004, 1–25.

Collinet, Raphaël. "Le rôle de la commission d'enquête." *Cahiers Marials* 135 (15 November 1982): 309.

Conway, Martin. "Building the Christian City: Catholics and Politics in Inter-war Francophone Belgium." *Past and Present* 128 (1990): 117–51.

– *Collaboratie in België. Léon Degrelle en het Rexisme, 1940–1944*. Groot-Bijgaarden: Globe, 1994.

Creusen, J. "Les faits 'merveilleux' de Belgique. Instructions de l'épiscopat belge (10.10.1933)." *La documentation Catholique* 16 (1934): 267–76.

Dannau, Wim. *Zo sprak Léon Degrelle*. Strombeek-Bever: Byblos, 1973.

Daston, Lorraine. "Comment." In *Debating New Approaches to History*, edited by Marek Tamm and Peter Burke. London: Bloomsbury Academic, 2019, 173–8.

Davis, Philip and Jacqueline Boles. "Pilgrim Apparition Work: Symbolization and Crowd Interaction when the Virgin Appeared in Georgia." *Journal of Contemporary Ethnography* 32, no. 4 (2003): 371–402.

de Beauffort, Geoffrey. "Miracle chez la Marquise." *L'Echo de Beauffort* 3 (2003): s.p.

De Bens, Els. *De Belgische dagbladpers onder Duitse censuur (1940–1944)*. Antwerp: Uitgeverij De Nederlandsche Boekhandel, 1973.

Decelle, Marie. "'Le scandale de Beauraing': À propos de la polémique autour des apparitions de Beauraing." CARHOP-Analyses (2006), https://www.carhop.be/images/Scandale_Beauraing_M.DECELLE_2006.pdf.

De Certeau, Michel. *The Practice of Everyday Life*. Berkeley: University of California Press, 1988 (first edition 1984).

De Greeff, Étienne. "Beauraing." *Saint-Luc Médical* 11, no. 4 (1933): 209–44.

– "Conclusions médico-psychologiques." *Études Carmélitaines* 19, no. 2 (1934): 262–310.

– "Notes sur les faits de Beauraing." In *Les faits mystérieux de Beauraing. Études, documents, réponses,* edited by Bruno de Jésus-Marie, Étienne De Greeff, Aloïs Janssens, Paul Van Gehuchten. Paris: Desclée De Brouwer, 1933, 31–88.

– "Rectifications, compléments, confirmations concernant les documents contenus dans les 'Notes.'" In *Les faits mystérieux de Beauraing. Études, documents, réponses,* edited by Bruno de Jésus-Marie, Étienne De Greeff, Aloïs Janssens, Paul Van Gehuchten. Paris: Desclée De Brouwer, 1933, 118–28.

– "Vers une explication naturelle des faits de Beauraing." In *Les faits mystérieux de Beauraing. Études, documents, réponses,* edited by Bruno de Jésus-Marie, Étienne De Greeff, Aloïs Janssens, Paul Van Gehuchten. Paris: Desclée De Brouwer, 1933, 129–76.

de Jésus-Marie, Bruno. "Introduction." In *Les faits mystérieux de Beauraing. Études, documents, réponses,* edited by Bruno de Jésus-Marie, Étienne De Greeff, Aloïs Janssens, and Paul Van Gehuchten. Paris: Desclée De Brouwer, 1933, 9–23.

de Jésus-Marie, Bruno, Étienne De Greeff, Aloïs Janssens, and Paul Van Gehuchten. "Avertissement." In *Les faits mystérieux de Beauraing. Études, documents, réponses,* edited by Bruno de Jésus-Marie, Étienne De Greeff, Aloïs Janssens, and Paul Van Gehuchten. Paris: Desclée De Brouwer, 1933, 7–8.

De Jongh, Willy. *Het mirakel van Beauraing.* Antwerp: Reynaert & Adriaenssens, 1935.

Delfosse, Annick. "De maagd Maria, een polymorfe figuur van het katholicisme." In *Devotie en godsdienstbeoefening in de verzamelingen van de Koninklijke Bibliotheek,* edited by Anne Morelli. Brussel: KBR, 2005, 74–96.

Derselle, C. *Et si c'était le diable?* Bruxelles: Ed. Universelle, 1933.

– *Beauraing. La vérité en marche du nouveau!* Charleroi: Souris F. & Ribaux, 1933.

Delvaux, B. "Naissance et développement d'un pèlerinage. Le cas de Beauraing 1932–1949." Unpublished master's thesis, Université Catholique de Louvain, 1981.

Delville, Jean-Pierre. "Le choc des images, la vision de la Vierge à Banneux par le ministre officiant juif de Liège Joseph Lepkifker, lors de la persécution des juifs en août 1942." In *Images et paysages mentaux des 19e et 20e siècles de la Wallonie à l'outre-mer*, edited by Luc Courtois, Jean-Pierre Delville, Françoise Rosart, and Guy Zelis. Louvain-la-Neuve: Presses Universitaires de Louvain, 2007, 201–52.

– "Marie apparue à Banneux (1933): figures et réceptions économiques, politiques et écologiques." In *Marie. Figures et réceptions. Enjeux historiques et théologiques*, edited by Jean-Pierre Delville, Joseph Famerée, and Marie-Élisabeth Henneau. Paris: Mame-Desclée, 2012, 83–100.

De Maeyer, Jan and Staf Hellemans. "Katholiek reveil, katholieke verzuiling en dagelijks leven." *Tussen bescherming en verovering. Sociologen en historici over zuilvorming,* edited by Jaak Billiet. Louvain: Universitaire Pers Louvain, 1988, 172–200.

De Maeyer, Jan. "De wending van de kerk naar het volk (1884–1926)." In *Het aartsbisdom Mechelen-Brussel: 450 jaar geschiedenis*, vol. 2*: De volkskerk in het aartsbisdom een vrije kerk in een moderne samenleving 1802–2009*, edited by Jan De Maeyer, Eddie Put, Jan Roegiers, André Tihon, and Gerrit Vanden Bosch. Anvers: Halewijn, 2009, 100–71.

De Merlier, Dirk. "Omer heeft niets gezien! Omer n'a rien vu." *Businarias* 1, no. 2 (1997): 17–26.

Deneckere, Gita. "Nieuwe geschiedenis van België 1878–1905." In *Nieuwe geschiedenis van België*, vol. 1: *1830–1905*, edited by Vincent Dujardin, Michel Dumoulin, Emmanuel Gerard, and Mark Van den Wijngaert. Tielt: Lannoo, 2005, 447–664.

Deneweth, Herman. *Kroniek van 50 jaar Brugge-Banneux.* Beernem: Depré-Printing, 1993.

Desmazières, Agnes. "Psychology Against Medicine? Mysticism in the Light of Scientific Apologetics." *Revue Belge de Philologie et d'Histoire* 88 (2010): 1191–212.

*De verschijningen van Beauraing en Banneux.* Louvain: Rex, 1933, s.p.

De Vroylande, Robert. *Quand Rex était petit …* Louvain: Les Editions Lovanis, 1936.

D'Hertefelt, Rita. "Analyse van het Belgisch tijdschrift van Onze-Lieve-Vrouw van Lourdes (1895–1914)." Unpublished master's thesis, University of Louvain, 1989.

Di Stefano, Roberto and Francisco Xavier Rámon Solans, "Introduction." In *Marian Devotions, Political Mobilization, and Nationalism in Europe and America*, edited by Roberto Di Stefano and Francisco Xavier Rámon Solans. Cham: Springer International Publishing/Palgrave MacMillan, 2016, 1–25.

Duffin, Jacalyn. *Medical Miracles. Doctors, Saints, and Healing in the Modern World.* Oxford: Oxford University Press, 2009.

Duvosquel, Jean-Marie, Hervé Hasquin, and Raymond Van Uytven (eds.). *Gemeenten van België: geschiedkundig en administratief-geografisch woordenboek.* Brussels: La Renaissance du Livre, 1980–81.

Dorola, F. (pseudonym of Fernand Remisch). *Les mystères de Beauraing: reportage critique,* Paris: Spes, 1933.

Eade, John. "Order and Power at Lourdes. Lay Helpers and the Organization of a Pilgrimage Shrine." In *Contesting the Sacred: the Anthropology of Christian Pilgrimage,* edited by John Eade and Michael Sallnow. London: Routledge, 1991, 51–76.

Eade, John, and Michael Sallnow. "Introduction." In *Contesting the Sacred: the Anthropology of Christian Pilgrimage,* edited by John Eade and Michael Sallnow. London: Routledge, 1991, 1–29.

Edelman, Nicole. *Les metamorphoses de l'hystérique. Du début du XIXe siècle à la Grande Guerre.* Paris: La découverte, 2003.

Elaut, Leon, "Professor Fransen en de Vlaamse geneesheren." In *Getuigenissen over professor emeritus Frans Fransen,* s.e. Gent: Davidsfonds, 1970, 36–8.

Emich, Birgit. "The Production of Truth in the Manufacture of Saints. Procedures, Credibility and Patronage in Early Modern Processes of Canonization." In: *Making Truth in Early Modern Catholicism,* edited by Andreea Badea, Bruno Boute, Marco Cavarzere, Steven Vanden Broecke. Amsterdam: Amsterdam University Press, 2021, 165–90.

Ernst, Robert. *Lexikon der Marienerscheinungen.* Altötting: Ruhland, 1989.

Ernst, Wilhelm. "Vertrauen." *Lexikon für Theologie und Kirche*, vol. 10. Freiburg: Herder, 2001, 745.

Etienne, Stéphane, Jean Pirotte, and Daniël Bauwens. *Gids voor bedevaartplaatsen in België*. Brussel: Licap/Creart, 1994.

Falleyn, Joanna. "Hysterie en de medische wereld in België, 1855–1914." Unpublished master's thesis, University of Louvain, 1999.

Feldt, Laura. "Marginality, Media, and Mutations of Religious Authority in the History of Christianity." In *Marginality, Media, and Mutations of Religious Authority in the History of Christianity*, edited by Laura Feldt and Jan Bremmer. Louvain: Peeters, 2019, 1–21.

– "Reframing Authority – the Role of Media and Materiality." *Postscripts* 8, no. 3 (2012): 185–92.

Fincoeur, Michel. "Le 'réseau rexiste' dans l'édition sous l'Occupation allemande (1940–1944)." In *Les Réseaux littéraires,* edited by Daphné Marneffe and Benoît Denis. Bruxelles: Le Cri/Ciel, 2006, 225–47.

Fransen, Frans. "Autour des faits de Beauraing." *Saint-Luc Médical* 11, no. 4 (1933): 155–84.

Frevert, Ute. "Über Vertrauen reden: historisch-kritische Beobachtungen." *Was ist Vertrauen? Ein interdisziplinäres Gespräch,* edited by Jörg Baberowski. Frankfurt: Campus-Verlag, 2014, 31–46.

– *Vertrauensfragen: Eine Obsession der Moderne*. Munich: Beck, 2013.

Gailly, Henri. "Les apparitions de Beauraing." *Saint-Luc Médical* 11, no. 4 (1933): 139–47.

– "À propos des événements de Beauraing, notes complémentaires." *Saint-Luc Médical* 11, no. 4. (1933): 193–205.

Geeraerts, Glenn. "Gewijde geschiedenis in beton: het Mariapark in Averbode (België)." Blog Donderberggroep, 2016. https://donderberggroep.nl/pf43-gewijde-geschiedenis-in-beton-het-mariapark-in-averbode-belgie (accessed 24 January 2023).

Geppert, Alexander and Till Kössler. *Wunder. Poetik und Politik des Staunens im 20. Jahrhundert.* Berlin: Suhrkamp, 2011.

Géradin, Amand. *Des apparitions à Banneux?* Louvain: Rex, 1933.

– *Banneux, page d'Evangile.* Louvain: Rex, 1933.

Gerard, Emmanuel. "Cardijn, arbeidersbeweging en Katholieke Actie (1918–1945)." In *Cardijn. Een mens, een beweging,* edited by Magda Pluymers and Luc Vints. Louvain: Leuven University Press, 1983, 119–45.

– "De democratie gedroomd, begrensd en ondermijnd, 1918–1939." In *Nieuwe geschiedenis van België,* vol. 2: *1905–1950*, Michel Dumoulin, Emmanuel Gerard, Vincent Dujardin, and Mark Van den Wijngaert. Tielt: Lannoo, 2006, 869–1099.

– "Grondlijnen van de katholieke verzuiling tussen 1914 en 1945." In *Tussen bescherming en verovering. Sociologen en historici over zuilvorming*, edited by Jaak Billiet. Louvain: Leuven University Press, 1988, 135–69.

– *De schaduw van het interbellum: België van euforie tot crisis 1918–1939*. Tielt: Lannoo, 2017.

Gerard, Léon. *Hâtez-vous, ou le message de Tilman Côme*. Liège: Rapid Press, 1933.

Gevers, Lieve. "Voor God, vaderland en moedertaal. Kerk en natievorming in België, 1830–1940." *Bijdragen tot de Eigentijdse Geschiedenis* 3 (1997): 27–53.

Gibson, Ralph. *A Social History of French Catholicism, 1789–1914*. London and New York: Routledge, 1989.

Gijbels, Jolien. "Medical Compromise and Its Limits: Religious Concerns and the Postmortem Caesarean Section in Nineteenth-Century Belgium." *Bulletin of the History of Medicine* 93, no. 3 (2019): 305–34.

Goedseels, L. "La question de Beauraing et les médecins catholiques." *Saint-Luc Médical* 11, no. 4. (1933): 245–7.

Goldstein, Jan. "The Hysteria Diagnosis and the Politics of Anticlericalism in Late Nineteenth-century France." *The Journal of Modern History* 54, no. 2 (1982): 209–39.

Gosseye, Alfons. "De verschijningen te Olsene." *Bijdragen tot de Geschiedenis en de Folklore van Machelen, Olsene en Zulte* 20 (2004–05): 109–21.

Grasmück, Oliver. *Eine Marienerscheinung in Zeiten der Diktatur: der Konflikt um Peñablanca. Chile: Religion und Manipulation unter Pinochet*. Berlin and New York: De Gruyter, 2009.

Halemba, Agnieszka. *Negotiating Marian Apparitions. The Politics of Religion in Transcarpathian Ukraine*. Budapest and New York: Central European University Press, 2015.

Halter, Deborah. "Field Notes – Charisma in Conyers: a Journey from Visionary to Apparition Site to Church." *Nova Religio* 14, no. 3 (2011): 108–14.

Hanlet, Camille. *Les écrivains belges contemporains de langue française, 1800–1946*, vol. 2. Liège: Dessain, 1946, 811–15.

Harris, Ruth. *Lourdes. Body and Spirit in the Secular Age*. New York: Viking, 1999.

Heimann, Mary. "Catholic Revivalism in Worship and Devotion." In *The Cambridge History of Christianity*, vol. 8: *World Christianities c.1815–c.1914*, edited by Sheridan Gilley and Brian Stanley. Cambridge: Cambridge University Press, 2006, 70–83.

– "Mysticism in Bootle: Victorian Supernaturalism as a Historical Problem." *The Journal of Ecclesiastical History* 64, no. 2 (2013): 335–56.

Hellemans, Staf. *Strijd om de moderniteit.* Louvain: Leuven University Press, 1990.

Henryot, Fabienne and Jean Pierre Chantin. "Apparitions." In *Dictionnaire Historique de la Vierge Marie. Sanctuaires et dévotions, XVe–XXIe siècle,* edited by Fabienne Henryot and Philippe Martin. Paris: Perrin, 2017, 40–50.

Hermkens, Anna-Karina, Willy Jansen, and Catrien Notermans. "Introduction: the Power of Marian Pilgrimage." In *Moved by Mary. The Power of Pilgrimage in the Modern World,* edited by Anna-Karina Hermkens, Willy Jansen and Catrien Notermans. Aldershot: Ashgate, 2009, 1–16.

Horsfall, Sara. "The Experience of Marian Apparitions and the Mary Cult." *The Social Science Journal* 37, no. 3 (2000): 375–84.

Hosking, Geoffrey. *Trust. A History.* Oxford: Oxford University Press, 2014.

Hynes, Eugene. *Knock. The Virgin's Apparition in Nineteenth-century Ireland.* Cork: Cork University Press, 2017 (reprint of 2008).

Jacobs, Frans, *De zienster van Onkerzele: Leonie Van den Dyck (1875–1949).* Malines: s.e., 1973.

Jelly, Frederick M. "Discerning the Miraculous: Norms for Judging Apparitions and Private Revelations." *Marian Studies* 44 (1993): 41–55.

Johanns, A. *Die Ereignisse von Beauraing: Wahrheitsgetreuer Bericht eines Augenzeugen über die Erscheinungen zu Beauraing, 29. November bis 3. Januar 1933.* Louvain: Rex, 1933.

Joset, Camille-Jean. *Dossiers de Beauraing,* 5 vol. Namur/Beauraing: Facultés universitaires Notre-Dame de la Paix, 1981–84.

– "Monseigneur Th.-L. Heylen évêque de Namur (1899–1941) et les apparitions de Beauraing." *Nouvelle Revue Théologique* 113, no. 2 (1981): 209–37.

Kane, Paula. "'She Offered Herself up': the Victim Soul and Victim Spirituality in Catholicism." *Church History* 71 (2002): 80–119.

Kaufman, Suzanne. *Consuming Visions. Mass Culture and the Lourdes Shrine.* Ithaca and London: Cornell University Press, 2005.

– "Les Miraculées de Lourdes: Sacred Celebrities in the Age of Mass Spectacle." *Journal of Religious History* 42, no. 4 (2018): 517–44.

Kerkhofs, Louis Joseph. *Notre-Dame de Banneux. Études et documents.* Liège: H. Dessain, vol. 1: 1950 and vol. 3: 1959.

– *Wat gebeurde er te Banneux?* Tielt: Lannoo, 1957.

Kevers, Pauline. "L'organisation religieuse de deux sanctuaries: Beauraing & Banneux." Unpublished master's thesis, Université Libre de Bruxelles, 2010.

Klaniczay, Gábor. "Louise Lateau et les stigmatisées du XIXème siècle." *Archivio Italiano per la Storia della Pietà* 26 (2013): 279–319.

Klein, Detmar. "The Virgin with the Sword: Marian Apparitions, Religion and National Identity in Alsace in the 1870s." *French History* 21, no. 4 (2007): 411–30.

Klimek, Daniel Maria. *Medjugorje and the Supernatural. Science, Mysticism, and Extraordinary Religious Experience.* Oxford: Oxford University Press, 2018.

Kotulla, Andreas. "Lourdes und die deutschen Katholiken: Über die frühe Rezeption eines katholischen Kultes im Deutschen Kaiserreich und die Anfänge der Wallfahrt bis zum ersten Weltkrieg." In *Maria und Lourdes. Wunder und Marienerscheinungen in theologischer und kulturwissenschaftlicher Perspektive,* edited by Bernhard Schneider. Münster: Aschendorff, 2008, 139–65.

– *"Nach Lourdes!" Der französische Marienwallfahrtsort und die Katholiken im deutschen Kaiserreich (1871–1914).* Munich: Meidenbauer, 2006.

Krieger, Leonard. "The Idea of Authority in the West." *The American Historical Review* 82, no. 2 (1977): 249–70.

Kselman, Thomas. "How Abundant is 'Abundant History'?" In *Recent Themes in American Religious History: Historians in Conversation,* edited by Randall Stephens. Columbia: University of South Carolina Press, 2009, 140–5.

Lachapelle, Sofie. "Between Miracle and Sickness: Louise Lateau and the Experience of Stigmata and Ecstasy." *Configurations* 12 (2004): 77–105.

Ladon, August. *Une épidémie mentale contemporaine. Les apparitions de Belgique.* Paris: Doin, 1937.

– "Over de psychologie der massa's (in verband met de zoogez. Verschijningen in België, 1933)." *Saint-Luc Médical* 17, no. 1 (1939): 27–44.

Lässig, Simone. "The History of Knowledge and the Expansion of the Historical Research Agenda." *Bulletin of the GHI Washington* 59 (2016): 29–58.

Laurentin, René. "Introduction: pourquoi ce dictionnaire?" In *Dictionnaire des "apparitions" de la Vierge Marie,* edited by René Laurentin and Patrick Sbalchiero. Paris: Fayard, 2007, 15–47.

Laurentin, René, and Patrick Sbalchiero. *Dictionnaire des "apparitions" de la Vierge Marie.* Paris: Fayard, 2007.

Laycock, Joseph. *The Seer of Bayside: Veronica Lueken and the Struggle to Define Catholicism.* Oxford: Oxford University Press, 2014.

Leclercq, Jacques. "La vie religieuse en Belgique," *La Cité Chrétienne* 172 (1933): 220–7.

Lecloux, Jos. *Les Apparitions de la Sainte Vierge a Hulteau-Chaineux. Réalité? Comédie? Jugez vous-même!* Jespers-Grégoire Dison, 1933.

Lindemans, Gertie. "Fransen, Jan Frans." *Nationaal Biografisch Woordenboek* 11 (1985): 228–36.

– "Jan-Frans Fransen, 1886–1975." Unpublished master's thesis, University of Louvain, 1980.

Louchez, Eddy. "Mariophanie." *Dictionnaire d'Histoire et de Géographie Ecclésiastiques* 196 (2022): 1123–1210.

Lourtie, Sabine. *Les apparitions en Belgique. Enquêtes sur les manifestations étranges.* S.l., Noir Dessin, 2008.

Maes, Gaston. *Beauraing. Réponse à la brochure* Et si c'était le Diable*? de C. Derselle.* S.l.: s.e., 1933.

– *Beauraing. Observations sur l'étude de M. De Greeff 19 novembre 1932–3 janvier 1933.* Louvain: Saint Alphonse, 1934.

Magain, Alfred. *Onze Lieve Vrouw bij de Vlamingen: de verschijningen van Onkerzele.* Louvain: Rex, s.d.

Maistriaux, Fernand. *Dernières apparitions de Beauraing.* Louvain: Editions Rex, 1933.

– *Wat gebeurt er te Beauraing?* Rex, Louvain, 1932.

– *Que se passe-t-il à Beauraing?* Louvain: Editions Rex, 1932.

Margry, Peter Jan. *Cold War Mary. Ideologies, Politics, and Marian Devotional Culture.* Louvain: Leuven University Press, 2021.

– "Global Network of Divergent Marian Devotion." In *Encyclopedia of New Religions: New Religious Movements, Sects and Alternative Spiritualities,* edited by Christopher Partridge. Oxford: Lion Publishing, 2004, 98–102.

– "Marian Interventions in the Wars of Ideology: the Elastic Politics of the Roman Catholic Church on Modern Apparitions." *History and Anthropology* 20, no. 3 (2009): 243–63.

Maître, Jacques. "De Bourneville à nos jours: interprétations psychiatriques de la mystique." Évolution *Psychiatrique* 64 (1999): 765–8.

Matter, E. Ann. "Apparitions of the Virgin Mary in the Late Twentieth Century: Apocalyptic, Representation, Politics." *Religion* 31, no. 2 (2001): 125–53.

Maunder, Chris, "The Footprints of Religious Enthusiasm. Great Memorials and Faint Vestiges of Belgium's Apparition Mania of the 1930s." *Journal of Religion and Society* 15 (2013): 1–17.

– "Marian Visionaries in Roman Catholicism as Popular Theologians: 'The Lady of All Nations' of Amsterdam." *Journal of Contemporary Religion* 27, no. 2 (2012): 291–304.

– *Our Lady of the Nations. Apparitions of Mary in 20th-century Catholic Europe.* Oxford: Oxford University Press, 2016.

Meulenkamp, Wim and De Nijs, Paulina. *Buiten de kerk. Processieparken, Lourdesgrotten en Calvariebergen in Nederland en België.* Soesterberg: Aspekt 1998.

Micale, Mark. *Approaching Hysteria. Disease and its Interpretations.* Princeton: Princeton University Press, 1995.

Monin, Arthur. *Onze Lieve Vrouw van Beauraing ontstaan en ontwikkeling van haar eredienst.* Beauraing: Pro Maria, 1953.

Mulsow, Martin. "History of Knowledge." In *Debating New Approaches to History*, edited by Marek Tamm and Peter Burke. London: Bloomsbury Academic, 2019, 159–73 and 179–87.

Narvaez, Louise. *Degrelle m'a dit.* Brussels: Editions du Baucens, 1977.

Noble, Henri-Dominique. "Confiance." In *Dictionnaire de spiritualité ascétique et mystique*, vol. 2. Paris: Beauchesne, 1953, 1406–10.

Orsi, Robert. "Abundant History: Marian Apparitions as Alternative Modernity." *Historically Speaking* 9 (2008): 12–16.

Östling, Johan, David Larsson Heidenblad, and Anna Nilsson Hammar. "Introduction." In *Forms of Knowledge. Developing the History of Knowledge*, edited by Johan Östling, David Larsson Heidenblad, and Anna Nilsson Hammar. Lund: Nordic Academic Press, 2020, 9–26.

O'Sullivan, Michael. *Disruptive Power. Catholic Women, Miracles, and Politics in Modern Germany, 1918–1965.* Toronto: University of Toronto Press, 2018.

– "West German Miracles. Catholic Mystics, Church Hierarchy, and Postwar Popular Culture." *Zeithistorische Forschungen* 6, no. 1 (2009): 11–34.

Park, Karen. "The Negotiation of Authority at a Frontier Marian Apparition Site: Adele Brise and Our Lady of Good Help." *American Catholic Studies* 123, no. 3 (2012): 1–26.

Pasture, Patrick. "Kerk, natie en arbeidersklasse. Een essay over collectieve identificatie, in het bijzonder m.b.t. de (christelijke) arbeidersbeweging in België." *Bijdragen tot de Eigentijdse Geschiedenis* 6 (1999): 7–36.

Perry, Nicholas and Loreto Echeverría. *Under the Heel of Mary.* London and New York: Routledge, 1988.

Petri, Heinrich. "Marienerscheinungen." In *Handbuch der Marienkunde*, vol. 2, edited by Wolfgang Beinert and Heinrich Petri. Regensburg: Pustet, 1996, 31–59.

Plavscic, Wladimir. *Le Cardinal Van Roey.* Brussels: Labor, 1974.

Porte, Cheryl. *Pontmain, Prophecy and Protest. A Cultural-historical Study of a Nineteenth-century Apparition.* New York: Peter Lang, 2005.

Reynolds, John. "The Templemore Miracles." *History Ireland* 17, no. 1 (2009): 41–4.

Rice, Jenny. *Awful Archives. Conspiracy Theory, Rhetoric, and Acts of Evidence.* Columbus: Ohio State University Press, 2020.

Rosart, Françoise and Guy Zelis. "Formation et apostolat dans l'Action catholique par la méthode des cercles d'études (1914–1939)." In *Images et paysages mentaux des 19e et 20e siècles, de la Wallonie à l'Outre-Mer: Hommage au professeur Jean Pirotte à l'occasion de son éméritat*, edited by Luc Courtois, Jean-Pierre Delville, Françoise Rosart et Guy Zelis. Louvain-la-Neuve: Academia-Bruylant, 2007, 295–318.

Rutten, René. *Histoire critique des apparitions de Banneux*. Namur: Les éditions Fidélité, Mouvement Eucharistique et Missionnaire – Apostolat de la Prière, 1985.

Sarasin, Philipp. "More than just Another Specialty: on the Prospects for the History of Knowledge." *Journal for the History of Knowledge* 1, no. 2 (2020): 1–5.

– "Was ist Wissensgeschichte?" *Internationales Archiv für Sozialgeschichte der deutschen Literatur* 36 (2011): 159–72.

Saussus, Roger. *Notre-Dame de Banneux*. Louvain: Editions Rex, 1933.

– *Le scandale de Beauraing. Réponse à* 'Si c'était le diable?' *de M. l'abbé ou M. le docteur Derselle*. Louvain: Editions Rex, 1933.

Sbalchiero, Patrick. *Enquête sur les miracles dans l'Église catholique*. Montréal: Novalis, 2019.

Scaillet, Thierry. "La religion populaire." In *Pour une histoire du monde catholique au 20e siècle, Wallonie-Bruxelles. Guide du chercheur*, edited by Jean Pirotte and Guy Zelis. Louvain-la-Neuve: Archives du Monde Catholique, Église-Wallonie, 2003, 111–60.

Scheer, Monique. *Rosenkranz und Kriegsvisionen. Marienerscheinungskulte im 20. Jahrhundert*. Tübingen: Tübinger Vereinigung für Volkskunde, 2006.

Scheer, Monique. "Verspielte Frömmigkeit: Somatische Interaktionen beim Marienerscheinungskult von Heroldsbach-Thurn 1949/50." *Historische Anthropologie* 17, no. 3 (2009): 386–405.

– "What She Looks Like. On the Recognition and Iconization of the Virgin Mary at Apparition Sites in the Twentieth Century." *Material Religion* 9, no. 4 (2013): 442–67.

Schellinck, Gustaaf. *Het wonderbare leven van Leonie van den Dijck*. Onkerzele: Komiteit, 1987.

Schneider, Bernhard. "Ein 'deutsches Lourdes'? Der 'Fall' Marpingen (1876 un 1999) und die Elemente eines kirchlichen Prüfungsverfahren" In *Maria und Lourdes. Wunder und Marienerscheinungen in theologischer und kulturwissenschaftlicher Perspektive*, edited by Bernhard Schneider. Münster: Aschendorff, 2008, 178–97.

Signori, Gabriela. "Die Wunderheilung. Vom heiligen Ort zur Imagination." In *Wunder. Poetik und Politik des Staunens im 20. Jahrhundert*, edited by Alexander Geppert and Till Kössler. Berlin: Suhrkamp, 2011, 71–94.

Sindic, Raphael. *Des apparitions en Flandre?* Louvain: Editions Rex, s.d.

– *Tilman* Côme, est-il un imposteur? Louvain: Editions Rex, 1933.

Smith Foster, Michael. "Canonical Considerations Regarding Alleged Apparitions." *Marian Studies* 46 (1995): 128–44.

Speleers, Frans. "Verschijningen te Anzegem in 1935–36." *Jaarboek van de Geschied– en Heemkundige Kring de Gaverstreke* 24 (1996): 29–40.

Stéphany, Pierre. *Les années 20–30. La Belgique entre les deux guerres. Deuxième Période: L'avant-guerre*. Brussel: Legrain, 1983.

Szabo, Jason "Seeing is Believing? The Form and Substance of French Medical Debates over Lourdes." *Bulletin of the History of Medicine* 76, no. 2 (2002): 199–230.

Taves, Ann. *Fits, Trances, and Visions. Experiencing Religion and Explaining Experience from Wesley to James*. Princeton: Princeton University Press, 1999.

– *Religious Experience Reconsidered. A Building-block Approach to the Study of Religion and Other Special Things*. Princeton and Oxford: Princeton University Press, 2009.

Thurston, Herbert. *Beauraing and Other Apparitions. An Account of some Borderland Cases in Psychology of Mysticism.* London: Burns Oates and Washbourne, 1934.

– *The War and the Prophets. Notes on Certain Popular Predictions Current in this Latter Age.* London: Burns and Oates, 1915.

Tihon, André. "Association des laïcs et mouvements d'action catholique en Belgique." In *Achille Ratti Pape Pie XI. Actes du colloque organisé par l'École française de Rome en collaboration avec l'Université de Lille III – Greco n° 2 du s, l'Università degli studi di Roma – "La Sapienza," la bibliotheca Ambrosiana (Rome, 15–18 mars 1989).* Rome: École Française de Rome, 1996, 641–56.

– "Les mouvements des laïcs aux XIXe et XXe siècles. Rapport général." *Congrès de Bucarest août 1980*. Brussels: Nauwelaerts, 1985, 143–77.

Tonquédec, Joseph de. "Apparitions." In *Dictionnaire de spiritualité: ascétique et mystique, doctrine et histoire*, vol. 1. Paris: Beauchesne, 1937, 806–9.

Toussaint, Fernand and Camille-Jean Joset. *Beauraing, les apparitions: le livre du cinquantenaire*. Paris: Desclée De Brouwer, 1981.

Van Acker, Karel. "Beauraing." *Vlaamsch Geneeskundig Tijdschrift* 14, no. 23 (10 June 1933): 445–54.

Vandendriessche, Joris and Van Osselaer, Tine. "Religion and Medicine." In *Medical Histories of Belgium. New Narratives on Health, Care and Citizenship in the Nineteenth and Twentieth Centuries,* edited by Joris Vandendriessche Benoït Majerus. Manchester: Manchester University Press, 2021, 65–98.

Van den Heede, Philippe. "Les maisons d'édition catholiques belges francophones." *Pour une histoire du monde catholique au 20e siècle, Wallonie-Bruxelles: Guide du chercheur,* edited by Jean Pirotte and Guy Zelis. Louvain-la-Neuve: Archives du Monde Catholique, 2003, 583–99.

Van den Steen, Christian. "Les apparitions de la Vierge à Beauraing, un jalon dans l'aventure Rexiste?" *Beauraing et sa Région: Archéologie, Histoire et Folklore* 4 (1992): 44–57.

– "Tilman Côme dit Côme Tilman ou l'aventure beaurinoise sans lendemain d'un 'miraculé'." *Beauraing et sa Région: Archéologie, Histoire et Folklore* 12 (1996): 22–36.

Vander Hulst, Reinout and Vandendriessche, Joris. "Physician-apostles for Christ. The Belgian Saint Luc Society and the Making of a Catholic Medical Identity, 1900–1940." *Histoire, Médicine et Santé* 17 (2020): 133–54.

Van Gehuchten, Paul. "Une lettre de Professeur Van Gehuchten." *Saint-Luc Médical* 11, no. 4. (1933): 185–6.

– "Quelques réflexions au sujet d'un témoignage sur Beauraing." In *Les faits mystérieux de Beauraing. Études, documents, réponses,* edited by Bruno de Jésus-Marie, Étienne De Greeff, Aloïs Janssens, Paul Van Gehuchten. Paris: Desclée De Brouwer, 1933, 177–9.

– "Un témoignage sur les faits de Beauraing." *Saint-Luc Médical* 11, no. 4. (1933): 128–35.

– "Un témoignage sur les faits de Beauraing." In *Les faits mystérieux de Beauraing. Études, documents, réponses,* edited by Bruno de Jésus-Marie, Étienne De Greeff, Aloïs Janssens, Paul Van Gehuchten. Paris: Desclée De Brouwer, 1933, 24–30.

Van Haver, Jozef. *Voor U, Beminde gelovigen. Het Rijke Roomse Leven in Vlaanderen 1920–1950.* Tielt: Lannoo, 1995.

Van Osselaer, Tine. "The Affair of the Photographs. Controlling the Public Image of a Nineteenth-century Stigmatic." *Journal of Ecclesiastical History* 68, no. 4 (2017): 784–806.

– "The Changing Face of the Enemy. The Belgian Apparition Sites in the 1940s." In *Cold War Mary. Ideologies, Politics and Marian Devotional Culture,* edited by Peter Jan Margry, 135–52. Louvain: Leuven University Press, 2020.

– "Mystics of a Modern Time? Public Mystical Experiences in Belgium in the 1930s." *Revue Belge de Philologie et d'Histoire* 88 (2010): 1171–89.

– "Op eigen houtje … De omgang met verschijningsbomen, boomrelieken en andere 'wondere' bomen." *Tijd-Schrift* 4, no. 2 (2014): 6–17.

– *The Pious Sex. Catholic Constructions of Masculinity and Femininity in Belgium, c. 1800–1940.* Louvain: Leuven University Press, 2013.

– "A Question of Competence and Authority. Lay Views on the Medical Examinations of the Marian Apparition Series in 1930s Belgium." In *Sign or Symptom? Exceptional Corporeal Phenomena in Medicine and Religion,* edited by Tine Van Osselaer, Kaat Wils, and Henk de Smaele. Louvain: Leuven University Press, 2017, 163–83.

– "Sensitive but Sane. Male Visionaries and their Emotional Display in Belgium in the 1930s." *Low Countries Historical Review* 127, no. 1 (2012): 127–49.

– "Uit de lucht gegrepen? Mariaverschijningen op het Naastveld." *Annalen van de Koninklijke Oudheidkundige Kring van het Land van Waas* 114, no. 1 (2011): 277–302.

Van Osselaer, Tine, in collaboration with Andrea Graus, Leonardo Rossi and Kristof Smeyers. *Between Saints and Celebrities. The Devotion and Promotion of Stigmatics in Europe, c. 1800–1950*. Leiden/Boston: Brill, 2020.

Van Osselaer, Tine, and Kristof Smeyers. "Divine Hysteria. Readings of the Sacred Disease in the Late Eighteenth and Early Nineteenth Centuries." Österreichische *Zeitschrift* für *Geschichtswissenschaften* 31, no. 3 (2020): 54–75.

Van Osselaer, Tine, Kaat Wils and Henk de Smaele (eds.), *Sign or Symptom? Exceptional Corporeal Phenomena in Medicine and Religion*. Louvain: Leuven University Press, 2017.

Van Ryssel, Daniël. *55 Vergeten Gentse schrijvers*, vol. 4. Gent: s.e., 2008.

Velle, Karel. "Het verenigingsleven van de Belgische geneesheer (19de en begin 20ste eeuw), een bijdrage tot de geschiedenis van het artsenberoep." *Annales de la Société belge d'Histoire des Hôpitaux et de la Santé publique* 26–7 (1988–89): 47–118.

– "De geneeskunde en de R.K. Kerk (1830–1940): een moeilijke verhouding?" *Trajecta* 4, no. 1 (1995): 1–21.

Ventresca, Robert. "The Virgin and the Bear: Religion, Society and the Cold War in Italy." *Journal of Social History* 37 (2003): 439–56.

Vervaeck, Louis. *Le rôle du médecin dans l'étude des guérisons considérées comme miraculeuses*. Liège: Pensée catholique, 1934.

Vervoort, Bert. *Het schandaal van Beauraing*. Alost: De Korenaar, 1934.

Vos, Louis. "Het dubbelspoor van de Katholieke Actie tijdens het interbellum." In *Vijftig jaar Chiroleven 1934–1984. Aspecten uit het verleden en heden van een jeugdbeweging*, edited by Maurits De Vroede and An Hermans. Louvain: Leuven University Press, 1985, 29–52.

Welskopp, Thomas. "Vertrauen. Drei Beispiele aus einer praxistheoretisch orientierten Geschichtswissenschaft." In *Was ist Vertrauen? Ein interdisziplinäres Gespräch*, edited by Jörg Baberowski. Frankfurt: Campus-Verlag, 2014, 49–72.

Wilmet, Louis. *Beauraing, Banneux en Onkerzele*. Tongres: Michiels-Broeders, 1935.

Wouters, Jens. "Transnationale spanningen in de katholieke schapenwei? Een onderzoek naar de transnationaliteit van de spanning én fluïde grens tussen religion as practised en religion as prescribed aan de hand van de Mariaverschijningen van Ham-sur-Sambre, 1936–1951." Unpublished MA thesis, University of Antwerp, 2021.

Wuillaume, Léon. "La reconnaissance officielle." *Cahiers Marials* 135 (15 Nov. 1982): 299–310.

Wuillaume, Léon. "Introduction." In *Histoire critique des apparitions de Banneux*, edited by René Rutten, V–XV. Namur: Mouvement Eucharistique et Missionnaire, 1985.

Zeyen, Georges. "La Vierge nous rend visite … Le saviez-vous?" *Présence* 350 (October 2013): 14–15 (http://www.ccdison.be/presence/Presence_350-10-2013_web.pdf, consulted August 26, 2020).

Ziegenaus, Anton. "Kriterien für die Glaubwürdigkeit." In *Marienerscheinungen. Ihre Echtheit und Bedeutung im Leben der Kirche*, edited by Anton Ziegenaus. Regensburg: Pustet, 1995, 167–82.

Zimdars-Swartz, Sandra. *Encountering Mary. From La Salette to Medjugorje.* Princeton: Princeton University Press, 1991.

– "Popular Devotion to the Virgin. The Marian Phenomena at Melleray, Republic of Ireland." *Archives des Sciences sociales des Religions* 67, no. 1 (1989): 125–44.

– "Religious Experience and the Public Cult: the Case of Mary Ann Van Hoof." *The Journal of Religion and Health* 28, no. 4 (1989): 36–57.

Zumholz, Maria Anna. "Die Resistenz des katholischen Milieus: Seherinnen und Stigmatisierte in der ersten Hälfte des 20. Jahrhunderts." In *Wunderbare Erscheinungen. Frauen und katholische Frömmigkeit im 19. und 20. Jahrhundert,* edited by Irmtraud Götz von Olenhusen, 221–51. Paderborn: Schöningh, 1995.

– *Volksfrömmigkeit und katholisches Milieu. Marienerscheinungen in Heede 1937–1949*. Cloppenburg: Runge, 2004.

# Index

*Note: Page numbers in italics refer to photographs or maps. Page numbers followed by the letter* t *refer to tables. Page numbers enclosed in square brackets denote textual references to endnotes.*